Translating Cultures

An Introduction
for
Translators, Interpreters and Mediators

David Katan

Routledge
Taylor & Francis Group

LONDON AND NEW YORK

First published 1999 by St. Jerome Publishing
Second edition 2003
Third edition 2004

Published 2014 by Routledge
2 Park Square, Milton Park, Abingdon, Oxon OX14 4RN
711 Third Avenue, New York, NY 10017, USA

Routledge is an imprint of the Taylor & Francis Group, an informa business

Notices
Knowledge and best practice in this field are constantly changing. As new research and experience broaden our understanding, changes in research methods, professional practices, or medical treatment may become necessary.

Practitioners and researchers must always rely on their own experience and knowledge in evaluating and using any information, methods, compounds, or experiments described herein. In using such information or methods they should be mindful of their own safety and the safety of others, including parties for whom they have a professional responsibility.

To the fullest extent of the law, neither the Publisher nor the authors, contributors, or editors, assume any liability for any injury and/or damage to persons or property as a matter of products liability, negligence or otherwise, or from any use or operation of any methods, products, instructions, or ideas contained in the material herein.

ISBN 13: 978-1-900650-73-1 (pbk)

Typeset by
Delta Typesetters, Cairo, Egypt

British Library Cataloguing in Publication Data
A catalogue record of this book is available from the British Library

Library of Congress Cataloging-in-Publication Data
Katan, David.
  Translating cultures: an introduction for translators, interpreters, and mediators / David Katan.--2nd ed.
     p. cm.
Includes bibliographical references and index.
  ISBN 1-900650-73-8 (alk. paper)
  1. Intercultural communication. 2. Translating and interpreting. 3. Language and culture.
I. Title.
  P94.6.K38 2003
  306--dc22

                                    2003018476

Contents

Preface

> "The book itself is only a tissue of signs, an imitation that is lost, infinitely deferred."
> Barthes (1977)

This book, now in its second edition, has had a long gestation. Many people have helped and given their valuable advice and time along the way. The first edition would never have seen the light of day without the firm guidance of John Dodds. Many other colleagues from the Interpreters' School in Trieste gave their support in many different ways, in particular, Federica Scarpa, Francesco Straniero Sergio and Chris Taylor. Eli Rota gave extremely useful feedback regarding NLP, and the Meta-Model in particular; while Carol Torsello's close reading was responsible for the improvements in the linguistic analysis. Many of the newspaper examples have been culled from Pat Madon's informal but effective cuttings service.

David Trickey has directed my reading in cross-cultural communication and has been a constant sparring partner on all things cultural for well over 20 years.

For the second edition, the book has been almost totally rewritten, and every single figure has been revised. My thanks go to Licia Corbolante for her help on localization, to my dissertation students who have all contributed in some way to the improvements, and I am also grateful for Lara Fabiano's studied comments. Finally, I'd like to thank Emanuela Mascarin for her enthusiastic and punctilious proofreading.

Inevitably, though, in ironing out inconsistencies, updating, and inserting new ideas, information and examples, new inconsistencies will have crept in. These may be interpreted as 'breaking news' in the lively new discipline of intercultural translation.

The book, naturally, is dedicated to Patty, Thomas and Robert.

HORATIO
O day and night, but this is wondrous strange!

HAMLET
And therefore as a stranger give it welcome.
There are more things in heaven and earth,
Horatio,
Than are dreamt of in your philosophy.

Introduction

'Translating across cultures' and 'cultural proficiency' have become buzz words in translating and interpreting. Mona Baker (1996:17) warns that many scholars have now adopted a "'cultural' perspective ... a dangerously fashionable word that almost substitutes for rigour and coherence". As the 21st century gets into stride, so does the call for a discipline combining culture and translation. In 2001, the CIUTI Conférence Internationale des Instituts Universitaires de Traducteurs et Interprètes opened its Colloquium with "Kooperationskonzepte für die multilinguale Gesellschafte" rather than on the word, the text and equivalence. The plenary sessions all focussed on transcultural communication and mediation. In 2004, the first international conference on "Translation and Intercultural Communication" was held, a landmark, at least in talk.

The aim of this book is to put some rigour and coherence into this fashionable word, and in doing so unravel the 'X' factor (see Dodds and Katan 1996) involved in teaching culture to translators, interpreters and other mediators. It is an introduction to current understanding about culture and its importance in communication, translation and interpretation. As such, it aims to bridge the culture-gap inherent in books or courses focusing on either translation theory and practice, language or 'institutions'. More importantly, in clarifying the 'X' factor, it aims to raise awareness of the role of culture in constructing, perceiving and translating reality.

This book should serve as a framework for interpreters and translators (both actual and potential) working between English and any other language, and also for those working or living between these cultures who wish to understand more about their cross-cultural successes and frustrations.

The book is divided into four main parts:
Part 1: Framing Culture: The Culture-Bound Mental Map of the World
Part 2: Shifting Frames: Translation and Mediation in Theory and Practice
Part 3: The Array of Frames: Communication Orientations
Part 4: Intercultural Competence: On Becoming a Cultural Interpreter and Mediator

Framing Culture: The Culture Bound Mental Map of the World

The 21st century arrived with a bang, awaking many to the increased tensions between cultures. Clearly, the task of translating cultures has so far not been successful.

Ethnic intransigence is making even more of a mark throughout the world. What is more, the usually quiet world of academic translators also woke up to a global rift.

Ironically, St Jerome, the publisher of this volume, which "supports the development of translation studies and other disciplines concerned with intercultural communication"[1] suddenly found itself embroiled in academic acrimony, if not communication breakdown, following various responses to the Israel/Palestine conflict[2] – and being eagerly reported by the world's press. According to *The Guardian* (13/07/2002), reporting in true hyperbolic tabloid journalism style, St Jerome even became "the most reviled little publishing company in the world".

Meanwhile, professional translators themselves, though, have been remarkably uninvolved. They are still battling to keep up with deadlines, with an increasing amount of their work part-translated by machine, and in search of *le mot juste*. It is also a shocking state of affairs that the EU, a respecter of languages and cultures has actually unconsciously encoded[3] the profession as follows:

> 74.8   Miscellaneous business activities n.e.c. 749×
> 74.81 Photographic activities 7494
> 74.82 Packaging activities 7495
> 74.83 Secretarial and translation activities 7499×

If we look in more detail at the translators' fellow travellers, the list is depressingly clear – translating and interpreting is perceived as text-based copying:

> 74.83 Secretarial and translation activities
> This class includes:
> – stenographic and mailing activities:
> – typing
> – other secretarial activities such as transcribing from tapes or discs
> – copying, blue printing, multigraphing and similar activities
> – envelope addressing, stuffing, sealing and mailing, mailing list compilation, etc., including advertising material
> – translation and interpretation
>
> This class also includes:
> – proof-reading

It is against this background that this book makes its start. The basic premise is that translators and interpreters need to change, both in how they are perceived and in how they work. They need to move away from being seen as photocopiers and

---

[1] St. Jerome Publishing 2003/2004 Catalogue, 2003, p.2.
[2] See Mona Baker's webpage for a clear statement: http://www.monabaker.com.
[3] EU Document 3037/90, "Nace Rev 1". The document is designed to provide a common basis for the statistical classification and analysis of economic activities within the EU.

working as human dictionaries to being perceived as visible agents in creating understanding between people. The aim of this book is to introduce the concept of the 'cultural interpreter' or 'mediator' and to illustrate what a mediator will need to know.

Part 1 continues by introducing the subject of culture. Culture is perceived throughout this book as a system for making sense of experience. The first task is to sort the various definitions of culture and approaches to teaching it, into one unifying framework. A basic presupposition is that the organization of experience is not 'reality', but is a simplification and distortion which changes from culture to culture. Each culture acts as a frame within which external signs or 'reality' are interpreted.

Part 1 concludes with an in-depth analysis of how individuals perceive, catalogue and construct reality, and how this perception is communicated through language. The approach is interdisciplinary, taking ideas from anthropology, such as Gregory Bateson's Logical Typing and Metamessage Theories; Bandler and Grinder's Meta-Model Theory; Socio-linguistics; Speech Act Theory; Sperber and Wilson's Relevance Theory, and Hallidayan Functional Grammar.

Shifting Frames: Translation and Mediation in Theory and Practice

Part 2 begins with a discussion of the strategies a cultural mediator needs to adopt to make the frames explicit. It includes a short synchronic and diachronic description of culture and theory of the translation process. Practical examples of translations with commentary are given.

Translation itself, following Nida (1976:65), is here viewed as "essentially an aspect of a larger domain, namely, that of communication". Steiner (1975:47) in his aptly titled *After Babel* takes an even wider view of translation: "inside or between languages, human communication equals translation". Hence, translation is discussed within the wider context of communication, extending ideas put forward by a variety of translation scholars such as Baker, Bassnett, Bell, Hatim and Mason, Holmes, Honig, Newmark, Neubert, Snell-Hornby and Wilss.

Newmark's (1995) two statements, "translation is the most economical method of explaining one culture's way to another" and "translation mediates cultures", take us back to the main concern of this book: improving communication across cultures.

The Array of Frames: Communication Orientations

Part 3 is an outline of the major influences culture can have on communication. It begins with a development of Edward Hall's theory of contexting, which discusses the changing importance of implicit and explicit communication between cultures in the transmission of a message.

The unconsciousness of basic British, American and other cultural orientations influencing the language is investigated from the viewpoint of social anthropologists working in a business context, with practical examples taken both from the national press and from translations.

Intercultural Competence: On Becoming a Cultural Interpreter and Mediator

The final part of the book is an attempt to model the translator and interpreter's changing identity, beliefs and strategies as s/he follows an idealised path towards intercultural awareness and mediation. The ideas are taken principally from Milton Bennett's Model of Intercultural Sensitivity and from NLP theory. The model gives a clear idea of what aspects of culture should be taught when and how; and the ideas have been developed for the training of translators.

The model has also been used here to benchmark translators and interpreters today in terms of intercultural competence. It clearly highlights the difference between ethnocentric and ethnorelative beliefs regarding language, communication and translation.

In demonstrating some of the reasons for our own cross-cultural frustrations and successes, the book as a whole highlights the way forward for future proficient and visible cultural interpreters/mediators.

Part 1. Framing Culture
  The Culture-Bound Mental Map of the World

Chapter 1. The Cultural Mediator

The aim of this chapter is to:
- discuss translation and interpretation problems in terms of 3 levels of culture
- introduce the concept of cultural mediator
- focus on the changes necessary for translators and interpreters to become cultural mediators

1.1 The Influence of Culture

- technical culture
- formal culture
- informal culture/out-of-awareness

As mentioned in the introduction, the words 'culture' and 'translation' are being increasingly linked. Questions regarding whether or not translations can account for culture, or to what extent culture is relevant to translation are very much at the centre of the debate. The two extreme views are that either everything can be translated without loss or that nothing can be translated without loss, as in the Italian expression *traduttore/traditore*/'translator/traitor'. These viewpoints are, in fact, both correct, and can be sensibly discussed by dividing the argument into three different levels. The three levels to be considered are: technical, formal and informal (or out-of-awareness) (Hall 1990).

There is no doubt that, today, conceptual terms are becoming easier to translate. Concerted international efforts are now being made to harmonise legislation and codes of practice across borders (the EU being just one case in point) and dramatic improvements are being made through ever-expanding on-line glossaries. Also, much that is new is developed internationally, and produced "translation ready" – in a way that was inconceivable before the advent of a global market.

In 1995, for example, there was one telephone per 200 houses in India, and terrestrial lines were few and far between. India has now invested resources in state-of-the-art satellite technology, allowing it to move directly from reliance on public to personal mobile phones. This technology is being imported from Japan, Europe and America. Translating or interpreting this (or any other) new technology across cultures, whether for the technicians themselves or for the end-user, for example, the unschooled Punjabi family, will certainly not pose a problem.

At a technical level, communication is explicit, and ideas are consciously transmitted. It is scientific. In terms of language, it is the proposition or the dictionary denotative meaning that needs to be translated. This form of culture is indeed now global, with business and industry working to the same standards throughout the world.

Negotiation of meaning is reduced to the minimum. The language provides, as far as possible, its own context. In fact, Peter Newmark (1988:6) is entirely correct when he states: "No language, no culture is so 'primitive' that it cannot embrace the terms of, say, computer technology".

The fact that it might be necessary to use more text to explain the concept, because the world is categorized in different ways, is certainly not a problem; neither for the translator as cultural mediator, nor for the target language reader. For example, "to watch sheep by night" sounds perfectly natural in English, yet requires five words. In Quiché (Guatemala), more advanced in this line of technology, only one word is necessary (Beekman and Callow 1974:54-55).

So, at the technical level little or no loss or distortion of meaning need ever occur. This is, as we have already mentioned, due to the fact that communication at this level has no extra-linguistic context: the text is the authority, and it is clearly spelled out. Anthony Pym (2000:189) calls translation at this level "NANS" or rather "no-addition-no-subtraction".

It is also at this level that the business community is most aware, and notices the shortcomings of a translator and interpreter. An interpreter without the technical language of, for example, aviation insurance, will clearly not be effective. As a result, many companies are improving their in-service language training instead of hiring interpreters (Kondo *et al.* 1997:161-62).

The translator, too, is fully aware of having the same problems, as any native speaker called upon to translate patent law, industrial plant specifications or medical papers will know. What can the non-specialist translator make of the following opening sentence from an article on computer systems, entitled "Location Awareness in Community Wireless LANs"?:

> We have developed a multi-user team awareness framework, CampusSpace, that on-the-fly and transparently collects and interprets position information of mobiles from the signal to noise ratio of IEEE 802.11 radios, and carto-graphically mapped RFID tags respectively.

"On-the-fly", here, clearly has nothing to do with fly fishing, but more importantly, nothing to do with being in a hurry or speed, the standard use of the idiomatic expression (as of 2003). In these cases, a successful interpreter and translator, at this level, will not only need to have a near-native command of both languages, but will also need to know where to find technical information efficiently: from concordances, dictionaries, encyclopaedias, glossaries, thesauruses, on paper, on the Internet and, of course, in human form. The internet has been of phenomenal assistance in providing not only on-line translation assistance in a variety of forms but also in providing immediate access to almost unlimited supplies of similar texts (or genres) written in the target language by native-language speakers. A *Google* search, in fact, came up with the meaning in IT as "dynamic" or "interactive".[1]

---

[1] The 2003 *Longman* dictionary (unpublished at the time of writing) also has an entry for the IT use of 'on the fly'.

The extract below poses further problems. It is taken from a steel rolling mill brochure, and is a fairly literal translation from the original (in Italian), but whether it is a good or bad translation is another matter:

> One of the main features of the complete machine are cantilevered tundish cars running on tracks on an elevated steel structure for rapid change of the tundish 'on the fly'.

Grammatically it is correct. However, very few native speakers would understand the meaning, and more importantly, they would not know if any *faux-pas* had been made. Comparison with other, well-written, technical texts would tell us that the translation at the level of discourse is not good. An improvement would be to break the sentence into two and at least add a verb:

> One of the main features of the (complete?) machine are the cantilevered tundish cars. These run on tracks on an elevated steel structure, which ensures a rapid change of the tundish 'on the fly'.

However, the native speaker, having decided that 'machine' implies the 'complete machine' and having simplified the sentences to a perfectly cohesive piece of discourse in English, will still have problems with "tundish 'on the fly'". With time, an Internet search will give the translator or interpreter an idea of what a 'tundish' is (a bath-tub shaped vessel), and will also tell us that 'on the fly' is the correct technical term, but probably with another specialist meaning (related to speed this time?). It would then take further reading to be able to decide whether "rapid" is tautologous and whether "the tundish" is preferable to "tundish" or "tundishes".

The problem of understanding the meaning remains. A non-native speaker, fluent in metallurgy and the continuous cast steel process, will almost certainly be able to comment on the translation at the level of meaning, and may well be able to provide a less accurate but more meaningful translation. Federica Scarpa's (2001: 155-56) volume, devoted to specialised translation, discusses the various problems of polysemy and (partial) synonymy, and concludes with the following warning: "There is then, the constant danger that a translator will confuse the specialised use of a word with the more common". Software programs are, in fact, now beginning to make these translations as good as, if not better than, the native human translator – and require only minimum post editing.

As the above examples illustrate, general translators and interpreters are always going to be at a disadvantage in a specialized field because they can never be sure, at a technical level, if "tundish 'on the fly'" is the right expression. We now move on to the formal level.

Technical concepts, such as satellite communications technology, have to be discussed, negotiated and implemented by people working within their contexts of culture. People, as representatives of their culture, do things in different ways, and usually out-of-awareness. Newmark (1988:156), in fact, cautions about "the possible

cultural and professional differences between your readership and the original one",
and explains that these will need to be taken into account when approaching a technical text.

Below is an example of a translation of food labelling. Received wisdom would
tell us that harmonised EU regulations and the labelling of ingredients would be a
simple case of word-for-word translation. We would naturally expect the same type
of lexical problem as we found above with translation at the technical level. However, the problems at this level are that each country has its own preferred way of
doing things, in this case labelling:

Italian	French	Portuguese
DESSERT A BASE DI YO-GURT E PREPARAZIONE DOLCIARIA ALLA FRUTTA	YAOURT AUX FRUITS	IOGURTE MEIO GORDO COM FRUTA
Ingredienti: yogurt (latte parzialmente scremato, fermenti lattici vivi) preparazione dolciaria alla frutta (24%) (frutta*, zucchero, amido mo-dificato, gelificante: pectina, aromi)*vedi coperchio per la specificazione della frutta.	Ingrédients: Lait demi-écrémé, préparation de fruits 24% (soit fruits: 12%), sucre, arômes, ferments lactiques.	Ingredientes: leite meio gordo fermentado (1.8% M.G.), preparado de fruta (11%), aromas, açúcar.
Da consumare entro: vedi coperchio.Conservare in frigo a +4°C.	Conservation à + 6°C maximum. A consommer jusqu'à (voir couvercle).	Consumir até: ver tampa. Com L. bulgaricus e S thermophilus. Conservar entre +0°C e +6°C.
Prodotto in Germania		Produzido na UE

The differences between the technical labelling required are notable, as are the
numerical discrepancies. Even though all countries follow the European food labelling laws and technical requirements, only some of the items on the label are
compulsory at an EU level, such as date of expiry. How countries deal with technical information, and what they deem to be important, is certainly not pan-cultural.

To what extent translators need to know about cross-cultural differences in legislation regarding food labelling, marketing and promotion is discussed by Candace
Séguinot (1995) in her paper and in the debate on "Translation and Advertising".
She notes (ibid.:65-6), for example, that in Quebec 'infant formula' is known as
'lait maternisé'. However, the Food and Drug Act specifies that the term has to be
'préparation pour nourissons', "which no speaker actually uses". In this case, the
dictionary correctly cites the term used by speakers, but the term itself is forbidden
by legislation. This is part of the 'something extra' a translator or interpreter will
need to know. Séguinot (ibid.:56) continues: "Translators are implicitly expected to
understand the requirements of different markets, and this means that translators
need to understand the cultures towards which they are translating".

An even more striking difference concerning consumer protection *within* the EU can be seen in the following labelling practices for a 'Whirlpool' Microwave cooker. In 10 European languages (excluding French) we have the equivalent of:

> OPTION: 8 YEAR GUARANTEE FOR SPARE PARTS: details inside.

In French, the 'translation' is as follows:

> *CETTE GARANTIE OPTIONNELLE DE 8 ANS NE S'APPLIQUE PAS EN FRANCE – Voir les modalités des garanties légales et contractuelles dans le livret d'information sur le SAV.*

As a final example, we can see how legal restraints, norms and socio-cultural differences can combine to produce what might, at first glance, seem a bizarre set of (non) parallel texts.

The "Super Disc Shot" – in page 12 – is made in Italy, and carries the usual safety warning in a number of languages. This shot is clearly marked as unsuitable for British or French children under the age of eight (for good measure, emphasised in bold in French), while in the country of production (allowing stereotypes to flourish), children on their 36th month may start shooting.

We then have the Swedish, Finnish, Danish, Norwegian and Dutch versions. Local norms have dictated the fact that, the Norwegian, for example, has an extra warning: "INCORRECT USE OF THIS PRODUCT MAY CAUSE PERMANENT HEARING DAMAGE TO CHILDREN". The Dutch, instead, are warned about throwing the caps into the fire at home. The Arabic version shows just how far culture, in particular, impinges on what information is to be highlighted. In Arabic, there is no trace or attempt at a translation, but rather a personal communication. The suitability of the shot for children is in the context, and can be presumed to left to the judgement of the buyer. What is important is that this product can be trusted, through the fact that it is made in Italy and can be vouched for by a personal agent.

Differences in technical consumer information provide just one example of the way each culture has its own appropriate ways of behaving. Translators and interpreters in particular, whether or not they are involved in IT, labelling or advertising, need to be well versed in the customs, habits and traditions of the two cultures they are mediating for.[2] Both the translator and the interpreter will also need solid background information about the cultures they are working with, particularly the

---

[2] There are many country or international guides explaining this level of culture, e.g. John Mole's (1992) *Mind Your Manners*, a business-oriented guide to appropriate behaviour in the individual European countries, Christopher Englehorn's (1991) *When Business East Meets Business West: The Guide to Practice and Protocol in the Pacific Rim*. Other publications will be mentioned in the following chapters. See also http://www.i18nguy.com/books.html#taylor for a fairly exhaustive list of books on internationalism, management and software localization.

Arabic:
This product is an original product made in Italy by "Edison Toys". Do not trust imitations. Exclusive Italian Edison company agent:
Mr. Mahmoud Ali Hasan
Alexandria, 4 Al Tahreer, Al Mensheya Square
Tel. Number: 810377 Fax no: 819028.

Italian
NON ADATTO AD UN BAMBINO DI ETA MINORE
DI 36 MESI
ATTENZIONE: NON SPARARE VICINO
AGLI OCCHI O ALLE ORECCHIE
NON TENERE LE CAPSULE SCIOLTE IN TASCA

French:
NE CONVIENT PAS A UN ENFANT
DE MOINS DE 8 ANS
ATTENTION: NE PAR TIRER A PROXIMITE
DES YEUX OU DES OREILLES
NE PAR GARDER DES CAPSULES EN VRAC SUR SOI

English:
WARNING: DO NOT FIRE INDOOR OR NEAR EYES.
DO NOT CARRY CAPS LOOSE IN A POCKET

Swedish
WARNING! DO NOT SHOOT CLOSE TO EYES OR EARS.
DO NOT CARRY CAPS LOOSE IN A POCKET

Finnish
WARNING! YOU SHOULD NOT SHOOT CLOSE TO EYES
OR EARS
DO NOT CARRY CAPS LOOSE IN A POCKET

Danish
WARNING! DO NOT SHOOT CLOSE TO EYES OR EARS
DO NOT KEEP CAPS LOOSE IN A POCKET

Norwegian
WARNING! DO NOT EXPLODE CLOSE TO EYES OR EARS
DO NOT KEEP CAPS LOOSE IN A POCKET
INCORRECT USE OF THIS PRODUCT MAY CAUSE
PERMANENT HEARING DAMAGE TO CHILDREN

Dutch
C. 15 B)-RID - DO NOT KEEP CAPS LOOSE IN A POCKET
                 - FROM 8 YEARS UP
                 - DO NOT THROW INTO FIREPLACE

English
NOT RECOMMENDED FOR CHILDREN UNDER 8 YEARS

Made in Italy by EDISON GIOCATTOLI S.p.a

geography and contemporary social and political history. These form the backbone of a culture's cognitive environment. This also means being aware of the popular culture (the culture's heroes, TV, films, personalities, etc.).

In fact, Akira Mizuno, a practising broadcast interpreter in Japan, states that popular culture presents one of the greatest challenges to Japanese broadcast interpreters (Kondo *et al.* 1997:155-56). He gives a list of some recurring American favourites that have caused him problems in interpreting:

• Superman	• the tooth fairy	• "Kilroy was here"
• Clark Kent	• the Brooklyn Bridge	• "I saw Elvis"
• Kryptonite	• the Checkers Speech	• "Just the facts ma'am"
• the Daily Planet	• Gilligan's Island	• "As Sergeant Joe Friday used to say"

However, it is 'localization', and what O'Hagen and Ashworth (2002) define as "Computer-Mediated Communication", that has revolutionised the theory and practice of technical translation, including the emphasis on the translation of popular culture. Microsoft, for example, has invested hugely in "localization", which O'Hagen and Ashworth define as a translation strategy specifically "addressing linguistic and cultural barriers specific to the Receiver who does not share the same linguistic and cultural backgrounds as the Sender" (ibid.:66-7). Microsoft spends well over 50 million dollars a year on overcoming these barriers. The examples in the table next page are taken from internal Microsoft documents[3] warning localisers of typical localisation problems when translating software and manuals from British or American English.

A recent 1000 page plus book on developing international software, published by Microsoft (International 2002:318), clearly states: "Those who are involved with software localisation need to consider these sorts of cultural differences. In contrast, when translating a book or a movie, there is no need to account for cultural variance".

Though we will disagree with the second part of International's statement, it is quite clear that not only the content but also the form of all IT translations are localized, which means that Pym's NANS have effectively gone by the board. O'Hagen and Ashworth (ibid.:67) go on to point out that other Web environments, such as on-line newspapers are being translated with localization strategies too. Local editions of *Time* and *Newsweek*, for example, "are often designed separately with specific local appeal".

Also, Computer Assisted Translation, Translation Memories and Machine Translation (MT) are beginning to take the purely 'technical' out of the translator's hands. Multiterm Glossaries, in particular, working in tandem with Translation Memory programs can mean that Fiat's next car manual will already be 50-75% 'translated' before the translator even lays hands on it. MT, such as SYSTRAN is a machine

---

[3] I am grateful to Licia Corbolante of Microsoft, Dublin for this information and for the opportunity to look at the internal documents.

translation system or, more precisely, a system which supports translators in their work, and according to the European commission's own website , in 2001, "260,000 pages were run through SYSTRAN proof enough that machine translation is here to stay".* The basic use is for a quick-and-dirty translation, a first draft that bureau-

Type of problem	Example Microsoft comments of culture-bound language or icon which will need to be localized
Fonts, sizes	Keyboard layouts, default paper and envelope sizes, character sets, text directionality (left-to-right; right-to-left; horizontal; vertical)
Format of technical strings (word order) :	Street name and number: US: 7 Kennedy Rd Italy: Via Garibaldi 7
	Date format: UK/France:17/03/05 US: 03/17/05
	Week format: UK/US: Sun-Sat Italy: Mon-Sun
	Time format: UK/US: am/pm France/Japan: 24 hr clock

	Separators: UK/US/Japan: 1,247.7
	                                Italian/Arabic: 1.247,7
	                                     France: 1 247,7

Multiple problems linking programming language to explanation in the text	Written text not necessarily related to keyboard actions: "Press the Assistant button", "Press CTR + U to underline"

Templates	CVs. UK/Italy: date and place of birth default
	                    US: optional
	          US/UK: sport and hobbies default
	                    Italy: optional
	'elegant' letters

Icons, artwork	Artwork should be adapted to local markets, i.e. pictures of baseball players should be replaced with pictures of soccer players; other recurrent pictures to be localized include pictures of US school bus, Wizard, Shakespeare.
Culture specific names	Localize names: "The update is filled with colourful themes ... from Cathy to Doonesbury"
Cultural (US) specific information	Delete country specific information: "All you need to do to get your local weather from MSN is inserting your zip code"; "These Microsoft products are available at Shop.microsoft.com, or from a licensed reseller"
Local (market) practices	Product comparisons are legal in UK and the US but not in all other countries: e.g. "the most powerful browser" should be changed to "a powerful browser".
	"Use your mother's maiden name as password" – In many countries, there is no change of name on marriage.
	Not all cultures find a "four-day holiday with an intercontinental flight" plausible: change to 8 days.
Style and Register: "is the US style suitable to the TL market (direct v indirect; personification of applications; colloquialisms, etc.)?"	Raise the register or eliminate (for Italy in particular): Clippit (Microsoft's first Office assistant); 'F.Y.I' (for your information); Post Mortem; "Sites that you're not so sure about go into another 'bucket'"; "Make your gaming experience a blast! Say cheese! Simple tools make it easy to import photos from scanners and cameras"; "Take the Web by storm!"

* (http://europa.eu.int/ISPO/docs/services/newsletter/98/may_june/ISPOMAY02.html).

crats and others can then decide to bin, take essential notes or have properly translated. Another area to be included at this formal level is 'corporate culture'. *The Economist* (10/9/94) published a story entitled 'The Trouble with Mergers', which discussed corporate cultures and the problems (not of international but of national mergers): "Even complementary firms can have different cultures, which makes welding them tricky". Each company, indeed each branch or department has its own accepted set of priorities. This means that accepted business practices vary not only at a national level and between companies (such as the well studied Apple Macintosh and IBM cultures) but between individual offices too.

A general interpreter and translator will again be at a disadvantage, as they will not be part of the in-group. Companies, again, are only too aware of this phenomenon. As a result, according to Stephen Hagen (1994, personal communication), author of a number of university and DTI sponsored research studies on the European business environment, "Companies are cynical about the use of university trained interpreters, and increasingly they are becoming more confident about handing over interpreting and translating tasks to their own department". The results of a University of Nottingham research report by Carol Arijoki (1993:20) echoes the same idea: "[Business] respondents were very much in favour of independence from interpreters". Though translation and interpreting take up a substantial portion of the EU budget, in many other areas the percentage is declining. This is particularly bad news for the traditional interpreter. However, there is a need for a new style of interpreter.

On a technical and formal level, "business is business" and, due to scales of economy and the exploitation of know-how, jointventures are becoming increasingly popular. Yet, at the same time, according to John Harper (1993:76): "in many instances, the evidence suggests that between 50% and 75% of joint ventures and mergers fail, without achieving the objectives for which they were formed". His paper on cross-cultural issues and the role of training highlights the fact that culture poses no problems at a technical level. However, at another level culture becomes an obstacle to communication:

> the researchers concluded that technical solutions were less instrumental in producing conflicts in work relationships than the difference between the two countries in the area of organizational behaviour ... More than 50% of the sample reported cultural differences at work and management production giving rise to tensions, but reported that these were often not regarded as important by headquarters management.

This is a problem of communication, but not one that a 'black-box' interpreter or translator can solve.

In theory, a joint venture or merger is based on cooperation and a convergence of interests. However, as Carol Taylor Torsello (1984:78) notes, conversations do not only converge; they also diverge and are inconsistent. Even more importantly: "convergence is probably impossible without cooperation, and even where cooperation exists, the world-views of the participants may fail to converge".

This takes us to the informal or out-of-awareness level of culture, the level at which the mediator should be able to intervene and mediate. Pym (2000:190), in discussing cooperation, comes to the same conclusion: "In short, our training programmes should progressively be oriented to the production of intercultural mediators, people who are able to do rather more than just translate".

The next section, in fact, discusses the potential role of a translator or interpreter as a cultural mediator, able to mediate the non-converging world-views or maps of the world, so allowing the participants to cooperate to the degree they wish.

1.2 The Cultural Interpreter/Mediator

The term cultural mediator was first introduced in Stephen Bochner's (1981) *The Mediating Person* and *Cultural Identity*. The idea of a translator as a mediating agent, however, is not new. George Steiner (1975:45) pointed out that: "The translator is a bilingual mediating agent between monolingual communication participants in two different language communities".

However, the emphasis is linguistic mediation. The 'cultural interpreter', on the other hand, is already an accepted term (in Ontario) for something that is more than linguistic mediation.

> Cultural Interpreting is defined as "communication of conceptual and cultural factors that are relevant to the given interaction as part of the lingual transmission". The important thing to keep in mind here is that the interpretation conveys messages in a way appropriate to the language and cultural frameworks involved. This means making choices – e.g., between literal or idiomatic usage – according to those factors as well as according to the situation. Cultural Interpretation did not simply come to be, but has a basis in theory and experience.
>
> A Cultural Interpreter is someone from a particular culture who assists a service provider and their client to understand each other. The focus is on effective communication and understanding between the service provider and client while respecting the client's cultural and language needs.[4]

The cultural interpreter, as understood above, is a community or public service interpreter, working principally to ensure that the client "receives full and equal access to public services" (Roberts 2002). The aim of this book is to investigate the conceptual and cultural factors relevant to all this living or working across language-cultures. Hence, I will use the term 'cultural interpreter' much more broadly, as does Artemeva (1988) in her article "The Writing Consultant as Cultural Interpreter". She clearly, though, distinguishes between the culturally aware 'writing consultants' and the culture-bound translators.

---

[4] http://www.kwmc.on.ca/services/cis.html

> The periodic engineering report can become a source of conflict and frustration when North American engineers collaborate with colleagues abroad. To overcome such difficulties, technical companies may hire writing consultants, who then take on the additional role of cultural interpreters, helping the partners bridge differences in both the practice of engineering and the language and culture of each country. As such a writing consultant, I worked with a Canadian engineering company, its Russian contractors, and a Russian translator to analyze the sources of difficulties in their reports. The language of the reports was English, but differences in tone as well as reader expectations about organization, format, and appropriate content caused misunderstandings among the collaborators. Contrastive rhetorical analysis helped to identify problems in both the conception of the report as a document and the translation of particular text.[5]

If the translators and interpreters do not include culture as part of their remit, then the 'writing consultant' and others will ensure that the translating profession will remain classified with the transcribers, copiers, stuffers and sealers.

The cultural interpreter's role is the same as that of the cultural mediator, and touches on the role of a mediator in any other field, from arbitrator to therapist. Taft (1981:53), in his contribution to Bochner's volume on the subject, defines the role as follows:

> A cultural mediator is a person who facilitates communication, understanding, and action between persons or groups who differ with respect to language and culture. The role of the mediator is performed by interpreting the expressions, intentions, perceptions, and expectations of each cultural group to the other, that is, by establishing and balancing the communication between them. In order to serve as a link in this sense, the mediator must be able to participate to some extent in both cultures. Thus a mediator must be to a certain extent bicultural.

According to Taft (1981:73), a mediator must possess the following competencies in both cultures:

- **Knowledge about society**: history, folklore, traditions, customs; values, prohibitions; the natural environment and its importance; neighbouring people, important people in the society, etc.
- **Communication Skills**: written, spoken, non-verbal.
- **Technical skills**: those required by the mediator's status, e.g. computer literacy, appropriate dress, etc.
- **Social skills**: knowledge of rules that govern social relations in society and emotional competence, e.g. the appropriate level of self-control.

---

[5] http://tc.eserver.org/13837.html

The mediator needs not only "two skills in one skull" (ibid.:53) but "in order to play the role of mediator, an individual has to be flexible in switching his cultural orientation". Hence, a cultural mediator will have developed a high degree of intercultural sensitivity, and will have reached the level of 'contextual evaluation'. We will return to these issues when discussing belief systems, particularly in Part 4, but now we should look more closely at the translator and interpreter as cultural interpreters or mediators.[6]

1.3 The Translator and Interpreter

Theories of the translation process itself are discussed in Part 2. Here, we will concentrate on what being a cultural mediator means for those involved in translating texts or interpreting for people.

• *The Interpreter*
The interpreter's role has long been thought of as a discreet, if not invisible, blackbox and as a walking generalist translator of words. As a cultural mediator, he or she will need to be a specialist in negotiating understanding between cultures.

A move in this direction has already been made. The endless debate between literal and communicative translation in the world of interpreting seems to be moving towards consensus. Masaomi Kondo (1990:62) has written a great deal on both interpreting and cross-cultural communication. He concludes (emphasis in the original): "*essentially speaking*, the debate is closed. The word-for-word correspondence between the source and the target has *virtually* no place in our work". This is a first move towards the more extreme communicative role of a cultural mediator who "may never be called upon to engage in the exact translation of words, rather he will communicate the ideas in terms that are meaningful to the members of the target audience" (Taft 1981:58).

However, the article Kondo wrote (emphasis added) is entitled 'What Conference Interpreters Should *Not* Be Expected To Do'. He raises the point that very often a cultural mediator is necessary during intercultural negotiations, but that also the interpreter would be out of a job if s/he took that role. His suggestion is to make both the role and the limits of an interpreter's intervention clear to participants before the interpretation begins. Kondo (1990:59) feels that the participants can then take it upon themselves "to achieve better results in interlingual and intercultural communications". However, due to factors at the informal level of culture, any improved communication results will be through accident rather than by design. This will also be the case if the Ontario Ministry of Citizenship Code of Ethics for the cultural interpreter is followed to the letter: As can be seen, the role is subservient to the will of the client and/or the professional worker:

---

[6] I will be using both terms, 'cultural interpreter' and 'mediator,' in the following pages. Neither, perhaps, is entirely satisfactory, due to their present connotations.

The interpreter will render the message by conveying faithfully its intent and spirit. The interpreter will transmit everything in the manner in which it is intended. This is especially difficult when the interpreter disagrees or feels uncomfortable with what is being expressed:

– The interpreter may be aware of the special circumstances surrounding the violent situation which the woman is being or has been subjected to and how those circumstances are perceived culturally. Where appropriate the interpreter may interject to help professional/worker and client understand cultural differences or sensitivity.

– If the interpreter's personal feelings interfere with rendering the message accurately, she will advise the persons involved and withdraw, when possible, from the situation.

– The interpreter will not counsel, advise or interject personal opinions related to the interpreting assignment, unless:
1. She is asked to do so by the client and/or the professional worker
2. She feels that it is appropriate or necessary to provide cross cultural information or personal assessment in order to ensure effective communication; any counselling, advice or personal assessment has to be communicated to the professional/worker
3. The interpretation contravenes the values and attitudes in the philosophy statements

Certain interpreters, such as Cynthia Roy (1993), suggest strategic intervention with regard, for example, to the organization of turn taking. Others also suggest a much greater active role. Richard Brislin (1981:213), a research associate at the Institute of Culture and Communication in Honolulu, takes up the idea of the interpreter informing the participants before the meeting to make the rules clear, and expands the role of the interpreter. His specific suggestions regarding "speculative strategies" (slightly adapted here) revolve around the interpreter as chair or referee:

- the interpreter works with all parties before the event to be interpreted. This means, for example, going through any texts to check for any possible cross-cultural problems;
- interpreters to be given explicit permission to stop a conference if they feel a misunderstanding is causing difficulty;
- interpreters to prepare materials for cross-cultural meetings for participants to read, including desirable behaviour, and intercultural communication points.

Annelie Knapp-Potthof and Karlfried Knapp (1981:183), in their contribution to Bochner's volume, suggest that the interpreter should become a visible third party, and "within certain limits may develop his or her own initiatives, introduce new topics, give comments and explanations, present arguments, etc.". This strikes against not only the Ontario Code of Ethics, but all Western cultural orientations with regard to the meaning of 'professional' in 'professional interpreter'. As Edward Stewart (1985:53) notes in his *American Cultural Patterns,* "In some cultures the interpreters' role may become a more active one, to the consternation of the American who is likely to interpret it as inefficiency or perhaps disloyalty". Nevertheless, in the business world there are those who realize that involving the interpreter can help in meeting negotiating goals. Gary Ferraro (1994:142), for example, underlines the importance of briefing the interpreter on objectives and that "The purposeful development of cordial relations with your interpreter can only help to facilitate the process of communication at the negotiation table".

More recently, research is showing quite conclusively that dialogue interpreters (Mason 2000), talk show interpreters (Katan and Straniero Sergio 2001) and, indeed 'cultural interpreters' (Favaron 2002) consistently intervene proactively, to ensure that communication continues smoothly across the cultural divide. Humphrey and Alcorn (1996) draw a "philosophical shift in the history of sign language interpreting". The barometer has left "machine conduit", is hovering on "communication facilitation", and is heading towards "bilingual/bicultural mediation". Another book, "Sign Language Interpreting", by Melanie Metzger (1999) actually has "Deconstructing the Myth of Neutrality" as its subtitle.

What is particularly disarming about this trend though is that the majority of the interpreters involved are still self-trained, barely visible, and are still treated as series B copiers. One shining exception that we know of is Olga Fernando. She is a professional, university-trained media interpreter, and has been praised in the Italian national press for her "sensitivity". Much more importantly, she is always addressed, and now known by, her name – and never as "the interpreter". We believe that she could well be a model to follow (Katan and Straniero Sergio 2001).

• *The Translator*

Taft (1981:58) asks whether a mediator is a translator. His own answer, as we have already seen, is that translating is one of the skills, but that a mediator is more than a translator. Basil Hatim and Ian Mason (1990:128, 223-24) also use the term mediation, suggesting that: "The notion of mediation is a useful way of looking at translators' decisions regarding the transfer of intertextual reference".

They continue, in the chapter entitled 'The Translator as Mediator', with the following:

> The translator is first and foremost a mediator between two parties for whom mutual communication might otherwise be problematic and this is true of the translator of patents, contracts, verse or fiction just as much as it is of the simultaneous interpreter, who can be seen to be mediating in a very direct way.

The authors conclude with two specific ways in which a translator is a mediator:

> • **bi-cultural vision**
>   The translator is uniquely placed to identify and resolve the disparity between sign and value across cultures.
> • **critical reader**
>   The translator is a 'privileged reader' of the Source Language [SL] text. S/he will have the opportunity to read the text carefully before translating, and therefore is in a position to help the target reader by producing as clear a text as the context would warrant.

Lance Hewson and Jacky Martin (1991:143), in their *Redefining Translation: The Variational Approach*, agree that the translator is also a critic. As they say, "Certain texts have been subjected to what one might call an intense and loving scrutiny, producing a 'hyper-reading' (Ladmiral 1979) of the original to the extent that people might well consult a translation in order to have a better (or more complete) understanding of the original". One particular example is the translation of Shakespeare, which will be discussed in Chapter 5.

Albrecht Neubert and Gregory Shreve (1992:54) go one stage further with the concept, suggesting that translations should serve as "knowledge breakers between the members of disjunct communities". Edwin Gentzler (2001:203) adds to this idea with the point that a text is always a part of history. He points out that the student of contemporary translation "is enmeshed in the entire network of multiple languages, discourses, sign systems, and cultures, all of which are found in both the source and translated texts and which mutually interact in the process of translation. The number of borders being crossed in one translation are always multiple".

With regard to who the translator is, Hans Vermeer (1978) described the translator as "bi-cultural", and Mary Snell-Hornby (1992) has described him or her as a "cross-cultural specialist". Hewson and Martin talk of 'The Translation Operator as a Cultural Operator' (1991:133-155, 160, 161) and discuss "the identity and motivations of the translation operator". Though they do not provide detail, they are clear on one point: "Our aim is simply to underline once again the [Translator Operator's] socio-cultural identity as being one of the many factors which account for translation being what it is". Hatim and Mason (1990:11) make the same point: "inevitably we feed our own beliefs, knowledge, attitudes and so on into our processing of texts, so that any translation will, to some extent, reflect the translator's own mental and cultural outlook, despite the best of impartial intentions".

Artemeva (1998:287) describes the difficulties she had working with technical (Russian to English) translators who first "expressed surprise at, and then rejected, my explanations about differences in the structure of English and Russian texts, different rhetorical patterns, and different emphasis on reader awareness". She concludes by saying "they need to be taught how to adapt to different ways of writing, how to learn on the job, how to understand other cultures, and the like to become better communicators". This means that, first, cultural interpreters/mediators need to be extremely aware of their own cultural identity; and for this reason they will need to understand how their own culture influences perception.

• *The Future*

Both translators and interpreters will have to be fluent in cross-cultural communication, otherwise, as Artemeva suggests, that role will be given to the writing consultant, and the translator may well truly become a technical word copier.

Also, as Kondo (1990) points out, an interpreter will have to tread very carefully when it comes to active participation in the communication process. Though, the academic world is, in theory, generally pushing for a more active and visible mediator, practical instances of it are, more often than not, met with ideological entrenchment. Pym, for example, asks: "are we really prepared to condone all those talk-show interpreters who truncate and twist the subjectivity of their foreign guests so as to slot them into the dictates of genre and Berlusconi commerce?" (Pym 2001:135).

The same is still true for the translator, where any idea of deliberately making changes to the form of the text, and manipulating the words to aid further understanding across cultures, is still viewed with suspicion. As we have stressed, the Western community at large still sees the translator and interpreter as a walking dictionary with fluent copying skills, and not as a cultural mediator.

In many other countries, both interpreters and translators are already carrying out some of the mediating functions. Fons Trompenaars and Charles Hampden-Turner (1997:60), intercultural management consultants, note that the interpreter "in more collectivist cultures will usually serve the national group, engaging them in lengthy asides and attempting to mediate misunderstandings arising from the culture as well as the language".

What is still needed in the West is a second development working in tandem with the wider role of the mediator: that of raising general awareness for the importance of the cultural factor. Leaving aside the EU classification of professions, there are signs that this is beginning to happen, particularly in the very pragmatic business community. One example is how advertising the concept of "global" is changing: from "one size fits all" to the slogan "think global act local", which HSBC is publicly broadcasting:

> HSBC Bank USA today announced the launch of a new branding campaign, which will leverage its status as one of the world's few, global financial organizations and highlight its unique ability to also operate as a truly local organization in each of the markets that it serves. This move is part of a branding initiative that HSBC Group has undertaken throughout the world.
>
> "The importance of knowing and understanding the local market is ingrained in our corporate culture," said John Carroll, Executive Vice President and Head of Marketing, HSBC Bank USA. ... HSBC's new tagline, "The world's local bank," is the synthesis of this positioning. "Being local means more than just speaking the language," noted Carroll, "Our offices around the world are staffed by local people who understand local customs and needs".
>
> Press Release 11/03/02

More importantly, there are a number of business publications focusing on the cultural factor, many of which will be quoted in these Chapters. Moreover, there is a steady increase in the number of business training courses on intercultural communication, both in Britain and abroad.

The British Department of Trade and Industry has also contributed with, for example, a series of sixteen-page handbooks distributed free to companies to heighten the awareness of the cultural factor in international business (D.T.I. 1994). One of the handbooks is entitled *Translating and Interpreting* and focuses on the need for a professional culturally aware interpreter and professionally trained translator for successful international business.

As the business environment itself begins to realize that culture, at all levels, is a fundamental issue in the success or failure of cross-cultural ventures, so it should be possible for the humble, university trained, general interpreter or translator to take a more high profile role in actively promoting understanding across languages and cultures. To do this, potential mediators should combine formal language and culture learning with a sojourn abroad, and hence, informal modelling of the target culture.

This brings us back to the teaching of culture for translators and interpreters. According to Newmark (1988:17), much of the analysis of the cultural aspect of the SL text "may be intuitive". The following chapters will investigate that intuition, and should form part of the formal learning about culture and the way it guides how we communicate.

Chapter 2. Defining, Modelling and Teaching Culture

The aim of this chapter is to:
- discuss the various definitions of culture
- introduce various models of culture
- discuss various approaches to the teaching of culture
- introduce the concept of ethnocentrism and culture-bound behaviour

2.1 On Defining Culture

> Whenever I hear the word 'culture' ... I release the safety-catch of my pistol.
> Hanns Johst, *Schlageter* (Palmer 1981:13); a quotation often attributed to Goering.

People instinctively know what 'culture' means to them and to which culture they belong. For example, in 1999 *Eurobarometer*[1] asked to what extent EU citizens felt attached to Europe. The (simplified) results were as follows:

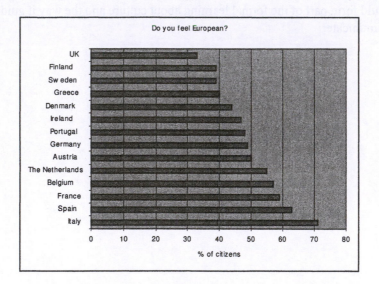

Figure 1. How European do Europeans feel

The results illustrate a number of interesting points about culture. First, individuals have a clear idea of where they belong culturally. Secondly, the mere fact of "being

---

[1] From the on-line book, *How Europeans See Themselves,* European Commission Sept. 2000, http://europa.eu.int/comm/publications/booklets/eu_documentation/05/txt_en.pdf

a member" does not necessarily mean that we feel attached – as the UK results show. Third, and more interestingly again, the differences highlight the fact that national groups tend to think along the same lines – i.e. as a culture. However, even though we all know to which culture we belong, definition of the word has been notoriously difficult.

One of the oldest and most quoted definitions of culture was formulated by the English anthropologist Edward Barnett Tylor in (1871/1958:1). It is, for example, used by the *Encyclopedia Britannica* (2000) to introduce the topic, and Edward Sapir (1994:35, 37, 40, 44) quoted it widely: "Culture is that complex whole which includes knowledge, belief, art, morals, law, customs and any other capabilities and habits acquired by man as a member of society".

By 1952, American anthropologists Alfred Louis Kroeber and Clyde Kluckhohn (1952:181) had compiled a list of 164 definitions. Their own lengthy definition was as follows:

> Culture consists of patterns, explicit and implicit of and for behaviour ac-
> quired and transmitted by symbols, constituting the distinctive achievement
> of human groups, including their embodiment in artefacts; the essential core
> of culture consists of traditional (i.e., historically derived and selected) ideas
> and especially their attached values. Culture systems may, on the one hand,
> be considered as products of action, on the other hand, as conditioning ele-
> ments of future action.

By the 1980's we have the following comment from *Teaching Culture* (Ned Seeleye 1978:413): "I know of no way to better ensure having nothing productive happen than for a language department to begin its approach to culture by a theoretical concern for defining the term". During the 1990's the 10 volume *Encyclopedia of Language and Linguistics* (1994:2001) confirmed that "Despite a century of efforts to define culture adequately, there was in the early 1990s no agreement among anthropologists regarding its nature".

Interculturalists, such as Trompenaars and Hampden-Turner (1997:21) admit that "In twenty years we have seldom encountered two or more groups or individuals with identical suggestions regarding the concept of culture". Today, the discussion is now enveloping ideology with many beginning to wonder if the definition of one also includes the other (Fawcett 1998:106).

Defining culture is important, not as an academic exercise, but because defining it delimits how it is perceived and taught. Put simply, if we define culture as "a particular civilization at a particular period" (*CED* 1991), then we will teach history, such as *England in the Nineteenth Century*. This definition of culture we might call high culture or culture with a capital 'C'. High Culture is not the concern of this book. This Culture is external to the individual and relates to a particular and restricted body of knowledge learned, and to a particular (upper) middle-class upbringing. It tends to be associated with 'well-educated', 'refined', 'a man of culture' (rather than woman), 'culture vulture', 'cultured', and so on. Culture for these people is fixed in time, and ended with the death of the novel, Evelyn Waugh, 'the old days' or some other appropriate time marker.

If, on the other hand, we define culture in terms of "the artistic and social pursuits, expressions and tastes valued by a society or class" (*CED* 1991) we will be teaching national literature, sports, hobbies, and some of the following:[2]

> The Frankenstein approach: A taco from here, a flamenco dancer from there, a gaucho from here, a bullfight from there
> The 4-F approach: Folk dances, festivals, fairs, and food
> The Tour Guide approach: The identification of monuments, rivers and cities
> The 'By the Way' approach: Sporadic lectures or bits of behaviour selected indiscriminately to emphasize sharp differences

The culture under discussion here is not visible as a product, but is internal, collective and is acquired rather than learned. Acquisition is the natural, unconscious learning of language, behaviour, values and belief through informal watching and hearing. Learning, on the other hand, is formal and is consciously taught. The culture we are interested in is acquired before the formal learning of Culture at school.

The word comes from the Latin *cultus*, 'cultivation', and *colere* 'to till'. The metaphorical extension is apt. Seeds continually absorb elements from the land, or rather the ecosystem, to ensure their development. In the same way, people continually absorb vital elements from their immediate environment that influence their development within the human system.

However, the traditional teaching of culture to translators, interpreters, and to language students in general, has not focused on culture as a shared system for interpreting reality and organizing experience (a possible definition for culture).

A course on the subject, in many academic institutions, includes a module on literature and history up to, but not necessarily including, the 20th century, and grounding in certain national bureaucratic and political institutions. What is fascinating is that the students graduate more proficient in these subjects than the vast majority of people they will be translating or interpreting for. Whether or not they are culturally proficient is another matter.

The definition of culture proposed here is in terms of a shared mental model or map of the world. This includes Culture – though it is not the main focus. Instead, the main focus here lies in 'what goes without being said' and the 'normal'. This 'normal' model of the world is a system of congruent and interrelated beliefs, values, strategies and cognitive environments which guide the shared basis of behaviour. Each aspect of culture is linked in a system to form a unifying context of culture, which then identifies a person and his or her culture.

Most of the 164 definitions cited by Kroeber and Kluckhohn, in fact, relate to a part of this definition of culture. As a first step in the organization of the various

---

[2] www.asialink.unimelb.edu.au/aef/shanghai/papers/ws4.html

approaches to culture, Gail Robinson (1988:7-13), from the Center for Language and Crosscultural Skills in San Francisco, grouped the various definitions into two basic levels: external and internal.

Culture definitions relating to...	
• *External* behaviours	– language, gestures, customs/habits
• products	– literature, folklore, art, music, artefacts
• *Internal* ideas	– beliefs, values, institutions[3]

She then suggests that each of the definitions can be seen in terms of a variety of approaches. Each of these approaches will affect the teaching style and content of a course on culture:

Definition	Approach focuses on ...
• Behaviourist	discrete behaviours or sets of behaviours, shared and observed
• Functionalist	shared rules underlying behaviour, and observable through behaviour
• Cognitive	the form of things that people have in mind, their models for perceiving, relating, and otherwise interpreting them
• Dynamic	the dynamic interplay of internal models and external mechanisms

We will now look at each of these approaches in turn, and briefly discuss the teaching methodology implied.

2.2 Approaches to the Study of Culture

• Behaviourist
• Ethnocentrism
• Functionalist
• Cognitive
• Dynamic

• *Behaviourist*

One book, which exemplifies the Behaviourist approach, is the very popular *Life in Modern Britain*. The book was originally published by (emeritus professor) Peter Bromhead (1985:6) in 1962, and by 1995 was in its 18th edition. The book opens with a panorama of Britain and its people, from which the following extract is taken:

---

[3] Robinson's understanding of 'institutions' is clearly different to that generally taught on a course of the same name.

> The British do not kill thrushes or blackbirds or sparrows. Cornish fishermen
> do not slaughter mackerel wholesale; nor are they happy when others deplete
> the sea to satisfy today's demands. In the past hundred years the British have
> done much to spoil their country, but they have done more to preserve its
> character, its green variety and its modest scale.

This is a good example of a Behaviourist approach: selected facts about what
people do and do not do. This approach can load the student with facts of dubious
relevance, banalities, and, of course, an implicit view that what the British choose
to do, or not do, is naturally better or superior. One wonders what a Pedro Bromcabeza
might have included if he ever wrote *La vida en la España moderna* about what the
Spanish have done to preserve the community, family life, regional cooking, and so
on. Britain, seen from this viewpoint would have won no points whatsoever. The
main problem with an approach like this is that it is ethnocentric.

• *Ethnocentrism*

Ethnocentrism is the belief that the worldview of one's own culture is central to all
reality (Bennett 1993:30). As a logical result, this belief in the intrinsic superiority
of the culture to which one belongs is often accompanied by feelings of dislike and
contempt for other cultures. An Ethnocentric approach to the teaching of British, or
any other culture, does not help the student to reason, let alone translate. Ethnocentrism allows for little or no contextualisation of described behaviour nor does it
foster an investigation as to why such behaviour might logically take place.

Beverly McLeod's (1981:47) definition of culture in 'The Mediating Person and
Cultural Identity' is an indication of what is at the heart of the problem in teaching
'culture'. Culture is, she says, "what seems natural and right". Joyce Valdes
(1986:vii), Director of the Language and Culture Centre at the University of Houston, agrees. She argues that people are culture-bound (which is also the title of her
book). Being culture-bound, people do not see the confines of their own culture, but
instead focus on those of other cultures: "Most people of whatever nation, see themselves and their compatriots not as culture but as 'standard' or 'right', and the rest
of the world as made up of cultures".

There has, of late, been a move to put Britain into a European context. *Profile
UK* (McLean 1993) was an early example with unit headings such as 'How European is Britain?' Students are actively encouraged to compare their own country
with Britain, but again, this approach concentrates on institutions. Even more recently, both the British Council and the University of Warwick have changed the
name of their courses from 'British Civilization' to 'British Cultural Studies'.[4]

---

[4] For a discussion, see Bassnett (1997); Bassnett was a key player in both the 'cultural turn' in
translation studies and the 'translational turn' in cultural studies. She is Professor at the Centre
for British and Comparative Cultural Studies, University of Warwick.

• *Functionalist*

The Functionalist approach to culture is a definite move away from Behaviourist ethnocentrism and purports to be above individual cultures. Such an approach looks at the reasons behind the behaviour. This is the realm of cultural studies as it is taught at present. Mona Baker (1996:13) points out that "However much they might differ in their attitudes to and understanding of the meaning of culture, scholars working within cultural studies tend to think of culture in political terms", and politics is seen in terms of good and bad ideologies. The Functionalist approach tends to stay locked within a judgemental frame based on one culture's dominant, or preferred, values; scholars tend to focus on power relations and the domination of one national culture, creed, gender or sexual orientation over another. The culture under investigation in this book is considered deeper than politics, and will orient a group of people towards dominating or accepting domination. Our task, as translators, interpreters and mediators in general, is to understand others; and to understand what makes sense (for them) rather than argue that we, and only we, have the truth.

Returning to Bromhead (1985:11), he does state the reason for the behaviour cited. In talking about London and how it has changed since 1921, he explains: "So much impermanence, change and movement have made the people more innovative, the place more lively, so full of surprises, that nothing is surprising".

As we shall see when discussing the Meta-Model, this type of language does not help to clarify culture. In this particular case it would seem that the substantive catalyst, i.e. "impermanence, change and movement", is also the underlying cause. 'Impermanence' in itself cannot *cause* London to be more lively – and 'liveliness' is only one of a number of possible responses to impermanence. The reaction to change depends on other factors, such as a culture's tolerance of uncertainty, whether it prefers to focus on the future rather than on the past, and so on. It is these factors that form the basis of the cognitive approach.

• *Cognitive*

This approach attempts to account for the way the brain works in linking a particular cause and a particular effect. It tends to use the concepts of modelling, and talks of mapping, underlying patterns and the culture-bound categorizing of experience. Howard Nostrand (1989:51), for example, talks of a culture's 'central code': "The central code ... involves above all the culture's 'ground of meaning'; its system of major values, habitual patterns of thought, and certain prevalent assumptions about human nature and society which the foreigner should be prepared to encounter".

Various authors have also used the analogy of computer programming to explain these habitual patterns of thought. For example, Geert Hofstede (1991:4-5), one of the most influential writers in the field, states:

> Using the analogy of the way computers are programmed, [we] will call such patterns of thinking, feeling, and acting *mental programs*, or ... *software of the mind*. ...Culture is the collective programming of the mind which distinguishes the members of one group or category of people from another.

Hofstede does accept that there are differences between a human brain and a computer, in that the human brain can react and change in unexpected and creative ways. His thesis is, though, that each culture will have a set software which every member of that culture will acquire, to a greater or lesser extent.

This view of culture suggests that, in learning about any other culture, one needs first to learn about how one's own internal programming functions in one's own culture. This is a move away from the Functionalist approach. Those who write or who are involved in intercultural training at this level (in marked difference to Bromhead) explicitly state who they are, and where their own preferred patterns lie. Claire Kramsch (1993:11, 188), for example, who has written a great deal on teaching culture, calls herself "a French woman, Germanist and teacher of German in the United States" (at MIT). She is convinced that language students cannot be expected to fully understand another set of institutions or even authentic material, such as newspaper articles, because the students (almost literally) cannot see past their own culture:

> The issue that is raised by the use of real-life materials is that culture is a reality that is social, political and ideological, and that the difficulty of understanding cultural codes stems from the difficulty of viewing the world from another perspective, not of grasping another lexical or grammatical code.

• *Summary of Behaviourist, Functionalist and Cognitive Approaches*

To summarize, the Behaviourist approach tends towards ethnocentricity. It is taught in terms of institutions and culture with a 'C'. The Functionalist approach attempts to look at what lies behind the behaviour and account for it. It does this though, through culture-bound evaluations, made within the context of one particular culture.

The Cognitive approach emphasizes the context and boundaries. It suggests that cultures model reality in different (rather than better or worse) ways. The teaching at this level includes the presentation of generalized models of culture. These are very useful models for providing a general framework of culture; and indeed, much of this book is devoted to explaining them.

However, all these models suffer to the extent that they treat culture as a frozen state. They also suggest that mediation between cultures is relatively straightforward. Valdes (1986), in fact, has the following optimistic words as the subtitle to her book: *Bridging the Cultural Gap in Language Teaching*. Kramsch (1993:228) categorically does not agree (emphasis in the original):

> What we should seek in cross-cultural education are less bridges than a deep understanding of boundaries. We can teach the boundary, we cannot teach the bridge. We can *talk about* and try to *understand* the differences between the values celebrated in the [American] Coca-Cola commercial and the lack or the existence of analogous values in its Russian or German equivalents. We cannot teach directly how to resolve the conflict between the two.

Though this might sound like an admission of defeat, it is in fact an acceptance that there is another approach to culture, what Gail Robinson (1988:11) terms the 'symbolic' definition of culture, which is the subject of the next section.

• *Dynamic*

The fourth approach to culture is to perceive it as a dynamic process. Robinson (ibid.:11) notes that "The concept of culture as a creative, historical system of symbols and meaning has the potential to fill in the theoretical gaps left by Behaviourist, Functionalist and Cognitive theories".

According to this theory, 'meaning' in culture is not an independent fact to be found by consulting books, cognitive maps or any other static system. It is, as described by French sociologist, Pierre Bourdieu, a 'habitus': "a system of durable, transposable dispositions", of "internalised structures, common schemes of perception, conception and action", the result of inculcation and habituation, simultaneously structured and structuring, and directed towards practice (1990:53-60). This may also be called a semiotic approach to culture (see Barthes 1993).

Culture, then, at this level is viewed as a dynamic process, constantly negotiated by those involved. It is influenced, but not determined, by past meanings and it establishes precedent for future meanings. However, this does not mean that culture is constantly changing, but that there is a dialectic process between internal models of the world and external reality. Clearly, teaching at this level cannot simply be reduced to a teacher explaining facts.

There are two important conclusions to be drawn from viewing culture at this level. First, rather than the teacher being the only active person, students or trainees become actively involved in learning about culture through 'hands on' experience. Howard Nostrand (1989:51), in fact, talks of the need for "inter-cultural encounters", thus making sojourns abroad an essential component of any course on culture. Encounters can also be simulated through cultural assimilators and critical incidents.[5]

The second point to note is that because culture is not static, change is possible not only individually but in society as a whole. In fact, many believe that, as the global village becomes more of a reality, so these changes in culture will lead to a levelling of difference, and move towards the lowest common denominator: McDonaldization.

2.3 McDonaldization or Local Globalization?

- McDonaldization
- Local Globalization

The dynamic process of globalization of culture can be clearly seen in the converging style of dress and eating habits among the young: "Customers know they

---

[5] See, for example, Brislin (1993:227-43).

can count on being served the same Big Mac whether they're at a McDonald's in Moscow, Idaho, or Moscow, Russia."[6]

National fast or cheap food places, the fish and chip shop, the traditional American diner, the Italian *osteria* and even the Malay satay centres are being spurned by the young in favour of the queue-to-be-served hamburger. In fact, at the 32nd World Sociology Congress[7] two of the ten sessions were dedicated to what in sociology is called 'McDonaldization'. It is, according to George Ritzer (1993:1) who coined the word, "the process by which the principles of the fast-food restaurant are coming to dominate more and more sectors of American society as well as the rest of the world".

The fast-food principles are those of rationalization: a studied programmable system which attempts to standardize both the process and the product. According to Ritzer, there are four major principles:

• efficiency	product ordered and consumed in minimum time;
• quantity	good supply for a good price;
• predictability	product range identical at home and abroad and reproducible worldwide;
• control	of both employees and customers in terms of standardized practices, e.g. waiting and sitting times, operational checklists.

Rationalization also pervades the language (verbal and non-verbal) to such an extent that counter-staff worldwide are observed for performance down to the last discrete detail. The box below is a much-shortened summary of the performance evaluation sheet used at McDonald's for service counter operations (Hampden-Turner and Trompenaars 1993:42-43):

	Yes	No
Greeting the customer		
1. There is a smile	____	____
2. It is a sincere greeting	____	____
3. There is eye contact	____	____
Assembling the order		
1. The order is assembled in the proper sequence	____	____
2. Grill slips are handed first	____	____
3. Drinks are poured in the proper sequence	____	____
4. Proper amount of ice	____	____
Asking for and receiving payment		
1. The amount of the order is stated clearly and loud enough to hear	____	____

---

[6] http://www.mcdonalds.com/countries/usa/corporate/info/studentkit/media/taste.pdf
[7] 'Dialogue between Cultures and Changes in Europe and the World', Trieste, 3-7 July, 1995.

> 2. The denomination received is clearly stated ____ ____
> 3. The change is counted out loud ____ ____
> 4. Change is counted efficiently ____ ____
> 5. Large bills are laid on the till until the
> change is given ____ ____
> **Thanking the customer and asking for repeat business**
> 1. There is always a thank you ____ ____
> 2. The thank you is sincere ____ ____
> 3. There is eye contact ____ ____
> 4. Return business was asked for ____ ____

The dynamic process whereby McDonaldization is changing the behaviour of consumers worldwide may also be seen at a deeper level. One example comes from Robert Dilts (1990). He is known for his work on human belief systems, and dedicates his book, on the subject of beliefs and change, "with deepest respect to the peoples of Eastern Europe who have shown the world the power and the reach of true belief change". The "true belief change" has been in terms not only of change in the political system but mainly in terms of a total embracement of a consumer-led capitalist economy.

However, not all agree that this particular dynamic process is the result of a change of belief. On the contrary, it may be that underlying cultural beliefs have been allowed to surface as a result of a weakening political culture (see Mead 1994). As James Ritchie (1981:222), Professor of Psychology at the University of New South Wales, points out: "Numerous and repeated changes may occur in, say, political systems without disturbance to the basic set of premises that lie behind behaviour".

Whatever the reasons, a dynamic process is going on. At the level of behaviour, the American hamburger, jeans and trainers, followed by Hollywood entertainment have, superficially, united the world. In fact, many authors believe, as does Kaynak (cited in Séguinot 1995:65) that:

> the growing significance of global communication ... blurs national differences. Age and lifestyle may be more important than national culture. Thanks to satellite TV, adolescents the world over have more in common with their peers in other countries in terms of their tastes than with other age groups from the same culture.

However, there are two main points to mention here. First, as we shall investigate in more detail later, the blurring of differences is at a visible level. What does not blur are the more important yet invisible elements of what actually make up a culture. As Kramsch (1993:227, emphasis in the original) says, "it is a fallacy to believe that because Russians now drink Pepsi-Cola, Pepsi *means* the same for them as for Americans".

Second, the four principles of McDonaldization are not, in fact, applicable worldwide. The sociologist Shannon Peters Talbott (unpublished), and cognoscente of

McDonald's in Moscow, points out that none of the four principles actually fit the Russian interest in eating at McDonald's. Below, is a summary of the differences found by Talbott. On the left is the McDonaldization theory according to Ritzer, and on the right the reality in the Moscow McDonald's in 1995:

Theory	Reality
• efficiency:	queues of up to an hour, even in 1995, and idem for time spent inside at the table
• quantity	many buy tea and not the food. The average cost of a meal is above the national average daily wage
• predictability	product range is different to daily food. Menu is not identical to an American McDonald's (no EggMcMuffin!)
• control	customers allowed to sit and chat.

His argument against Ritzer's third point regarding predictability (lack of EggMcMuffin) may be considered weak. Yet, the official McDonald's site, itself, in reaction to falling consumer interest, vaunts the fact that:

> Internationally [McDonald's] occasionally develop other items which appeal to our host country's cultural preferences. For example, some McDonald's restaurants serve rice dishes and fried chicken in Japan; beer in Germany; Kiwi burgers in New Zealand; spaghetti in the Philippines; salmon sandwiches, called "McLaks," in Norway; and in Islamic countries, like Saudi Arabia, our restaurants offer a "Halal" menu.[8]

In fact, the American Quintin Tarantino found similar small differences in Europe worth mentioning in his film *Pulp Fiction*:

> "But you know, the funniest thing about Europe?"
> "What?"
> "It's the little differences .... In Paris you can buy a beer in a McDonald's ....
> And you know what they call a quarter pounder with cheese in Paris?"
> "No. They don't call it a quarter pounder with cheese?"
> "No, they've got the metric system. They wouldn't know what the fuck a quarter pounder is ".
> "So, what do they call it?"
> "They call it a Royale with cheese".
> "A Royale with cheese?"
> "That's right".
> "And what do they call a Big Mac?"
> "A Big Mac's a Big Mac, but they call it Le Big Mac".
> "Le Big Mac ".
> [laughter]

---

[8] http://www.mcdonalds.com/countries/usa/corporate/info/studentkit/media/taste.pdf

More importantly, Peters Talbott's other points show that Muscovites do not go to McDonald's for the same reasons as the Americans, nor do they behave at McDonald's in the same way as would be expected in America. Also, McDonald's management in Moscow have adapted to Muscovite ways by allowing clients to make McDonald's a 'slow-drink' rather than a fast-food outlet.

Bill Gates[9] knows to his cost that "When it comes to 'localizing' information, nuance matters". He describes the "hundreds, sometimes thousands of new articles" that were written when localizing the Encarta encyclopaedia into 5 different languages. Below is how the US and British "local, educated, realities" (Gates' words) talked about the same event: the invention of the incandescent light bulb:

> US: In 1878 and 1879, British inventor Joseph Swan and American inventor Thomas Edison simultaneously developed the carbon-filament lamp.
> GB: In 1878 [Swan] demonstrated an electric light using a carbon wire in a vacuum bulb. Thomas Edison arrived independently at the same solution the following year.

It may be relatively easy to accept that history is open to interpretation and local adaptation – but this is just the tip of the iceberg. The American anthropologist Edward T. Hall (1990:83) gives us a nice example of local, Mexican, adaptation of what should not have been open to interpretation – at least as far as the visiting Americans were concerned. Urban speed limits of 15 mph had been introduced in Mexico in the 1930s. The Americans working there were constantly getting speeding fines from a particular traffic policeman when they were driving one mile an hour above the legal speed – and, in rage, paid the fine.

The principle of fines for speeding had been interpreted differently in Mexico, according to the local informal way of doing things. In Mexico, at that time, almost everyone knew someone who could help in tearing up the ticket once it had been written. Hence, except for the most serious of offences, it was possible not to pay. The American understanding and application of the rule starts from another viewpoint. The traffic police will only give a ticket for the most serious of offences, i.e. not at sixteen miles an hour, but at over twenty. At which point there is no discussion.

What happens is that an imported system, such as enforced speed control or eating at McDonald's, dynamically adapts to an already existing way of doing things. According to Talbott and others, there will always be global localization (or glocalization), and successful individuals and multi-nationals like McDonald's will always dynamically adapt to local cultures. In fact, the global MTV pop music channel "soon learned that success depended on creating local versions" (*Economist* 5/4/ 2003). So far, there are 38 independent local MTVs:

---

[9] http://www.microsoft.com/billgates/columns/1997essay/essay970326.asp (3/26/97)

> Each is tailored to local tastes, literally: a top show on MTV Italy is 'MTV Kitchen', where musicians show off their favourite recipes. In Indonesia, MTV broadcasts a 'funky but respectful' call to prayer five times a day'...

An important second point regarding the invasion of McDonald's is that although there is now a McDonald's on platform one at the Bologna train station in Italy, on platform 2 the local traditional snack, *piadine*, is also doing very good business. McDonald's has also adapted on platform one by sharing its premises with a well-stocked Italian bar, and does not even attempt to compete with Italian coffee. According to many (Waters: unpublished), chains such as McDonald's have already reached their limits, in America at least. The result of global localization is, in fact, a potentially richer culture, with the choice of whether to go global or local being decided on a day-to-day basis.

This dynamic process of interaction between the global and the local culture has been taken up in recent business development models. In fact, as we are seeing, the importance of local cultures is being taken extremely seriously by big business, and the models underline the fact that the more a company develops, the more important the cultural factor becomes.

The diagram below is an adaptation of a typical model, taken from a training management course (Brake *et al*. 1995:20). It shows five stages in the growth and development of a company. A typical company begins life operating exclusively on the domestic market. Cross-cultural communication will already be a key factor for management within cosmopolitan markets such as Australia and the United States, due to their multi-ethnic workforce. A good example of the effects of culture at the domestic level is given in an Australian video entitled *Cultural Diversity at Work: The Business Advantage* (SBS 1996). When the company begins to export, the culture factor affects every department, from research and development of new products and services to sales and after-sales service. Not only are departments affected, but each individual working across cultures will react to the fact that he or she is communicating with a foreign tax or legal system, agent or customer. The foreignness will be compounded by language, and how it is used to communicate.

When the company becomes a multinational, it is again operating mainly with locally recruited personnel working within their respective domestic cultures. The next stage is global. The global company experiences the effect of cultural diversity within its own departments. The company, working with diverse cultures, brings them together, and the market is global. The product, such as the Ford *Mondeo*, also has a global name. The final outcome, though, transcends the "one global market, one global product" stage. The transnational company consciously responds to the needs of local cultures and exploits the strengths of cultural diversity within its own departments. The intensity of competition will help to ensure that if a company is to succeed, it will need to understand and take advantage of these cultural differences. This business theory fits more closely to the reality of HSBC, MTV and McDonald's than does Ritzer's McDonaldization Theory:

Domestic	Export/ International	Multinational	Global	Transnational
Domestic multi-culturalism making an impact	Crosscultural negotiations. Must adapt approach, products and services to local cultures. Cultural diversity has big effect on external relationships	Localized structure reduces need for cross-cultural awareness	Need to manage cultural diversity inside and outside the company. All levels need cross-cultural management skills for maximum flexibility	Global structure requiring networked multinational skills and abilities with a critical understanding of local responsiveness, integrating and coordinating mechanism of corporate culture on a global basis

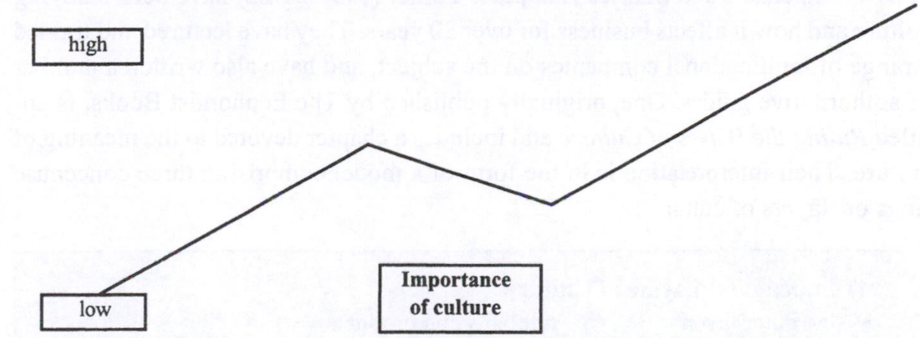

Figure 2. Organizational form and the Importance of Culture

2.4 Models of Culture

- Trompenaars' Layers
- Hofstede's Onion Model
- The Iceberg Theory
- Hall's Triad of Culture

The approaches to culture we have just discussed are not mutually exclusive, and none of them by themselves totally cover all aspects of culture. The various theories, Behaviourist, Functionalist, Cognitive and Dynamic, operate at different levels, in much the same way as translation and the cultural factor, which we discussed earlier. We will now look at a number of models, which aim to unite these approaches. They have all been suggested by social anthropologists who are also as it happens, business consultants.

Modelling is a process that simplifies how a system functions. We have mentioned in the dynamic approach to culture that learning facts is not enough, and
that bridges between cultures cannot be taught. Models, on the other hand, can be
taught and are much more useful in understanding how culture functions. The
business training programmes now available include courses on communication
and culture, and they generally provide models of culture and cross-cultural (or
change-management) communication skills rather than simply facts about a country or rules of conduct.

The models discussed below come from some of the major influences on training in culture for the business community: Trompenaars and Hampden-Turner;
Hofstede; Brake, Medina Walker and Walker, and E.T. Hall. All the models provide useful ways of understanding culture, and they will be referred to later in
the book.

• *Trompenaars' Layers*

Fons Trompenaars and Charles Hampden-Turner (1997:21-22) have been studying
culture and how it affects business for over 20 years. They have lectured and trained
a range of multinational companies on the subject, and have also written a number
of authoritative guides. One, originally published by The Economist Books, is entitled *Riding the Waves of Culture* and includes a chapter devoted to the meaning of
culture. Their interpretation is in the form of a model comprising three concentric
rings or 'layers of culture':

Trompenaars' Layers of Culture	
• the outer layer	artefacts and products
• the middle layer	norms and values
• the core	basic assumptions

The outer layer is the most visible layer. Trompenaars calls this 'explicit'. This
is the level of culture with a capital 'C': the artefacts and products. The organization of institutions, such as the legal system and bureaucracy, are included here.
The middle layer differentiates between norms and values. The norms relate to social rules of conduct. They concern, and to a large extent dictate, how one should
behave in society. Values, on the other hand, are aspirations, which may never actually be achieved.

Finally, we have the core, which as the word suggests, is not visible. Trompenaars'
term is 'implicit'. This is the heart of culture, and the most inaccessible. It contains
basic assumptions about life which have been handed down unconsciously from
generation to generation. These unquestioned assumptions may have little to do
with the present, but they have much to do with long-forgotten survival responses to
the environment:

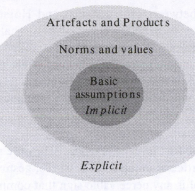

Figure 3. Trompenaars' Model of Culture (1993:23)

• *Hofstede's Onion*

Geert Hofstede is one of the most influential authors in the field and has been quoted by many,[10] including Trompenaars and Hampden-Turner (1997:x), who say the following in the 'Acknowledgements':

> And obviously, we could not be stimulated more than by the comments of Geert Hofstede. He introduced Fons to the subject of intercultural management some 20 years ago. We do not always agree, but he has made a major contribution to the field, and was responsible for opening management's eyes to the importance of the subject.

Hofstede's (1991:7, 9) chapter on defining culture is actually entitled 'Levels of Culture', and specifically uses the metaphor of "skins of an onion" not in reference to any tears, but simply because there are superficial and deeper layers, which he suggests are as follows:

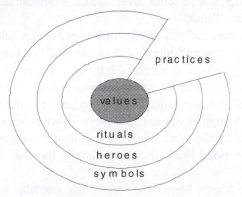

Figure 4. Hofstede's Levels of Culture

---

[10] e.g. by Victor (1992), Brake *et al*. (1995), Mead (1990, 1994), Adler (1991).

The main difference between Trompenaars' and Hofstede's model is that Trompenaars has a tripartite view of culture (like Hall as we shall see), while Hofstede has two main layers: practices and values. Hofstede groups symbols, heroes and rituals under practices (as compared with Trompenaars' artefacts and products, norms and values) and makes it clear that "the core of culture is formed by *values*" (emphasis in the original). We will first look at 'practices' in a little more detail.

• *Practices*

The 'symbols' represent the first level of practices. They are semiotic signs recognized as belonging to a particular group such as words, gestures, pictures, objects, dress, and so on. A symbol is any perceivable sign that communicates a meaning. Hofstede includes these in the outer, most superficial layer because, like a hairstyle, they can be changed easily.

For those who speak two or more languages, changing the language is also easy, but does not necessarily mean that there has been any cultural switch. Comedians, in fact, take great stock in sending up the English who manage to speak French while remaining English in every other respect. Many bilinguals find themselves in the same position: they are bilingual but not bi-cultural, and hence lay themselves open to being "fluent fools" (Bennett M. *et al.* 1999:13).

Next come 'heroes'. Hofstede is unusual (in the intercultural field) in highlighting the importance of real or imaginary heroes. Semioticians, instead, such as Umberto Eco and Ronald Barthes focus much of their work on how screen heroes construct cultural identities. Hofstede focuses on the advent of national film and television, and the creation of culturally diverse role models. It is certainly true that Clint Eastwood, Rambo and Superman provide (and reflect) one particular culture's belief in the superhero: the outsider who single-handedly defeats evil in society. It would be difficult to imagine any of these as being the national heroes of any other culture. On the other side of the Atlantic Ocean, Ian Fleming's British secret agent is anything but an outsider, and he could never take on American behaviour and say "My name's Bond, Jimmy Bond".

On the other hand, superficially, a number of heroes are pan-cultural. If we look at Italy and the US and compare children's heroes, we find that they travel between the cultures, highlighting cultural similarities. Italy has adopted Mickey Mouse (or rather *Topolino*) as its own Italian hero; with his own Italian written and produced magazine, which is "still the best-selling Disney magazine in the world". What is particularly interesting, though, is that all the Disney characters, all with local names, are much more part of the Italian collective memory than in the US. *The Phantom*, too, having outlived his useful life in the USA, happily lives on in Europe and in Australia.[11]

According to Italian *Martin Mystery* writer Alfredo Castelli, even though 80% of domestic comic production in Europe is European-made, local writers all follow

---

[11] http:/www.khepri.com/i-bvzm-3.htm

the "iron rule", and comics continue to be characterized by "American" main characters and settings. Castelli continues, "Though many of [Martin Mystère's] adventures are set in Italy, Mystère 'is' American and 'lives' in Washington Mews, NY, where he has been a lecturer". In fact, Italian fans of this particular French-named American rang the doorbell of 3 Washington Mews looking for the hero. Alfredo Castelli wrote to the real resident apologising: "The real resident – a Mr. Claxton, working for NYU – was very kind with me, and answered that, indeed he was surprised by the strange pilgrimage to his home, still stranger as the pilgrims were Italians".[12]

On the other hand, Pinocchio (outside Italy) is associated with Disney rather than with Collodi, and is a major Hollywood hero in his own right, having netted two Academy awards: "Count the number of truly classic animated films and the list would begin with *Walt Disney's Pinocchio* ... a timeless adventure for all who have a dream in their heart".[13] What remains to be seen is whether Roberto Benigni's version will change *Pinocchio's* epicentre in any way.

Finally, under 'practices' we find 'rituals'. According to Hofstede (1991:8), these are "technically superfluous in reaching desired ends, but, within a culture, are considered as socially essential". Rituals permeate all communication. For example, in any conversation (except for restricted or artificial language talk) there is a ritual 'ice-breaking' or introductory rapport building chat, whether the context is an international conference, a negotiation, a presentation or a casual encounter.

Each context will have its own culturally appropriate introductory ritual. In Italian there is a tendency, in casual conversation, to comment on personal appearance, health and family. In English, the accent is on the weather and activities (work, routines, etc.); while in Malay, conversations tend to open with a food question ("Have you eaten yet?"). Communicative interference is the term used in linguistics to describe the problem of using L1 rituals in L2.

Mode of address is another example of ritual, from "doffing one's cap", bowing, shaking hands, to modes of address. The examples in the following table show how often there is no direct translation. The examples are from Italian, though the same if not more complex non-equivalents occur with every other language.

Many other examples of formulaic expressions that form part of more elaborate language rituals are to be found in phrase books. Even dictionaries are now beginning to include sections on these rituals. The Collins bilingual dictionaries have now published French-English and Italian-English dictionaries each with over 60 pages on how a language-culture has ritualised what is to be communicated.

Rituals are often so much a part of our way of doing things that we could have difficulty identifying them, let alone understanding that another culture might have a different ritual system altogether. At times, though we do make comments such as "[the meeting] is a bit of a ritual". Thus we accept that such ritual activities do take place and have little to do with the stated desired ends.

---

[12] http:/www.bvzm.com/english/conferenzaeng.html
[13] Back cover text to Walt Disney video *Pinocchio*. Emphasis added.

	English + Literal Italian	Actual Italian used	Explanation
titles	Mr./Signore	signore/dottore/professore/ ingegnere/avvocato	Signore (Mr.) would only be used for a complete stranger or for a man with no university degree.
	Mrs./Ms./Signora	signora dottoressa professoressa ingegnere/avvocato	Signora still connotes 'married' though now (in theory) doubles as the equivalent of Ms.
	your honour vostro onore	signor giudice/Mr. judge	
	You (singular)/Tu	Tu or lei/You or she	A decision must be made to position addressee in terms of social distance and relationship. Tu is close, lei is distant
letter writing	Dear Sir/Madam	Gentile signore/signora/ Kind sir/madam Spettabile Ditta Messrs. Company	
	Yours sincerely/ faithfully	Distinti saluti Distinguished greetings	
on the phone	Good morning XYZ department, can I help you?	Pronto? Ready?	
	It's George Brown here...	Sono George Brown... I am George Brown	

The important point that Hofstede (1991:8) makes is that symbols, heroes and rituals are visible, and can therefore be subsumed under practices: "their cultural meaning, however, is invisible and lies precisely and only in the way these meanings are interpreted by the insiders. The core of culture ... is formed by values". The idea of the visible/invisible in culture is certainly not new, and one of the most enduring metaphors is that of the iceberg.

• *The Iceberg Theory*

The Iceberg Theory has, in fact, been used to describe culture for many years. In the 1950s, the theory was popularised through the works of Edward T. Hall, and in particular in *Silent Language* ([1952] reprinted in 1990). As Hall notes, the concept was one of many being used to explain that the most important part of culture is completely hidden, and what can be seen is, as the cliché has it, 'just the tip of the iceberg'.

Other (visible/hidden) divisions included Clyde and Florence Kluckhohn's 'explicit' and 'implicit', and Ralph Linton's distinction between 'covert' and 'overt'. Linton was one of the most influential psychologists regarding role-theory, and revered by Hall as "the late great Ralph Linton". The two American anthropologists, Clyde and Florence Kluckhohn have been similarly lauded, and their individual and joint works are still considered authoritative texts.

Hall remains one of the great popularisers of 20th century anthropology and was also, well before Hofstede and Trompenaars, a highly successful business consultant, cross-cultural skills trainer and writer. He is certainly the most widely respected in his field, and deservedly so. Hall also provides the essential link between studies on meaning in language and meaning in culture. His theory on contexting is discussed in detail in Part 3.

Another development of the Iceberg Theory has been made by a team of American management consultants, Brake *et al.* (1995:34-39). They suggest a division as follows:

> Laws, customs, rituals, gestures, ways of dressing, food and drink and methods of greeting, and saying goodbye. These are all part of culture, but they are just the tip of the cultural iceberg.
>
> The most powerful elements of culture are those that lie beneath the surface of everyday interaction. We call these value orientations. Value orientations are preferences for certain outcomes over others.

The term 'value orientations' was in fact, first coined by Florence Kluckhohn in 1953 (Kluckhohn and Strodtbeck 1961). The orientations, as listed by Walker *et al.*, are shown below the waterline and will be discussed in detail in Part 3:

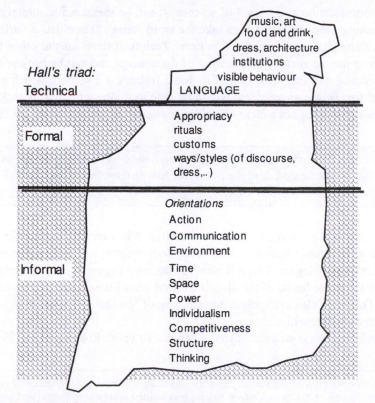

Figure 5. Adapted from Brake et al. (1995:39)

• *Hall's Triad of Culture*

Hall, as we have mentioned, has written a great deal on culture, though only some of what he has written is quoted today. In *The Hidden Dimension* (1982), he proposed an extension of the Iceberg Theory and suggested the addition of a third level, which lies sometimes above, and sometimes below the waterline. This model, which he termed a 'Triad of Culture', deserves a great deal more attention. It is mentioned in passing in a book entitled *Managing Cultural Differences* by Philip Harris and Robert Moran (1991:39-40). It is probable, however, that Trompenaars has been influenced by the idea.

We have already used Hall's Triad in discussing the importance of culture in translation. We will look here in more detail at this theory of levels specifically with regard to culture and communication.

> **Hall's three levels of culture**
> • technical culture
> • formal culture
> • informal culture *or* out-of-awareness culture

• *Technical Culture*

This is communication at the level of science. It can be measured accurately, and has no meaning outside itself. Let us take the word 'time'. 'Time' has a variety of meanings, depending on context and culture. Technical time, on the other hand, refers only to the technical understanding of the concept and can be broken down into its 'isolates' and analysed. One of its basic isolates is a second, which we all have a feel for. However, very few would be able to define a second. A technical 'second' has no feeling but a clear unambiguous scientific definition (*CED* 1999):

> A second is the basic SI unit of time: the duration of 9 192 631 770 periods of radiation corresponding to the transition between two hyperfine levels of the ground state of caesium-133.2.

Textbooks[14] and manuals, in theory, are written at this level of culture. In practice, as we have already seen with *Life in Modern Britain*, and software manuals, there is a lot more going on. Yet, it is also true that two engineers, for example, can discuss the tolerance levels of metals at this level with little or no communication problem. They will also extrapolate the meaning of 'on the fly' better than a non-expert native speaker will.

In linguistics, this is equivalent to the denotative level. Roger Bell's (1991:98-

---

[14] Though textbooks may, on the surface, give the impression of belonging to technical culture, we have already seen that *Life in Modern Britain* was written within both formal and informal frames, and that software manuals are written with a good deal of hidden cultural meaning.

99) *Translation and Translating* explains very clearly the concept of the denotative meaning of a word, utterance or complete text; the meaning is "referential, objective and cognitive and, hence, the shared property of the speech community which uses the language of which the word or sentence forms a part". 'Denotation' tends to be described as the definitional, 'literal', 'obvious' or 'commonsense' meaning of a sign. In the case of linguistic signs, the denotative meaning is what the dictionary attempts to provide.

Teaching at this level isolates the parts, analyses and then recombines them. This is how grammar, or rather syntax and semantics (which is the study of idealized meaning) are taught. The language, at this level, is taught as an independent and idealized system. Some languages are, by their very nature, 'technical'. These are the restricted languages such as Seaspeak. As David Crystal (1987:56) says, "The language is so tightly constrained by its context that only a small degree of variation is permitted .... They usually consist of routinely formulaic constructions, with a conventionalised prosody or typographical layout, and a limited vocabulary".

The idea of English as an international language and the use of a standardized international technical language are attempts at making both language and culture technical. The most extreme examples of this are the artificial or auxiliary languages, such as Esperanto, which are culture-free. The fact that they are culture free may well account for their lack of success in practice.

As we have seen with the McDonald's example, it is possible to analyse the isolates of conversation technically, breaking down the interaction into a series of mechanical moves:

Thanking the customer and asking for repeat business	Yes	No
1. There is always a thank you	___	___
2. The thank you is sincere	___	___
3. There is eye contact	___	___
4. Return business was asked for	___	___

Technical culture, then, is scientific, analysable and can be taught by any expert in the field. In a technical culture (apart from the study of theoretical areas such as particle physics) there is only one right answer, which will be based on an objective technical principle.

• *Formal Culture*

Hall calls his second level of culture 'formal'. It is no longer objective, but is part of an accepted way of doing things. It can, and indeed is, taught. This is the culture of traditions, rules, customs, procedures and so on. We are generally not aware of the conventions surrounding (in Hall's words) the routines of life, but awareness is immediate when the convention is flouted. For example, if a child (brought up in Britain) forgets to say "thank you" at the appropriate moment, an adult will invariably prompt him or her with a question such as "What do you say?" or "What is the magic word?" Children, in fact, learn this form of culture through trial and error with their family, and then later in school. They soon learn the accepted way of doing things. The language of these routines of life would now, in linguistics, be called genres.

Though genres are not usually analysed in everyday life (and hence are part of formal rather than technical culture) they can be scientifically studied and technically taught to others. A service counter conversation, for example, contains much that is routine. Guy Aston (1988), for instance, made an extensive study of this particular genre deciphering the different Italian and English patterns in requesting information in a bookshop. One of the researchers, Laura Gavioli (1993:390) points out that, "the analysis shows that in presumably similar settings like self-service bookshops in England and Italy, different patterns of action are 'proper'".

Once analysed, like the McDonald's sequence, these patterns become technical. So, this level of culture is sometimes above and sometimes below the conscious waterline.

• *Informal Culture*
By suggesting the term 'informal' for his third level of culture, Hall means that there are no 'rules' as such. This form of culture is neither taught nor learned, but acquired informally and, even more importantly, 'out-of-awareness'. According to Hall, this term was coined by the Washington psychiatrist Harry Stack Sullivan to distinguish that part of personality that we are conscious of (in-awareness), and that part which is visible to others but is outside our own awareness. This concept relates back to Freud who believed that the conscious self is not, in fact, 'master of the house'. We are, he claimed, governed by the Unconscious (the out-of-awareness) which is formed from crucial memories in childhood and guides our adult life.

It is this out-of-awareness level that we respond to emotionally and identify with. It is the "not what-he-said but how-he-said it" level. In terms of Speech Act Theory it is the illocutionary force of a proposition that we respond to, rather than the locution. As Hall suggests, we react out-of-awareness at this informal level – and not at the technical level. Margherita Ulrych's (1992:254) publication on translation also stresses that we judge and react to words at the level of connotative meaning. These are "the culturally or socially determined value judgements that are implicit in the semantics of a word".

It was Barthes who first coined the terms denotation and connotation (1967). He pointed out that connotation, unlike denotation, depends on knowledge of the context to understand the full meaning. 'Connotation' is used to refer to the socio-cultural and 'personal' associations (ideological, emotional, etc.) of the sign. Connotations will change according to class, age, gender, ethnicity and so on. Signs are more 'polysemic' - more open to interpretation. There is no longer an authoritative dictionary meaning, and effectiveness of connotation lies in the writer's and reader's ability to link the text to the out-of-awareness shared map or model of the world. Christopher Taylor's (1998:41) volume, subtitled "A practical and theoretical guide for Italian/English translators" contains an extremely useful (technical) guide to using dictionaries, while always aware of the fact, as he says: "it is difficult for the lifeless page to capture all possible uses of word, and even more difficult to provide a list of all possible translation options".

An extract from almost any novel (or recording of any conversation) brings out the fact that it is the unconscious part of our brain that dictates our response. The extract below, from Tom Wolfe's book *The Bonfire of the Vanities*, captures the 'out-of-awareness' emotive force of communication. The book is set in present day New York, and Wolfe (1990:xvii) explains in his 'Introduction' that his objective was to produce "highly detailed realism based on reporting, a realism that would portray the individual in intimate and inextricable relation to the society around him".

In the first few pages of the book, we find the protagonist, Sherman McCoy, leaving his luxury apartment to take the dog for a walk. After entering the lift (or rather elevator), he is joined by a neighbour, Pollard Browning:

> Browning looked Sherman and his country outfit and the dog up and down and said, without a trace of a smile, 'Hello, Sherman'.
> 'Hello Sherman' was on the end of a ten-foot pole and in a mere four syllables conveyed the message: 'You and your clothes and your animal are letting down our new mahogany-panelled elevator'.

Only someone steeped in the culture of a Park Avenue co-op apartment could appreciate and react to Browning's "Hello Sherman". Sherman's reaction was not governed by his conscious mind, but by something much deeper:

> Sherman was furious but nevertheless found himself leaning over and picking the dog up off the floor.

In terms of Speech Act Theory, picking up the dog is the perlocutionary effect. This effect is produced, as Sherman finds, out-of-awareness.

• *The Triad*

Any activity can emphasize any of the three levels. It is also possible to change level almost instantly, as the following dialogue illustrates. It is an illustration of a typical parent-child interaction. As the parent becomes more aware of the need to focus consciously on the situation, so his language moves from the informal to the formal, and finally, spelling out the situation, the language becomes technical:

•	**informal**	Pookins, pick up your clothes, will you? (no reply)
•	**formal**	Steffy, please pick up your clothes. (no reply)
•	**technical**	Stephanie Tinker, I have so far asked you twice to pick your clothes up and put them on the chair. I am warning you that I have no intention of asking you a third time. Is that clear?

The next chapter looks in detail at frames and levels. It explains how they interact and help to orient individuals in attaching meaning to what they hear, see and feel.

Chapter 3. Frames and Levels

The aim in this chapter is to:
* introduce the idea of the 'meta-message' and framing
* introduce the theory of Logical Levels
* link the various levels to theories of culture
* introduce the concept of congruence
* differentiate between culture-bound and non culture-bound behaviour

3.1 Frames

* meta-message
* context
* Bateson's frames
* Tannen's frames
* prototypes

We have already discussed the fact that culture exists on a number of levels. Here we will take up the nature of levels themselves and how they function in communication. The "Hello Sherman" example from the previous chapter illustrates how even the simplest of messages come with another message. The English anthropologist Gregory Bateson (1972:178; 1988:122-37) pointed out that all animals communicate about their communication, and this 'communication about' (1988:124,) he called 'meta-communication' (following Whorf). More specifically, it is this metamessage which carries the force of the message and provides a clue to its interpretation.

The Greek suffix *meta* originally meant 'after, between or among'. In linguistics it now means 'about'. Hence, 'meta-language', for example, is language used to talk about language: 'verb', 'noun', 'actor', 'parataxis', etc. For Bateson, and in this book, *meta* is a higher order Logical Level which provides the key to interpreting the meaning of the level beneath.

Bateson (1972:184-92) also discussed the closely related term 'frame', originally in the 1940s, as did Goffman (1974). For a full discussion of the history and the various meanings of the term 'frame', see Deborah Tannen's *Framing in Discourse* (1993a, 1993b) and, in particular, her introduction: 'What's in a Frame?'. 'Meta' and 'meta-levels' have been widely developed in Neuro-Linguistic Programming (e.g. O'Connor 2001:221-37). This discipline, a branch of cognitive psychology, grew directly out of the teachings of Bateson. It adopts frames to help clarify problems in human communication. Robinson (1988:52) also discusses the same concepts from a cross-cultural point of view.

The relationship between the 'context' and 'frame', as understood by Bateson (1972), is that 'frame' is an internal psychological state and makes up part of our map of the world, whereas 'context' is an external representation of reality. A frame is not 'real' in the same way as our map of the world is not the actual territory it represents. It is more of an indication of the "sort of thinking in interpreting" (ibid.:187). Erving Goffman (1974:10) follows suit by defining frames as "principles of organization which govern events".

Following Bateson, a frame can be thought of as a picture frame, though he also warns that "the analogy … is excessively concrete". What is within the picture, and hence the frame, is to be understood in terms of the title of the picture while what is outside the picture and its frame is to be understood from a wider frame. This wider frame will, however, affect our interpretation of the picture. Each frame will in turn be subject to a yet wider frame. These frames can be added to, each affecting the interpretation of what is framed below. The example Bateson used to explain the theory of frames is (simplified here) as follows.

The two sentences in the frame create a paradox and are basically nonsensical. It is no accident, in fact, that Bateson's original work on framing came from his study of schizophrenia:

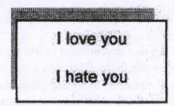

Figure 6. A Paradox

However, if we frame the statements, we have the beginnings of a hierarchy of meanings. Once 'I love you' frames 'I hate you', we can begin to see a hierarchy of interpretations. The outer frame will explain how the inner frame is to be interpreted. In this case, we might entitle the 'I hate you' frame 'play':

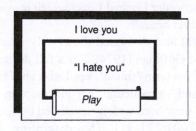

Figure 7. Paradox Framed and Resolved

Further, larger frames will similarly bring in more important reference points. For instance, the frame may be framed by a response: "You're always saying that". Hence, 'play' has been met with 'derision', reducing its value. In general, as Bateson (1972:187) says, the picture frame tells the viewer that a different form of interpretation is necessary. There are always at least two possible interpretations: one from inside the frame, and one from outside. For example, at an art gallery, we can either associate totally with the picture and forget the wider context of the gallery itself, or we can focus on the gallery as a whole and interpret the picture in relation to the other pictures. When we associate totally with the picture, there is the possibility that we mistake it for reality. The picture is a symbol, yet sometimes the symbol, as Bateson (ibid.:183) again notes, becomes as important as the reality it represents:

> Finally, in the dim region where art, magic, and religion meet and overlap, human beings have evolved the 'metaphor that was meant,' the flag which men will die to save, and the sacrament that is felt to be more than 'an outward and visible sign, given unto us'. Here we can recognize an attempt to deny the difference between map and territory.

We have already mentioned, as a basic presupposition, that the map is not the territory. The map, a series of signs, as Barthes (1993) explains, is a myth. Barthes' focus was on exposing the myth as a misrepresentation, if not a lie. His objective was to weaken the power of the myths and the ideologies feeding them. For our purposes, thinking in terms of maps is a more useful metaphor when considering culture and translation, because our first task is (continuing the analogy) to chart the reality as perceived by others. A map is designed to cover a specific area. It tells us what to expect and it also orients us inside that area. A map also has very definite borders, in the same way as our understanding of an event has a culture-bound frame.

Tannen (1993a:9) is clear that frames are culturally determined, as is Goffman (1974:18). She follows Bateson in understanding a frame as an interpretative device, though she would probably prefer the metaphor of a moving film rather than a static picture or a map. Tannen and Cynthia Wallet (1993:73) define frames and schema in the following terms:

> [A frame] refers to participants' sense of what is being done.
> [Schema:] patterns of experience and assumptions about the world, its inhabitants and objects.

Another term related to frame, used by linguists, is 'prototype',[1] which is the ideal or idealized example held in a frame. For communication to take place there will have to be some form of matching between the event in reality and the internal representation. This means that there will be a relevant prototype, in a frame.

To summarize, every message contains another message: the meta-message. The meta-message is located at a higher level and frames the message, and hence houses connotations. The frame itself is an internal mental representation, which can also

---

[1] Prototype theory was developed by Eleanor Rosch (see, for example, Rosch 1978) and discussed in detail by George Lakoff (1987). Snell-Hornby (1988) was the first to formally apply the theory to translation. See also Bell's (1991) 'ideal type', and Tymoczko (1998) on prototypes in 'Computerised Corpora and the Future of Translation Studies'.

contain an idealized example or prototype of what we should expect. Many of these frames together make up our map of the world.

3.2 Logical Levels

- Russell's Logical Typing
- Bateson's Logical Typing
- Dilts' Logical Levels

One of the originators of the concept of hierarchical levels of meaning was Bertrand Russell, who introduced the theory of 'Logical Typing' (Whitehead and Russell 1910). He postulates the fundamental principle that whatever involves all of a collection cannot be one of the same collection. Many solutions to problems of miscommunication rest on this very principle, and will be referred to often in this book especially when discussing culture, language and translation. Bateson (1972:280, 289) worked on the theory further (emphasis in the original):

> the theory asserts that no class can, in formal logical or mathematical discourse, be a member of itself; that a class of classes cannot be one of the classes which are its members; that a name is not the thing named; that 'John Bateson' is the class of which that boy is the unique member; and so forth ....
> The error of classifying the name with the thing named – or eating the menu card instead of the dinner [is] an error of *logical typing*.

He also noted that context, if it were to remain a useful concept, must be subject to logical typing: "Either we must discard the notion of 'context', or we retain this notion and, with it, accept the hierarchic series – stimulus, context of stimulus, context of context of stimulus, etc ...".

Tannen (1993a:6) notes that Bateson's findings have been more keenly taken up by researchers in communication and psychology than by linguists; in fact, the development discussed below has its roots in communication systems and family therapy. One of the pioneers in the development of Bateson's findings is Robert Dilts, a co-founder of Neuro-Linguistic Programming (NLP). The stated aim of NLP is the study of excellence and the modelling of how individuals structure their experience, i.e. how individuals construct their map of the world. As a relatively new discipline, it has still to be accepted by mainstream communication scholars or by psychologists. It is often seen as a get-rich-quick manipulation tool.[2] As the communication techniques work, it is hardly surprising that results driven areas such as advertising, marketing and selling have taken the ideas on board. NLP is also making an important contribution to education. Though the scholarly journal, *NLP World: the Intercultural Journal on the Theory and Practice of Neuro-Linguistic Programming* (1994-2002) is, alas, no more, NLP has a great deal to offer linguistics, culture

---

[2] See, for example 'Framing Psychotherapy' by Nick Owen, http://www.transitions.com/files/Framing_Psychotherapy.rtf.

and translation – as the original definition (Dilts *et al.* 1980:2) of the discipline illustrates:

> 'Neuro' stands for the fundamental tenet that all behaviour is the result of neurological processes. 'Linguistic' indicates that neural processes are represented, ordered, and sequenced into models and strategies through language and communications systems. 'Programming' refers to the process of organizing the components of a system to achieve a specific outcome.

One of the guiding principles behind NLP is Dilts' work on Logical Levels, which he developed after Bateson to explain how individual learning, change and communication function. Dilts initially isolated five levels, a hierarchy of frames that all biological or social systems operate within. The same levels operate whether we are talking about an individual, an organization or a culture.

Similar frameworks for the organization of the communication process have been created by linguists and ethnomethodologists.[3] One of the principal differences, though, between this particular classification and others is that here, following Russell (1903; Whitehead and Russell 1910) and Bateson (1972:279-308), the levels are *hierarchically* ordered and interrelated, in that the higher level organizes the information on the level below. The reverse can happen, but this is less usual. (See, though, O'Connor 2001:29, for a more systemic view of the levels). The levels are as follows:

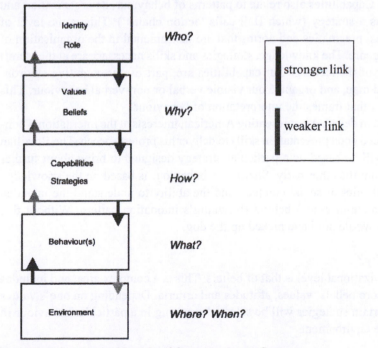

Figure 8. Dilts' Logical Levels of Organization in Systems

---

[3] M. A. K. Halliday, for example, has proposed a communication model, 'the context of situation',

Before discussing how the logical levels relate to culture or communication we should explain in a little more detail what each level represents.

• *Environment: Where? When?*
The basic level is the surrounding environment. This is the sum of external factors or constraints affecting an organization or process. It is who or what can be seen, heard, or felt through the senses, in time and space. The environment could be an international conference, a one-to-one meeting, or, in the case of Sherman McCoy, an oak-panelled elevator in a luxury co-op apartment in New York.

• *Behaviour: What?*
Organizations and individuals react to and operate on the environment through their behaviour. Behaviour can be verbal or non-verbal, and will generally (but not always) be visible to interlocutors such as Pollard Browning – who is on hand to watch Sherman stooping down to pick up the dog. Behaviour by an organization could be a verbal protest by the Americans about an international conference resolution. Alternatively, an individual Brazilian negotiator might decide to get up and walk away from a meeting.

• *Capabilities: How?*
Without appropriate skills or knowledge (capabilities), desired behaviour cannot be accomplished. Capabilities also relate to patterns of behaviour, its organization and repeated use as a strategy (which Hall calls 'action chains'). This is the level of appropriateness, pragmatics and norms that are instrumental in the organisation of discourse and genre. The knowledge, strategies and skills necessary are at the (semi) invisible layer of the iceberg. Our capabilities are, part of our cognitive environment or mental map, and organize our visible verbal or non-verbal behaviour. This is the first level that frames the interpretation of behaviour.

The American delegate (representing American interests at the international conference) will need good presentation skills to deliver his protest speech. The Brazilian 'walk away' will be based on a particular strategy designed to bring about further concessions from the other party. Sherman's behaviour is based on the knowledge of the informal rules of social conduct, and the ability to understand the intended meaning (the meta-message) behind Browning's intonation pattern. Without this knowledge, he would not have picked up the dog.

• *Beliefs: Why?*
The next organizational level is that of beliefs. This is a complex area, and includes many facets: core beliefs, values, attitudes and criteria. Depending on one's values and beliefs, certain strategies will be selected resulting in a particular behaviour in response to the environment.

---

which, as he says (1989:12) "serves to interpret the social context of a text, the environment in which meanings are being exchanged"; see discussion in Chapter 10.1.

Beliefs are mental concepts, theoretical constructs, held to be true or valid, and are formed in response to perceived needs. They provide the idealized examples (for instance of conduct) for the frames, and as such provide us with expectations about what the world should be like. For example, the American will need to believe that a crisp, clear and logical presentation of his views will be the best way to convince the delegates. The Brazilian will believe that direct expressive action will help him achieve his target. Sherman believes that he is a good citizen and that good citizens should follow the rules of social conduct. If he did not believe this, even if he had the knowledge, he would not have picked up the dog.

We should also remember that the application of beliefs will of course, depend on capability. The American delegate will actually need to have good presentation skills, have prepared his speech, have good background knowledge (apart from the authority), and be prepared for difficult questions, to convince anyone listening that he speaks for America. Similarly, we may, for example, believe we can speak a language. But if we do not have a sufficient command of it, then, objectively, our performance will be limited.

Beliefs are the vital motivational factor and can stimulate capabilities to such an extent that one can, in fact, bluff one's way through areas where there is no genuine capability. Students who learn this learn not only to perform well at oral exams but in many other areas of life. A belief in one's capabilities to do something in a particular environment, whether it be in the booth interpreting at a conference, translating a manual, or mediating a negotiation, will enable capabilities, skills and encyclopaedic knowledge to be employed to their maximum.

On the other hand, beliefs can be limiting rather than permitting. For example:

I can't do (*the presentation*)
It's impossible to do (*the exam*)
I'm not up to doing (*the interpretation*)
What if I can't do (*the job*)?

No matter what one's actual capabilities are, if one has such limiting beliefs resulting performance will tend to fulfil the negative prophesies because the capabilities will, to a large extent, be blocked.

• *Values: Why?*

Beliefs embody values. Our core values are the basic unconscious organizing principles that make up who we are. Once they are formed, they very rarely change. If they do change, then our identity, who we are, will also change. Attitudes, on the other hand, are the most superficial and can change in time or through force of argument without affecting core values.

Values embody what is important to us and act as fundamental principles to live by. They are polar opposites and tend to be expressed as nominalizations. As Hofstede (1991:8) aptly puts it, "values are feelings with an arrow on it: they have a plus and a minus side". The values with a plus sign are what motivate us.

NLP distinguishes between general guiding values and values in a particular situation. The latter they call 'criteria'. Criteria guide choice in a context, as in the previous examples, and motivate us either 'away-from' or 'towards' particular options. The decisions to be made can include everything from general lifestyle to which TV programme to watch, and from type of career choice to menu decisions. The specific behaviour that satisfies a criterion (a contextualized value) is termed a 'criterial equivalent'. In general, we will use the all-embracing term 'values' when talking about general values or criteria, though we will also use the term 'criterial equivalent'. This will be particularly useful when discussing the different ways cultures interpret the behaviour they witness. People see a behaviour and assume that it is equivalent to a particular criterion or value. This 'assumption' is, of course, only valid within individual maps of the world.

To find an individual's criterial equivalent we can ask the following question: "How do you know that [a value in a particular context] is being achieved?"

> Q: How do you know that [successful communication with X in context Y] is being achieved?
> A: When I see nodding/smiling/...; when there is no interruption; when X talks about self/when X asks me questions; when X listens and doesn't talk/when I feel good; ... /when X tells me, etc.

• *Identity: Who?*

Values and beliefs will be determined by the type of person, organization or culture in that particular context. In linguistic terms, this corresponds to the role that is being played (e.g. person holding authority, specialist or information giver/seeker). In organizational terms, we have, for example, a state petrochemicals company, a limited partnership, a university or a committee. We have already stated the identities of our example cases: Sherman McCoy, Brazilian negotiator and American spokesperson.

There is nothing to stop us from investigating the logical levels of the various, and at times, conflicting roles of Sherman McCoy. In this particular scene, Browning may well have labelled him as 'slob' and not – as Sherman would have preferred – 'respected member of a Park Avenue co-op apartment'.

• *Levels of Culture*

With regard to a definition of culture, we can see that the approaches discussed earlier define aspects of culture at only one or some levels, and that culture, like any other organization or process, operates at all levels. Saville Troike's (1986:47-48) ethnomethodologist definition of culture most closely encapsulates the theory of interrelated logical levels: "Culture encompasses all of the shared rules for appropriate behaviour that are learned by individuals as a consequence of being members of the same group or community, as well as the values and beliefs that underlie overt behaviours".

Below is a table linking the NLP Logical Levels to the theories of culture discussed so far:

NLP	Robinson	Hofstede	Trompenaars	Hall
Context	*External*	*Visible*	*Explicit*	
Environment		Symbols/ Heroes	Artefacts & Products	Technical
Behaviour	Behaviourist	Rituals/ Practices		
Frame	*Internal*	*Invisible*	*Implicit*	Formal
Capabilities Strategies	Functionalist		Norms & Values[4]	
Beliefs	Cognitive		Basic Assumptions	Informal or Out-of-aware-ness
Values		Values	Core Values	
Identity	Symbolic			

3.3 Culture and Behaviour

> - culture is only one of the filters affecting behaviour
> - individuals are members of many cultures
> - culture is a cline
> - congruence
> - ecological fallacy

• *Culture is a Filter*

The first point to be made is that culture is only one of the filters responsible for affecting behaviour. This is rather like saying that members of a political party may accept the underlying party culture but, at the same time, may well vote against the party line for personal reasons. There will also be times when there is no party line, and a free vote takes place. In this case, members may act or vote according to individual conscience.

• *Individuals are Members of Many Cultures*

Second, we are all members of a number of different cultures. So, while we are in the environment of one culture we may well be responding as members of a second culture. Men and women, for example, are as different in their ways of doing and being as any other cultures. The problems in translating meaning from woman to man, and vice-versa, are highlighted in Tannen's *You Just Don't Understand: Women and Men in Conversation* (1992). Her first chapter is tellingly entitled 'Different Words, Different Worlds'.[5] In fact, in 'A Cultural Approach to Male-Female

---

[4] For the sake of clarity, the levels have been harmonized. However, Trompenaars, for example, places his 'norms and values' between 'implicit' and 'explicit'.

[5] Since then, a number of even more popular books have appeared, each highlighting the differences, such as: *Men are From Mars, Women are from Venus* (Gray 1993) and *Why Men Don't Listen and Women Can't Read Maps: How Are We Different And What To Do* (Pease and Pease 2001).

Miscommunication' Maltx and Borker (1992:171) "prefer to think of the difficulties in both cross-sex and cross-ethnic communication as two examples of the same larger phenomenon: cultural difference and miscommunication".

Cultural difference can be manifested in a wide variety of ways. Some of the differences we have little or no choice over (such as ethnic group), while other cultural differences may be the result of more personal choice:

little/no choice	more personal choice
• race	• neighbourhood
• gender	• friends
• family	• education
• region	• corporate culture
• social class	• profession
• religious background	• generation

Adapted from Brake et al. (1995:72)

• The Distribution of Culture

The third point to remember with regard to culture and behaviour is the fact that every culture allows for a certain deviation or eccentricity. Hence, we will find a distribution of behaviour ranging from totally stereotypic of culture A to atypical, and then finally as unrecognizable as culture A behaviour. Between the two there will be fuzzy cut-off points:

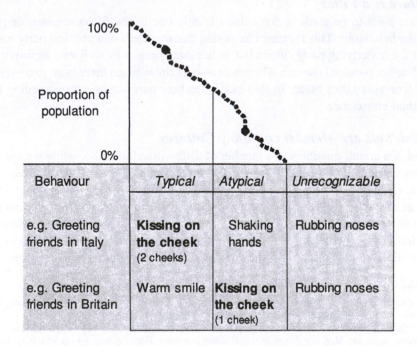

Behaviour	Typical	Atypical	Unrecognizable
e.g. Greeting friends in Italy	**Kissing on the cheek** (2 cheeks)	Shaking hands	Rubbing noses
e.g. Greeting friends in Britain	Warm smile	**Kissing on the cheek** (1 cheek)	Rubbing noses

Figure 9. Culture-Bound Behavioural Distribution Curve: Greeting Friends

A second culture will display the same type of behaviour curve, but the typical behaviour will have shifted, as for example with regard to time (figure 10) below. Both cultures recognize kissing on the cheek as a sign of friendship, though the behaviour is atypical in Britain. The modality of the kiss is also different. Both cultures, though, would feel the same way about rubbing noses. So, there will be people within each culture who behave in the same way, but also many who do not. As a result, the behavioural distribution curves will not quite overlap.

The answer to the question "When is late, late?" and subsequent tolerance of 'lateness' will depend upon what is typical within a culture. For culture 'A', it is normal or typical to consider 5 minutes late (for a meeting, a dinner appointment) as late. Culture 'B', on the other hand, typically considers 20 minutes after the agreed time as late. Clearly, in both cases, there will be a large portion of the population who will be more or less flexible in their toleration of late arrivals. So, there will be culture 'A' people who act like culture 'B' people – but they will be in the minority. The vast majority will already have stretched their toleration of lateness after 30 minutes. Likewise, there will be a minority of culture 'B' people who are sticklers for time. The vast majority, though, will find 30 minutes comfortably within their toleration of difference.

Interestingly, in particular with regard to the equivalence debate in translation, behaviour that is deemed equivalent will almost invariably be at a different point in the distribution curve of the other culture, as figure 10 illustrates:

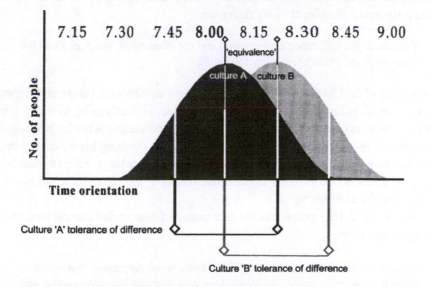

Figure 10. Behavioural Distribution Curve

• Congruence

An important point in the Logical Levels Theory concerns congruence. We act according to our beliefs and values, but the levels may not all be working congruently. Incongruence occurs when there is an internal conflict of values or beliefs.

Returning to Tom Wolfe's book and Sherman McCoy, life begins to turn sour on him when he has to juggle two incongruent beliefs. In the extract below, he is attempting to prove to his wife that he is not in the middle of an affair (emphasis in the original):

> [*Sherman's wife, Judy*] 'Please don't bother lying'.
> [*Sherman*] '*Ly*ing – about *what*?'
> She was so upset she couldn't get the words out at first.
> 'I wish you could see the cheap look on your face'.
> 'I don't know what you're *talking* about!'
> The shrillness of his voice made her laugh.

His incongruence shines through both visually and audibly and is due to a clash of two incompatible beliefs. One important belief comes out in the following short conversation Sherman imagines he might have with his wife (emphasis in original):

> Look, Judy, I still love you... and I don't want to change any of it – it's just that I, a Master of the Universe, a young man still in the season of the rising sap, deserve *more* from time to time, when the spirit moves me.

Here his identity is 'Master of the Universe', which permits him to believe that he can deserve more than just his wife (albeit only from time to time). However, this belief about himself clashes with another fundamental belief, as explained to him by his girlfriend – the object of his rising sap:

> You know the difference between you and me, Sherman? You feel sorry for your wife, and I don't feel sorry for Arthur.

A Master of the Universe cannot feel sorry, but a sensitive husband can. Sherman believes that he is both. So, the only way he can act logically is by verbally lying about the existence of another woman, thereby (a) protecting what he believes he deserves, and (b) at the same time attempting to avoid upsetting his wife. However, the metamessage his wife receives is that he himself is unable to believe what he is saying. And this is non-verbally crystal clear through "the cheap look" on his face and "the shrillness of his voice".

Bateson (1972:412) points out the supremacy of non-verbal communication in conveying sincerity:

> When boy says to girl, 'I love you', he is using words to convey that which is more convincingly conveyed by his tone of voice and his movements; and the girl, if she has any sense, will pay more attention to those accompanying signs than to the words.

This type of external incongruence is part of daily life but actually has its own internal congruence and is not normally thought of as a thought disorder. Instead, as Sherman admits to himself:

The Master of the Universe was cheap, and he was rotten, and he was a liar.

So, his behaviour was, in fact, congruent with a slight modification to the beliefs he had about his identity. He is still a Master of the Universe, but sitting uncomfortably with this identity is the realization that he is 'a liar'.

This triple identity (Master of the Universe, sensitive husband, liar) is reminiscent of schizophrenia, which is in fact generally categorized as an incongruent thought disorder. Yet, even here, there is internal congruence. Branca Telles Ribiero (1993:110) is one of the contributors in Tannen's *Framing in Discourse*. She found in her discussion on psychotic discourse that as the patient in question underwent her psychotic crisis, so her role (identity) and her behaviour changed. The patient alternately took the role of a variety of participants: a patient talking to the doctor (present); a daughter talking to her mother, a sister talking to her sister, and a variety of other people – none of whom were present. "What emerges is that [the psychotic patient] uses language to mirror the different functions that each participant has in her discourse. On this level of analysis, she never 'misfires' ... a rather unexpected accomplishment for a 'thought disordered patient'!".

It was J. L. Austin (1962) who introduced the concept of 'misfiring'. He has had a very considerable influence on the development of analytical philosophy since the Second World War. He points out that certain conditions have to be met before words can mean what they say and for successful communication to take place. These he termed 'felicity conditions'. One of his 'infelicities' was 'insincerity', which resulted in what he called an 'unhappy' situation'. His pupil John Searle (1969:39-43) developed Austin's ideas, terming one of the felicity conditions 'the sincerity condition', i.e. the belief that the proposition is true.

If we turn now to the Logical Levels of culture, we can only (in general) be members of a particular culture if, as a first condition, we believe we are. We also need to share 'sincerely' some beliefs about values, strategy, behaviour and appropriate environments. In the same vein, if behaviour is to be seen as part of culture it will have to be congruent with a set of beliefs shared by that culture. Edward Sapir (1994:36), in his posthumously published lecture notes, points out that "culture is not mere behaviour, but significant behaviour" and goes on to say: "We might even say that the test of whether a type of behaviour is part of culture is the ability to historicize it ... as meaningful". What he is suggesting is that culture-bound behaviour is part of an analyzable historical tradition. So, for behaviour to be culture-bound, it will have to be proved to be congruent with that tradition of observable culture-bound behaviours. Barthes (1993:129) was to say something very similar: "We reach here the very principle of myth: it transforms history into nature".

• *Ecological Fallacy*

Finally, we should be aware of what Hofstede (1991:112) calls the 'ecological fallacy'. It would be a fallacy to say that all the underlying cultural values are held to be true by every person in that culture. What is true however, is that every person within a particular culture is likely to identify certain underlying cultural values and associated beliefs and patterns of behaviour as congruent with that same culture. He or she would necessarily identify *with* all those values.

So, the examples given in the following chapter will illustrate the various levels of culture that lie within the cognitive environment of that culture rather than within every individual member.

• *Summary*

All communication is bounded by frames, and it is these frames that orient the addressee as to the metamessage. The metamessage is non-verbal, but relayed through the quality of the voice, gestures, or may simply be implicit from the context.

The Logical Levels function as a hierarchical series of metamessages linking behaviour in an environment to a pattern of strategies (how), and organized by a set of values and beliefs (why). These are all framed at a higher level by the role or the identity. The Logical Levels Model provides a unifying framework within which all the approaches to culture can function. There will always be congruence between the levels.

There are many cultures one will be a member of, and any of these may act as an important frame responsible for behaviour. Finally, culture is not the only factor influencing behaviour; and culture-bound behaviour itself is on a cline from typical, through atypical to unrecognizable.

Chapter 4. Logical Levels and Culture

The aim of this chapter is to:
- give a comprehensive view of how culture reveals itself at each Logical Level
- give practical examples of cultural differences
- introduce translating and interpreting issues in terms of Logical Levels

4.1 Environment

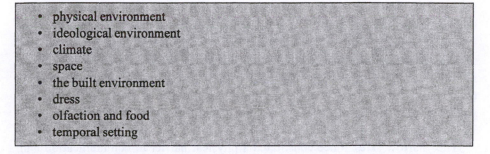

- physical environment
- ideological environment
- climate
- space
- the built environment
- dress
- olfaction and food
- temporal setting

What follows is a brief discussion of some of the isolates of the environment responsible for influencing culture-bound behaviour. Hall (1990:27) adopted the term 'isolates' to describe the individual building blocks of culture, which he also likened to a musical score. These will also include culture with a capital 'C'. Here, though, we will focus only on an example list of the environment related isolates to provide some practical examples of the variety of factors that determine culture at this level.

• *Physical Environment*

Until recently, physical barriers such as rivers, seas, and mountains constituted cultural barriers due to the lack of physical contact. Today there are very few cultures physically cut off from other cultures. Yet, still today, there are many cultures that continue to regard their physical boundaries as cultural boundaries. One example of the physical environment having a direct bearing on culture are mountains. The Alpine mountain chain, for example, has witnessed massive emigration and, as a result, a migrant culture.

The words of Leonardo Zanier (1995:17), poet from a mountain community in the North-Eastern tip of the Alps (Carnia, Italy), clearly express the close relationship that is felt between the enclosed valleys and the unfulfilled desire of the inhabitants to be free of their surrounding environmental constraints. The extract below comes from a collection of poems which dwell on the life of the Alpine emigrants who were obliged to find work abroad, and is entitled *Free ... To Have to Leave*. The English translation (discussed in Katan 2001a) follows the original Friulian dialect more closely than the Italian, which reduces the metaphor *tra un cîl cussì strent* ('between a sky so narrow') to the more prosaic *in valli così strette* ('in valleys so narrow'):

Friulian	Italian	English
a chel desideri di libertât	*a quel desiderio di libertà*	to that desire to be free
ch'a nu vîf denti	*che ci vive dentro*	which within us lives
encja se nassûts	*anche se nati*	even if born
tra un cîl cussì strent	*in valli così strette*	under such a narrow sky

With the advent of mass-transportation and communication links these physical barriers have become less of an obstacle. Communication between people can now be instant, and the world has indeed not only become a global village but a global multi-medial living room. We should bear in mind that the response to the environment is not necessarily based on the present environment. As Sapir, from his lecture notes again points out: "A people's response to their environment is conditioned by their cultural heritage; *it is not an immediate response.* We see nothing beyond what we are trained to see" (1994:73, emphasis added). As we have already noted, Trompenaars made a similar point.

The "narrow skies" once constituted a physical barrier to communication and social interaction. By the beginning of the 20th century metalled roads linked mountain areas. By the end of the Second World War, motorways and tunnels began to criss-cross the barriers. By the 60's televisions and telephones had linked every house, and nowadays Alpine web sites communicate with the world. Yet the people still see and react *as if* they were enclosed by "narrow skies". The power of *as if* in modelling our perception of the world has not gone unnoticed. The philosopher Vaihinger (1924) entitled his book on the subject as "The Philosophy of 'As If'"; and NLP uses this sleight of mind as an effective tool in taking more effective control of the human ability to believe that myths are reality.

It seems to be part of western culture, at least, to need to anchor the interlocutor to a particular physical environment. One of the first questions to ask someone on a first meeting is "Where are you from?" With the answer to this question we begin (and also often conclude) our membershipping of the interlocutor's culture. Though we may never have had any direct or indirect contact with that individual, we will construct a set of behaviours for him or her based on certain value judgements and beliefs that we have about people living in that particular place. So, we tend to attach an identity to an address. This may be even more true in America than in Britain. The addresses in *The Bonfire of the Vanities* identify the people talked about. The hero is introduced via his address in the first paragraph of the second chapter:

> At that very moment, in the very sort of Park Avenue co-op apartment that so obsessed the mayor ... Sherman McCoy was kneeling in his front hall.

And other characters are introduced in a similar way ...

from the swell-looking doorway of 44 West Seventy-Seventh Street emerged a figure that startled him.

[The 3 assistant district attorneys] had been born a million miles from Wall Street, meaning the outer boroughs, Brooklyn, Queens, and the Bronx. To their families, their going to college and becoming lawyers had been the greatest thing since Franklin D. Roosevelt.

As Hall (1982:138) points out:

In the US we use space as a way of classifying people and activities, whereas in England it is the social system that determines who you are. In the US your address is an important cue to status (this applies not only to one's home but to the business address as well).

   Addresses, such as those above, can be translated at the technical level, but the metamessage, i.e. any identifying connotations, may be totally lost. The nonsensical result of the translation may then easily discourage the reader from reading any further. The 'us' and 'them' in many countries revolves first around a north/south or east/west divide, and then by region, district and finally by neighbourhood. With time, many stereotypic comments such as the following lose their historical force:

North/South/East/West	Translation/Explanation
Civilization ends at Watford Gap	There is no civilization North of London
Northerners call a spade a spade	The direct, blunt style of talking in the north of England
Southerners are arty-farty	The Northerner's negative view of London and the Southeast, and its emphasis on appearance, fashion and sophistication
Da Roma in giù è tutta Africa	From Rome down it's all Africa
Terroni ladri/scansafatiche	Dirty Southern thieves/the workshy south
Nordici tutti polentoni	Northerners are all fat polenta eaters, and therefore without personality
Regional	
Essex man	young, right-wing politics, low education, loudly dressed, fast car ...
Essex girl	"loud, vulgar, stupid and too willing to have sex" *Longman* (1992:435)
I vicentini mangiagatti	People from Vicenza eat cat
Neighbourhood	
Sloane Ranger	Rich, superficial and young residents of the Sloane Square area, London
Hampstead Socialist	Educated left-wing sympathizer, living in up-market village atmosphere in north London
The wrong side of the tracks	Living in the poor (usually black) shanty area on the underdeveloped side of the railway track (US) Workers in Starbeck (Harrogate, UK) living downwind of the station.

• *Ideological Environment*

Today, fundamental religious (Muslim, Christian and Zionist) and ethnic beliefs are dividing the world. Within each religious or ethnic group, too, the internal ideological and territorial divisions are just as strongly entrenched. Only 50 years ago, though, the divisions were more political, and the world was divided with larger brush strokes. When British Prime Minister Winston Churchill famously stated that an "iron curtain has descended across the Continent" he was describing one ideological division – that between the area of American influenced capitalist democracy in the West and the area of Soviet influenced communism to the East. The terms 'East' and 'West' had suddenly taken on political identities.

The strength of belief regarding the importance of territory is epitomized by the Balkan states. Historically these states have been at war over territory, to such an extent that we have since used the verb 'to balkanize', to mean 'divide a territory into small warring states'. The more a group of people identify their beliefs with a physical environment the more Balkanization will take place. The settlement of the Israeli-Palestinian conflict will depend on the extent that the Israelis and the Palestinians are able to loosen their identity/territory beliefs.

It is when political or religious ideology is not the subject of discussion, but part of the general background environment, that it can create tensions for the translator and interpreter. Like intercultural communication in general, the background ideology will provide a profoundly different interpreting frame on the behaviour.

What was the Italian interpreter to do, for example, in the following situation? The setting was the Institute of International Theoretical Physics, in Trieste, on the occasion of the 25th anniversary celebrations of the Institute. On 31 October 1989, there was a formal ceremony in the presence of the then Prime Minister of Italy, Giulio Andreotti (and other leading exponents of his Christian Democratic Party), the then Director General of International Atomic Energy Agency, Dr. Hans Blix, 5 Nobel Laureates, and all those who had contributed to the growth of the Institute of International Theoretical Physics.

The Pakistani Nobel physicist, Dr. Abdus Salam, director of the Institute, finished his presentation with these words:

> ... and finally I would like to thank Allah, through Whom, and thanks to Whom,
> I was able to study physics, and without Whom I would never have had the
> opportunity to do this small amount I have done in my life; praise be to Allah.

The Italian simultaneous interpreter was left with two interrelated culture-bound problems given the fact that the environment was a state-of-the-art physics centre (ideological environment: western science, the supremacy of Man and his ability to gain knowledge through personal endeavour). The audience was composed of a mixture of international scientists and Italian (Catholic) politicians. First, reference to religion and moreover to the importance of deities is not traditionally a part of this genre in the western world, and second, could 'Allah' become 'Dio'? Unfortunately for the interpreter concerned (personal communication, and Viezzi 1996:69-70) He did. The interpreter also 'appropriately' shortened the length of praise for the domestic audience.

It was now Andreotti's turn to speak. He warmly commended Dr. Salam for his timely reminder of the importance of 'Dio'. The very same interpreter sweated through his interpreting into English. What became of 'Dio' is not clear.

• *Climate*

The environment is not only visual or auditory but also sensory. We receive information about culture through our senses. The dampness of much of Britain and the heat in the Italian *mezzogiorno* has an effect on, and is part of, the culture. Climate, and the meaning of the weather, is not immediately pan-cultural. The weather, stereotypically a national British preoccupation, is the subject of headlines at much milder levels than would be the case in Southern Europe or in any of the Americas.

According to Bill Bryson (1991:5), himself a naturalized American in Britain and writer on both language and travel:

A Londoner has a less comprehensive view of extremes of weather than someone from the Middle West of America. What a Briton calls a blizzard, would in Illinois or Nebraska, be a flurry, and a British heat wave is often a thing of merriment to much of the rest of the world.

He also regales his readers with the following headline from an old London Evening News, which, if literally translated, would result in merriment for much of the rest of the world:

> BRITAIN SIZZLES IN THE SEVENTIES[1]

However, in 1995 Britain really did sizzle at ninety-five degrees Fahrenheit, and for two solid months there was no rain. There were hosepipe bans and people swam in the lochs in Scotland, while they fled the Mediterranean resorts under a torrent of rain. In a special ten-page feature, *The Independent Magazine* (02/09/95, 14-26:19) focused on 'The Summer of 95' (emphasis added):

'All round the coast languid air did swoon'. The grey smudge of sludge that passes for the ocean turned a Mediterranean blue ... *Britain wasn't Britain anymore,* but a land where it is always afternoon.

Here the climate defines a country, and certainly behaviour changed radically in response to the sun.

When a definite change in climate occurs so can cultural priorities at the level of values. Brislin (1993:5-6) cites an article by Arsenault which discusses how the introduction of air-conditioning (a man-made change to the local climate) in the Southern States of America made an impact on "the cultural value of Southern

---

[1] 70 degrees Fahrenheit is approximately 21 degrees centigrade.

hospitality". Originally, in response to the hot and humid summers, people used to sit outside on the porches and would chat to one-and-all. After the 1950s, with the introduction of air-conditioning, the focus of attention changed from the outdoors and the community to the sitting room and the concerns of the immediate family.

• *Space*

The natural environment can be oppressive, as Zanier illustrated: high valley sides and enclosing mountains frustrating "that desire to be free". On the other hand, one of the stereotypic images of America is that it is a country where there is space to do everything. At least part of this stereotype is borne out in reality, as Hall (1990:141) notes: "The size and scale of the United States and the feeling of open spaces are overpowering to visitors who are accustomed to the smaller scale of Europe".

Hall also suggests that the presence or absence of physical space is a determining factor in the culture-bound meaning of 'private' and 'public' space. Physical space needs are discussed at length in Hall's *The Hidden Dimension* (1982:123), which also includes a useful chart of approximate accepted mainstream North American distances (in feet and inches) and the associated language:

	US	example	language
• intimate	touch - 18"	family in private	intimate
• personal	18" - 4'	family in public	informal
• social	4' - 12'	business	formal
• public	25'+	speech making	frozen

Hall noted that these distances, or space 'bubbles' as he calls them, are culture-specific. The more Mediterranean and Arab cultures will find these distances too restrictive, while Asian cultures, for example, will regard these distances as too close, especially when gender is taken into account. The British place a high priority on private space. In comparison with the Americans, they are particularly restrictive as to who is allowed into those private spaces. According to Hall, this is a strategy in response to the lack of physical space in Britain. Dialogue (or liaison) interpreters, involved in face-to-face interpreting, will need to be acutely aware of how their physical presence and organisation of the three-cornered space will influence communication.

We now move on to briefly discuss some of the more man-made aspects of the environment which influence culture, and our response to it.

• *The Built Environment*

Individual buildings set the scene for the identification of institutions or social groupings: the campus, the company offices, and in particular the reception. We all tend to size up an institution by its entrance: 'imposing', 'warm', 'run down', and so on. This feeling is then generalized to the whole institution and to the people working there.

We also automatically change behaviour according to building. On entering mosques, churches and temples, and clubs (gentleman's, golf or dance), there are usually specific written rules about appropriate dress and behaviour. The same is also true, but with unwritten rules, from the managing director's office to a friend's living room.

In business, the size and position of the office, the type of furniture, and indeed whether or not one has an office, is an indication of one's corporate identity. The criteria, though, are culture-bound. In an open plan office, for example, the 'window people' (Mead 1990:149) would be regarded as having a better position in the West. In Japan, however:

> the employee moved to a window desk is being discreetly told that his or her services are no longer crucial, and that if he or she should decide to find some other job in preference to fruitless hours spent staring out of the window, this would not be regretted.

• *Dress*

Dress style can be seen as part of the environment, and is usually the first sign of identity. The level of formality in clothes usually coheres with formality in behaviour, though the meaning of 'informal or 'casual' is strictly culture-bound.

American dress style, for example, is regarded as (too) informal by European standards. 'Sneakers' for instance have become universal footwear, but only in America worn universally, i.e. by most of the people most of the time, whether for work or play. Statistically, in America, one in two shoes sold is an athletic shoe. As the American NBC 20/20 report (18/08/88) stated:

> Sneakers: everybody has them and everybody likes them. They're a symbol of fun and joy – a natural obsession and you can do almost anything in them. Sneakers have acquired a special mystique in our modern-day culture. Rock stars perform in them, so do TV and movie stars. In our culture, women walk to work in them for two reasons: comfort and equality.

The American magazine *Business Week* (25/4/94) gave the figures for relative sales: "In Europe, where sneakers are not widely worn for casual street-use, there is only one pair of Nikes sold for every twenty people. In Japan it is one pair for every fifty people. In the US it is one in four".

This level of informality is totally foreign to Europeans, and to the Italians and French in particular, who have a formal set of rules about the appropriateness of the athletic shoe. On the other hand, it is not unusual for American politicians or business people to be pictured wearing sneakers. For the French and the Italians, the wearing of casual dress signifies non-professional behaviour. The distinction between professional and non-professional contexts in these countries is less clear-cut. In general, casual dress for professionals in Europe remains formal (by American standards), even if the environment and the subject of conversation is not related to work. However, at the 1997 Denver Summit of the G8, all leaders (including the French and the Italian) gamely dressed up as cowboys for Bill Clinton. The only exception was Germany's Helmot Kuhl, who refused. He felt that he would look ridiculous. This may well have been a personal belief, given his particular size and shape.

Dress not only delineates national cultures, but almost all other cultural groups. The most immediate and obvious case is that of men and women. There is even a word for the infringement of the unwritten Western gender dress code: 'cross-dressing'. However, what counts as cross-dressing is culture specific. For instance, the *sarong* or *pareo*, a wraparound skirt-like garment, is equally worn by women and men throughout Southeast Asia. This would be considered inappropriate wear for men throughout the West – though the Scottish kilt is nothing but a skirt. The hand or shoulder bag, *il borsello*, carried by (older) men in Italy, is still considered effeminate in Britain.

Dress also delimits class in Britain, to such an extent that the language categorizes class by dress: blue or white-collar worker. There is a literal equivalent in many languages: *colletto blu/bianco* (It), *col bleu/blanc* (Fr). In Italian there is another identification by clothing: *tuta blu*/blue overalls. Turkish, apart from having borrowed the same expressions, has "the poor man particular in his dressing wears white in winter", which means to look ridiculous when trying hard to be appropriately dressed.

At a practical level, all those involved in face-to-face cross-cultural encounters, such as interpreters, will have to dress appropriately if they are to be regarded as professional and competent. However, what 'appropriate' means is culture specific. Italy and France will tend to the more formal in comparison with Americans. General cultural orientations will need to be checked (see Part 3), but more importantly, open eyes, previous contact and the use of a cultural advisor will always be the best strategy in deciding what is appropriate.

Translators, who deal with texts rather than face-to-face encounters, need to be aware of the culture-bound meaning behind references to dress, as in the following texts. Often a literal translation will be of little help to a target audience. This is quite simply because each culture has very strong beliefs about the identity portrayed through dress style. For many, "you are what you wear" – as the following two extracts show. The first is from a *Sunday Times* series on *Wordpower* (1994, 3:21; emphasis added):

> While some people would not be seen dead in a **shell-suit**, some feel equally uncomfortable in **Lagerfeld** or **Armani** creations. Yet over recent decades certain modes of leisurewear have become widely adopted for situations that do not require **business dress**. There are still subtle distinctions (**Lacoste, Gap** and **BhS**).

Behind each of the emphasized words are culture-bound beliefs regarding identity. The same is true with this second extract, which explains change in beliefs in terms of dress. It is from an article entitled 'Ruled by the Sixties', which appeared in *The Sunday Telegraph* (8/3/92):

[John Major, ex-leader of the Conservative party] speaks ... in that neutral South-East voice which defies the listener to make class judgements. For this was one characteristic of the Sixties: even the apolitical young adopted egalitarian modes of speech and **dress.**

The change was sudden. At Cambridge in the late Fifties, **jeans** were rare. (I can recall only two undergraduates who habitually wore them) ...

The standard dress was still **sports jacket** and **flannel**, **corduroy** or **cavalry twill trousers**. **Suits**, even **tweed suits**, were frequently worn ...

Beneath the **double-breasted suits** and the **sober-coloured shirts** [of British political party leaders today], there lurks a **T-shirt** with a Sixties slogan: "Do your own Thing".

Translators and interpreters also need to be aware that clothes change their symbolic meaning as they cross borders. For example, the Barbour jacket in Britain is worn especially by people who live or spend time in the country, and especially so by the genuine country 'Green Wellie Brigade'.[2] The Barbour jacket has also attracted the attention of the Sloane Ranger described below (emphasis added):

A stereotype of a young person, esp. a woman, who comes from an upper middle class family, esp. from the country areas in the south of England, and a particular set of conservative values. Sloane Rangers typically wear designer clothes and spend a lot of time on their social lives, esp. in fashionable places such as Chelsea. People often joke about them driving Range Rovers, wearing **Barbour jackets** and green wellies and saying "OK yah" and calling their parents "Mummy and Daddy" past the usual age for using these terms. Their lifestyle is thought to be very shallow.
Longman (1992)

The Barbour jacket in Italy has a completely different message, and price tag. It has never been worn by country people, but by those who wish to have a 'casual' jacket that can be used both for the office and outside. It would be more likely to be worn with Fendi rather than Wellington boots. There is also a certain social status gained from the fact that Barbour symbolizes aristocratic English. It has even been suggested that it is better to wear a Barbour jacket at a formal social event in Italy rather than a run-of-the-mill dinner jacket.[3]

---

[2] "A name given to the richer classes of British society who enjoy country life esp. hunting, horse riding, etc ..." *Longman* 1992.

[3] Fashion trends according to *Finissaggiotessile* http://board.finissaggiotessile.it/tendenze/1034429168/index_html (19/01/03).

Quando si acquista un Barbour, non si compera soltanto un giaccone impermeabile, bensì un pezzo di stile di vita internazionale. ... Per quanto possa sembrare assurdo, è meglio presentarsi a una serata mondana con pullover, jeans e Barbour piuttosto che con le scarpe sbagliate o uno smoking di fattura[4] mediocre. In Europa il Barbour è una sorta di biglietto.	When you buy a Barbour, you're not just buying a waterproof coat. You're buying a slice of the jet-set style … However crazy it might seem, it's better to show up for an evening event with a pullover, jeans and a Barbour rather than a run-of-the-mill smoking jacket. In Europe, the Barbour is a sort of entry ticket into society.

What counts as 'business dress', 'sober-coloured' and indeed 'casual' varies across cultures, even though the words may remain the same. Though business may be global, dress is not. According to the Charter Institute of Purchasing and Supply, UK: "Gone are the days when workers could be identified by their bowler hats and briefcases". Casual is now the buzzword in many offices … [5] In the US, according to a 1999 Jackson Lewis poll of over 1,000 human resources executives from a broad range of businesses, "more than 70% say their companies have adopted some version of 'dress down days'". Apart from the problem of translating "dress down Friday", the concept of 'casual' itself varies from country to country. The following email posting, for example, would create, once again, a double-take for a reader from most non-Anglo-American cultures:

> I started the day off 'right' by catching my 'dressdown Friday' Hawaiian shirt on the office door latch, ripping two buttons off and thereafter trying to keep a low profile so no one would notice the single pin keeping my protruding stomach covered.[6]

The problem is not so much the pin, but the fact that, in Italy, for example, 'casual' office attire typically means a well-ironed (Lacoste or similar) 'polo shirt'. Hawaiian shirts are worn on the beach.

• *Olfaction and Food*

The variety of food and drink and the taste is also a facet of culture. The olfactory organ is particularly efficient at registering smells. But what constitutes a 'smell', 'perfume' or 'odour' depends on one's cultural upbringing. Dialogue interpreters

---

[4] The original comment "*smoking di fattura mediocre*" translates literally as "smoking jacket of mediocre quality (of workmanship)". Note the Italian appropriation through nominalization and deletion of the English "smoking (jacket)". In the same vein: *un camping* (site) and *un parking* (lot).
[5] http://www.casualpower.com/innews40.htm
[6] http://pages.prodigy.net/crotty/

working full days (and often obliged to work through dinner) take note.

As milk products are rarely consumed by Asians, they can perceive the fermentation of dairy products emitted by sweat glands. Hence, westerners 'smell' as far as Asians are concerned. Westerners, on the other hand, complain about the smell and taste of the Asian (particularly Malay) speciality, Durian fruit. Most Westerners describe the experience of eating it as a cross between chewing gum and inhaling lavatory cleaner. Yet, this fruit is treated with the greatest of respect in Malaysia, and selected fruits are often brought by friends when invited for dinner. Understandably, in more cosmopolitan Singapore, Durians are not allowed on the spotlessly clean and odour free underground system.

The British stereotype of the Mediterranean (and the French in particular) includes the smell of garlic. 'Garlic' for the British collocates with the verb 'to reek' (i.e. to have a strong and unpleasant smell). Whatever the culture, olfaction is part of what Hall (1982:47) calls 'the hidden dimension'. He observes that "The body's chemical messages are so complex and specific that they can be said to far exceed in organization and complexity any of the communication systems man has yet created as extensions [such as the computer]". O'Hagen and Ashworth (2002:150) are not so sure. They see translators involved in producing web sites "to include both sensory and olfactory information. [Also] a future bakery web site could be furnished with olfactory and tactile sensations whereby the visitor could smell the freshly baked bread and feel its texture. This in turn will allow translators to better understand the verbal descriptions and in fact may eliminate the need for language facilitation altogether in some cases".

• *Temporal Setting*

In Western cultures, time can be seen to pass – and ingenious devices have been devised to measure it. Though time cannot actually be observed, change can be, so we reasonably talk about 'the 60s culture', 'the Thatcher years', 'the Me generation', 'the caring and sharing nineties', and so on. Each period has an identity that constitutes a framework for that culture.

Literary and artistic styles change, and literary critics argue as to whether a text needs to be analyzed with respect to its temporal setting. Structuralists argue that there is no meaning outside the text and that the time of writing, or the time of reading, has no effect on interpretation. But the number of new interpretations of classic texts over time shows that accepted response patterns do change with time as the following examples taken from book catalogues illustrate.

Feminist Readings in Middle English Literature
The Wife of Bath and all her Sect.
Ruth Evans and Lesley Johnson
• How has feminist criticism changed the way that medieval literature is read?
Routledge Literature Catalogue (1994:41)

> FRENCH LITERATURE
> ... recent stage adaptations of *Liaisons Dangereuses* and Hugo's *Les Misérables* show that there is much to rediscover in one of the world's richest cultures, through a continuing process of translation and re-evaluation, vital to our understanding of our nearest neighbours and of ourselves.
>
> *Penguin Classics Catalogue* (1995:35)

In conclusion, to quote from Sapir's lecture notes once again (1994:73): "What is important is environment as defined by culture – what the natives have unconsciously selected from the environment, and their cultural evaluation of it".

4.2 Behaviour

This level of culture informs us about what a culture does, its perceived actions and reactions. It is the level of do's and don'ts that a culture tells itself, through proverbs or old wives' tales. In the following table is some good behavioural advice on bringing up a daughter and getting her married (in Turkey).

Traditional do's and don'ts in Turkey	Meaning
Kyzyny"dö ̂ ömeyen dizini döver/ dööer	If you don't beat up your daughter you will end up beating yourself up!
Kyz"y kendi haline byrakyrsan ya davulcuya varyr ya zurnacyya	Do not leave it to your daughter; she'll either marry the drum player or the clarinet man. [The implication is that they may look and sound interesting but they don't earn good money or have a high status].
Yki bayram arasy evlenmek uðursuzdur.	It is unlucky to marry between the two fêtes. [Ramadan and fête of Sacrifice].

It is also at this level that stereotypes about other cultures are most prominent. The following examples of 'behavioural' comments made by the Italians and the English about each other are taken from Jocelyne Vincent-Marrelli's (1989:465) article on the subject:

Gli inglesi sono freddi/The British are cold	Italians are too emotional
Gli inglesi sono distanti/The British are distant	Italians are too personal
Gli inglesi sono ipocriti/The British are hypocrites	Italians are untrustworthy
Gli inglesi sono pignoli/The British are pedants	Italians are devious
Gli inglesi sono ottusi e ingenui/The British are mentally slow and naive	

These reactions are totally natural and normal, though not particularly useful for cross-cultural encounters or as strategies for improving communication.

Each culture has its own rules of behaviour, and this observation has been noted for some time. The traditional aphorism for both tourists and business people, "when in Rome do as the Romans do", comes from St. Ambrose (c. 339-397), the bishop of Milan. He was asked the following question by St. Monica and her son St. Augustine: "In Rome they fast on Saturday, but not in Milan; which practice ought to be observed?". He actually said *"Si fueris Romae, Romano vivito more; si fueris alibi, vivito sicut ibi"*. *The Concise Oxford Dictionary of Quotations* (1981) translates the response as "If you are at Rome live in the Roman style; if you are elsewhere live as they live elsewhere".

The French have also adopted the aphorism *à Rome il faut vivre comme les Romains*. Interestingly, the Italians themselves have decided to ignore sant'Ambrogio. Their 'equivalent' is *Paese che vai, usanze che trovi* (*CID* 1995), "the countries you go to, the customs you find", or "different country, different customs". This advice is at the level of environment – there is no explicit advice on how to behave.

Since St. Ambrose's day, guides to behaviour can be found everywhere. They tend to be categorical, laying down behavioural rules. Below is a deliberately extreme example of what tourists should and should not do in Reggio, Italy:

GIUSTO E SBAGLIATO A REGGIO	RIGHT AND WRONG IN REGGIO
GIUSTO	RIGHT
A cena si va al London Bistrot, al Boccaccio o da Giovanni.	Dinner at the London Bistrot, the Boccaccio or Giovanni's.
SBAGLIATO	WRONG
Non si va più a teatro, perché, praticamente, una vera stagione non c'è più.	The theatre. Basically, there's no real season anymore.
(*Corriere della Sera, Sette*, N. 25, 1993)	

There are innumerable guides to conduct, and many of these socially accepted rules of behaviour change from time to time. One well known guide in England was entitled *U and non U*, a guide to upper class language usage published originally by Alan Ross as an essay, and then incorporated in Nancy Mitford's highly popular *Noblesse Oblige* (1959). It was U then (according to Ross) to say 'looking glass' and non-U to say 'mirror'. Today, his U forms have become obsolete, and this includes much of his 1969 update: *Who Are U?* In 1969 (he claims) it was still considered non-U to say 'toilet', while the U form was 'lavatory'.

According to *Il Vero Galateo Moderno* ('The Real Guide to Modern Manners'), published in 1996, Italian etiquette has also changed recently. It is now not appropriate to say "buon appetito" at formal lunches whether in the restaurant or at home (Montorfano 1996:82). In theory, this should obviate one cultural translation problem noted by Bassnett (1991:22) – at least in part. She rightly points out that there is no English equivalent for the continental invitation to have a good appetite.

Advice on appropriate behaviour has recently spread from what is etiquette in society to what is etiquette (rather than just good style) in professional and academic writing. The advice reprinted here comes from *The Open University* (1993:8). It tells the potential writer what he or she should do and not do when writing about ethnic groups:

> Avoid patriarchal or white philanthropic approaches to black people, for instance equating white as civilized or best, or black with backward or of less worth ... Make sure that cultures and societies are represented accurately, not from the author's ethnocentric point of view.

Observable behaviour (or advised behaviour) is part of a larger pattern, which is the subject of the next level.

4.3 Capabilities/Strategies/Skills

> * language channel and style
> * rituals
> * strategies

This is the first level of interpretation of behaviour or environment. The focus here is not on what is read, seen, heard or felt, but on how a message is transmitted and how it is perceived. It is also at this level that culture-bound frames are accessed. The frames tell us what to expect; and we tend to assess or judge in terms of what we expect.

• *Language Channel and Style*
With regard to how a message is sent and understood, there are a number of culture-bound factors affecting interpretation. These are discussed in depth in Part 3. However, it will be useful to give an idea of a number of practical differences before going into detail.

The medium is the means by which a message is conveyed from one person to another. There are three main channels:

* written
* spoken
* non-verbal

The choice of medium, and how it will be used, will depend on a number of factors, such as:

> * audience and formality of occasion
> * complexity and importance of message
> * message function
> * physical and social distance between interlocutors

- time
- expense
- need for accuracy and legal considerations

However, we must stress, as Mead (1994:175) does, that:

> cultural factors also play a part, and you cannot jump to the conclusion that the same factors that influence your perception of the appropriate medium are significant for the other culture. In other words, you need to consider the cultural implications of your selection before committing yourself.

Maria Sifianou (1989:527), for example, reports different strategies regarding the use of the phone. Her conclusion is that "In England, the primary function seems to be *transactional*, whereas in Greece, the principle function seems to be *interactional*" (emphasis in the original).[7]

As we shall see in Part 3, the use and meaning of, for example, direct face-to-face communication rather than more indirect formal written memos will depend on a culture's priorities in terms of text and context. Not only is an appropriate use of the channel culture-bound, but the style is too. A common remark about another person in many cultures begins with "It's not *what* he says but *how* he says it that I like/hate". When this happens in a cross-cultural encounter, very often, individual personality will have little to do with the evaluated behaviour. The observable visible behaviour will simply be an example of conforming to a different cultural pattern (Mead 1990:162):

> A voice feature that is stereotyped positive in one culture may strike the outsider very differently. The listener reacts in terms of his or her own cultural preferences, and hence is in danger of stereotyping the speaker on the basis of voice.

Hall (1982:142), for example, notes that distance between people is maintained partly through appropriate loudness, and that what is considered appropriate varies from culture to culture: "In England and in Europe generally, Americans are continually accused of loud talking". For the Americans, loudness is part of their openness showing that they have nothing to hide. The English, on the other hand, interpret loudness from within a different cultural frame. We have already mentioned that space is an important variable affecting culture, and Hall believes that soft speaking is another important strategy for the English as a response to the lack of space. As the lexico-grammar changes according to space bubble, cultural

---

[7] 'Transactional' and 'interactional' refer respectively to communication exclusively for the transmission of facts and communication which has a personal, social or phatic component. See Brown and Yule (1983).

interpreters need to be particularly aware of how their own space bubble will be interpreted and tune their voice and language accordingly.

Finally, Hall and Hall's advice (1989:28-29) to those hiring interpreters is to make sure that the interpreter's accent and dialect is acceptable to both parties, and that their use of language reflects "a good level of education". They point, in particular, to problems with the Japanese who simply may not be 'forthcoming' if the interpreter has an inappropriate style. The French and Germans are also mentioned as sticklers for a "well-educated" and "well-mannered" style. The authors finish by noting that "This facet of communication cannot be overstressed, yet it is one of the most frequent violations of the unwritten laws of communication abroad".

In British English, in particular, 'how' we speak has been the subject of earnest debate for some time. An article on 'Estuary English'[8] explains: "The way we speak says just as much about ourselves as the clothes we wear" (*The Sunday Times Wordpower Series* 1993, 3:21). The way we speak is immediately interpreted according to ready-made frames. Most of the (British) frames contain negative stereotypes about accent, as George Bernard Shaw famously remarked in the Introduction to *Pygmalion*:

> It is impossible for an Englishman to open his mouth without some other Englishman despising him.

Fortunately, foreign accents do not always generate such an automatic negative response among the British. Indeed, many are used to promote products, such as French for perfume and Italian for ice-cream. Anna and Giulio Lepschy (1988:12) note the class connotation of accent in Britain and confirm that "The situation is quite different in Italy ... The distinction between Italian and dialect has no formal correlation with social hierarchy ... and cuts right across class barriers".

The 'how' of speaking, once learned, tends to fossilize. The British in general acquire one dialect, either the preferred national (a small minority) or a regional dialect (the vast majority). If they do change dialect it is generally incongruent with identity and understood usually as an imitation of someone else or another culture. Interestingly, the same is not true in other countries such as Italy, where most of the population acquire both the national and the local dialect and can therefore switch between the two.

• *Rituals*

We have already noted the existence of rituals in Chapter 2.4. Communication acts are often formalized, and indeed fossilized as a set of rules or action chains. Each culture, for example, has its own way of conducting business. In Japan, a formal

---

[8] Estuary English is a term coined by David Rosewarne of Birkbeck College in the 1980s. It is a variety of modified regional speech grouped between RP (Received Pronunciation) and London speech. The danger, according to him and a number of other influential people, is that the Thames Estuary speak is engulfing large parts of England. One example is the 'loss' of the 't' sound in all but the word-initial substituted by the glottle stop, and of 'l' in the word-final or near final position.

business introduction begins with a bow and an exchange of business cards. No mention is made of position in the company. In the West, it is usual to shake hands and to exchange names and company position verbally. The business card in the West will usually be exchanged during leave taking.

• *Strategies*

Guides to behaviour can either be at the level of isolated 'do's' and 'don'ts' or they can be at the level of strategies. Strategic rules are more useful than behavioural rules because they can be applied to a number of contexts, and they involve a variety of behaviour. The following tourist guide, an extract from *Italy: The Rough Guide* (1990:14, emphasis in the original and added), gives strategic rules on how a pedestrian should act in front of Italian motorists:

GETTING AROUND

However you get around on the roads, bear in mind that the traffic can be appalling. **The secret is to make it very clear what you're going to do**, using your horn as much as possible, **and then do it with great determination**. Just walking around, too, don't assume that as a pedestrian you're safe, and *never* step off the pavement without looking first. Italian drivers aren't keen on stopping when they can simply swerve, and even on pedestrian crossings you can undergo some close calls. **Again the answer is to be bold**, and stride straight out with great determination.

Much strategic (or patterned) behaviour occurs out-of-awareness. The meta-messages are clearly understood within the intended cultural frame. However, in cross-cultural encounters misunderstanding of the unconscious strategy (or pattern) can easily take place.

If we take business as an example, the maxim 'business is business' may well be true, but the meta-messages received while discussing business may well be misperceived, and can affect the business itself. Three short examples will suffice. The removal of the business jacket is perfectly acceptable behaviour in many business situations, but the meta-message differs significantly. In Anglo-Saxon countries (Britain, America and Germany for example) removal can often signify getting down to work in a warmer, more cooperative atmosphere. If this is associated with rolling sleeves up/ *die hemdsaermel hochkräempelm*, then the meta-message is that the participant is ready to "get down to business" and work hard on the subject at hand. In Italy, there is the same expression for rolling sleeves, but it is only used in professional situations figuratively. The same strategic behaviour (removing the jacket) can actually mean "let's relax and get more comfortable", and tends to take place only among people who know each other. Rolling sleeves up is simply unprofessional.

Leaving the office door open at work is another, usually unconscious, strategy with a number of alternative meta-messages. If you are American, it will suggest "I'm open for business". A closed office door, on the other hand, signifies privacy, and may well be viewed negatively. If, on the other hand, the office door is closed in Germany, the signal is "everything is in order, and it's business as usual". An open door here suggests disorder, untidiness, and maybe disrespect (Kramsch 1993:209).

Finally, as Sapir (1994:105) points out in his lecture notes, what counts as appropriate business strategy in one country may well be regarded as banditry in another. Below is an example of two interpretations of the same act. The Italian words (in the left hand column) can be interpreted as either good or bad business practice. To a large extent this connotation will depend on one's values or cultural orientation:

Italian word	positive interpretation	negative interpretation
raccomandazione	recommendation	string-pulling
tangente	cut/commission	bribe/kickback
regalo	gift	palm-greasing
clientelismo	patronage	nepotism

4.4 Values

Our map of the world contains many values. These will be in a hierarchy of 'feeling' or importance. We have already noted one difference between a British and an American hierarchy. The British tend to value privacy over openness, while the Americans value openness over privacy. Hence, given the choice of talking to a stranger about the weather or about your private life a British person will tend towards the former and an American towards the latter.

An important distinction can be drawn between a hierarchy of values (such as openness before privacy) and a cluster of values. A hierarchy will mean that one value will prevail over another. A cluster, on the other hand, is a group of values that act together and determine a particular orientation or, in Hofstede's terminology, cultural 'dimension'. Groups of people tend to behave according to particular orientations, and it is at this level that culture can be observed.

An interesting point made by Florence Kluckhohn (Kluckhohn and Strodtbeck 1961:1-49) in her work on value orientations is that in any culture there will be both a dominant and a variant orientation.[9] The dominant orientation will tend to be the orientation held by those in power. The variant orientation will tend towards the opposite end of the orientation cline and will be held by those who historically do not have power. We will be focusing later on the dominant/variant orientations of the professional and the working classes.

4.5 Beliefs

The fact that people who are part of different cultures do things differently in similar environments is determined by a system of values articulated in terms of beliefs.

---

[9] These concepts were originally discussed by Kluckhohn between 1950 and 1953. The original article is reprinted in Kluckhohn and Strodtbeck (1961).

Beliefs provide the motivations and the reasons for doing or not doing things. Hence they provide the reasons for following certain strategic rules of conduct. These beliefs will determine which particular guide to follow, whether it be *The Bible, The Torah, The Koran* (or *Qur'an*), *Das Kapital* or even *How to Win Friends and Influence People*.

Culture-bound beliefs can be analyzed through common sayings and proverbs. Nancy Adler (1991:79,80), a cross-cultural specialist at McGill University, suggests listening for these and asking oneself "What does a society recommend, and what does it avoid?" She goes on to produce an interesting list of North American proverbs. These embody beliefs that Americans hold to be true. However, according to the *CED* a proverb is more than just a belief, it is a "commonplace fact of experience". Believing a proverb to be a fact of experience rather than a belief means that the frame of interpretation for the *CED* is 'reality' rather than 'a saying' or 'a proverb'. Hence, we can agree with Adler that proverbs contain beliefs which are very deep-seated and, in the case of the *CED*, so out-of-awareness that they are believed to be true. Adler lists the general values attached to the proverbs, and I have added an example of criterial equivalence for each general value:

Proverb	Value	Criterial Equivalence
Cleanliness is next to godliness	Cleanliness	A shower every day
A penny saved is a penny earned	Thriftiness	adverts/coupons with 10 cents off
Time is money	Time/Thrift	'billable time'
Early to bed, early to rise, makes one healthy, wealthy and wise	Diligence/Work ethic	'Partying' restricted to weekends
God helps those who help themselves	Initiative	The self-made man
No rest for the wicked	Guilt/Work ethic	Working lunches
You've made your bed, now sleep in it	Responsibility	3rd party liability insurance for all
The squeaky wheel gets the grease	Aggressiveness	Lobbying
Don't count your chickens before they're hatched	Practicality/Time	Working for short-term profits
A bird in the hand is worth two in the bush	Practicality/Time	High pro-capita consumption, low pro-capita savings

The values in this table have culture-bound meaning or criterial equivalents. So, values can be interpreted in different ways. If we take 'practicality' as an example, a criterial equivalent regarding a business lunch might well be a sandwich in the office, because it saves time. The criterial equivalent for other cultures (French, and to a certain extent Italian) may well be in terms of a restaurant where there is a quiet corner to talk, or where service is efficient.

We also notice that Americans believe practicality to be linked with the idea of the present, and that the future is not practical. Other (Anglo) American proverbs show similar beliefs about 'present time':

> Time flies
> There's no time like the present
> Take care of today, and tomorrow will take care of itself
> Time waits for no man
> Time and tide wait for no man
> Never put off till tomorrow what may be done today

Other cultures, the Japanese for instance, believe that practicality includes the future.

> Fall seven times, stand up the eighth time.
> Vision without action is a daydream. Action without vision is a nightmare.
> When you have completed 95 percent of your journey, you are only halfway there.

Highly practical and successful company policy in Japan, for example, stretches over decades. Hampden-Turner and Trompenaars note (1993:135): "One of the consistent competitive advantages attributed to the Japanese is that of strategizing long-term".

Culture-bound beliefs affect the meaning we assign to language and to behaviour, and are the basis for cultural misunderstanding. However, this is not only a problem for face-to-face encounters but is just as important in translation, as the Bible translators John Beekman and John Callow (1974:160-61) point out: "A statement made in the translation – even if grammatically and lexically correct – may still clash with the belief system or the cultural viewpoint of the readers". One example they give is Jesus' washing of the disciple's feet. The translation into Vietnamese resulted in laughter. The Vietnamese readers believed that appropriate behaviour for Jesus might include the washing of hands, but not the washing of feet. As far as they were concerned the only logical congruent explanation for Jesus washing feet that coincided with their map of the world was a typing error – hence the laughter.

Meaning attached either to a visible behaviour as above or to a word itself has little or nothing to do with reality; it has to do with individual and collective beliefs. As we discussed earlier, word meaning can be understood on one of three levels: a technical (denotative) level, a formal level, or an informal (connotative) level. The informal, out-of-awareness level is the one we react to. The connotative meanings below, for example, depend on one's territorial, political and religious beliefs:

Word	Meaning according to belief
The IRA	terrorist
	freedom fighter
Fundamentalist	saviour
	fanatic
Capitalism	freedom to manage property for profit
	exploitation of man by man
Privatization	the country is better off
	the country is worse off
(the political) left	Communism (and danger to freedom)
	freedom
(the political) right	Fascism (and danger to freedom)
	freedom

In 1997, the British Conservative party banked on the belief that "the political left represents communism" mounting a poster campaign showing Tony Blair with red eyes, and the slogan: *New Labour. New Danger*. However, this particular belief was shown to be held by a tiny minority, which does show that strong beliefs can, indeed, change. Yet, later in Italy, in 2003, a similar poster campaign was mounted. To begin with the following posters appeared side by side, showing polar beliefs encoded in the same word in exactly the same time and place:

1. *VOTA COMUNISTA*	VOTE COMMUNIST
2. *VOTA PER ILLY E VINCONO I COMUNISTI*	VOTE ILLY AND THE COMMUNISTS WILL WIN

The *Vota Comunista* was clearly in favour of the local Neo-Communist Party. *Vota per Illy* referred to Ricardo Illy, the businessman and heir to the *Illy* coffee empire. He is a charismatic new-left politician. This particular poster, however, has the centre-right *Casa delle Libertà* logo, and clearly banked on exactly the same belief as the British Conservative party six years earlier – showing equally that strong beliefs tend not to learn from (the British) experience nor from current Italian reality. Italy has grown up with a strong Communist party, and the only thing Communist about it is its name – for the rest it is culturally Italian, and ideologically it is social-democratic.

Causes of external events are also dependent on belief:

Event	Cause
recession	bad government
	bad industrial management
	high energy costs

	lack of skilled workforce inflexible infrastructure ...
corruption/sleaze	basic human condition the need to do business and cement relations the legislation which is impossible to follow lack of enforcement

The problems that arise in translation of meaning here are twofold. First, meaning is not inbuilt but interpreted according to individual and culture-bound beliefs. Second, there is the widespread belief that translation of the denotative meaning automatically assures a good translation. However, as Séguinot (1995:60) points out, "the motivating force is generally carried by the more hidden messages, the connotative meaning ... And connotations are notoriously culture-specific". Newmark (1988:123) gives a number of examples of political and historical connotative word meanings and suggests "where appropriate it is the translator's duty to show which sense such words have in the SL [source language] text".

4.6 Identity

Culture, as we have seen, is what we identify with. At the highest level, 'mankind' is a culture that we all belong to, though there are many, particularly those at war, who choose to focus on other levels of identification and identify the enemy as 'non-human'. We have mentioned identification at the level of continent (America, Europe, Asia), country, region and so on. Cultures also traverse geographical and political borders and are sometimes more usefully categorized ethnically, linguistically or religiously.

To be a member of a culture, one will need to share beliefs at every level of culture. Below is a sample set of beliefs congruent with being British. That being said, we should remember the 'Ecological Fallacy', which suggests that these beliefs have to be part of our cognitive environment rather than active beliefs:

Belief at the level of...	Belief in ...
Value:	fair play democracy compromise privacy
Strategy:	internalization of feelings
Behaviour:	queuing
Environment:	an Englishman's home is his castle a little bit of dirt never did anyone any harm there's nothing like a good cup of tea

A set of beliefs congruent with an Italian identity would be on the following lines:

Belief at the level of...	Belief in ...
Value:	*la famiglia*/the family
	la mamma è sempre la mamma/ mother is always mother – whatever
	il forbo o il fesso/wise up or be had
	il rispetto/respect
	l'estetica/aesthetics
Strategy:	*saperne una più del diavolo*/to know one more than the devil
	fare bella figura/to make a good impression
	l'arte d'arrangiarsi/the art of making the best out of any situation
Behaviour:	*mangiar bene*/eating well
Environment:	*la casa brilla come uno specchio*/the house shines like a mirror
	la buona cucina/good cooking

Anna Wierzbicka (1992:31-116) notes the fundamental importance of three Russian values: *duša*/'soul', *sud'ba*/'fate/destiny', and *toska*/'yearning/a painful feeling/ nostalgia'. These three concepts permeate Russian conversation, language and literature. The range of meaning is wider, and the effect of these words deeper, than in English because they are core values. The mediator or cultural interpreter will be extremely aware that these, and all, core values are directly and inexorably connected to identity. In translating the core value, the mediator will be concerned about compensating for the lack of connection in the mind of the target culture reader. This will be discussed later in Chapter 7.

4.7 Imprinting

- Lorenz's Imprinting
- Maslowe's Hierarchy of Need
- Dilts' Developmental Model
- Bernstein's Codes theory
- Hasan's HAP/LAP theory
- Enculturalization

Beliefs about identity are such an important aspect of culture that it is useful to look at how they are formed. The Austrian zoologist and founder of ethology, Konrad Lorenz (1954/1977), is credited with first discovering that early experience is crucial in forming life-long beliefs about identity and relationships. He discovered that

ducklings on seeing him first, rather than the mother duck, happily 'believed' that
he was their mother. Every time he moved they followed. Later introduction of the
real mother could not overturn that first experience. The ducklings were convinced
that Lorenz was the mother, and that the real mother an outsider. Reality, as Lorenz
realized, had very little to do with the matter. He called this type of process 'imprinting'. Dilts (1990:102), among others, has extended this idea to people, defining
an imprint as "an identity-forming experience ... It is a reflection on your identity".

Imprints generally become core beliefs. They are the highest, or deepest, frame
of reference, and all day-to-day living is carried out within these frames. There are
no further frames readily available from which imprints can be viewed. As such,
imprints are difficult to identify, as they are completely out-of-awareness.

Like ducks, people are ready to process certain inputs from the environment at
certain times of development. For example, a human child can recognize its mother
within 24 hours but is unable to distinguish the dog from the cat until much later.
Clearly, it is more important for the child to locate its mother (assuming she is the
provider of food and security) than the cat or the dog.

According to the psychologist Abraham Maslowe (1970), the acquisition of beliefs about the world occurs according to a hierarchy of need. Physical survival
(physiological needs) is the first need to be satisfied, and any beliefs relating to
higher, less fundamentally necessary needs will have to wait. Maslowe proposed a
five-fold classification of motives and needs as below. It should be remembered
that this triangle is to be framed within Maslowe's own model of the world, which
perceives 'self-actualization, as the final stage. There are those who see this stage a
necessary stage before 'spiritual mission' or 'enlightment'. In theory, the framing is
infinite:

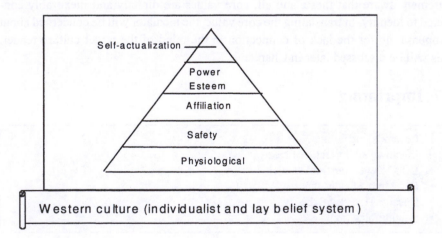

Figure 11. Maslowe's Hierarchy of Needs

Dilts (1990:135) has adapted Maslowe's hierarchy, relating it specifically to Logical Levels. His levels are discussed below.

• *Biological Level*

As we have already mentioned, the first imprinting is 'biological'. The human baby's first needs are to survive in an environment, and it learns very quickly how to deal with dependency on food. How it deals with this reality will have long-term effects.

• *Emotional Level*

The second stage is 'emotional': "Where are my bonds? What is my territory?". This stage develops at home and forms much of the cultural imprint. A two-year old will be aware of his/her private space and possessions, including "*my* toy", "*my* room" and "*my* mummy".[10]

   Later, as the child's perception of his/her environment grows, the reality of group territory (whether it be Sarajevo; the Falls Road, Belfast or the Gaza Strip) and the 'us/them' divide will be inculcated through parents and tested with peers. Ethnic conflict has its roots here. Well before school age, a child will already respond appropriately to culture-bound beliefs about the family, privacy, socially accepted distances, possession and eating habits.[11] Italian children, for example, who have lunch at kindergarten, learn to say *buon appetito* before eating their meal. With parental encouragement, this is repeated until it becomes an automatic response at every meal.

• *Intellectual Level*

The next stage is 'intellectual'. This is equivalent to the Logical Level of capabilities, strategies and skills. At this stage, the child (particularly at school age) begins to develop the ability to understand symbols and process them efficiently.

   During adolescence, the child is ready to consolidate decisions about his or her 'social' role. This is the level of beliefs, and in particular beliefs about identity. The educational sociologist Basil Bernstein (1972) and systemic linguist Ruqaiya Hasan (1989; 1991; 1992) have both found that the prerequisites for decision-making about role are learned through the parent's language input. Bernstein's original thesis, that social class influenced language, caused much controversy, particularly as it became clear that he effectively said lower-class children had a more restricted language (restricted code), and that this restricted language resulted in a more restricted view of the world. However, his findings have been defended by Halliday (1992: 70-71) and by Hasan. Hasan, in particular, has developed Bernstein's theory through her studies of mother and child language from the two traditional social classes, renaming them as 'high' and 'low autonomy'. She came to the conclusion that children from Lower Autonomy Professions (LAPs) learn from their parents that they too have low autonomy in the world.

   Clearly, it would be simplistic to suggest that all LAPs learn that they have low

---

[10] Personal observation. See also Aitchinson (1989:119) and her discussion of two-word sentences at this age.
[11] See also Samovar and Porter (1991:55-56) and Brislin (1993:6-8).

autonomy, or even that their use of language determines their position in society. What we can say is that language (as we shall see in Chapter 6) is one of the filters through which we learn about the world. Hasan suggests that the way in which mothers explain the world and its rules becomes a strong model for the children to follow. Her results show that the LAP mothers' conversations tended to follow a particular pattern: rules are laid down, but not explained. If we take this finding to its logical conclusion, children may learn that rules are a fixed reality – and not to be questioned.

This possible hypothesis takes us insidiously close to Aldous Huxley's (1932/1955) distopia, *Brave New World*. In his book, children were born pre-programmed in test tubes; production was divided into alphas, betas, gammas and deltas; each group was destined to a higher or lower level of autonomy in work, and every individual was genetically adjusted to their predestined level. However, the quote below is not from science fiction but from Hasan (1992, emphasis in original):

> Both the HAP and the LAP groups are adjusted to their social positioning: *In natural everyday discourse, speakers speak their social position.*

The presuppositions of NLP therapy are very close: people in need of help speak their limited world; and through precise linguistic intervention, therapists can help their clients have more options in life. Bateson's (1975: x) introduction to *The Structure of Magic* explains how the originators of NLP "succeeded in making linguistics into a base for [human interaction] theory and simultaneously into a tool for therapy. ... Grinder and Bandler have succeeded in making explicit the syntax of how people avoid change and, therefore, how to assist them in changing".

Children from Higher Autonomy Professions (HAPs) have learned the language of change. They learn that rules have contexts and justifications (further frames), and that therefore, like the picture in the art gallery, these rules can be admired or criticized from a distance. The difference is that for many LAPs rules *are* the world and cannot be questioned. HAPs, instead, learn that rules are part of the wider world and can be changed in response to wider world needs. These children, through language forms learned from their parents, have a richer model of the world, one that furnishes them with beliefs about their power to influence change. The two worlds can be shown as below. The LAP world on the left is smaller and has rules as its frame. The HAP world, on the right, is larger, as there is a wider frame of reference through which rules can be interpreted.

In psychology, this learning of the rules is known as socialization; in culture-studies, it is known as enculturation: "the modification from infancy of an individual's behaviour to conform with the demands of social life" (*CED* 1991). Modification, as we have already suggested, begins at home (see also Brislin 1993:95) through what Bernstein originally referred to as parental appeals. According to Sapir (1949:197) and Bernstein (1972:485), these appeals are a principal means of social control.

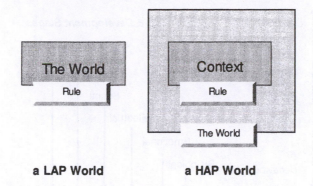

Figure 12. A HAP and LAP View of the World

• *Aesthetic Level*

The next level is the 'aesthetic'. At this level people begin to "develop awareness of things for what they are" (Dilts 1990:135). This is the level of self-realization and is equivalent to personal identity in the Logical Levels Model. According to Maslowe, Dilts and others (see Guirdham 1990:21-30), only when these lower level needs have been satisfied does one have the time to look at the world and appreciate it. At the lower levels, the chief concerns are using or exploiting the world for biological, survival or role needs. In the 'civilized' world, this higher level of imprinting takes place at school.

• *Meta Level*

The final level goes beyond the satisfaction of self and looks towards purpose in life. This is the 'meta' level. At this level, identity and evolution are considered not only from a personal but also from a social point of view. At this stage, the person begins to look for a higher purpose. This is equivalent to the spiritual level or 'mission' in the Logical Levels Model, and will be discussed in the following section.

The various levels of imprinting, Logical Levels and the developmental stages are shown below. Along the horizontal axis, from left to right, is the time line, from birth to adulthood. By the time one is an adult, one is expected to have moved from concern with biological needs to concern for the aesthetic needs and beyond. Vertically, we can see how the Logical Levels Model links with the developmental model. Biological need is at the level of behaviour (all attention is focused on doing). At the capabilities level, intellectual imprinting takes place (the focus is on how). The following level, beliefs, relates to societal imprinting while identity relates to aesthetic imprinting (realization of self). The final stage, not yet discussed as part of the Logical Levels Model, is the spiritual level, which compares to the meta-development stage.

It should be remembered that these models are all culture specific, relating only to those cultures that place individual self-realization, for example, over social belongingness.

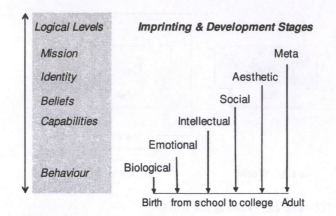

Figure 13. Dilts' Imprinting and Development Stages

4.8 The Model as a System

- Role Changes
- Level Changes
- A Dynamic Model of Culture
- Habitus and Logical Level clashes

We can now use the Logical Levels Model in a variety of ways. First, we can identify the differences between a traditional view of a translator and a cultural interpreter or mediator, then we can look at how the levels interact within the system.

• *Role changes*

Below is an example of the congruent Logical Levels associated with being a translator:

Identity:	a translator
Values:	language, text, words, general knowledge, precision, perfection, solitude, patience ...
Beliefs:	equivalence, accuracy and fidelity to the text, *le mot juste*
Capabilities:	language, translation, know-how (library and e-resources, computer skills)
Behaviour:	reading, writing, accessing, checking, correcting, rewriting...
Environment:	a source text, a computer, desk, dictionaries/internet, quiet area ...

When beliefs about role identity change, and the translator becomes a cultural interpreter, all the other levels are affected. Also, the visible behaviour of a traditional interpreter, for example, will change from the discrete 'black-box' approach mentioned earlier to more active participation and control. The translator, as mediator, should become more active in obtaining information. This will include involving the participating agents to clarify the frames of the translation. Gentzler (2001:79) notes the importance given recently, for example, to 'the initiator' of the translation process and also to the translation brief. Aspects in the brief to be clarified will include: reasons for the translation (the skopos), information on the target reader, the target culture, and similar target-culture texts. With regard to the translation of promotional material, Séguinot (1995:60) lays great stress on the fact that "without access to the product or information about the service" a translator cannot do his or her job. Christina Schäffner (1995:81), citing the Finnish translator Justa Holz-Mänttäri, says the same: "You can't give quality without access to all the information available. [Holz-Mänttäri] never signs a contract unless she has a guarantee that she can talk to the producers, and that they will take her to the factory for example".

I have already mentioned that the translating-interpreting habitus is still extremely restricted. As mentioned, the EU itself still identifies the professions in terms of "secretaries", and logically, their capabilities in terms of "copying" (see also Katan 2002:185). So, most translators are clearly not in a position to expect such a level of cooperation. Following Dilts and Maslowe, they (along with fledgling interpreters and mediators) will be at the biological level: survival in a small and competitive market. The aesthetic level, that of quality, will be the desired aim – but insistence on all the information at all costs will not ensure survival. In the not too distant future, as the market becomes increasingly aware of the importance of culture, so a mediator's insistence on information *will* be essential for survival.

There are, of course, many other aspects to being a mediator. Most of the changes will be internal, requiring little change in the external environment. Strategies will be different. The cultural mediator will need to be able to demonstrate cognitive flexibility, be able to change viewpoint (disassociation) and be able to mind-shift (see Part 2). Capabilities will include a conscious understanding of cultures as well as language.

Values, for both translators and interpreters, will change. No longer will they focus exclusively on language and the text (whether source or target), but on culture, text function, communication and mutual understanding. There will be two values in particular which will permit a mediator to work well. First, the cultural interpreter will have a high tolerance for difference, and secondly, s/he will believe in the relativity of values, i.e. the principle that no culture has an inherently better or worse hierarchy of values. Clearly, though, cultures will have more or less beneficial values in particular contexts, and mediators will also have their own personal feelings. At the level of identity, as we have already mentioned, a mediator will be able to identify with both cultures.

Finally, referring back to Dilts' meta-level, a sixth Logical Level, 'mission', will be more evident. The mission goes beyond identity and answers the question "What is my role in society?" In the case of the mediator, the mission will be to improve mutual understanding between people.

Example Logical Level changes from translator to cultural interpreter/ mediator	
Environment:	a client, an initiator, a brief, a model reader; a source text, a computer, desk, internet, …
Behaviour:	proactive asking for clarification, involvement with other agents in

	the translation process; reading, writing, accessing, checking, correcting, rewriting
Capabilities:	language and culture, communication, social, technical, translation
Strategies:	disassociation, mind-shifting
Values:	culture, understanding, difference, mediation, flexibility
Beliefs:	integrity of cultures, cultural relativity of values, contextual translating principles
Identity:	cultural mediator, bicultural person
Mission:	to bring further mutual understanding

• *Level Changes*

In general, any change in a higher level will affect all lower levels (less so the other way round). Let us imagine, for example, an Eastern European who has grown up and believed in communism. He now believes himself to be a capitalist. A successful change in identity ('who') involves a complete change in 'mission', one's place and role in society. In this case the communist, who saw his role as satisfying or furthering the interests of the group (political, family ...) now sees his mission as an explorer, out to stake new territories for himself. He will no longer be motivated by the group, and its welfare, but by personal success and entrepreneurship. This will mean a change of direction in strategy and the need to learn new capabilities. The result will be an action, a change in behaviour, for example working overtime and risking personal investments in his new capitalistic environment. Finally, the environment will react differently compared to when it was a centrally planned market, possibly encouraging him to further explore the market.

The following diagram is a schematic illustration of how Dilts (1990:209-210) understands the changes in the Logical Levels:

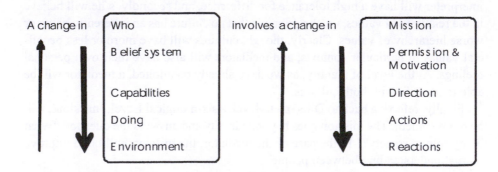

Figure 14. Dilts' Logical Levels and Change

• *A Dynamic Model of Culture*

We can now put the component levels together to identify a person as a member of a dynamic system, i.e. culture. The necessarily stereotypic example below shows how the various levels interact at a particular moment. Two people are talking in a pub on a crowded Saturday night as they go to the bar:

A (on jostling people to get to the bar):	Excuse me.
Those being jostled:	Sorry.
A (to B)	What would you like to drink?
B:	Sorry? What did you say?
A:	What are you having?
B:	It's my round.
A:	Let's go halves.

For a full picture of how the culture is operating dynamically we should analyze the Logical Levels, looking first at the environment, working up finally to identity at the top. Clearly, the environment will change constantly but is both the most visible element and also the least important. The environment can radically change, but if there is no change in the belief and identity, strategy (use of abilities) may not necessarily change.

Level	Example	Criterial equivalent
Identity	British	Speaking English.
Values/Beliefs	Fair play	It's my round.
	Compromise	Let's go halves.
	Privacy	Defensible space, "Excuse me".
Strategies:	Language:	Use of conditional,
(Use of) **Abilities**	Conversation rules	polite question forms,
		high use of modals,
	Politeness strategies	question forms
Behaviour	Indirect offers	"What would you like to drink?"
	Non-threatening questions:	"Sorry, what did you say?"
	Explicit politeness markers	
Environment	British institution	Country pub, full of people on a Saturday night.
	Weather	Damp outside.
	Food	Baked potato, lasagna, chicken curry, vegetarian dishes,
	Architecture	Low ceilings, open beams, small rooms; fireplace

• *Attribution Theory*

Our ethnocentric approach to other cultures and the basic principles of cross-cultural communication can be analyzed through the Logical Levels model. 'Ethnocentric' means that we tend to blame the individual people and their culture for our own internal response. This process is known in psychology as the attribution process and is discussed below.

The Attribution theory[12] was first discussed by Fritz Heider in 1958. Citing research, he suggests that perception of behaviour depends on our own personal position, i.e. attributor or attributee. When interacting with others, we will tend to attribute their behaviour in terms of volition or other personal factors regarding their personality. On the other hand, we will tend to attribute our own behaviour in terms of the situational.

A good example of the attributor position is that of the manager or university professor who is unable to complete a job on time due to overwork, pressing engagements, etc. The subordinate, or student, who likewise is unable to complete his or her task, will, on the contrary, be thought of (as an attributee) as being lazy, badly organized or untrustworthy.

The importance of this theory cannot be underestimated in crosscultural communication. Native speakers can hear grammatical inaccuracy and can therefore contextualize any errors in terms of language learning. However, they are unlikely to have the same conscious awareness of linguistic or behavioural *appropriacy* (rather than accuracy), especially when the non-native speaker has a reasonable command of the language. As a result, the native speaker is likely to attribute the inappropriacy to some personal factor rather than to the speaker's – or their own – communication or cultural (in)competence. Every time we have a negative reaction to someone's behaviour we are attributing our own meaning to that behaviour, and hence we apply an aspect of our own congruent Logical Level system to the behaviour. A few seconds thought will allow us to realize that this is a form of mind reading and that behaviour, like language, makes sense in its own context.[13]

The iceberg diagram below shows how the logical levels and attribution combine to produce intercultural misperception, misattribution and miscommunication. As the diagram illustrates, a culture B hearer (for example, British) hears an imperative such as "tell me!" (the formally correct translation of either the formal subjunctive *mi dica* or the informal imperative *dimmi*) from an interpreter or directly from a culture A speaker. In the British culture the imperative is appropriate in certain situations only, for example to indicate anger, authority or urgency. If this is not the context, then various values important to culture B may not be satisfied, such as deference, indirectness and so on. The resulting (mis)attribution of these imperatives is impoliteness, rudeness or aggression.

On the other hand, in culture A (Italian, for example) directness in language may well be positively valued. Hence, what is a positive communication behaviour in culture A is interpreted as a negative personal trait by a culture B observer. When culture B observers notice a repetition of the negatively valued behaviour, the trait becomes generalized to a form of negative stereotype. Scollon and Scollon (2001: 43-59) devote a complete chapter to miscommunication due to inappropriate politeness strategies and suggest that when an inappropriate politeness strategy is used

---

[12] For a discussion of other work on Attribution see Selby (1975) and Lalljee (1987).
[13] See also Mansur Lalljee's study on Attribution theory and intercultural communication: "evaluative meaning is influenced by context" (1987:41).

the event will be interpreted in terms of power. Politeness strategies are discussed further in Chapter 11.

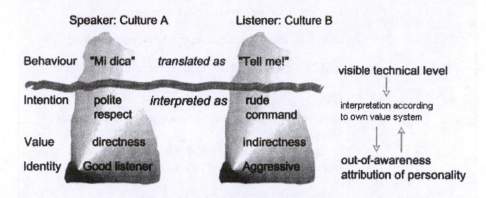

Figure 15. Culture-Bound Misinterpretation

Culture-bound communication can be analyzed with the Logical Levels Model through a simple set of clarification questions. There is a specific question form to be used relating to each level, which then helps to distinguish the various aspects of culture:

Where/When	Environment
What	Behaviour
How	Capabilities
Why	Beliefs
Who	Identity

These clarification questions are not entirely new. One of Rudyard Kipling's *Just-So* Stories (1902/1966:42) calls them the six honest serving men:

> I keep six honest servingmen
> (They taught me all I knew);
> Their names are What and Why and When
> And How and Where and Who.

Roger Bell (1991:7-10) also uses these clarifications, taken directly from Kipling, to investigate a text: its semantic meaning, communicative value, place in time and space, and participants involved. The important point to remember is, as we have already mentioned, that these questions relate to a hierarchy of levels – which would have taught Kipling even more.

Let us now see how we can apply these questions to clarify the context of culture. We can imagine a visible behaviour such as kneeling in a particular environment, as in a church on Sunday at 9.00 am, with a group of other people all kneeling at the same time. With this information, we can begin to construct a cultural identity that is congruent with this behaviour using the clarification questions below:

Where and When	• church during a religious service.
What	• kneeling, reciting words: an act of prayer.
How	• according to a set procedure; formally; concentrated.
Why	• to follow the implicit and explicit rules involved in the service. • belief in humility. • because this is the way to communicate with a superior being. • because of a deep-seated belief that this superior being exists and can answer the prayer satisfactorily.
Who	• a member of this religious group. • a believer. • a Christian.

This hierarchical system of Logical Levels is a step towards contextualizing culture. A number of linguists have considered communication in similar hierarchical systemic terms. Peter Mühlhäusler and Rom Harré (1990:29, 30), for example, have proposed what they call a moral order. The important point they make is that when change is introduced at the top, so change is induced further down the order: "A person taking on, or being thrust into, a role is like a change coming to be located at a certain point in physical space and engendering a field in its environs".

They continue by explaining that only a certain number of speech acts are possible in the surrounding space. In NLP terms, the surrounding space is at the level of the environment while the speech acts are behaviour. The speech acts in the surrounding space, according to the authors, are oriented by "the system of rights, duties and obligations – that is, by the conversational force field". The system of rights, duties and obligations is at the level of beliefs, and the force field can be compared to the logical element in the logical levels theory. They envisage speech acts as being constrained by a moral order that changes with changing roles. For the moral order to function, they emphasize the importance of speaker sincerity, which is closely related to the NLP concept of congruence between levels.

• *Habitus and Logical Level clashes*

Another way of describing the system is to use Bourdieu's (1990:78) habitus, which he describes as people's "ordinary relations to the world" and includes "cultural comfort zones and characteristic ways of acting" (Lull 1995:69). When change takes place, and we move out of our traditional habitus and comfort zone, tension is created. The idea of a system, a habitus influencing all its components, can be developed not only to investigate the links between language and culture, but also to show at what hierarchical level(s) tensions between the systems themselves (cultures, texts and so on) are more apparent.

As the systems are, for the most part, hidden, so it takes time to understand how internal maps of the world will need to negotiate those aspects of the external reality that clash. The example below shows how the traditional identity of the media interpreter (on Italian talkshows) is still tending to clash at a number of logical levels both with the habitus of the broadcaster and that of the TV audience.

As can be seen from the model (developed in Katan and Straniero Sergio 2001), it is the traditional interpreter's beliefs about invisibility, the supremacy of the text and equivalence that are being challenged by the relatively new habitus of Italian TV talkshows. What appears to be happening is that the interpreter is being judged, no longer on source text/target text criteria, but in terms of audience share and entertainment value. In particular, the traditional media interpreter is having to come to terms with the need to satisfy the audience's "comfort factor" through entertainment, rather than rely primarily on fidelity to the text. This is due also to the broadcaster's active control of the interpreter's abilities. The interpreter is visible and 'directed' on stage. S/he will be told when to intervene, may well be truncated, paraphrased and at times 'overruled' by the presenter or other guests who may offer their own translations. Even more importantly, the interpreter is also 'required' to perform as a participant. The verb "to require" suggests a clash with a traditional interpreter's model of the world. As far as the broadcaster and the viewers are concerned, though, the interpreter has 'an opportunity' to become visible and perform. The real clash, is that evaluation of interpretation quality is no longer restricted to the interpreting profession and to the interlocutors directly concerned, but to the deadly use of the remote control to change channel, and to the consequent repercussions in terms of audience share.

Clearly, to be a successful professional interpreter (on Italian talkshows) the hierarchy of values must also embrace those of this newfound TV habitus. Many will see this habitus as a threat to professionalism (see Pym 2000), while others will understand the opportunities available in *combining* the 2 or even 3 sets of values, along with *developing* their abilities to include those of performance. As successful mediators, they will be able to choose when entertainment needs will override those of fidelity, and when the opposite will also be true. See figure 16 next page.

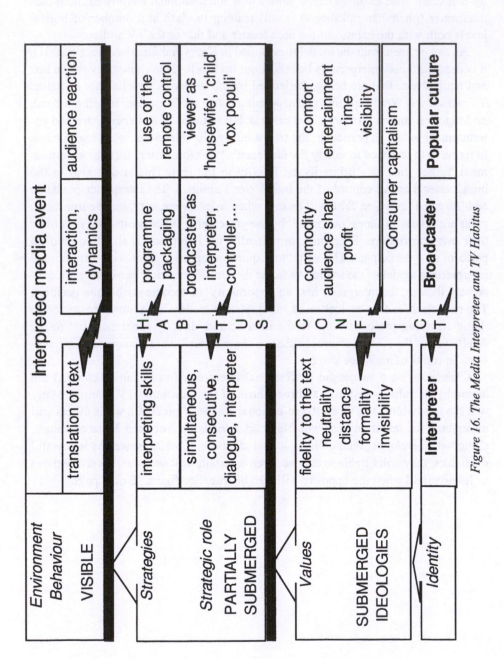

Figure 16. The Media Interpreter and TV Habitus

Chapter 5. Language and Culture

The aim in this chapter is to:
- identify the links between language and culture
- introduce Malinowski's contexts of situation and culture
- discuss the Sapir-Whorf hypothesis (strong and weak, lexical and grammatical versions)
- discuss political correctness in terms of language and culture
- develop the idea of categorization
- discuss lexical gaps, borrowing and coining

5.1 Contexts of Situation and Culture

Culture is still hardly a respected area of study for linguists. Fortunately though, anthropologists respected the study of language. In 1911, Franz Boas (1986:7), a German and one of the fathers of modern anthropology, discussed the links between language, thought and (primitive) culture. Boas felt that language was not in itself a barrier to thought but that there was a dynamic relationship between language, culture and thought. His key point was succinctly put as follows: "the form of the language will be moulded by the state of that culture". Seventy-five years later, his thoughts are still very relevant, and in fact serve to introduce Valdes' publication on culture (1986:1). In her Preface to the book, she stated: "his work inspired a generation of anthropologists and sociologists before the applied linguists took up the subject of the effect of culture on language and vice versa". And it is to him that we owe the term "cultural relativism".

Like Boas, Bronislaw Malinowski, who was Polish, was also a founding father of anthropology and an outsider (Eriksen and Nielsen 2001:38). They were also both interested in language. Malinowski coined the terms 'context of situation' and 'context of culture', and noted that a language could only be fully understood, i.e. have meaning, when these two contexts (situation and culture) were implicitly or explicitly clear to the interlocutors. He actually coined the term 'context of culture' in his 1935 work (1935:18), but, as the 1938 republication of his original 1923 paper illustrates, he was already discussing the meaning of language in terms of a wider context of culture:

> [...] language is essentially rooted in the reality of the culture [...] it cannot
> be explained without constant reference to these broader contexts of verbal
> utterance. (Malinowski 1938:305)

He studied the inhabitants of the Trobriand Islands and their language (Kiriwinian), and felt that he would have to make a number of changes in translating Kiriwinian conversations into English. Most importantly, he realised that he would need to add a commentary to make explicit what was implicit for the Trobrianders. Below is his first translation of a native monologue:

Tsakaulo	kaymatana	yakida;	tawoulo	ovanu;
We run	front-wood	ourselves;	we paddle	in place;
tasivila	tagine	soda;	isakaulo	ka'u'uya
we turn	we see	companion ours	he runs	rear-wood
oluvieki	similaveta	Pilolu		
behind	their sea-arm	Pilolu		

He realised that he still needed to explain the immediate situation of the conversation to the English audience. Otherwise, the English reader would not have understood that the Trobriander was, for example, sitting round with a group of eager listeners, recounting the day's fishing trip, and, in this extract, talking about guiding the boats home. A version for outsiders might have sounded something like this:

> In crossing the sea-arm of Pilolu (between the Trobriands and the Ampphletts), our canoe sailed ahead of the others. When nearing the shore we began to paddle. We looked back and saw our companions still far behind, still on the sea-arm of Pilolu.

Thirdly, though, Malinowski realised that not only the immediate environment needed to be clarified for the English, but also that Trobriand traditions and beliefs were encoded in the texts, and were not immediately understandable in translation. These included the fact that the fishing expedition finished in a race, and that the speaker was evidently boasting. Only when these two factors were taken into account could the texts be said to have meaning:

> **Front-wood** is a technical term for competitions, as in 'leading canoe', and includes "a specific emotional tinge only comprehensible against a background of their tribal ceremonial life, commerce and enterprise".
> **Paddle** signals the fact that the sail is lowered as shallow water is reached and is used metaphorically to mean that the race is all but over.

Though Malinowski was primarily an anthropologist, he was much more interested in the role of language in producing meaning than his fellow linguists writes Lyons (1981:16, emphasis in original): "There have been times in the recent past, notably in America in the period between 1930 and the end of the 1950s, when *linguistic semantics*, – the study of meaning in language – was very largely neglected". The reasons were due to the linguists' focus on the technical level of language: the word and in how words combined (syntax). Meaning, of course, is highly subjective, changeable and indeed vague, hardly a subject for technicians. The word 'meaning' itself is open to a number of different definitions (ibid.:30-31). Semantic meaning may be part of formal culture, but 'the meaning' in the sense of what the interlocutor understands is part of the informal culture – and therefore was not regarded as worthy of study. Translation, too, suffered in the same way. It was largely taught, not in terms of meaning, but as a behaviourist grammar-translation activity.

'Context' began to receive more attention in 1933 when the American linguist Leonard Bloomfield (1984:139) published *Language*. He drew on behavioural psychology for his understanding of meaning, which he illustrated with Jack and Jill. The example, summarized here, is as follows. Jill spies an apple tree. She makes a noise with her larynx, tongue and lips, and the obedient Jack vaults the fence, climbs the tree, takes the apple, brings it to her and places it in her hand. So, according to Bloomfield, meaning depends on "the situation in which the speaker utters it and the response which it calls forth in the hearer". The definition of meaning in NLP (O'Connor and Seymour 1993:18) is very similar: "The meaning of the communication is the response that you get". The social background is important for Bloomfield (1984:23), though he does not actually mention culture and its effect on the act of speech: "The occurrence of speech ... and the wording of it ... and the whole course of practical events before and after [the act of speech], depend upon the entire life-history of the speaker and of the hearer".

Sapir, on the other hand, an anthropologist like Malinowski, and also a student under Boas, was convinced not only of the importance of the social background but that future language studies would turn to a 'concept of culture'. He introduced his essay on 'Language Race and Culture' (1949:207) with these words: "Language has a setting ... language does not exist apart from culture". In Britain, the linguist J. R. Firth developed a number of Malinowski's ideas, but focused principally on the concept of a context of situation.

According to Halliday (Halliday and Hasan 1989:9) the importance of a cultural framework in linguistics was not extensively studied until thirty years later with Hymes' work and his definition of the ethnography of communication in 1962. This led to a renewal of interest in the different ways in which language is used in different cultures. Hymes (1974:4) dedicated one of his books in memory of Edward Sapir and pointed to the importance of examining cultural values and beliefs for their bearing on communicative events. More recently, NLP has also taken the view that meaning in communication is culture-bound (O'Connor and Seymour 1993: 23, 89). Independently, one of the axioms of semiotics is that the meaning of a sign is arbitrarily assigned according to context.

Halliday (Halliday and Hasan 1989:47), a former pupil of Firth, takes up Malinowski's notions of context of situation and control of culture. However, it is context of situation that is explained in detail, not context of culture. He explains why below:

> We have not offered, here, a separate linguistic model of the context of culture; no such thing yet exists ... But in describing the context of situation, it is helpful to build in some indication of the cultural background and the assumptions that have to be made if the text is to be interpreted – or produced – in the way ... the system intends.

The Logical Levels Model discussed earlier should go some way towards clarifying the factors (linguistic and non-linguistic) involved in the cultural background.

Two of the most vigorous exponents of the role of culture in language were, of course, Sapir and his pupil Benjamin Lee Whorf. It is a testimony to their groundbreaking and controversial ideas that they are still discussed today. The Sapir-Whorf hypothesis has an obligatory place in all contemporary text books that touch upon the subject, even though the hypothesis was first published before the Second World War. Indeed, as Eriksen and Nielsen (2001:66) put it, even when the theory wasn't being discussed in the fierce anthropological debates in the 1990s, this "can only be understood as a serious case of collective memory loss".

The next sections look at the theories of Sapir and Whorf and how they can help contribute to the discussion on the context of culture.

5.2 The Sapir-Whorf Hypothesis

- the strong/weak versions
- the lexical/grammatical versions
- examples of the hypothesis:
  - categorization
  - political correctness

That the world is *my* world, shows itself in the fact that the limits of that language (*the* language I understand) mean the limits of *my* world. (Wittgenstein)

In this section we will discuss the Sapir-Whorf hypothesis in terms of its relevance today. The quote above is from Ludwig Wittgenstein's *Tractatus Logico-Philosophicus*, originally written in 1921 and now included in *The Wittgenstein Reader* (1994:25, emphasis in the original). His words have been used by many, both in linguistics (e.g. Hasan 1984:133) and in translation (e.g. Ulrych 1992: preface). They also serve as a backdrop to this and the following chapters.

Sapir (1929:214), as mentioned earlier, like Malinowski, was convinced that language could only be interpreted within a culture. However, he went further, suggesting "no two languages are ever sufficiently similar to be considered as representing the same reality. The worlds in which different societies live are distinct worlds, not merely the same world with different labels". This well-known extract forms part of what is loosely known as the Sapir-Whorf Hypothesis, of which there have traditionally been two versions: the strong and the weak. In the strong view, language actually determines the way the language user thinks, which would suggest, for example, that bilinguals would automatically change their view of the world as they change language. This view has few supporters today. Steven Pinker (1995:57) in *The Language Instinct* is adamantly critical of the theory: "The idea that thought is the same thing as language is an example of a conventional absurdity: a statement that goes against all common sense".

Hatim and Mason (1990:29), among many others, have come to the same conclusion. They say that if the strong version of the Sapir-Whorf Hypothesis were accepted, this would mean that people, hence translators and interpreters too, would be 'prisoners' of their native language and would be "incapable of conceptualizing in categories other than those of our native tongue. It is now widely recognized that such a view is untenable".

Many others also believe that acceptance of this version of the Sapir-Whorf hypothesis means that we can only ever think what our language allows. Halliday (1992:65) would also not call himself a supporter of this strong version of the hypothesis, though he does state that "grammar creates the potential within which we act and enact our cultural being. This potential is at once both enabling and constraining: that is, grammar makes meaning possible and also sets limits on what can be meant". This is an example of the weak version of the Sapir-Whorf theory, which suggests that language influences thought. This version of the theory has many more supporters in anthropology, linguistics and translation. For example, R. J. Reddick (1992:214), in an essay in honour of the linguist Robert E. Longacre, states: "We cannot foreground reality in discourse unless we have unmediated access to it, and we never do. Our perceptions are always mediated by our assumptions, our beliefs, and, in fact, by the language we speak".

Supporters of the weak version suggest that language is one of the factors influencing our understanding of reality, but it is not the determining factor. Hatim and Mason (1990:105), in fact, accept the weak version: "languages differ in the way they perceive and partition reality". Importantly they also add "This situation creates serious problems for the translator". According to the Logical Levels Model, the determining factors are, as Reddick suggests, beliefs and values.

We will now focus on how language does influence our perception and look in a little more depth at what Sapir and Whorf actually had to say. Apart from there being a strong and a weak version of their theory, they had a different approach. The two approaches are now known as the lexical and the grammatical versions of the Sapir-Whorf Hypothesis.

5.3 Lexis

- lexical labels
- an example: political correctness
- categorization
- lexical and conceptual gaps

Sapir and Whorf had a different understanding of the term 'language'. For Sapir, at least in his early years, the key to cultural reality was in the lexicon. As far as he was concerned language was a case of labelling lexis, and behind that label was a different reality rather than simply a different label.

How far this is true has been a subject of discussion for three-quarters of a century. One recent in-depth study on lexical labels was carried out by Rogelio Diaz-Guerrero and Lorand Szalay (1991:24-25). They interviewed 100 Mexican and 100 North American college students and asked them to make a list of words they associated with a headword, or what they called 'stimulus themes', such as 'equality' and 'the United States'. The "rather lengthy response lists are particularly informative in revealing what a particular group feels is important, what they pay attention to, what they feel sensitive about, and what they are collectively predisposed to overlook and ignore". Below is a 'semantograph' of Mexican and American responses to the labels 'United States' and 'Estados Unidos'.

The results show that the 'psycho-cultural distance' between the labels 'United States' and 'Estados Unidos' represents different realities. For the North Americans, 'United States' has a fairly technical meaning in terms of 'states' and 'America'; there is also a strong feeling of love and patriotism. For the Mexicans, 'United States' is anything but technical. The lexical item cues historic frames of exploitation and war, as well as comparative frames with their perception of their present context of culture. 'United States' represents what Mexico does not have: money, wealth, power and development. Maps of the world, for the lexicon at least, are culture specific. These differences in meaning, as we discussed in 'Beliefs' (Chapter 4.5), make life very difficult for a cultural mediator:

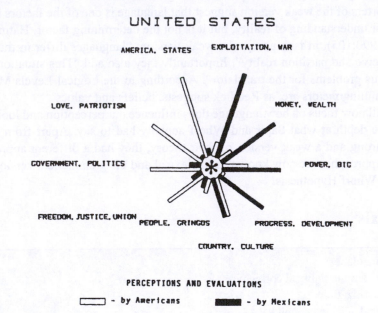

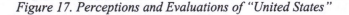

Figure 17. Perceptions and Evaluations of "United States"

• *Political Correctness*

However, we do not have to travel to two different languages to see how the lexicon channels thought. In the eighteenth century, an English editor, a certain Thomas Bowdler, published an expurgated edition of the works of Shakespeare. He felt that Shakespeare's use of language was at times offensive to the reader. Since then, the term 'to bowdlerize' has denoted the attempt to remove or substitute language deemed to be indecent, i.e. language that might offend. Those who believe in the effectiveness of this approach believe that by using a euphemism, or leaving implicit an explicit word, the reader will be directed to think in a different way.

More recently there has been a great deal of bowdlerizing both in Britain and in America under the guise of bias-free language, or politically correct (PC) language, and this necessarily affects the acceptability of a translation. The target is not so much 'decency' as 'sensitivity' in general. The aim of the PC movement is, according to Bryson (1994:425), "to make language less wounding or demeaning to those whose sex, race, physical condition or circumstances leave them vulnerable to the raw power of words". The PC view is that if an evaluative or offensive word is substituted by a standard or technical term, then the evaluation or the offence is also removed.

As we have seen, the American based localization industry has been particularly sensitive to the translation of potentially politically incorrect terms. An early Microsoft thesaurus, for example, contained both 'savage' and 'man-eater' as synonyms for 'Indian'. Spanish-American users complained and the words were erased. Some examples of the types of changes being sought are outlined in the style guide for academic writing produced by The Open University (1993) in England. We have already mentioned its own style, which includes a series of behavioural "do's and don'ts", in Chapter 4.2. The guide dedicates two pages to language style and a further seventeen pages to writing which

> aims to create the conditions whereby people are treated solely on the basis of their merits, abilities and potential, regardless of gender, colour, ethnic or national origin, age, socio-economic background, disability, religious or political beliefs, family circumstance, sexual orientation, or other irrelevant distinction.

The Open University, according to its official publication, is convinced that "language reflects and enshrines the values and prejudices of the society in which it has evolved, and is a powerful means of perpetuating them". The areas specifically covered with regard to political correctness are:

• **age** "Language is a powerful method of structuring attitudes about old age"	
Words to avoid	
mutton dressed as lamb	
dirty old man	
old fogey, old codger, old dear, old folk	
the elderly	
• **cultural diversity**	
Words to avoid	*Words to use*
Blacks, non-white, coloured	words denoting ethnic origin; e.g. Afro-American, Black American, etc.
Red Indian	Native American
Eskimo	Inuit

- **disability**

Words to avoid	*Words to use*
X is a polio victim	X has polio
the disabled	disabled people
mental handicap	people with learning difficulties
'blind spot'/'deaf to entreaties'	isn't attentive/doesn't listen

- **gender**

Words to avoid	*Words to use*
unspecified he/she	s/he, he or she, they
modifiers: e.g. woman doctor	doctor
generic 'man'	people/humanity

Mühlhäusler and Harré (1990:235-38) devote an entire publication to the use of pronouns, and they cite research that establishes that (the English) language is biased against women. The examples they give concern gender indeterminate nouns and pronouns ('man' as in 'mankind'; 'doctor'; the generic 'he', etc.). Though these are generic words, they generally give rise to thoughts of men rather than women. This, the authors state, gives rise to what they term 'indexical offence'.

Whether or not we have indexical offence, the use of language does affect thought. The first response *is* determined by the language. One only needs to look at a list such as the one supplied below by Bryson (1994:25-26), borrowed from Martin Montgomery (1986:178), to see how language takes on meaning within a culture and tends to condition our thoughts. In each paired opposite, there is a difference in connotation:

master	mistress
bachelor	spinster
governor	governess
courtier	courtesan

In all cases, these paired sets of words do not simply denote gender differences but power (on the left), and submissiveness and inconsequence (on the right). As Montgomery (ibid.:178) says, reflecting on the same gender pairing, "It is striking … that words associated with women should be consistently downgraded in this way. Such a tendency lends support to the claim that English, at least, is systematically skewed to represent women as the 'second sex'".

However, there are many, especially the more conservative, who believe that changing the form will not change the offence. They believe that 'a shop assistant' is still (just) 'a shop girl', 'an office manager' is a glorified 'secretary', and 'between jobs' is, in fact, 'unemployed'. Many publications are now very careful to be technically politically correct. However, (unconscious?) slip-ups occur, belying the fact that adhering to correct in-house style has little to do with a writer's actual mental model of the world. This example (emphasis added) is taken from a 1997 *Financial Times* publication:

Contrary to popular belief, the tax**man** does not always want to bleed you dry of your pound of flesh. Peel away **his (or her)** mask, and underneath you may be surprised to find a fairly decent, understanding sort of **chap**.
(*The International*, July 1997:31)

For many, particularly right-wing thinkers, PC is seen as limiting intellectual and artistic freedom. Jane Gordon (English) describes with dismay in the conservative *Daily Telegraph* (03/03/95) how her (American) book editor tried to change a number of words in her first book. The reason given by the editor was that the words were not politically correct and might upset or offend. She also cites other changes 'demanded' from other first-book novelists:

Original	Copy editor remark
The only other woman I had seen walk like that was a lesbian	delete line
Irish drunk	omit nationality
'You old scrubber'	change to "You ex-cleaning woman you"
(for an adult) girl/lady	change to "woman"

Established novelists have also been hit. Enid Blyton's children's *Noddy* books, written in 1949 (and immensely popular in Britain) had to go through a number of rewrites after the end of the 1980s. To counter criticisms of sexism in their animated series, the BBC introduced a character called Dinah Doll to Toy Town. She was "a black, assertive, ethnic minority female". The character "Big Ears" became "White Beard", and "Mr. Plod the policeman" became "officer Plod" (for the American market). The most important rewrite, though, involved the deletion of one of the principal characters, a loveable soft black-faced doll, named "Gollywog". He had to go, because part of his name, 'wog', connotes "a black or dark-skinned person or an immigrant who does not speak English". However, "Pleasing every sensitivity is often difficult. When the Golliwogs became goblins in 1989, protests were received from Scandinavian countries who believed their trolls were being insulted".[1]

Gordon continues with another writer's thoughts on the matter:

Eradicating certain words from fiction does not mean that the feelings they reflect in the real world cease to exist. Children nowadays are described as having learning difficulties and what has happened? Other children have started to refer to them as 'LDs', which is no different from calling them 'morons or 'spastics' is it?

Mühlhäusler and Harré (1990:247) would certainly agree that neutral words take on their own connotations. They describe the attempt to find a PC equivalent of

---

[1] news.bbc.co.uk/1/hi/uk/531557.stm

'Mr' for women. The problem that needed solving was that there is a sexual connotation (or meta-message) of 'unavailable' with 'Mrs' and 'available' with 'Miss'.
The solution was the technical 'Ms'. However, like all technical words used informally, there is a meta-message. 'Ms' "has now come to mean in many instances not
married or unmarried woman, but unmarried feminist person".

In the Anglo-Saxon countries in particular, the idea that language should not
offend or demean (particularly with regard to gender, race, appearance or behaviour) is basically accepted, even if the conservative press complains about the extreme
applications. Halliday (1992:72, emphasis in original) notes that:

> We [in Australia] have a Scientific commission on Language and Sex to deal
> with the situation (and note in this connection that it is *assumed* that by work-
> ing with language you can change social reality, which makes sense only if
> you accept that reality is construed in language).

There are three important points to be made here with regard to crosscultural
communication. First, surface lexical choice clearly does influence thought. Second, surface structure does not necessarily mirror underlying thought. Thirdly, what
is most interesting about the PC phenomenon is not the debate itself but the fact that
it is treated in different ways in different cultures.

In Italy, for example, the PC movement is almost non-existent. As Tobias Jones
(2003:118) explains to his British readers: "It quickly becomes clear that Italy is the
land that feminism forgot". The leader of one of Italy's most important political
parties uses language that no politician or influential party leader could ever use in
America or Britain:

> Umberto Bossi of the Northern league ... is a growling, blustering, regional
> populist just like Ian Paisley. But he is crude to a degree that would horrify
> the Ulster cleric: "the Northern League," he is fond of saying, "has got a
> hard on".
> *The Guardian Weekend* (3/12/94)

The Italian news-magazine *Panorama* (24/03/95) published a cover story on the
PC phenomenon, which helps to illustrate the frame within which the PC philosophy is interpreted. The cover of the magazine has a photograph of a number of
unclothed top models. The article notes that all the major Italian news magazines
will continue to use the same strategy to increase sales – and that this is not in line
with PC thinking. The inside story describes (and treats) PC as a fashion rather than
a serious problem: *la più radicale e discussa moda culturale americana*/the most
radical and talked about culture-fashion yet from the States.

What the British conservatives feel about PC is what mainstream Italy feels. To
use Kluckhohn's terms, the variant British orientation is the dominant Italian. So,
different cultures respond to the politically correct movement in different ways;
only some cultures believing that the use of language has a significant direct bear-

ing on thought. Séguinot (1995:61, 68) makes the same point and, citing Boddewyn, notes that only the following countries had legislation on sexism in advertising: Canada, the Netherlands, India, Scandinavia, the UK and the US. No other country deemed it necessary to intervene on behalf of politically correct language. The PC phenomenon is felt most in the United States, and in fact most of the complaints raised by copy editors and publishers in the Gordon article were American – and most of the complaining writers were British. More than anything else, this demon-strates Sapir's main point that there are different realities behind different languages. As mentioned earlier, these must be mediated if translators are not to offend (or bemuse) their readers or editors.[2]

• *Categorization*

One fundamental aspect of Sapir's theory is that of categorization. Though not all writers agree with the Sapir-Whorf hypothesis, it is generally accepted that we do organize our perception so that we put what we see into a predefined category. For example, when looking at something for the first time in a shop window we are able to say "Look at that chair. Isn't it unusual?" Thus, it is possible to talk about the unusuality of something never seen before. This leads us to the importance of ex-pectations, which have already been discussed in Chapter 3 in terms of frames and prototypes.

Sherlock Holmes was a master in categorization. Without this skill he would have lost most of his clients. He followed Abelson and Black (1986:1) who state:

> A fundamental supposition throughout our work is that knowledge is schematised, that is, organised in chunks or packages so that, given a little bit of situational context, the individual has available many likely inferences on what might happen next in a given situation.

On watching a woman hesitating outside his front door from his upstairs win-dow, Holmes casually mentions to Watson:

> I have seen those symptoms before. Oscillation upon the pavement always means an *affaire de coeur*.

According to psychology professor Edward Smith (1990:33-34), categorization is paramount: "We are forever carving nature at its joints, dividing it into categories so that we can make sense of the world ... Coding by category is fundamental to human life because it greatly reduces the demands of perceptual processes". George Lakoff (1987:5) devotes his book, *Women, Fire and Dangerous Things: What Categories Reveal about the Mind*, to the subject: "Categorisation is not to be taken lightly; there is nothing more basic than categorisation to our thought, perception, action, and speech".

---

[2] See also Taylor's advice regarding PC and Italian/English translation (1998: 86-8).

But there is a fundamental distinction to be made between categorization or labelling referential meanings and labelling where culture is involved. Both Lakoff
and Pinker agree that the categorization of snow in the Sapir-Whorf debate is a red
herring:

> Possibly the most boring thing a linguistics professor has had to suffer ... is
> the interminable discussion of the 22 (or however many) words for snow in
> Eskimo.
> (Lakoff 1987:308)

> No discussion of language and thought would be complete without the Great
> Eskimo Vocabulary Hoax. Contrary to popular belief, the Eskimos do not
> have more words for snow than do speakers of English. They do not have
> four hundred words for snow, as it has been claimed in print, or two hundred,
> or one hundred, or forty-eight, or even nine.
> (Pinker 1995:64)

The origin of the hoax makes for fascinating reading, and is basically a case of
Chinese whispers and wishful thinking. What is more important is that categorization at this level is technical. 'Snow' is categorization of the environment. This, in
Dilts' hierarchy, is the lowest level, and as such has little influence on higher levels
of values and beliefs.

Those who spend the winter months skiing will also have a higher number of
special words for snow. This fact will not make the skiers see the world in general
any differently; though, as with any technical specialization, they will see snow
differently. So, both Eskimos and skiers will know more about snow, but as Lakoff
underlines, no change of values is involved. Real labelling of packets in supermar-
kets is another example of categorization at the level of environment. For example,
the labelling of spaghetti in Britain simply states "Italian spaghetti". In Italy, spaghetti is sold in a variety of prominently labelled sizes: *spaghettini n. 1*, *2* or *3*;
spaghetti n. 5, and so on.

However, a change in labelling does become important when it is, to use Lakoff's
words, conceptual – i.e. when higher Logical Levels (beliefs and values) are involved. We have already noted that "United States" is conceptually different to
Estados Unidos and that a *raccomandazione* and *comunista* can be conceived in
different ways according to beliefs. Most of the examples in the following chapters regarding crosscultural meaning and translation focus on different conceptual
labels.

• *Lexical and Conceptual Gaps*
Apart from different ways of categorizing what is seen, such as 'snow', 'spaghetti',
and the 'United States', languages can actually lack the concept itself. In this case
there are a number of alternatives. The language can either borrow the language
label, do without the concept, or invent its own label. A number of countries have
academies whose job it is to keep a check on language borrowing, and periodically

recommend their own national labels. The *Académie francaise* is a case in point. To help the academy in its task, the French government actually passed a law, in 1977, banning the use of English loan words in official texts. However, as David Crystal (1987:4) points out, "it is a law honoured more in the breach than in the observance". Yet, this is not stopping more traditionally liberal countries such as Norway and Denmark implementing the same measures to stem the inflow.

A mediator would be wise to check the current political mood of the (national, corporate, and any other) culture being translated into, particularly with regard to translation from English – and respect the preferences of that reality. Microsoft, as we have already noted, is particularly aware of the repercussions of not taking account of the local political climate. But sensitivity regarding Anglo-American (lexical) hegemony is not only one-way. One conference interpreter (Viezzi, personal communication), for example, was handed a note (while still in the booth) from an irritated delegate explaining to him that the Italian term for "the budget" was not *la finanziaria* but rather *il budget*.

A number of translation scholars[3] have offered lists of translation procedures for culture-bound terms, all of which include 'borrowing' (as in *il budget*). Bilinguals often make use of a second language to fill in the lexical gaps. This is also known as adoption, importation, transfer or transference. Typical examples of English-Italian late bilinguals speaking are as follows:

Expression	Partial dictionary meaning
He's very *simpatico/in gamba*.	nice, friendly/ smart
It was a real *casino/brutta figura*.	mess up/bad impression
Have you got your *lasciapassare/libretto*?	resident's pass/official university booklet with record of exams
The *questura* want to see my *permesso di soggiorno*.	police station/ permission to stay document
Fancy a *digestivo* at the bar?	digestive liquor
You can always wait for a *condono*.	remission of penalty (i.e. a change in the law, making what was illegal, legal by means of a small payment)
Ask the *bidelli* for the key.	university porter, janitor, caretaker.

[3] See, for example, Newmark's translation practices for proper names and institutional and cultural terms (1981);Vinay and Darbelnet's (1958) procedures and techniques; Ivir's (1987) procedures for the translation of culture; Malone's (1988) trajections; Van Leuven-Zwart's (1989/90) microstructural shifts; Hervey and Higgin's (1992) degrees of cultural transposition; Aixela's (1996) procedures for the translation of culture-specific terms; Mailhac's (1996) procedures for cultural references, and Gottlieb's (1997) strategies for rendering idioms; Scarpa's (2001) *metodi e procedure di traduzione*; and Taylor's translation strategies and culture-bound language. Particularly useful is Piotr Kwiecinski's (2001) synthesis of all but the last two mentioned authors.

These are cases of borrowing where there is no real equivalent single label. 'Nice' or 'friendly', for example, is too weak a sentiment for *simpatico*. For *casino* (literally a brothel), there are a variety of partial equivalents: 'cock-up', 'balls-up', 'hell' or 'mess'. Though they carry the right force they either lack something of the noise, confusion or lack of control. Other examples relate to institutions and bureaucratic procedures that simply do not exist in the second language. However, a translation will always be possible. Often circumlocutions or glosses will be necessary. A lengthy gloss to enter the Collins Italian/English dictionary (1995) is below:

> ***circolazione a targhe alterne*** (Aut) anti-pollution measure whereby, on days with an even date, only cars whose numberplate ends in an even number may be on the road, while on days with an odd date, only cars whose numberplate ends in an odd number may be on the road.

Examples of words from other languages which have no conceptual equivalent in English are as follows:

Danish	*hygge*	instantly satisfying and cosy
French	*sang-froid*	composure, self-possession in a difficult moment
German	*schadenfreude*	delight in another's misfortune
Russian	*glasnost*	the policy of public frankness and accountability
Spanish	*macho*	exhibiting pride in demonstrating typically masculine characteristics: prowess in strength, sex ...

Bryson (1991:4) suggests, "we must borrow the terms from them or do without the sentiment". And in fact all but *hygge* have been borrowed and assimilated into the English language.

However, as many who are concerned about Anglo-American hegemony note, other languages throughout the world are borrowing English to such an extent that many local people are feeling cut off from their own language-culture. There was a public outcry in Denmark, for example, when the web page of the SAS Airlines appeared in English only. As a result, the government in 2002 began an enquiry into how to limit this English invasion. In Holland, the *Peptalk* dictionary (Koenen and Smits 1992) is devoted to the explanation of the conservatively estimated 3600 English words and phrases currently in use in Holland. One of the reasons for this number of words is as above: there is no equivalent lexeme for the sentiment in the language: "Often an English word gives a different meaning. *Peptalk* sounds a lot stronger than just 'an encouraging talk' and therefore seems to give you something more" (ibid.:5, personal trans.). The authors suggest that these loan words are not only practical, but also add variety and humour to the language. Newmark (1981:82) adds a further reason, what he calls 'local colour'. In these cases, an equivalent exists for the concept, but the source language is retained to remind the reader of the context of culture, e.g.:

loan-word used	Italian equivalent	Literal translation
il fair-play	*la correttezza*	correctness
gentleman's agreement	*l'impegno sulla parola*	commitment on the word
le ladies (di Bond Street)	*le signore (di Bond Street)*	the ladies (of Bond Street)

However, there is something more at play during the following overheard conversation:

A: *"Quella volta lavoravamo night and day [sic] – come dicono gli inglesi".*	A: That time we were working "night and day" – as the English say.
B: *"Sì, e anche giorno e notte come diciamo, e facciamo, noi".*	B: Yes, and also day and night as we say, and do.

The intended meta-message of speaker A was to impress the overhearer (English) with his command of the language, and to include him in the conversation. It seems, though, that important and sensitive beliefs about identity were touched upon. The first speaker's meta-message, as interpreted by speaker B is that the Italians, not having an expression for hard work, do not work hard. The listener's reply emphasizes the fact that there is both the expression and the concept supporting it. He also makes it clear that *noi* do work hard whereas the English (only) talk about it.

Bryson (1991:174) also notes the use of English to impress. In all the cases he cites the message is nonsensical. The following are all Japanese products sold (understandably) on the home market only:

> I FEEL COKE AND SOUND SPECIAL (Coke can)
> O. D. ON BOURGEOISIE MILK BOY MILK (t-shirt)
> ELEPHANT FAMILY ARE HAPPY WITH US. THEIR HUMMING
> MAKES US FEEL HAPPY (shopping bag)
> SWITZERLAND: SEASIDE CITY (shopping bag)

And, finally, a fashion boutique in Bologna successfully sold a pink blouse to a highly amused Canadian with what seemed a romantic poem written in English:

> She stood in the evening-close
> and he came to her
> and socked her in the bra

The reason why this and other creative uses of English help to sell products emerges from a comment the owner of the Bologna boutique made to me: "Who cares what it says as long as it looks good". Séguinot (1995:57) makes a similar point: "cultures view the functions of texts differently. [It] is related to the importance they give to the visual aesthetic. In other words, combinations of words are selected for their graphic value rather than their meaning".

Italian, Japanese and many other languages tend to borrow, either to fill a lexical gap, to impress or because "it looks good". English, on the other hand, tends to invent. The English lexico-grammar system lends itself to the short and simple. The coining of new words from old is common particularly in American English. The first settlers to America literally invented new compound words from old, partly to categorize aspects of their new environment unseen or rare in England. Below are some compound examples, sewing two familiar concepts to produce a new one:

> jointworm, glowworm, eggplant, canvasback, copperhead, rattlesnake, bluegrass, backtrack, bobcat, catfish, bluejay, bullfrog, sapsucker, timberland, underbrush.

As Bryson (1994:26) points out, "These new terms had the virtue of directness and instant comprehensibility – useful qualities in a land whose populace included increasingly large numbers of non-native speakers – which their British counterparts often lacked".

The way the American language has developed also reflects a different way of thinking. There is an emphasis on transparency and clarity in the individual words themselves whereas the English is more obscure:

US	GB
sidewalk	pavement
eggplant	aubergine
doghouse	kennel
bedspread	counterpane (now listed as 'old-fashioned' in *CED*, 1995)
frostbite	chilblains

The fact that the English and the Americans feel uncomfortable in each others' linguistic shoes is further testimony to different ways of thinking. Here, for example, is a comment from the British *Weekly Telegraph* (No. 197, 1995) about one expatriot's response to life in Florida:

> We greeted people with 'Hey, how yowl doing?', learned quickly that it is cheaper to pump your own gas than to request service and that you go to the store to buy supplies. But I have still never been able to bring myself to end a conversation with 'Have a nice day'.

This same out-of-awareness response is felt by many of those who identify themselves with Britain, and leads us to a discussion of the patterns of language, and how they are related to culture.

5.4 The Language System

- Whorf's Theory
- an example: advertising
- interplay between language and culture

Whorf's understanding of the interface between language and culture was not so much in the lexis (the labelling) but in the underlying patterns. His main interest was in the grammar – or language as a system. According to Mühlhäusler and Harré, Sapir was also moving towards a more grammatical or pattern approach to language in his later writings. They cite the following extract from a Sapir lecture in 1931(Mühlhäusler and Harré 1990:3):

> Language is not merely a more or less systematic inventory of the various items of experience which seem relevant to the individual ... but is also a self-contained, creative symbolic organisation, which not only refers to experience largely acquired without its help but actually defines experience for us by reason of its formal completeness.

Whorf built on Sapir's later work, and based his theories on the form and the function of language tense systems. He was able to show that there existed two types of languages: temporal and timeless. In Hopi, a native American-Indian (Amerindian) language, the tense system is not organized primarily by time whereas the Indo-European system is. Pinker (1995:63), on the other hand, cites the anthropologist Ekkehart Malotki who was equally able to demonstrate exactly the opposite. The controversy continues. We are fortunately not particularly concerned with Hopi, but we will find that within the Indo-European system the use of language reflects cultural priorities not only with regard to time but also with regard to every other aspect of the environment. In the next section we will see how the structure of the language itself does have an effect on the translation of certain cultural values.

• *Advertising*

A striking example of how the language system reflects different realities comes from advertising. The linguistic label, or strapline, in an advertisement cannot simply be translated. In fact, few, if any international marketing strategies have ever been successful using a translator for a major campaign or to translate the slogan. Instead, the whole text has to be redesigned, because selling the same product to different countries is not the same as selling to the same world with different labels (Bassnett 1991:28-29; Séguinot 1995).

We have already mentioned in Chapter one that translators and interpreters will always be at a disadvantage compared to mother tongue speakers with regard to culture-bound styles and meaning. This is even truer when translating into their second or 'B' language. Some well-known examples of gaffes in the (non) translation of advertisements are reported in a variety of publications and widely on the internet.[4]

Non-Translated Imports	Origin	Destination	Connotation
Kinki Nippon Tourist Agency	Japan	US/UK	sex tourism
The Ford 'Pinto' car	US	Portugal	small penis (slang)
Colgate's 'Cue' toothpaste	US	France	title of French porno magazine
'Koff' Beer	Finland	US/UK	a cough
'Bich' biro	France	US/UK	a bitch
Translated imports			**Back translation**
GM slogan 'Body by Fisher'	US	Belgium	Corpse by Fisher
Come Alive with Pepsi	US	Taiwan	Pepsi brings your ancestors back from the grave
Nothing sucks like an Electrolux	Sweden	US	Electrolux is the worst quality Electrolux performs good oral sex

Séguinot (1995:58-59) gives a number of examples of other ways to produce advertising gaffes. These have less to do with the translator's skill but much more to do with his or her control of the design, layout and destination of the final translated text. Pitfalls include automatic hyphenation of electronic texts, non-sensical chopping or shortening of sentences to fit in with layout, and arbitrary selection and use of pictorial material. All of these pitfalls point towards the need for the translator to become a mediator, and take a more active part in the process of communicating with the target culture.

A report in the American magazine *Business Week* (25/4/92:32) brought to light a very real problem in communication across cultures. The Nike athletic shoe company wanted to translate their slogan "Just Do It". The problem was that this three-syllable action-packed slogan has no syntactic or semantic equivalence in many of the languages that they wished to translate it into. Phil Knight, the CEO, "was dismayed when he previewed an advertising campaign that didn't measure up". "Rather than 'Just Do It', he says, 'it could have had the tag line of Toyota or Gillette or a lot of different companies'".

---

[4] e.g. Seeleye and Seeleye-James (1995:15-16), http://www.i18nguy.com/translations.html
A high number of examples in the literature are actually urban legend. The Chevrolet *Nova* car, quoted by Seeleye, is closer to *nueva* than it is to "no va" (doesn't go), which would not be the Spanish term anyway (*no funciona*). Yet, as Dave Taylor in "Global Software", says: "Similar to much of internationalization, there are glimmers of truth in the story, yet upon further examination, it is difficult to see how much is misunderstanding within the market, and how much is more of a misunderstanding of the marketplace". David Rickes, however, notes that General Motors did in fact change the name of the automobile to "Caribè," with a resultant increase in sales". http://www.intuitive.com/globalsoftware/gs-chap5.html
See also http://spanish.about.com/library/weekly/aa072301b.htm and http://www.i18nguy.com/translations.html

The problem was that the slogan did not catch the dynamic feel of "Just Do It". However, worse was to follow in Japan. The company headhunted a successful Japanese manager, Yukihiro Akimoto, and brought him to America "for a four-month immersion in Nike culture and operations". The result was that he stopped smoking and began to run. His employees even followed suit:

> But in many respects, Akimoto just didn't get it when it came to the Nike brand. As he was preparing to leave for Tokyo, Knight says, he began presenting Nike executives with possible Japanese translations for 'Just Do It'. One alternative sounds more like 'Hesitation makes Waste'. The Nike team were horrified. "We said 'No! Don't translate it!'"

In Japanese, as *Business Week* points out, the language system cannot create a "just do it' semantic equivalent. However, this is not just a semantic problem. As we have already noted, Japan's competitive advantage is due to long-term thinking, and not to just doing it. So, neither the concept nor the language comes naturally to Japanese culture.

This takes us back to Whorf's (1956:212) (stronger) version of the Sapir-Whorf hypothesis:

> The background linguistic system (in other words the grammar) of each language is not merely a reproducing instrument for voicing ideas but rather is itself the shaper of ideas, the program and guide for the individual's mental activity, for his analysis of impression, for his synthesis of his mental stock in trade.

Further evidence of the problems involved in translation is the NIH syndrome. An article from *The New York Times* entitled "Continental Divides on the Box" focuses on the translation of TV commercials: "Films that aren't home-grown are referred to by advertising executives as NIHs – 'not invented here' – and are frowned upon". The advertising executives generally feel that something is missing in a translation, and that a translated advertisement would not be as well accepted as a home-grown one.

This feeling was actually tested in a European study, which asked 600 consumers from Germany, Britain, France, the Netherlands and Italy to watch 48 TV commercials from all over Europe, all of which had already won international awards. The article concludes with the following statement: "Even though the ads had been translated, the consumers liked the films from their own country best". Clearly, domestic culture images or ideas expressed through the home culture language provide the most congruent and effective message.

• *Interplay between Language and Culture*
It does seem clear that there is a link between language and the context of culture. Indeed, as Bateson remarked (in Eriksen and Nielsen 2001:66) "the main problem may be that the Sapir-Whorf hypothesis cannot – on some level or other – *not* be

true". As Peter Farb (1973:186-87) says in *Word Play: What Happens When People Talk*, "The true value of Whorf's theories is not the one he worked so painstakingly to demonstrate", but "the close alliance between language and the total culture of speech". It is also clear that, at a lexical level, though English does not have a single dictionary entry to express *simpatico* or *targhe alterne*, this does not mean that the concepts cannot be thought or understood. Roman Jakobson (1959:236) went further in his much-quoted paper 'On the Linguistic Aspects of Translation': "Languages differ in what they must convey and not in what they can convey".

This is certainly true, up to a certain point. However, even though "Hesitation Makes Waste" might technically denote the values behind "Just Do It", it cannot convey the out-of-awareness feeling. There are two points to be made here. First, *how* languages convey meaning is related to the culture. Secondly, though languages *can* convey concepts from other cultures, people (including translators and interpreters) tend not to realize that their perception (through language) is, in fact, bound by their own culture. And here Pinker actually does agree (1995:57):

> Finally, culture is given its due, but not as some disembodied ghostly process or fundamental force of nature. 'Culture' refers to the process whereby particular kinds of learning contagiously spread from person to person in a community and minds become coordinated into shared patterns.

And it is to the creation of these shared patterns that we now turn.

Chapter 6. Perception and Meta-Model

The aim of this chapter is to:
- discuss the filters affecting perception of reality
- introduce the Meta-Model as a tool for analyzing perception and meaning
- give practical examples of how language acts as both a means of – and a limitation on – communication

Two Americans, John Grinder, professor of linguistics, and Richard Bandler, his student, with a particular interest in cybernetics were approached by Bateson to model the language of some successful therapists. The result of this project was the Meta-Model (Bandler and Grinder 1975): a model to explain systemically how the therapists used language to enlarge their client's perception of reality, and how their clients equally used language to limit perception. Bateson's introduction to their book is as follows: "It is a strange pleasure to write an introduction for this book because John Grinder and Richard Bandler have done something similar to what my colleagues and I attempted fifteen years ago... to create the beginnings of an appropriate theoretical base for the describing of human interaction. [They] have succeeded in making explicit the syntax of how people avoid change and, therefore, how to assist them in changing". The thesis proposed in this volume is that multicultural communication also involves change and requires a wider perception of reality. Those who require the services of translators and interpreters will need mediators who can, like therapists, assist them in assimilating discourse, spoken or written from within another context of situation and culture.

Grinder and Bateson followed the same semiotic school of thought: the sign is not the thing itself and the mental map is not the territory. The originators of the metaphor (according to Bandler and Grinder) were two philosophers. The first was Hans Vaihinger (1924:159-60):

> It must be remembered that the object of the world of ideas as a whole is not the portrayal of reality – this would be an utterly impossible task – but rather to provide us with an instrument for finding our way about more easily in the world.

The second source of the map/territory metaphor was Albert Korzybski (1958:58-60), who was also a scientist, linguist and founder of the Institute for General Semantics in America: "A map is not the territory it represents, but, if correct, it has a similar structure to the territory, which accounts for its usefulness". In any communication, according to this theory, there is a universal modelling of reality that functions in the same way as a map.

A map-maker has to make choices about how much information is to be processed and what aspects need to be highlighted to make the map meaningful and useful. The result is, clearly, deletion of some of the material that is deemed irrelevant for the map. There will also be distortion of the relevant material. For example, roads and landmarks will be made disproportionately large. Their features will also be generalized to fit a standard recognizable pattern in terms of colour, shape and size. Rivers are a standard blue on many maps. On British maps, motorways are a darker blue. On Italian maps, they are green.

We buy different maps according to need. Walking maps distort the size of the mountain huts. A motorist's map has no huts but identically sized service stations. Tourist maps represent ruins all of the same shape, larger than the towns or villages that they are in, and, for that matter, often more visible on the map than in reality. The rest of the town, countryside or even country, will be omitted to highlight what is of interest.

Human representation, like cartographic representation, will always be a scaled-down model of reality, and so the model of the world like any other model involves three necessary and basic changes:

GENERALIZATION
DISTORTION
DELETION

Apart from different, individual and culture-bound ways of perceiving, human perception itself distorts and deletes much of what objectively exists in the outside world. We will look first at the various perception filters.

Hofstede (1991:6) sees perception as involving "three levels of uniqueness in human programming":

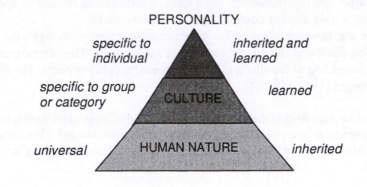

Figure 18. Hofstede's Perception Filters

We will now discuss these three filters, and add a fourth: language.

6.1 Filters

- 1. Physiological
- 2. Social Engineering/Culture
- 3. Individual
- 4. Language

• Filter 1: Physiological

The first level, or filter, is universal. Our only contact with the outside world is through the way we interpret information relayed by our senses. Hall (1982:41) quotes the psychologist Franklin P. Kilpatrick on the perception of space: "We can never be aware of the world as such, but only of ... the impingement of physical forces on the sensory receptors". To make matters worse, our sensory receptors are not even the best on the evolutionary market. The rods and cells in our eyes are able to collect information from the visual spectrum, but only from the 380 to 680 million microns wavelength, which is only a part of the actual visual field. We cannot, for example, unlike nocturnal animals, see in the dark; and hence, in common with many languages, we use 'dark' metaphorically for the unknown, the difficult or the dangerous:

• to be kept in the dark	• a dark horse
• to darken with anger	• darkest Africa
• the darkest hour	• The Dark Ages

Our hearing is equally limited. Our ears do not hear sound above 20,000 cycles per second, but dogs' ears, for example, can. The human world of hearing and vision is a constant limitation. The world of touch, however, is not only limited but is also not a constant. Different areas of skin vary in sensitivity to touch, pressure and pain. For example, our sensitivity to pressure is so acute on the forehead that displacement of air is felt before even the lightest touch. The thick soles of our feet, on the other hand, need a pressure of 250g/mm before the nerves start responding. They are 100 times less sensitive than the forehead. It is, in fact, this variety of filters helps us make sense of the world and survive within it: the soles of our feet have developed a lack of sensitivity to allow us to walk; and our eyes are more sensitive to daylight than to low light, which complements the body's other daytime needs.

So, as members of the human race, we all select the same limited reality. Most of the time we are not aware of the limitation: it is our world, to which our sensory receptors are perfectly adapted. These are our neurological constraints (Bandler and Grinder 1975:8).

• Filter 2: Social Engineering/Culture

However, even after having selected only part of the natural environment to be aware of, our neurologically accessible world is still very large. Accessing everything that is perceivable would lead to severe mental overload. It would, for example, be overbearing to actually process every sound within hearing distance at a party, so the brain unconsciously makes decisions about what to listen to. Selective listening is also called 'the cocktail-party phenomenon' (Crystal 1987:147). In short, perception has to be limited to make sense of the world.

The particular perception we have of reality varies from individual to individual, but not at random. There are, in fact, a variety of loosely aggregated groups of people who tend to share the same perceptions. For example, a group of timber merchants walking through a forest will tend to agree on what they are looking at and how to evaluate the forest. Naturally, there may be some discussion over their conclusions, but in contrast with a group of wild life conservationists (or still-life artists, picnickers and trials bike enthusiasts) there will be remarkable agreement.

Each 'culture' will have a different impression of the same forest because they will select to see, hear and feel different aspects of it according to perceived need. We should also remember, as we have already noted, that perceived need may have little to do with the present environment. This selection process has been called 'social engineering' (Bandler and Grinder 1975:12) and is the process that begins to distinguish us from others. Following Confucius, we may say that we are all born similar but learn to be different.[1]

• *Filter 3: Individual*

We also, of course, react according to individual identity. Individual constraints depend on the genetic framework we were born with and our own unique personal history. In the nature/nurture controversy, both are seen here to affect perception. Even identical twins growing up in the same family will have their own identity, and their own individual reactions to the same environment.

• *Filter 4: Language*

However, it is also through language that we hear and learn about the world. As Halliday (1992:65) explains, language itself construes reality. This construction is subject to the universal modelling of reality and is modelled to our needs. So, in communicating our understanding of the world, a further filter, language, constrains and distorts reality, as Alice discovered:

> [Humpty Dumpty] "There's glory for you!"
> "I don't know what you mean by 'glory'", Alice said.
> "I meant, 'there's a nice knock-down argument for you!'"
> "But 'glory' doesn't mean 'a nice knock-down argument'", Alice objected.
> "When I use a word", Humpty Dumpty said in a rather scornful tone, "it means just what I choose it to mean – neither more nor less".
> (Carroll 1981)

In the previous chapter, we noted that language influences rather than determines thought. However, the language label does determine our first response, just as it did for Alice. In the next section we look at further examples of how the language labels filter the way we think.

---

[1] *Ren zhi, cui, xing ben shan/ Xing xiang jin, xi xiang yuan* (Man, by nature is good/People's inborn characters are similar, but learning makes them different), from Scollon and Scollon (2001:138).

6.2 Expectations and Mental Images

Reality is what our language says it is.[2]

We have already discussed the principles of categorization. Here we will focus on how much we depend on making use of our own internal categorization rather than actually listening to what we hear or reading what we see. Experimental evidence to demonstrate this (at least with regard to our default response) can be found in research carried out by psychologists. One of the first significant results came from the work of the American psychologists Carmichael, Hogan and Walter in 1932. They conducted an experiment with what they called stimulus figures, to gauge the effect of language on visually perceived form. The stimulus figures they used are reproduced below:

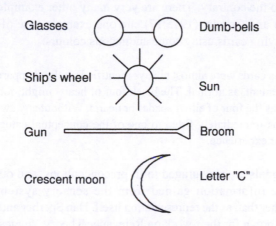

Figure 19. The Original Stimulus figures

They divided volunteers into two groups. In each group, one person described what s/he saw while the other drew what s/he heard the other describe. The first group was given the symbols with the labels on the left hand side, while the second group was given the same symbols but with the labels on the right hand side. The resulting pictures drawn invariably reflected the linguistic label rather than the drawing instructions. For example, the 'dumb-bells' were drawn with a double line between the two circles, while the 'glasses' were drawn with double circles:

Figure 20. The Reproduction as Dumb-bells and Glasses

---

[2] M. A. K. Halliday's opening statement at a conference on 'Scientific English', University of Trieste, 25/10/1995.

In all cases, the reproductions were influenced by the linguistic label. This implies that the word 'heard' is made to fit a pre-existing image of what, for example, 'dumb-bells' or 'glasses' look like. It is this strategy, which makes correction of our own spelling mistakes, and proofreading, such a difficult activity.

Consider the following well-known expressions:

PARIS IN THE THE SPRING	ONCE IN A A LIFETIME	A BIRD IN THE THE HAND

We tend not to 'see' the repetition of the definite and indefinite articles, as the linguistic cue is made to fit an internal lexico-grammatical pattern. We unconsciously take more notice of what we believe should be the pattern, overriding any actual visible evidence to the contrary. There are very many other examples of this in the literature. Bandler and Grinder (1975:17) cite one example case of an experiment with a pack of playing cards using some anomalous colours:

> the anomalous cards were almost always identified, without apparent hesitation or puzzlement, as normal. The black four of hearts might, for example, be identified as the four of either spades or hearts. Without any awareness of trouble, it was immediately fitted to one of the conceptual categories prepared by prior experience.

So, sensory signals are encouraged to fit preconceptions, and our general strategy is to use the information gained from the sensory system as a cue for representation, rather than as the representation itself. Dan Sperber and Diedre Wilson (1995:186), best known for their work on Relevance Theory, suggest that the interpretation process is not only instant and unconscious, but so automatic that it is generally a relatively peripheral process. They suggest that perception of reality depends on closeness of fit with, or accessibility to, an "internal organization of a stereotypical event"; in other words, a prototype.

The ideas of closeness of fit and stereotypical event follow closely Gillian Brown and George Yule's (1983:64-67) framework. In *Discourse Analysis*, they introduced the 'Principle of Analogy', suggesting that we interpret according to past experience of similar genres, and that we naturally expect things to conform to previous experience.

Closure is another well-known aid to perception, which again tends to limit what is perceived to what fits recognized patterns. This involves automatically and unconsciously closing any gaps, filling the spaces with internal representations. Cloze tests rely on this ability. The word 'cloze' itself is an adaptation of the idea of closure (*CED*).[3] These language tests delete every fifth or seventh word. The student

---

[3] The tests were originally developed in Gestalt theory. They are discussed by W. Taylor (1953) in his article 'Cloze Procedure: a New Task for Measuring Readability'.

then has to close the gaps relying on his or her internally generated understanding of the lexico-grammatical pattern:

> Cloze Test:
> It took Alan Turing, the brilliant _____ mathematician and philosopher, to make the _____ of a mental representation scientifically respectable. _____ described a hypothetical machine that could _____ said to engage in reasoning.

All the examples discussed in this section on perception and language are linked to prototype theory, which, as we have mentioned, is based on typical cases and expectations. On this point Pinker (1995:72) agrees. In fact, in his effort to disprove the fact that language determines thought, he demonstrates that meaning is determined very largely by mental images.

As our understanding of the world depends on a previous construction of a suitable mental image it is consequently very difficult to be objective about reality, or to state what is actually, objectively and intrinsically true 'out there'. This is particularly evident when we find ourselves in a new situation. As George Lakoff and Mark Johnson (1980:162) state, "truth is relative to understanding, and the truth of ... a sentence is relative to the normal way we understand the world by projecting orientation and entity structure onto it".

So, we have firmly established that the real world and our understanding of it are two different things. First, there are neurological constraints limiting our capacity to perceive; and secondly, we tend to take more notice of what we expect, our internal image, than what we could theoretically perceive. In the next sections we will examine how this universal modelling of reality applies to language.

6.3 The Meta-Model

Modelling, as Margaret Berry (1989:17) states in her introduction to *Systemic Linguistics*, is now considered an important tool in linguistics, and is also central to Systemics. As she points out, "the term *model* has for the last few years been an extremely fashionable word in disciplines ranging from the sciences to education and theology". Not only are models fashionable but they have revolutionized work in cybernetics and information theory. The study of language went through a revolution when Noam Chomsky presented his model; and today Hallidayan (systemic or functional) grammar is still attempting to model language. The problem, as with all models or maps, is that these model-makers are attempting to make the model more detailed to account for all variation and change.

An old story has it that when the map-makers tried to show the king his territory on a map, the king was not satisfied. He wanted a better map. The map-makers continued to improve their map, but to no avail as it still did not contain everything on it. At this point, the building that housed the map was simply not large enough.

Eventually the walls of the map institute were taken down to allow space for all the detail. Finally, of course, the map was so detailed that it could not be seen: it was indistinguishable from the territory it was mapping.

So, for a map or a model to be useful, it must generalize, distort and delete what is real. Bandler and Grinder (1975) suggest this is central to the way humans perceive, interpret and communicate. They have made this process of simplification explicit through another model – which they termed the Meta-Model. It identifies those language patterns which are generalizations, distortions and deletions, i.e. simplistic models of meaning, and it clarifies the shorthand we use to communicate. The Meta-Model also checks for where simplistic communication obscures meaning, and includes specific questions to clarify and challenge imprecise language.

Chomsky's formalist model, on which the Meta-Model was originally based, suggests that for every surface structure there is a more complete deep structure. As native speakers speak or write, they make a series of choices. In his theory, these choices are basic patterns or transformations of the form that speakers use to communicate their experience. Chomsky suggests that native speakers intuitively know if the surface structure is well-formed grammatically, irrespective of whether it is meaningless. For example, native speakers intuitively accept that "the slithy toves did gyre and gimble in the" is syntactically incomplete, even if they have never heard of Lewis Carroll's work.[4] Native speakers also know that "the slithy toves did gyre and gimble in the wabe" is complete, or in Chomsky's terms well-formed.

The Meta-Model does not specifically use Chomsky's phrase grammar or transformational rules, but it does make use of the basic principle of 'well-formedness' to investigate meaning, which Chomsky's model deliberately excludes. Sperber and Wilson (1995:188) also adopt a similar approach to investigate meaning. They analyze semantic rather than syntactic incompleteness, as does Eugene Nida, the father of modern translation (Newmark 1995). Nida simplified and adapted Chomsky's model to include the context for his translation theories. In one of his many articles on the subject he calls for "a deep structure approach ... to fully identify the extent of equivalence and the need for supplementation or redistribution of semantic components" (1976:72-73).

The speaker only needs to refer to what is shared – the rest of what is shared can be inferred (Taylor Torsello 1987:5). This is the basis of conversational inference (Gumperz 1977) and is essential to communication. However, as Scollon and Scollon (2001:63) also point out, one of the greatest problems in crosscultural communication is the fact that speakers and writers assume that the surface language refers the reader or listener to the same shared semantic base.

The example below illustrates the difference between semantic well-formedness and shared information, and comes from a personal conversation which took place in a delicatessen in Trieste.

---

[4] This is from the nonsensical poem 'The Jabberwocky', in Carroll's (1981) *Alice Through the Looking Glass*.

Client:	*Un panino con prosciutto.*	A ham roll.
Assistant:	*Cotto?*	Cooked?
Client:	*Sì.*	Yes.
Assistant:	*Misto?*	Mixed?
Client:	*Mi scusi?*	Sorry?

In every utterance, information is missing from the surface structure. However the interlocutors are able to refer to a shared full representation – except in the last instance, where the utterance is both semantically incomplete and unshared. The full representation of the language, with little or no inference, might be as follows:

Client:	(I would be obliged if you could prepare me) a bread **roll** with some slices of **ham** inside.
Assistant:	You would, I presume, prefer **cooked** rather than raw ham inside the **roll?**
Client:	**Yes** (thank you, I would prefer cooked ham inside the roll).
Assistant:	Am I also right in thinking that you would prefer **mixed,** lean and fatty pieces of ham as they come off the bone, rather than lean ham**?**
Client:	I am **sorry** but I was not able to make a full semantic representation or indeed infer meaning from your last utterance due to a lack of a sufficiently shared model of the world. Would you kindly give me a more explicit surface structure so that I may be able to access a relevant frame of interpretation, make a mental representation and then decide how to answer your question? Thank you.

The function of the Meta-Model is to bring to the surface what is hidden. We should anticipate the fact, however, that the Meta-Model itself in clarifying complete representations can only point towards what is actually happening between speaker and hearer (or writer and reader). To quote Sperber and Wilson (1995:176) again, "Semantic representations of natural-language expressions are merely tools for inferential communication".

Yet, a full semantic representation is more than just a tool. It gives us the full representation of an individual's (culture-bound) underlying beliefs and values. The cluster of beliefs and values will fit logically into a model of the world, rather like joining the dots to form a picture. What is particularly interesting is that this process is largely unconscious. As Roger Fowler (1977:21) points out in *Linguistics and the Novel*, "'choice' and 'favour' are not necessarily conscious. A writer's construction may betray his patterns of thought without his intending that they do so. These, generally unconscious, 'choices' and 'favours' will not only reflect a speaker or writer's individual thought patterns but will also be influenced (constrained or directed) by the meaning potential of the grammar system itself, the particular context of situation to hand, and the underlying context of culture.

The processes involved, following the universal process of modelling, can be

seen in the following diagram. It shows how the three filters delete, distort and
generalize reality so that it can fit our map of the world. The model of reality, as we
have said, can be fully expressed semantically:

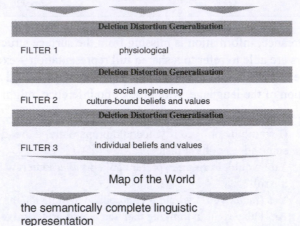

Figure 21. Creation of the Map of the World

In general, much of this information (potentially available as a complete linguistic representation) is not conveyed in speech or in print, either because some of the
representation will be assumed to be shared, or because the grammar and stylistic
considerations actually encourage a change or a reduction of the representation.
Hence we have the fourth filter, language which also deletes, distorts and general-
izes what could be more completely represented. The result is a surface structure
which is semantically incomplete:

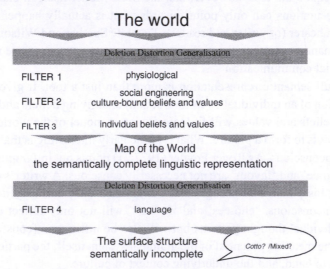

Figure 22. Representation of the Map of the World

The main function of the Meta-Model is to reverse the sequence of the arrows and to point to which filters are most responsible for the resulting surface representation. By focusing on explicitness we can raise awareness of the ambiguity and vagueness in language and communication. Most of the time, as Joanna Channell (1994:4) notes,

> Most speakers of English are not particularly aware of the frequency of vague language use (until it is pointed out to them) and this fact is in itself of interest. It shows that vagueness in communication is part of our taken-for-granted world, and that we normally do not notice it.

Cross-cultural communication is an extreme example of the fact that the world cannot be taken for granted. The Meta-Model is designed to clarify vagueness; can alert the interlocutor to any potential miscommunication, and can also clarify the limits of the system of possibilities that language and thought itself are created from. It can also help in unravelling the speaker or writer's culture-bound map of the world and hence improve the mediator's ability to understand texts in terms of culture-bound attitudes and beliefs. With regard to translation, Candlin (1990:viii-ix), following Steiner (1975), places the discipline "beyond the apposite selection of phrases" and suggests that the act of translation "asks us to explore our ideologically and culturally-based assumptions about all those matters on which we utter". Since then, translation studies (rather then practice) has undergone a real revolution, with entire volumes being dedicated to ethics (Pym 2000) and ideology (Pérez 2003).

Clearly, any instruments that can aid in making speaker or writer assumptions more explicit can help in translation studies and practice – and in all other aspects of cross-cultural mediation. Candlin continues, expanding on what a translator needs to be capable of:

- an understanding of the cultural and experimental worlds that lie behind the original act of speaking or of writing;
- an understanding of the potential of the two semiotic systems in terms of their image making;
- a making intelligible of the linguistic choices expressed in the message;
- an exploration of the social psychological intentions of the originator of the message matched against one's own;
- an ability to match all of these with our appropriate response in our semiotic and linguistic system, and our culture.

The following sections explain in more detail how the analysis of the three universal modelling processes – generalization, distortion and deletion – can increase the understanding of the cultural and experimental worlds at the basis of the original act of speaking or of writing. As a consequence, we can more definitely point towards the psychological intentions of the originator of the message.

6.4 Generalization

> - the need for generalization
> - universal quantifiers (explicit and implicit)
> - clarification questions

> Our experience is in fact organized on many levels at once, and we abstract
> from it a whole lot of different layers of generalization. (Halliday 1968:100-1)

A generalization occurs when one example is taken as representative of a number
of different possibilities (O'Connor 2001:132). For example, an utterance such as
"Cats are nice" will be the result of a specific learning or experience relating, possibly, to a reaction to a particular cat at a particular time. This experience is then
expanded to the level of the universe.

Frederic Bartlett (1932:206), one of the founders of modern psychology, was
among the first to note that an individual "has an overmastering tendency to sim-
plify, to get a general impression of the whole". He is cited by many linguists today.
Tannen (1993b:15), for example, notes that he was the first to popularize the term
'schema'. Brown and Yule (1983:61) also give him the credit for having first put
into print the idea that "effort after meaning" involves "the attempt to connect something that is given with something other than itself".

So, as Brown and Yule point out, Bartlett had already noted the phenomenon of
generalization, "the importance of relating a particular experience to other similar
experiences", over 70 years ago. He also noted that if we did not generalize we
would have to spend an inordinate amount of time explaining and specifying, and
we would not be able to benefit from learning. The whole of prototype theory and
frame analysis discussed in Chapter 3.1 depends on our ability to generalize reality
to fit our model of the world.

The less positive aspect of generalization is that it limits the model of the world,
so reducing choice. The idea that everything is immutably as stated, logically, reduces any possibility of an alternative. "Cats aren't nice", for example, allows for
no exceptions to the rule.

Specific, explicit, linguistic signs of generalizations are universal quantifiers (as
described below). Also, many of the deletions and distortions, discussed later, become implicit generalizations.

• *Universal Quantifiers*

Universal quantifiers, by their very name, are all encompassing. They do not allow
for any exception. Typical universal quantifiers are as follows:

> all, always, each, every, any, never, nowhere, none, no-one, nothing,
> nobody.

Many famous quotations are generalizations stating a rule (emphasis added):

> **Every** country has the government it deserves.   J. D. Maistre
> *Trois heures, c'est **toujours** trop tard ou trop*
> *tôt pour tout ce qu'on veut faire.*
> Three o'clock is **always** too late or
> too early for anything you want to do.   J. P. Sartre (trans., OUP)

or a general truth:

> Let's be frank about it; most of our people
> have **never** had it so good.   H. Macmillan
> **Never** in the field of human conduct have
> so many owed so much to so few.   W. Churchill

In advertising, the use of universal quantifiers is also common:

> *Liquido Detergente Johnson and*   Johnson and Johnson Liquid Detergent has
> *Johnson nasce dall'esperienza che,*   evolved from experience which has **always**
> *da **sempre**, prende cura di te.*   taken care of you.
>
> *Per l'uomo che non deve chiedere **mai.***   For the man who **never** has to ask
> (Aftershave)
>
>   American Express: **Never** leave home
>   without it.

Also, of course, by translation scholars:

> **All** translation implies a degree of manipulation of the source text for a cer-
> tain purpose.   (Hermans 1985:11)
> Translation **always** involves a process of domestication.
>   (Venuti 1995a:203)

Often the universal quantifiers are implied, as in much persuasive language such as political discourse:

> My aim as Chancellor is simple. I want people to feel secure about their jobs,
> their standard of living and their future.
>   Kenneth Clarke, *News of the World* (26/2/95)

The implication is that:

> My **only** aim as Chancellor is simple. I want **all** people to feel **totally** secure
> about their jobs, their standard of living and their future.

Clearly, the full semantic representation is untenable – particularly when uttered by a conservative minister whose party philosophy is based on non-intervention and the use of market forces to determine the employment rate. So, by not overtly stating the untenable, this full re-presentation of the ex-chancellor's thoughts passes unnoticed and hence unevaluated.

The universal quantifier is often implicit in stereotypes. We have already seen examples of British and Italian stereotypes in Chapter 3, where the implication is that either all the British or all the Italians behave in a stereotypic manner all the time. A report by *The Weekly Telegraph* (1995, No. 191) of a court case regarding a Briton suing his French boss in New York over 'racist' remarks reveals the importance of omitting the quantifier, which would otherwise have further ridiculed the whole proceedings:

> "The remarks alleged in the lawsuit ... span the catalogue of traditional nationalistic prejudice":
> * Britons dress badly
> * French women are better looking than British women
> * French schools are better
> * The English are soccer hooligans.

• *Clarification*

In generalization, the specific context is lacking, and the implication is that the utterance is of universal validity. The man in the shaving lotion advert never has to ask anything from anybody, at any time. The first point to clarify would be the context or contexts in which the above statement is true. Alternatively, we could challenge the limiting belief that 'to ask' is, in fact, an obligation.

With regard to English hooligans, are all the English (men, women and children) soccer hooligans all the time? By challenging the statements with the same universal quantifier we can begin to contextualize the utterance to within what is actually objectively verifiable:

> * All the English?
> * Always?
> * (Absolutely) never ask anything?

6.5 Deletion

> * Modality: Intrinsic and Extrinsic
> * Unspecified Referential Index
> * Missing Performatives
> * Value Judgements
> * Comparatives and Superlatives
> * Disjuncts

6.5.1 The Use of Deletion

Deletion takes place on two levels: syntactic and semantic. The first is lexico-grammatical. We have already mentioned that "Slithy toves did gyre and gimble in the" is syntactically incomplete. Also, "I like" will leave the listener waiting for the object, whether it be a pronoun or a noun phrase. As it stands, it is ill-formed. On the other hand, "I like cheese" is syntactically well-formed. A native speaker would also realize that though we now have all the necessary elements,[5] others could be added to give a full representation of the 'who', 'what', 'when', 'where' and 'how' exactly concerning cheese. A further expansion of "I like cheese" could be: "I usually like a few slices of Dutch Gouda cheese with my toast for breakfast at weekends". This full representation is unlikely to coincide with another's understanding of "I like cheese".

With regard to deletion, the meaning of a sentence may be implied, vague or even ambiguous, as in the following well-known examples:

Investigating FBI agents can be dangerous	('investigating' as an adjective or gerund)
Time flies	('Time' as an imperative or a noun)

This type of ambiguous specification is often at the basis of jokes, as more than one interpretation is possible. It is also an important device in literature and is the basis of poetic effect.[6]

Linguistic deletion, in fact, allows the hearer to create an array of possible closures, and hence fully participate in the communication act. Let us take two examples from Shakespeare. The first is from *Othello*, where the trustworthy and down-to-earth maid Emilia is giving her sound opinion of men:

> Tis not a year or two but show us a man,
> they are all **stomachs** and we all but **food**;
> They **eat** us **hungerly**, and when they are **full**,
> They **belch** us. (iii, iv)

The use of metaphor is an example of semantic incompleteness. According to the *CED* (1991) a metaphor is "a figure of speech in which a word or phrase is applied to an object or an action that it does not literally denote in order to imply a resemblance". In this case the metaphor operates as follows:

---

[5] A fully formed syntactic sentence can contain up to five of the following elements: subject (S), lexical verb (V), complement (C), object (O) and adverbial (A). The ordering and possible acceptable combinations are strictly limited and depend on basic sentence-structure rules. For a complete list, see Quirk and Greenbaum (1990:204).

[6] See Dodds (1994) for an exhaustive discussion of the poetic effect.

> • word: stomach
> • object: men

By only applying a resemblance we have an incomplete surface representation of what Emilia meant exactly. The rich possibilities implied by this resemblance are, of course, the basis of poetic effect. Diane Blakemore (1992:9), one of the developers of Sperber and Wilson's Relevance Theory, says with regard to the same passage: "It is impossible to spell out what she meant without distortion or loss of meaning. There is no single proposition that Emilia meant". Poetic effect is not only achieved through metaphor but also through the use of unspecified language, as in the second quotation from Shakespeare:

> To be or not to be: that is the question. (Hamlet, III, I, 55-56)

One of the most unspecified verbs in the English language is, of course, the verb 'to be'. It is used three times in this extract. In recreating a fuller representation as below, we lose all other possible inferences, i.e. the poetic effect:

> To live or to die. That is the question.

One might think that such individually unpoetic and basic words would always be literally translated. However, Franco Zeffirelli's Hamlet includes the following translation (see Taylor 1990:4-5):

> *Essere o non essere. Tutto qui.*
> To be or not to be. That's it/That's all [literally: 'all here']

The deletion of specific language ('the question') may well have been an attempt to return to the original non-specificity of Shakespeare's English. At a semantic level, neither the Italian *questione* nor *domanda* allow for the same array of inferences as 'question'. *Domanda* is a simple question, whereas *questione* is serious, sombre and problematic. In fact, a number of translators have opted for *dilemma* ('dilemma'). Here, any decision taken at the level of word results in some deletion of possible meaning. However, paradoxically, some deletion of the source text language *can* result in maintaining an equivalent array of inferences. By using the clarification questions (discussed later in this chapter) we can more clearly understand the array of inferences intended by Shakespeare.

As we have already mentioned, it is not only in poetic language that deletion exists; deletion is also an essential feature of all language. The following is a fairly random selection, taken from an interview, a publisher's brochure, and a novel:

> I didn't like **getting my hands dirty** and I loved dressing up and making model theatres out of Shredded Wheat packets.

> Ned Sherrin, director, novelist and writer talking about his youth (*The Times Magazine* 12/8/95)
>
> Low level English learners present special needs. Most have busy schedules and a limited time to study English. All have one aim: **to become operative in English fast**. (Longman Publishers Newsletter September 1995)
>
> — *Signorina – chiese.*   'Signorina' he asked.
> — *Dimmi.*   'Yes?'
> — *Perché piange?*   'Why are you crying?'
> — *Perché sono* **sfortunata in amore**   'Because I'm **crossed in love**.'
> — *Ah!*   'Ah!'
>
> Italo Calvino, *Pesci grossi, pesci piccoli*, trans. Archibold Colquhoun

All the above examples seem clear enough. There is no obvious vague language, yet much of the full semantic representation has been deleted. In 'getting my hands dirty', for example, we immediately understand enough of the meaning to follow the text, but we do not know exactly what sort of getting hands dirty he is talking about: is it through doing household chores, working on the family allotment, playing with play-dough, painting or playing outdoors with friends for instance? The same is true for the other emphasized examples. A common request amongst second language learners is that they wish "to become operative in English". This means different things for different people. Being operative in English at the supermarket checkout is not the same as being operative in English to set-up a joint venture. But in general we feel that we have enough information, as does the boy in the third example from Italo Calvino, who appears to understand ("Ah!") with the minimum of information.

The usefulness of deletions is clear in everyday talk once they are compared to registers of language that attempt to render, in the surface structure, a faithful mirror of the total possible representation. A perfect example is legal text, which is so explicit as to render it unreadable for the layperson. Below, for example, is an extract of Lord Diplock's words outlining, as clearly as possible, what constitutes a crime (Russell and Locke 1992:176):

> Conduct which constitutes a crime consists of a person's doing or less frequently omitting to do physical acts, and the definition of the crime also contains a description of physical acts or omissions, though it may, and in English law generally does, also require that the physical acts or omissions which constitute the described conduct should be done with a particular intent, either expressly cited in the definition or to be implied from the mere fact that Parliament has made the described conduct punishable.

Though the language contains no legal terminology, its completeness makes for opaque reading. This is an 84-word sentence – though not the longest in the English language. Pinker (1995:86) cites a *Guinness Book of Records* report of a 1300-word sentence in William Falkner's novel *Absalom, Absalom*. The point, however, is not so much the length, but the high 'fog' factor, or lexical density (Halliday 1987:60).

The aptly named Fog Index[7] is an index of the clarity of a text. As a rough and ready guide, the higher the number of words, and the higher the proportion of three or more syllable words per sentence, the thicker the fog. One technical formula is the average number of words per sentence (in this case 84) added to the number of words of three syllables or more per 100 words (20 in this case, which makes 23.8 per 100) multiplied by 0.4. Reasonably clear writing has a Fog Index of between 9 and 12. Lord Diplock's words are decidedly foggy with an index of 43.12. Paradoxically, by making the text less explicit through deletion, the meaning is rendered more clear to a non-legal audience:

> Conduct which is a crime consists of a person doing (or omitting to do) something with intent, either expressly cited or implied by Parliament as punishable.

We have now reduced the number of words in the sentence to 25, the Fog index has gone down to 16.4 – and we understand. Both Scarpa (2001:38) and C. Taylor (1998:38-40), though, point out that expected lexical density patterns will depend not only on language but also on text type. Taylor also suggests, "the measuring of lexical density can provide a parameter in assessing whether a translator has achieved the right register and balance of technical expression. It is also useful with corpus-based devices, to see whether different parts of texts are more term-dense than others, and organise a translation accordingly". Apart from reducing lexical density, another important use of deletion is cohesion (see Halliday and Hasan 1976).

Deletion can, however, also interfere with communication, either because the surface representation is no longer connected to a speaker's model of the world (linguistic deletion) or because the speaker's particular model of the world itself has deleted much of the world.

The following sections will focus on those deletions in the surface structure that point to a speaker's map of the world rather than deletion due to cohesion or shared understanding. They will cover the following areas:

- intrinsic modal possibility
- intrinsic modal necessity
- missing referential index
- restricted codes
- missing performative
- value judgements
- missing comparatives and superlatives
- disjuncts

---

[7] This particular example is taken from O'Connor and Seymour (1994:274-75).

6.5.2 Modality

According to the *University Course in English Grammar* (Downing and Locke 1992:382), modality is one of the most important ways in which interpersonal meaning can be expressed. It is the expression of an attitude of the speaker towards a reality: "modality is said to express a *relation* to reality, whereas an unmodalized declarative treats the process *as* reality" (emphasis in original). Generally, modality is expressed either through an auxiliary verb (can, may, should, etc.) or through a full lexical verb (wish, need). Other possible ways are through adverbs and adverbial clauses (possibly, probably, certainly) and adjectives (it is necessary/vital that).[8]

Modality can be divided into two basic areas: extrinsic (or epistemic) modality and intrinsic (root or deontic and dynamic) modality. Extrinsic covers the possibility, probability or certainty that a proposition is true according to one's own model of reality. In each of the following cases, we can add 'as far as I know':

Assessment	reality/fact	
It can't be	raining	
You can	get coffee on the train	as far as I know
They might just	be right	

Intrinsic modality, on the other hand, is a sign of an individual's personal involvement. The speaker 'does' or 'performs an act' while uttering. The performance (Austin 1962) will generally be in terms of the speaker's attempt to influence or controlling self and others:

Control	reality/fact	
You can	have an ice-cream now	
We can't	go on meeting like this	*I* have decided.
I can't	allow myself any more chocolate	

More than anything else, the difference between the two modalities is of Logical Level. Extrinsic modality is an utterance at the level of environment or behaviour, while intrinsic modality is a surface sign that the speaker is (re)acting at the level of beliefs and values. Both levels can provide us with much information about our constructed model of the world.

We will divide intrinsic modality into necessity and possibility.[9] Both intrinsic modal possibility and necessity set the individual and culture-bound limits of choice, either by implying (limiting) beliefs about the world or by stating what is considered possible.

---

[8] See also Falinski (1989:292) for a list of modal expressions.
[9] Bandler and Grinder (1975) use the terms 'model operator of possibility' and 'modal operator of necessity'. However, model operators only include the modal auxiliaries, and not the other means of expressing modality described above. Here, we will follow Downing and Locke's (1992:383-84) list of those forms which can realize modality.

• *Intrinsic Modal Necessity*

Modal necessity expresses levels of obligation. It can range from advisability through to inescapable duty or requirement:

> must, have to, need, should, ought to, it is necessary ...

Here are some requirements handed down to us from translation scholars in history:

> Only an idiot would go ask letters of the Latin alphabet how to speak German, the way these dumbasses [the papists do]. You**'ve got to** go out and ask the mother in her house, the children in the street, the ordinary man at the market. Watch their mouths move when they talk, and translate that way.
> (Martin Luther, in Robinson 1997:87)
>
> The translation **should** give a complete transcript of the ideas of the original.
> (Tytler, in Robinson 1997:211)
> [The translator] **must** be our tour guide.
> (Herder, in Venuti 1995a:99)

The necessity is often expressed through rules. For example:

> ... society **needs** some regulations, and these **must** mean some restriction of personal freedom.
> *The Weekly Telegraph* (1995, No. 193; emphasis added)

> *quando un paese ha un debito pubblico* when a country has an astounding public
> *impressionante,* ***deve*** *rimettere ordine* ... debt, it **must** bring order about again ...
> *sono questioni che devono essere* these are questions that have to be tackled.
> *affrontate. Il Corriere della Sera* (12/4/95)

All the extracts above lay down what appear to be universal truths. However, these truths are, in fact, no more than intrinsic modal necessities – limiting beliefs held by the speaker in relation to reality.

• *Intrinsic Modal Possibility*

Intrinsic modal possibility includes ability and permission, and sets the limits to options as perceived by the speaker or writer. It is realized principally through 'can', 'could', 'may' and 'might'. When permission is denied, those responsible for the denial are often not stated, as in the following example:

> The police know who many of the crooks are, but **cannot** touch them.
> *The Independent* (15/12/93)

From our exophoric[10] knowledge we know that, in this case, parliament has decided by law what is the right and proper approach with regard to police apprehension of suspects, and that police behaviour is limited by these laws.

Permission to act in a particular way may be refused because of social rather than written rules, as in this apocryphal confrontation between a Maitre d'hôtel and a trouser-suited woman:

> I'm sorry madam; you **cannot** go into the dining room like that. Ladies in trousers are not properly dressed.
> *The Independent* (15/12/93)

In both these cases there is clear reference to accepted rules. In both cases, one could contest the rule, but the important point is that there is a written or house rule that can be cited.

There is, as we have mentioned, the extrinsic meaning of 'can/cannot'. Extrinsic modality is also known as epistemic modality; 'epistemic' comes from the Greek word 'knowledge'. As such, extrinsic modality concerns the modality of propositions and the degree of truth or certainty to be attached to them. Here is an example:

> We **cannot** all detect the same odours ... the smell of cooking pork **cannot** be detected by about 50% of adult males and 10% of adult females.
> *The Independent* (21/12/93)
>
> Whereas historians tend to privilege single story lines, map-makers **can** stack, multiply and combine maps.
> Hermans (1999:123)

The use of the intrinsic modal possibility is often hidden in the surface structure and can often appear to describe the world as it is. 'Can' and 'cannot' in particular are often used by speakers to give the impression that what they are saying is extrinsic when, instead, they actually refer to a personal (and maybe unshared) belief. For example, the comment below demonstrates a personal understanding or model of the world, which is presented as a universal rule. Needless to say some groups of people act is if it were:

> ***Non si può*** *ottenere nulla per le vie legali.*
> You **can't** get anything using the legal channels.
> Enzo Biagi (1995:175)

---

[10] 'exophoric': referring to elements outside the text itself; 'endophoric': referring to elements within the text itself.

Below is another personal belief which appears to be extrinsic. Again, the modal impulse does not come from 'knowledge' but from the speaker's conviction and desire to control events:

> We **cannot** repair the American community and restore the American family until we provide the values, the discipline and the reward that work gives.
> Bill Clinton, *The Independent* (19/12/93)

The last example concerns a person who has just won a court case. He is discussing the damages he has been awarded as a result of police conduct during a raid on his house:

> This case was never about money. It was about clearing our names once and for all and about showing the police they **cannot** act in this fashion.
> *The Independent* (21/12/93)

This is a further example of a personal desire to influence events (intrinsic modality). Again, the surface structure regarding conduct is stated as an established extrinsic rule.

In the examples above, the language of limiting rules through intrinsic modality has been used to express a personal belief about behaviour in society. In other cases, the limits actually define the limits of the speaker's world, which are then generalized (through deletion) to become a universal rule for the whole of society:

You **cannot** take seriously how Hollywood at its worst will see you. You just **cannot**.	Sigourney Weaver *The Independent* (31/10/93)
You **can** only take things for so long. I have stood up to be counted. Changes are being made here which go against my principle.	Disc Jockey, Dave Lee Travis formerly of *Radio 1* telling his audience why he was leaving the BBC.
This stinking situation **can't** go on like this forever.	*The Independent* on the Middle East (16/12/93)
You **cannot** send tank regiments to patrol Mogadishu streets.	*The Independent* on Somalia (24/10/93)
The party **needs** to bed down now. You **cannot** go on changing your leader when their style is out of fashion.	*The Independent* on the Conservative government (16/6/93)

These intrinsic modals of (universal) possibility and necessity have the general logical form as follows: S1 prevents/makes S2 possible or necessary.

Modals of:	S1		S2
possibility	something	**prevents**	something **from being possible**
			you taking things for so long.
			sending tank regiments.
necessity	something	**makes**	something **necessary**
			some regulations necessary.
			it necessary for the party to bed down.
surface structure	**deleted**	↓	↓
	It	is/isn't possible/ necessary	(for me/them/…)
			↓
			You can't …

The **S1** *something* is deleted from the surface structure. Clarification of the full representation would contextualize the utterance and would help decide if the speaker is describing his or her own internal beliefs and is therefore performing (being intrinsic) rather than describing (being extrinsic).

At times, speakers do make the limits of their perceived world explicit as surface structure:

Neil Back on why he was not selected for the England Rugby team:	I just **cannot see** why this should place a question mark against my ability to perform at international level.
And Dave Lee Travis continues:	Changes are being made here which go against my principles and I just **cannot agree** with them.

The limits in the above cases have been restricted, from universal application to the speaker. However, they are still incomplete representations of the speaker's reference point. The yardstick (values) against which they are able to decide "thus far and no further" is missing. According to Downing and Locke (1992:393), "That something [missing] in each case represents a set of laws, whether natural laws, moral laws, laws of physics, of good manners, and perhaps many more".

• *Clarification*

There are a number of key questions that can be used to contextualize the speaker's point of view and to clarify the speaker's world and its borders:

(1) By challenging with universal quantifiers: never/ever/always/all:
• *Must these regulations* always *mean some restriction of personal freedom?*

> (2) By looking for exceptions, which again illustrate the existence of boundaries:
>   • Can you imagine any circumstance in which *X* would not be true?
>
> (3) By making the reason explicit:
>   • What makes it impossible *to agree to the changes*?
>   • What prevents (you) from *agreeing to the changes*?
>   • What would happen if *you did agree to the changes*?

Answers to these questions will show the rules by which a person lives and which filters are most responsible:

	Example
• Filter 1 physiological	Penguins can't fly.
• Filter 2 cultural/social engineering	You can't wear that jacket.
• Filter 3 individual	You can't see me now, I'm busy.
• Filter 4 linguistic	(a witness to a bomb explosion): I couldn't believe it.

6.5.3 Unspecified Referential Index

Lyons (1981:220) begins his chapter on reference with the title 'Worlds within Worlds: the subjectivity of utterance'. 'Reference', as he explains, is "the relation that holds between linguistic expressions and what they stand for in the world", whereas the 'index' is the point of reference. The referential index may be missing either due to the language filter (e.g. cohesive and other stylistic reasons) or to culture/social engineering.

The use of the pronoun is generally a clear index (hence a linguistic deletion) pointing to a referent, as in the well-known (to some) "We are not amused". The reader, though, will only be able to attach the index to a referent through his or her knowledge of the context. In this case the knowledge is culture-bound: 'We', the 'royal we', refers to Queen Victoria, but only because native-speakers share that exophoric knowledge.

• *The Language Filter*
Generally available information is deleted because it is assumed to be shared (Halliday and Hasan 1976:33, 142; Taylor Torsello 1987:29-30). As another example, let us look at this protest song popularized by *The Proclaimers* in 1988 (emphasis added):

> I can't understand
> why **we** let **someone else** rule **our land**.
> **We** fight when **they** ask **us**.
> **We** fought then **we** cower.

The specific referential indices have been deleted, and we are left with universal generalizations. The context here (both linguistic and extra-linguistic) points to the more specific referential indices of 'the Scots' (for "we", "our" and "us"), 'English person' (for "someone else") and 'English people' (for "they"). We have clarified the deletions, but we still have generalizations, and hence we still do not know 'who' this protest song refers to. Further clarification is necessary. For example, is 'an English person' anyone, an example of a group, or does the expression refer to a particular English man or woman?

The grammarians Quirk and Greenbaum (1990:85) distinguish two types of reference: generic and specific. If the reference is generic, then the implication is that the English in general (i.e. ALL the English ALL the time) are involved in asking ALL the Scots to fight. On the other hand, the reference may be specific. In this case, the implication is that a specific group of English and Scots are involved. Until we arrive at the heart of the beliefs about who exactly is involved we will not have a full semantic representation of the world as perceived by the writer or singer of this song.

In this particular case, the extra-linguistic context makes it clear that we are talking about the English (rather than British) prime minister and his/her government. A generalized negative feeling about a different people has now been contextualized to a smaller specific group of individuals, and more importantly to an organization: parliament. This is precisely where pressure was exerted to effect change. As a result the Scots (and the Welsh) now have their own Assembly. The current popularity of the song highlights the fact that 'Assembly' still does not 'refer' to 'ruler'. And home-rule for the Scots is still not a reality.

• *Clarification*

To clarify unspecified referential indices, the procedural questions are:

- Who specifically *is ruling*?
- What exactly *is our land*?

• *Culture/Social Engineering*

The second reason for deletion of the referential index in the surface representation is due to social engineering. 'Restricted' and 'elaborated' codes are terms used by Bernstein for the different ways of conveying meaning in a social context (which were briefly discussed in Chapter 4.7). Restricted code users, for example, delete nouns from the surface structure. Bernstein's (1972:478) study of the language of middle-class and working-class children showed that "The working class children are more likely to select pronouns as heads (especially third person pronouns). Where pronouns are used as heads, the possibility of both modification and qualification is considerably reduced". This lack of modification occurs when there is no deeper semantic representation. The use of 'we' or 'they' is not actually connected to a specific referent, to any first-hand experience, but to vague and unchangeable 'them' and 'us'. However, as both Bernstein and Hasan report, it is not only in terms of unspecified referential indices that people (and in particular the working class) limit their map of the world, and hence choice in life.

Hasan's more recent work (1992:32) on HAPs and LAPs (see Chapter 4.7) also shows how deletion limits a child's possible world. The example below shows how a LAP mother tends to reply to a child's question in the LAP world:

Mother:	put it up on the stove and leave it there.
Karen:	why?
Mother:	'cause.
Karen:	that's where it goes?
Mother:	yeah.

When the mother then asks questions, the children already have a model response, effectively limiting whatever innate language potential they might have (Hasan 1989:256):

Mother:	but you'd be glad when you go back to school, won't you?
Karen:	no.
Mother:	**why?**
Karen:	**'cause.**
Mother:	'cause why?
Karen:	'cause Rebecca don't go to my school any more.
Mother:	who's Rebecca?
Karen:	the little girl in my school.
Mother:	did she leave?
Karen:	yeah.
Mother:	**why?**
Karen:	**'cause.**

Hasan's research shows clearly that the "why/'cause" routine lies firmly within the LAP world and that Karen, for example, has already learned to delete a host of possibilities. Hasan's (1991:107) conclusion is as follows (emphasis in original):

> The children learn something from the typical absence or irrelevance of what mothers say a propos their questions ... But if a why question typically draws no answer, or if it draws the simple response, *cause*, then is it really reasonable to expect that one will go on believing in the efficacy of *why*?

HAP children, on the other hand, will learn to link references to an individual source, thus constantly enriching their view of the world (Hasan 1992:14):

Julian:	when I get as old as you and Maree likes me could we marry each other?
Mother:	no because Maree is your cousin.
Julian:	oh.
Mother:	'cause cousins aren't allowed to marry.
Julian:	why?
Mother:	'cause the law says they're not.

According to Hasan (1989:258): "The implication is that [HAP] mothers would be likely to provide additional and fuller information to explicate and make precise the referential application of their questions and replies".

This is a refined extension of Bernstein's (1972:480-81) elaborated and restricted code theory which caused so much controversy in the 1970s. Even more controversial was his more forthrightly stated fact that "the relative backwardness of many working-class children ... may well be a culturally induced backwardness transmitted by the linguistic process".

According to Brislin (1993:99-105), various other ethnomethodological researchers studying class in a variety of cultures have noticed the same differences with regard to parent/child interaction. The working class throughout the world tend towards reducing interaction between children and adults, while the middle class tend to encourage interaction. Brislin (ibid.:102) concludes with the following:

> Children of working class learn to be comfortable with external standards in contrast to their own, internally set goals. They learn to accept what other people consider to be good manners, and they have limited experience in making suggestions and requests to authority figures.

Brislin (ibid.:104) also mentions how difficult it is to comment objectively on class. Like Halliday, he believes that it is important not only to accept that class difference exists, but also to comment objectively on the advantages and disadvantages that class brings. In 1992, Halliday (1992:69) made the following statement during his keynote speech entitled 'New Ways of Meaning: The Challenge to Applied Linguistics' at a world conference on applied linguistics:

> I hope by now we are beyond the point where we have to pretend that everybody's world view is alike, just in order to protect ourselves from a foolish accusation of prejudice by those who cannot distinguish between 'different from' and 'better (or worse) than'. The task for applied linguistics here is to interpret the grammatical construction of reality.

6.5.4 Missing Performatives

> Grammarians have not, I believe, seen through this 'disguise' and philosophers only at best incidentally. (Austin 1962:4)

Austin introduced the concepts of 'performative utterances' in the early sixties, and his ideas were widely adopted through to the end of the seventies. He believed that a performative act takes place when an utterance performs an act, as in: "I name this ship Mr. Stalin" – and the ship is effectively named as a result of these words. However, this principle has been extended by Austin himself, among others, to the effect that behind every sentence there lies a hidden performative. Quite simply, in saying something one is also performing an act.

Austin (ibid.:103) believed that the illocutionary force of an utterance "could be made explicit by the performative formula". P. F. Strawson (1964:451) agreed, saying that the performative can "make explicit the type of communication intention with which the speaker speaks, the type of force the utterance has". J. R. Ross's (1970) 'Performative Hypothesis' suggests the same idea. There are few supporters of this view today, as pointed out by Geoffrey Leech (1983:174-75) in his 'Performative Fallacy'. Leech (1985:325) rightly says "it seems unnatural to argue that every single direct statement is fundamentally an indirect statement".

However, making the cross-cultural (or rather, the culture-bound) aspect of communication explicit entails framing the statement with its performative reference. For example, the following direct statement, from an on-line gift flower catalogue[11] is presented as a generalized (and not culture-bound) rule: "These autumn classic chrysanthemums will make for a warm, wonderful feeling anytime". We do not know, at this stage, anything about the writer's identity: 'a warm, wonderful feeling', according to whom? Is the writer also the original creator of these thoughts, the animator/interpreter or reporter? Are these beliefs individual or corporate? Have they been handed down as a tradition, do we know the source? Once we have made the source explicit, we can have a clearer idea of the applicability and (relative) universality of the statement. In this particular case, the "warm, wonderful feeling" is certainly culture-bound. In fact, if we take a fairly random Google hit for the Italian translation of the flower, *crisantemo*, we find:

Minestra di crisantemi e ginseng. ... E non lasciatevi suggestionare dall'idea di morte associata al crisantemo...[12]	Chrysanthemum and ginseng soup ... And don't let yourself be influenced by the idea of death associated with chrysanthemums...

We now have two contradictory statements:

Chrysanthemums	will make for a warm, wonderful feeling anytime are associated with the idea of death.

The solution is to mediate these two opposing beliefs by framing the statements in the same way as discussed in Chapter 3.1: In some cultures/For Americans/According to Italian tradition....

This explication of the full semantic representation in normal speech is generally unnecessary, because, as Austin (1962:141) says, it is "too obvious to be worth saying". Again, this reminds us of the "taken-for-granted world" in Channel's *Vague Language*. "Obvious" is itself a deletion of Austin's (possible) full semantic representation. The question, to clarify the deletion, is "obvious to whom?"

Leech (1983:181), in his discussion of the 'Performative Fallacy', explains clearly

[11] www.1800USAFlowers.com.
[12] www.cookyland.it/ricette/512_minestra_di_crisantemi_e_ginseng.asp

when and why the performative is made explicit: "it occurs, understandably enough, when a speaker needs to define his speech act as belonging to a particular category". Generally, as Leech makes clear, a speaker does not need to consider his or her utterance as belonging to a particular category because the category, in this case the culture, is taken for granted. Whenever we speak about social or culture-bound rules (the dos and taboos, manners, etiquette and so on), we do not connect them to a particular speaker or category because the rule is all encompassing and includes every speaker. In short, these are imprinted rules. Bernstein (1972:485) categorizes three principal types of parental appeals that become imprinted rules:

Imperative form	Don't do that.
Positional appeals	Little boys don't cry.
Personal appeals	I know you don't like X but [*reason*] Y.

In all these cases, the form of language used "transmits those aspects of culture that are not to be questioned" (Saville-Troike 1986:48). This is a form of instrumental conditioning, the child being usually rewarded or punished in some way depending on his or her response.

Of the three examples, the personal appeal is the most explicit allowing for what Bernstein (1972:486) calls "the individualized interpersonal context". In this case, the hearer understands that there is a rule, and that the rule is part of the external world. The imperative is also implicitly clear about limits being dictated by the speaker. However, the positional appeals are the most difficult to unravel: "The essence of a positional appeal is that in the process of learning the rule, the child is explicitly linked to others who hold a similar universal or particular station". This type of appeal presupposes a universal rule to which both speaker and hearer must obey. Apart from there being no exceptions, there are also no limits. For example, in "little boys don't cry", information has been deleted which would reveal which little boys exactly, in what situations exactly, until what age, and also the reasons and beliefs underlying the expected behaviour.

However, the most important deletion is the performative, to be clarified by asking "according to whom?" By disconnecting the surface structure from its original reference structure, specific parts of the society's contextualized experience have been deleted. It is, of course, very likely that the speakers will be repeating the same surface structure that they heard from their home environment and had simply internalized without question. As we have already mentioned, present behaviour is often related to a historical response to past perceived needs.

As a result of lack of specification, meaning in discourse is generalized to imply that the rules are the same for all people and cultures all the time – and that rules are unchangeable. Though it may seem paradoxical, translation scholars, themselves, are not immune to falling into the same universal (i.e. culture-bound) trap – as we shall see later.

• *Clarification*

To clarify a missing performative and relativize the utterance to the speaker, or to his or her culture, we need to ask the following questions:

• According to whom specifically	*chrysanthemums are associated with death?*
	little boys don't cry?
• According to what	*regulations*
	rules of conduct specifically?
	traditions

6.5.5 Value Judgements

> e.g.: good, bad, correct, right, wrong, true, false, only (as in 'the only way')

Value judgements[13] are opinions expressed as facts. For example, Herman's personal opinion of Jose Lambert's writing is stated as fact:

> "Many of his articles are **marred** by **woolly** phrasing, **circuitous** statements and **tortuous** lines of arguments".

More importantly, value judgements tend to delete the performative and the criteria used to make the judgement.

Where we do not know who is performing the judgement, the implication is that the values behind the judgement are shared by all concerned. In the first case below, we do not know what constitutes a "good" translator, and we are free to attach our own criteria. In the second extract, we are encouraged to take as shared the "success", "aggression", and "unreceptiveness" of British and American publishers. In both cases it would be useful for the critical reader to frame such judgements with the author's name, and add "according to":

> A **good** translator will almost invariably supply extra information in the L2 text.
> (Neubert and Shreve 1992:76)
>
> [British and American publishers] have reaped the benefits of **successfully** imposing Anglo-American cultural values on a vast foreign readership, while producing cultures in the United Kingdom and the United States that are **aggressively** monolingual, **unreceptive** to fluent translations that invisibly inscribe foreign texts with English-language values and provide readers with the narcissistic experience of recognizing their own culture in a cultural other.
> (Venuti 1995a:15)

---

[13] Bandler and Grinder (1975:107) list the words in the box under lost performatives but call

Value judgements, such as those above, rarely further cross-cultural communi-cation. This is because the values will be held either by a limited faction, or the values will be culture-bound – as the following example heard on ZFM American Forces Radio News (7/1/96) illustrates. The extract is from a news report of a snow-bound Sunday in Washington D.C. The President of the United States was reported going to church:

The President was well dressed for the event in blue-jeans and a flannel shirt.

Many Europeans would have difficulty in agreeing to this value-judgement, bear-ing in mind the discussion on dress in Chapter 4.1. Contextualizing the statement, we can say that the President of the United States of America was well dressed according to an American set of values of individual practicality, comfort and universalism.

• *Clarification*

To connect these judgements to the speaker or writer's mental representation we need to clarify them by asking:

> • *right/wrong/well*   according to whom?
> according to which set of culture-bound values

• *Comparatives and Superlatives*

Any sentence that uses comparatives or superlatives without stating 'in comparison to what' is deleting some information from the surface representation. John Morley (1993:412) notes the advertising strategy of deleting the point of comparison. The industry makes ample use of this style as seen by the endless number of examples that range from: "OMO washes whiter" to "Vortex kills germs longer". The fuzziness of the surface strapline allows the listeners or readers to fill in the missing details for themselves. Morley, in fact, attempts to retrieve the missing comparative for Vortex: "Longer than what? Longer than any other product? Longer than it did last year? Or longer than a barrowful of horse manure would?"

Superlatives are also very much part of the advertising genre, with 'best' possi-bly as the most recurrent. Another washing powder advert sums up how much can be done with the comparative and superlative of 'good'. It is difficult, reading the text, to believe that this can be anything else but a spoof on washing powder adver-tising, yet the voiceover, as Morley notes, depicts an intelligent, successful woman talking to equally intelligent and successful people:

---

them simply 'cue words'. O'Connor (2001:144) uses the term 'judgements'. Here we will use the term 'value judgements' to indicate that the judgements are related to a (culture-bound) set of values.

Most washing powders tell you they're **good.** Even **better**
and they're right.
But I'll tell you Radion Micro is the **best** yet.
New Radion Micro
Better than **good**
Better than ... even **better**
It's the **best** yet.

If we were to retrieve the missing comparatives and superlatives (among other deletions) from our knowledge of the genre, and in particular of other washing powder commercials, we would have the less effective version below:

> Most producers of washing powder tell you their product is good enough to wash clothes (according to minimum washing standards as laid down by EU directive xyz).
> They will also tell you that their products perform even better than the minimum standards (*or* perform even better than last year) and we think these producers are right.
> But I'll tell you Radion Micro is the best washing powder on the market beating the minimum washing standards by at least x%, which is y% more than the best other washing powder performance.
> This means that the new Radion Micro product is better than any of the good washing powders on the market today.
> We also believe (*or* have scientific evidence to prove) that Radion is better than the Persil washing powder which is advertised on TV as "even better than all the other washing powders on the market today".
> So, we have reason to believe that Radion is the best washing powder on the market – so far.

Many if not all the statements above will be untenable; hence, the advertiser does not explicitly state them. Instead, the advertiser relies on the never failing, but wholly unrealistic, human ability of closure.

• *Clarification*

To fill in the deleted comparative or superlative, the questions to ask are:

> • Compared to what?
> • According to what yardstick?

Very often, the clarification will lead to culture-bound differences, for example:

Statement		According to...	more specifically...
The meeting	went on for too long	*our* idea of use of time	our company's *modus operandi*
	was badly handled	the way *we* handle meetings	the Anglo-American way

6.5.6 Disjuncts

> e.g.: naturally, hopefully, in fact, in reality, obviously, to be frank, if I can be frank with you...

The three adverbs in the extract below appear to be describing what the writer could see. However, one of the three adverbs is not stating a fact but a value judgement:

> ... three men, **obviously** locals, were eating their lunch **steadily** and **silently**. *The Observer* (12/1/1992)

The two adverbs after the second comma, 'steadily' and 'silently', describe how the three men were eating. 'Obviously', though, is not describing a 'how' but is an evaluative comment made by the writer of the article. Eating steadily and silently is directly observable, whereas the fact that the men were locals was obvious to the writer.

A comment by a speaker on the content of the clause, as with 'obviously', is called a disjunct (Downing and Locke 1992:62-63). Disjuncts are most often realized (as in the boxed example above) by adverbs, prepositional groups and by both non-finite and finite clauses. Disjuncts are usually clearly positioned before or after the clause they are commenting on, as a sign that they are a comment, e.g. "Naturally, he spoke to me when he saw me". However, the unconscious brain tends not to notice the position of the disjunct, but does take note of the sound and look. As a result, disjuncts can interfere with communication. The surface structure (e.g. 'naturally', 'obviously') looks like an adverb describing an observable 'how'. In reality, these disjuncts represent an author's personal evaluation.

• *Clarification*
First, it is necessary to check if the adverb can be transformed into an 'anticipatory it' in the form "It is X that". If this is the case then we have an example of a disjunct. For example: "Naturally, he spoke to me" can be transformed into: "It is natural that he spoke to me". Also, "obviously" can be transformed into "it is obvious that ...", while "steadily" makes little sense as "it is steady that ..."

Second, we need to recover the performative, and so the clarifying question is: "To whom is it *X* that ...?" For example: "To whom is it *obvious* that the men were locals?" The full representation is now: "It was obvious to **me** that the men were locals".

6.6 Distortion

Both generalizations and deletions distort reality in the sense that what is said reduces the detail, making it progressively more difficult to connect to the full representation or specific frame. The following section, instead, focuses on language that actually distorts or transforms what is real or objectively verifiable. The reader, or listener, in this case is led to a different – though equally specific – frame of reference. We have already mentioned the human need to make sense of the world, and one way that this is done is to distort it to fit our preconceptions. Guirdham (1990:68) notes in her volume *Interpersonal Skills at Work*:

> We are very hesitant to accept any information that does not fit with our existing ideas and beliefs. We therefore select and distort our new observations, so that the initial impression can be preserved. There is a lot of evidence that impressions once formed are resistant to change.

This universal tendency, which Guirdham terms 'the locked-in effect', is very similar to the Principle of Analogy mentioned earlier. It is, in general, a useful strategy – otherwise values and beliefs might radically change, resulting in an identity crisis. The other side of the coin is the ease with which speakers can manipulate their audience, as Sperber and Wilson (1995:63) point out: "Journalists, professors, religious or political leaders assume, alas often on good grounds, that what they communicate automatically becomes mutually manifest".

6.6.1 Nominalization

Halliday (1992:68) uses the term 'thinginess' to describe nominalization. This useful term can be used to ask about the degree of thinginess a thing (noun) has. The thinginess of 'hill', for example, is very different from that of 'sky'. Even more different is the thinginess of 'chair' compared with 'war', 'government', 'shopping' and so on. Some of these nouns are not really things but are ongoing processes which have been frozen. The sky changes in a way that a hill does not, and 'wars', 'governments' and 'shopping' are all dynamic processes that have been momentarily frozen. Individuals actively fight, govern and shop.

According to Downing and Locke (1992:149-52), nominalizations are transformations of verbs (de-verbals), attributes (de-adjectivals) and circumstances, into things or rather nouns. This process is clearly a distortion of reality. The distortion in these cases also hides a deletion: the subject of the nominalization. Take for example the following sentence:

> The war in [*location*] is terrible.

As we have noted, it is fighting which hurts, but not even fighting in itself. People fight. The full representation should be:

> [*named people*] fighting [*named people*] is terrible.

The de-adjectival nominalization "terrible" is, of course, also incomplete. It is a value judgement, which will need clarifying by locating the missing performative and the terms of measurement. Clearly, there will almost always be good reason for using this language shorthand, as usually we know who is fighting whom, or we may be using language more phatically.[14] Nominalization, in fact, is a particularly efficient way of reducing time spent on explicit communication. However, according to O'Connor and Seymour (1993:96), "By turning processes into things, nominalizations may be the single most misleading language pattern".

Halliday (1992:77-79) is also concerned about "the trend towards thinginess". Though he limits his discussion to the rise of scientific and bureaucratic English, his conclusions regarding the rise in the use of nominalizations are relevant to any discussion on clarity and contextualization in language: "The reality construed by this form of discourse [thinginess] became increasingly arcane and remote from the common-sense construction of experience ... it had already come to be felt as alienating, a world made entirely of things".

As we have noted, nominalizations delete the subject. As a result, responsibility for utterances can be omitted. This phenomenon has been put to good use by those who prefer not to name names, such as in politics where the surface structure deletes any common-sense construction of experience as Halliday (1992:77-78) also points out.

The following is an example of political discourse. Kenneth Baker (Home Secretary at the time) gave a speech to a packed parliament and to about six million people watching television. He was discussing the legal system in England after 16 years of public protest against the wrongful imprisonment of a number of Irishmen and others. One particular group of four Irishmen (The Guildford Four) had been given life sentences for their involvement in an IRA attack. Sixteen years later, they were released: victims of a miscarriage of justice. Kenneth Baker's words on that occasion were as follows:

> It is of fundamental importance that the arrangements of criminal justice should secure the speedy conviction of the guilty and the acquittal of the innocent. When that is not achieved public confidence is undermined.

In these two sentences there is no actor. The listeners to these words have no idea *who* or *what* exactly has undermined public confidence or *who* believes that the issue is important now (rather than before). In short, references to specific individuals responsible for imprisoning the four Irishmen were deleted.

• Clarification

To check if a word or expression is a nominalization it should fit into the blank in the following phrases:

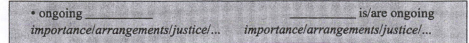

* ongoing _____   _____ is/are ongoing
importance/arrangements/justice/...   *importance/arrangements/justice/...*

---

[14] Phatic communication, as coined by Malinowski (1923/1938), means language used to establish atmosphere or maintain social contact.

The nominalization is then clarified by turning it into a verb, adjective or circumstance and clarifying:

> • Who *or* What is *arranged/important/*...?

6.6.2 Presupposition

Presuppositions are also hidden distortions of reality. They play tricks with what is theme and rheme, given and new. Each clause is organized as a message into a theme and a non-theme or rheme (Taylor Torsello 1987:150). In English, the theme is at the beginning of the clause and normally coincides with 'given' information. In fact, according to Wolfgang Dressler (1992), the *ordo naturalis* is to move from given to new information – especially in English. Taylor Torsello (1984:152, 153) follows Halliday in suggesting that thematic organization in English is extremely important, more so than in other languages. She also goes on to suggest "It is the assignment of 'given' and 'new' which serves primarily to relate the stretch of text to what has gone before in the text".

The 'what has gone before' will be assumed to be shared. So, the presupposition is that there was something that had gone on before, and 'that something' is shared information. This is precisely where distortion can take place.

For example, a frequent question in Mediterranean countries, which many British people have problems replying to is: "Which do you prefer? The sea or the mountains?" The question is posed by people from hot climes. The reason for the problem is a difference in presupposition, which is culturally based. In general, (the summer of 1995 notwithstanding) the British go on holiday looking for the sun, continental Europe being a favourite destination. Italians and other Mediterranean Europeans go on holiday too, but generally *away from* the heat to the sea or to the cooler mountains. So, the Mediterranean question presupposes that the interlocutors have already suffered the stagnant heat in towns or at least in the plains and wish to move to the two most convenient places that offer respite.

Taylor Torsello's (1987) *Shared and Unshared Information* covers presupposition in detail and itemizes some of the syntactic, semantic and prosodic options that necessarily invoke it. (I have added example elements to her summary below):

> Not entirely fictitious discussion between customer (C) who had bought socks, assistant (A) and manager (M) in a department store at Christmas time:
>
> C: I want to see the manager.
> A: She isn't in today.
> C: Hmmmf! The fact that I slipped on the ice outside your store hardly surprises me. Why didn't you do anything to help? When the manager returns, tell her I will sue.
> (*Later*)
> C: The manager's office is a bit small. (*Enter manager*) Look, I bought these socks and now they are all ruined! As we all know they are now completely worthless, so what are you going to do about it?

> M: Well...
> C: The store manager **is** responsible ...

Part of speech	Presupposing element taken as given or true	'new' element
definite noun phrases: "I want to see the manager"	The manager [there is a manager in, e.g., a department store]	I want to see
cohesive elements (reference, substitution, ellipsis)	She	isn't in today
embedded clauses (e.g. the fact clause, the defining relative)	The fact that I slipped on the ice outside your store	hardly surprises me
wh-questions	do anything to help.	Why didn't you
sentence-initial subordinate clauses	When she returns	tell her I will sue
the specifying genitive	The manager's office [She has an office]	is a bit small
some uses of the simple past	I bought [compare 'I have just bought']	these socks, and now they are all ruined
lexical indicators: clearly, obviously, etc.	As we all know they are now worthless	so what are you going to do about it?
rising tones, tonic stress	The store manager	**is** responsible

• *Clarification*

The presuppositions can be clarified or challenged by asking what objective evidence there is to suggest that X is the case:

• How do you know specifically that	*(fill in with the presupposition)*
• What leads you to believe that	*there is a store manager?*
	something is going on?

6.6.3 Mind Reading

Mind reading occurs when someone presumes to know about another person's thoughts (ideas, beliefs or feelings) without any objective evidence. We depend on this strategy in our day-to-day communication, as Channell (1994:161) illustrates in the following extract of a conversation:

> C: or have something completely different
> B: yeah that's right
> C: like a barbecue with a you know a
> B: yeah
> C: whatsit theme
> B: yeah

B is literally reading C's mind at every turn, yet will be following his/her *own* picture of what B is talking about. So far in the conversation, B's mental representation is not clashing with C's words. And, as we have mentioned earlier as a general principle,[15] B will tend to fit C's words to his/her own frame. This makes communication much quicker, but on the other hand, there is no guarantee that the two mental representations are similar, unless there is feedback, as in the following example where "whatsisname" is named by the listener:

> 'Where's Sandra? ... did she come in?'
> 'Gone t'bed. Came in a while ago.'
> 'And whatsisname?'
> 'Cliff went home.'
> David Lodge (1988), *Nice Work*

In both the above examples the speaker is explicitly asking the interlocutor to mind read ("you know?" and "whatsisname?"), and the communication is successful. One further point needs to be made in favour of mind reading before discussing the dangers in communication. Mind reading may not be explicit yet may still be a conscious activity; in which case, a label of 'intuition' or 'sixth sense' may well be added. This sixth sense is not actually mind reading but more often the result of heightened sensitivity to non-verbal cues (see also Pease and Pease 2001:27-28). As Bateson (1972:412) among others points out, the non-verbal channel is a stronger channel of communication. We have already noted in the section on Cultural Congruence (Chapter 3.3) the importance of non-verbal communication and Bateson's warning:

> When boy says to girl, 'I love you,' he is using words to convey that which is more convincingly conveyed by his tone of voice and his movements; and the girl, if she has any sense, will pay more attention to those accompanying signs than to the words.

Clearly, there is a difference between listening and watching for non-verbal signals and believing that one can 'know' another's mind. Hasan's study of mother and child talk demonstrates that LAP mothers tend to resort to implicit mind read-

---

[15] See 'Principle of Analogy' in Chapter 6.2 and the 'Locked In Effect' in Chapter 6.6.

ing more frequently than HAPs. Hasan (1991:101) noted, in particular, the LAP preference for 'assumptive' questions. A speaker selecting an assumptive question "believes she knows the other so well as to assume knowledge of the likely, normal, and/or desirable behaviour on the other's part". In any communication this can be dangerous, but in cross-cultural communication it is a recipe for misunderstanding at all levels. Hasan suggests that HAPs have beliefs that allow them to communicate more effectively. The belief is based on what Hasan (ibid.:100, emphasis in original) calls 'the principle of individuation', which states that:

> Each of us as an individual is a unique being, and the intentions, beliefs, opinions of each one of us are private to each; they are, in principle, inaccessible to our conversational *others* without verbal mediation. Unless relatively specific and explicit verbal exchanges occur, the *other's* subjectivity cannot be accessed: one cannot assume *reflexive relation*, acting on the presumption that the other is just like us, ourselves.

LAPs and culturally incompetent speakers, on the other hand, tend to behave as if the opposite were true: i.e. they can read someone else's mind. Examples of mind reading are as follows:

I know what you're thinking.
I know what you mean.
He's deliberately dragging his feet.
They always want to delay the meeting.

Questionnaire replies from a French/American group of engineers
Nikola Hale (1996:108):
Why do they [the Americans] think they've solved a problem when they've written it down?
Why do they [the French] not listen to American suggestions?

• *Clarification*
The clarification question for mind reading is as follows:

	Mind reading statement
• What specifically	do they not listen to?
• How do you know	they don't listen?

The answer to 'how do you know' will clarify the evidence that the speaker has. The belief may be subject to the culture filter, or, alternatively, the distortion may be part of an objective evaluation that has been generalized, deleted or distorted by the language filter.

6.6.4 Cause and Effect

The existence of cause and effect, an agent causing a change, is part of the natural world. In physics, the universal rule is that every action has a reaction. An extreme example is the Butterfly Effect. This was named after a talk by the American meteorologist Edward Lorenz entitled 'Does the Flap of a Butterfly's Wings in Brazil Set off a Tornado in Texas?'[16] He pointed out that a tiny change in the right place can have huge consequences. Not only in the physical and animal world is there cause and effect, but in the human too. People too can cause, coerce and manipulate.

What is not universal, though, is the perception, scope and conditions for something or somebody to directly affect another. According to Nancy Bishop (1992:300-2), in her essay in honour of Longacre, "What can cause what is defined by a culture's worldview ... What is considered coercion or manipulation is also culturally defined". In linguistics, Downing and Locke (1992:115; see also Palmer 1996:147-69) add that "The notion of agency is a complex one, which includes such features as animacy, intention, motivation, responsibility and the use of one's own energy to bring about an event or initiate a process". The complexity of the notion is very rarely conscious, it is part of our out-of-awareness culture. When we say, "lightning damaged the house" or "prices are affecting trade", at the surface level we are attributing varying degrees of animacy, intention, motivation and responsibility to 'lightning' and 'prices'. According to Downing and Locke, these roles are easily accepted as metaphorical transfers from normally inanimate and unwitting agents to animate agents.

However, at times we have more of a problem separating the metaphor from the reality (see Lakoff and Johnson 1980). Below are two examples from Italy of good advice or old wives' tales, depending on whether you believe in the cause and effect framework or believe that the surface structure is a distortion of reality:

Old wives' tale or good advice	Translation
Se bagni i piedi prendi il raffreddore	If you wet your feet, you'll catch a cold
La corrente ti fa male	The draught is bad for you [literally: the draught will hurt you]

The above examples concern environmental cause and effect. However, neither of the above environmental conditions can actually cause, for example, a cold. They may, indirectly, provide a context that would allow agents, such as bacteria, to cause a particular effect. Alternatively, a specific context can be generalized to provide a fictitious or superstitious cause and effect. In 862, according to legend, the bishop of Winchester was to be canonized as St. Swithin on July 15th. However it rained that day, affecting the proceedings – and rained for a further forty days. The proverb has it that:

---

[16] Reported in O'Connor and Seymour (1993:207). This example is a useful metaphor to describe the cause-effect process, but it deliberately ignores two fundamental aspects of reality: gravity and friction.

> If it rains on St. Swithin's Day, there will be rain for forty days.

However, the present July 15th, St Swithin's Day, is based on the Gregorian calendar; whereas, the July 15th of the rains was Julian. Believers in this particular proverb conveniently forget that Pope Gregory put the clock forward 10 days.

Other cause/effect distortions are to do with human behaviour and psychological states. Statements such as "the behaviour of the French caused the meeting to break up" are semantically ill-formed. The behaviour of an individual cannot directly cause a response in the way that if you boil water it will turn to steam. The response will always depend on how the behaviour is interpreted. So, some of the responsibility for the response lies with those responding – as it is they who decide how to respond. For example, we can refer back to Chapter 2.2 and Bromhead's cause and effect remark about London: "So much impermanence, change and movement have made the people more innovative, the place more lively, so full of surprises, that nothing is surprising". As we have already noted, the 'impermanence' is the stimulus, not the agent. The response in this case, according to Bromhead, is positive. However, this particular distortion of reality is especially dangerous for communication when we have a negative response. And this is what happens during culture shock. We make other people responsible for our feelings (whether positive or negative). Some semantically ill-formed ethnocentric examples are given below:

> The disorganization of [*culture B*] **makes** me frustrated.
> Their habits **revolt/ disgust/ upset** me.
> It **makes** me so angry that they can never say what they mean.
>
> **Questionnaire replies from a French group of engineers**
> Nikola Hale (1996:108):
> I like their [American] habit of staying focused on the topics of the agenda at meetings, but **it drives me crazy** because this reduces their ability to be flexible, innovative and open to new ideas.

And below is an all purpose generative cause-effect culture shock sentence:

> Their total disregard for [*fill in the noun of your choice*] really [*fill in with suitable emotive verb of your choice*] me.

By the same token that change could not cause London to be exciting (a highly relative value judgement anyway), it is highly unlikely that one person or culture can actually technically cause a certain response. With regard to both positive and negative effects of other people's behaviour, O'Connor and Seymour (1993:103) state: "Thinking that you can force people to experience different states of mind, or that other people can force you into different moods is very limiting, and causes a great deal of distress".

• *Clarification*

We can clarify the supposed cause and effect by asking this question:

> • Does the act/event technically **cause** the response or is the response due to other factors such as social engineering?

In general, cause and effect can be challenged by asking:

> • How specifically *does X cause Y*?
> • What would have to happen *for X not to be caused by Y*
> • Does X always (in all contexts) *cause Y*?

6.7 Example Text

We will now look at an example text to investigate how distortions, deletions and generalizations are unconsciously adopted in texts. The specific examples outlined below can begin to give us an insight into the author's view of the world, and where its limits lie. We will immediately note that the article itself is a distortion of Tuscany in that it highlights only a part of it for the reader. The author also presupposes a certain kind of reader, and we can note from the deletions what is assumed to be shared knowledge.

Sensuous Secrets of Tuscany	**Sensuous Secrets of Tuscany:** ill-formed title (Tuscany itself cannot have secrets) **sensuous:** imprecise figurative/metaphorical language **secrets:** nominalization
Eric Newby and his wife Wanda were in Umbria thirsting for a supply of wine on tap, when **serendipity** let them into the **hidden** Italian world of *Agriturismo* – farmhouse food and rooms. Here they **take a rustic tour** through the Tuscan landscape.	**Eric Newby and his wife…:** missing performative (Eric Newby and his wife were in Umbria according to whom? Newby himself? The editor of the article?) **serendipity:** cause and effect (serendipity cannot cause them to find hidden Italy) **hidden:** deletion (hidden to who? hidden how?) **take a rustic tour:** nominalization ('take a tour', they toured)
A couple of autumns ago, while driving through Umbria, **we were brought to a standstill by a tremendous rainstorm,** outside a **solitary** farmhouse, on a **lonely** road near the Lago di Corbara eastwards of Orvieto.	**we were brought…:** cause and effect deletion (the rainstorm affected their car, their vision or their psyche?) **rainstorm; standstill:** nominalizations **lonely:** distortion (**solitary**, however, is objectively verifiable); cause and effect (it made who feel lonely?); value judgement (lonely according to who? or to which culture-bound parameters?)
We were in this part of Umbria because	**We were in this…:** fairly complete seman-

we were trying to find a farmer prepared to sell us some Corbara, which is a red wine made from Sangiovese grapes cultivated near the shores of the lake.

Corbara is nothing **great**. A little-known wine, it is at its best when between three and four years old. **The difficulty is to find it** *sfuso*, that is literally loose, on tap. It is particularly difficult just before **the** *vendemmia*, when stocks of the previous year's wine are low, as we were discovering.

We wanted to buy it *sfuso*, because **we could then take it back to England in 25-litre containers, where we could bottle it**. This is something we have been doing since we **made** our own vineyard in Tuscany more than 18 years ago. **In such containers the wine takes up far less space than in bottles beside being about half the price.**

A sign outside the farmhouse, which was stone-built and **austere, announced** that it was the Azienda Pomonte and that meals were served – a rarity in Italy where a *trattoria* may sometimes be part of a village shop, but never a farmhouse.

We were given **a warm welcome** by the signora, the farmer's wife, and taken to a small, plainly furnished room in which three men, **obviously** locals, were eating their lunch steadily and silently.

That they were doing so was **sufficient recommendation** and soon we found ourselves being **served** with a **delicious** Umbrian meal: home-made salami of several sorts, *congilio in potacchietto*, casserole of rabbit cooked with garlic and olive oil, followed by *pere al forno*, cooked pears. The wine was Corbara sfuso, **we had**

tic representation, apart from:

trying to find: unspecified verb (trying how, in what way? with/without a map, following verbal instructions?)

trying: suggests difficulty (how was it difficult trying?)

great: value judgement (great for whom? Great in comparison to what?)

the difficulty is…: presupposition (one wants to find or drink a wine that is *sfuso* or rather 'nothing great')

the *vendemmia*: presupposition (understood through use of the definite article and no translation; part of a shared model of the world); nominalization (through use of the definite article)

we could then…: well formed sentence (it gives indication of value, size, DIY, economy…)

made: unspecified verb (made how exactly? Constructed from bare earth, built with their own hands?)

In such containers…: incomplete comparison (half the price of what?); presuppositions (only the price changes, the quality remains the same as in bottles; price is an important and positive value shared by the readers)

a sign […] announced: distortion (a sign is normally inanimate)

austere: deletion; value judgement (austere for whom? For the Italian farmer or for the English writer? What objective evidence is there?)

trattoria: presupposition (shared understanding of the word)

a warm welcome: nominalization; value judgement (how was the welcoming exactly? according to whom was the welcoming warm? the *signora*, her culture or only Eric Newby? "warm" by English, Italian or which standards?)

obviously: distortion (it was obvious to whom? what evidence is there?)

sufficient recommendation: distortion; deletion (who is responsible for the recommending? sufficient for whom, in comparison to what?)

served: deletion (served by whom exactly? served how, exactly?)

delicious: deletion (delicious for whom, and how?)

run it to earth at last. There was no menu and no choice, which is always **the best** way to eat in rural Italy.	**we had run it…:** figurative language (tells one about how the representation is visualized); convert to simile (it was like in a chase, smelling-out a rabbit) **the best:** universal quantifier (always the best, there are no exceptions?); superlative (best according to whom, and according to what yardstick?)

It is the culture-bound deletions that will help us construct the Newbys' (shared) world. Beginning with the title, Eric Newby sets up an idea that Tuscany has secrets, which when unravelled, or rather run to earth, will be perceived as sensuous for his audience. The locals, on the other hand, will not find Tuscany particularly secret, and what he describes as sensuous is likely to be perceived as "normal".

Newby's secret frame is strengthened through a set of lexical chains, all of which are value judgements: 'hidden', 'solitary', 'lonely', 'trying to find', 'the difficulty is', 'austere', 'rarity'. What the Newbys are looking for is hidden, right up to the end, in a small, plainly furnished room. If we ask what frames could be opened with this set of cues it would not be too far fetched to suggest a detective story, maybe even Sherlock Holmes. We could even add a touch of Gothic horror: (super)natural agents had organised the tremendous rainstorm which brought them to a standstill in the middle of nowhere.

Readers from more Mediterranean climes may be bemused by this vision of Tuscany, and even more so when told that the challenge or the hunt is to try to find a farmer prepared to sell them a wine, which is "nothing great". On the surface, we have nothing but a series of negatively valued comments about Tuscany, yet they clearly must set up positive expectations for the intended reader (according to travel writing norms). So, we need to organise a set of Logical Levels that would cohere positively with these comments. The identity depicted in this extract is "detective". The figurative language ('run to earth') helps us understand that Newby was also thinking in terms of a foxhunt.

Values that cohere would indeed be "challenge" and "difficulty": the greater the difficulty, the greater the prize. In fact, having overcome the obstacles Newby can claim his prize: a warm welcome and a delicious meal. However, what logical model of the world would aspire to this form of challenge within the general environment of 'holiday' and 'travel' given that his real prize (the object of his mission) was Corbara sfuso, which "we had run to earth at last"?

To find the logical values, we need look no further than his own words:

    take back in 25 litre containers
    to bottle (rather than 'to buy ready bottled')
    take up less space,
    half the price.

The values that logically cohere with these behaviours cue basic Anglo-Saxon pragmatic values: quantity, space, economy and practicality. These values become even clearer when we pit them against their (unstated) opposites: quality, taste, cost and so on. Apart from the values we have already mentioned (the challenge and practicality) we could also notice that there is an accent on 'doing'. The holiday is active, and is positively valued due to the fact that he had to struggle to merit his prize. Extrapolating, we might notice how well this fits in with Protestantism and the Utilitarianism ethics (see Scollon and Scollon 2001).

The culture-boundness of Eric Newby's view of Tuscany is clearly visible from the array of distortions we have discussed above, such as his value judgements and nominalisations, and also from his universal quantifier generalisation: "*always* the best way to eat in rural Italy". The deletions, on the other hand, more than anything else point to his shared Anglo-Saxon world, and to what he presupposes his reader already knows about Italy (geographical names, *vendemmia*, *trattoria*, and so on).

To sum up, we can show Eric Newby's shared culture-bound model of the world in this particular context of travel and travel writing for a British readership as follows (*the terms 'HCC', 'particularist' and 'utilitarianism' are explained in Part 3):

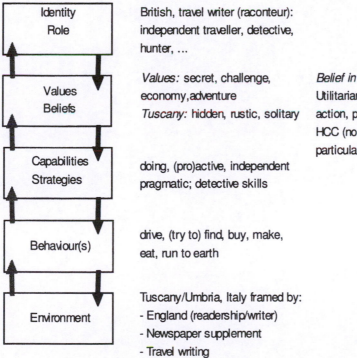

Figure 23. The culture-bound Logical Levels of Eric Newby's model of his Tuscan/ Umbrian world

Part 2. Shifting Frames
Translation and Mediation in Theory
and Practice

So far, we have established that meaning is dependent on the frame, and that the context of culture is an important frame from within which we perceive, interpret and communicate. We have also discussed what a Cultural Interpreter or Mediator should be, and how he or she should view culture.

Part 2 focuses on the mediator's ability to change frame. As cultures operate within different interpretative frames, so a cultural mediator must be able to mind shift between possible frames.

Chapter 7 illustrates how the universal process of modelling and the Meta-Model function in translation, and describes the translator/interpreter's active role in the interpretation process.

Chapter 8 offers a detailed explanation of Chunking. The technique is used to change the focus of interpretation, whether from word to meaning, from text to context (and vice versa) or from one cultural frame to another.

Chapter 7. Translation/Mediation

The aim of this chapter is to:
- discuss two models of translation: decoding-encoding and frame
- illustrate how frame theory is relevant to the translation process
- underline the fact that translation is a form of cross-cultural communication
- point out that translation is subject to universal modelling and can benefit from a conscious use of the Meta-Model
- define 'manipulation', 'mediation', 'interpreting' and 'facilitation'

7.1 The Translation Process

- The Decoding-Encoding Model
- The Importance of Frame
- The Cognitive Creation Model
- The Translation Process and Culture

• Decoding-Encoding or Cognitive Creation

A number of models describing the translation process have been suggested over the past thirty years. The model proposed by Eugene Nida (Nida and Taber 1969:484) has been particularly influential. This model (and the many other models that followed) depends on the conduit metaphor:[1] the source text language is broken down into smaller parts, analyzed, and then reformulated in other words – as if the text were being processed through a pipe. The emphasis either can be on the surface level, or, as Nida proposes, on the fuller representative deep level (see figure 24).

More recently, other theorists have suggested a different process. Bell (1991:21),

---

[1] Michael J. Reddy (1993) coined the term in 1979.

in fact, suggests that between the SL and the TL text, the translator creates a "semantic representation" of the text. Neubert and Shreve (1992:14) are more explicit suggesting that in the translator's mind there is a "virtual translation", which is "a composite of the possible relations between a source text and a range of potential target texts". The virtual translation "accounts for [author and translator] knowledge, thoughts, and feelings. It includes their aims, intentions, needs and expectations". The idea of a virtual translation will be used here to describe that out-of-awareness understanding a mediator has of the text and the feel s/he has of the text that has yet to be created in the target language.

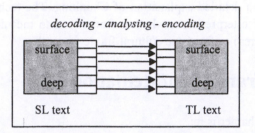

Figure 24. The Decoding-Encoding Translation Model

James Holmes (1988:96) proposed a similar theory regarding the translation process. His "mapping theory" adopts a similar map metaphor to Bateson and others before him:

> I have suggested that actually the translation process is a multi-level process. While we are translating sentences, we have a map of the original text in our minds and at the same time a map of the kind of text we want to produce in the target language.

Wolfram Wilss (1989:140-42) also draws attention to the "Multi-Facet Concept of Translation Behaviour". He takes a culture-oriented approach to translation and focuses extensively on the importance of context, but disagrees with the idea of a mental map. Though he notes Charles Fillmore's (1977:61) suggestion that "one mentally creates a kind of world" he only fully agrees with Fillmore on the subject of frames. This, he says with regard to translation, is "more to the point".

More importantly, Wilss highlights two very different strategies for translating. The first strategy uses algorithmic knowledge: "If X in Source Text, then Y in Target Text". Wilss points out, even if he does not agree with the map or the virtual translation theory, that the second strategy involving "heuristic procedures" and "frames" must be employed to solve translation problems.

Mary Snell-Hornby (1988:29), in her *Translation Studies: An Integrated Approach*, also advocates a heuristic approach. Her integrated approach is actually based on Lakoff's (1982) ideas and Eleanor Rosch's (1978) research on prototypes and categorizations. Rosch identified two levels of category. Her research showed that at the lower level, categorization is based on the function, as in 'a chair' is for sitting on. At the higher level (e.g. 'furniture'), the category is less functionally detailed but carries greater cultural significance. "The essential point", according to Snell-Hornby (quoting Lakoff 1982:20 and adding her own emphasis), is that "At that [higher] level things are perceived holistically, *as a single gestalt*, while for identification at a lower level, specific details have to be picked out".

Many translation theorists are now convinced of the importance of frames and of a gestalt approach to translation.[2] According to Neubert and Shreve, a good translator reads the text, and in so doing accesses grouped linguistic and textual knowledge. At the text level, translation theorists have assigned this 'grouped' knowledge various names, which include 'text type' and 'genre'; and levels of grouping have been subdivided into frames, schemata, plans and scripts. However, the main area of interest is the frame. Neubert and Shreve (1992:60), for example, define frames in terms of organization of experience and knowledge repertoires (emphasis in the original): "This organization of experience may be referred to as *framing* and the knowledge structures themselves as *frames*".

Unfortunately, Mia Vannerem and Snell-Hornby (1986:190), following Fillmore's categorization, use the term 'frame' to signify "the linguistic form on the page", while they reserve the term 'scene' for what we have been calling 'frame': "the reader/translator's personal experience". The ideas expressed, however, fully coincide with those of other translation theorists: that the frames activated by the text "are very closely linked to the socio-cultural background of the language user in question".

Hans Hönig (1991:79-80) simplifies Fillmore's 'scene-and-frame' distinctions suggesting "*Scheme* and *frame* stand for different parts of the reader's expectation structures, they are structured domains of long-term memory". His understanding, also following Tannen's definition, is that frames are a combination of prior knowledge, generalizations and expectations regarding the text. As the text is read so it is checked against expectations and degree of fit with other similar known or possible texts. As this process unfolds, a meaningful, but still virtual, text begins to develop in the mind of the translator (though Wilss, as we have noted, dissents here). From the meaningful but wordless text, the translator then sketches a pattern of words in the target language. The traditional interpreter does the same. In what is known as the "blah blah" theory, the professional interpreter forms a basic idea of the moves of, for example, the conference delegate. S/he will make some opening remarks, agree, disagree, propose and conclude. As the delegate speaks, so the virtual text begins to take on form. The interpreter will already have a number of prototypical scripts, organised by genre, setting, culture and so on, ready to give substance to the virtual text.

The difference between the coding-encoding approach and the more recent

---

[2] See Neubert and Shreve (1992:36-68); Bell (1991:199-228); Hatim and Mason (1990:138-64); C. Taylor (1998:7); Vennerem and Snell-Hornby (1986); Kussmaul (2000:61-64); Nord (2003:101-8)

frame-driven approach is summed up by Bell (1991:161), who states that "Current thinking among translation theorists ... insists that a translated text is a new creation which derives from careful reading; a reconstruction rather than a copy" (*pace* the EU). The diagram below shows the difference between the decoding-encoding (copy) model, and the map or virtual text (creation) model. As can be seen, there is a looser connection between SL and TL text. Both texts feed into and out of the virtual text. This approach suggests that someone takes holistic control and coordinates the frames.

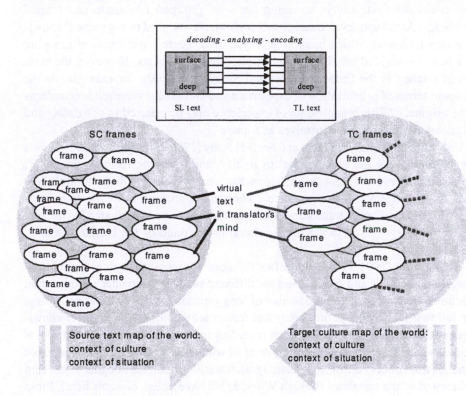

Figure 25. The Cognitive Creation Translation Model

• *The Translation Process and Culture*

This particular translation process approach is of notable importance to the cultural interpreter and mediator. Snell-Hornby (1988:39-64), for example, in her chapter "Translation as a Cross-Cultural Event" states that the translation process can no longer be envisaged as being between two languages but between two cultures involving "cross-cultural transfer", integrating the scenes-and-frame concept of Fillmore. Candlin (1990:ix) points out in his introduction to Hatim and Mason:

> [The translation process] allows us to put language into perspective by asserting the need to extend beyond the apposite selection of phrases to an investigative exploration of the signs of culture ... It asks us to explore our

ideologically and culturally-based assumptions about all those matters on which we utter, in speech or in writing, or in signs.

Bassnett (1991:13) also believes that translation must take place within a framework of culture, and began her publication *Translation Studies* with the following title "Central Issues: Language and Culture". In fact, an essential difference between a traditional translator and a mediator is the mediator's ability to understand and recreate culture-bound frames wherever necessary. The mediator will be able to understand the frames of interpretation in the source culture and will be able to produce a text which would create a comparable (rather then equivalent) set of interpretation frames to be accessed in the target reader's mind.

Of course, 'comparable', itself, is a deletion of the criteria and in some ways is no more helpful than its outmoded predecessor 'equivalence'. The major shift though is in orientation. A mediator accepts that difference is the norm, and that there is no single 'correct' translation. The word 'correct' will always need to be contextualised: "correct for whom, in what context, according to what norms?" The translation scholar, Gideon Toury (1980, 1995) ably answers the question: the constantly changing, and conflicting, socio-cultural norms in the receiving culture.

The language of negotiations might help in explaining the mediator's task. Both texts (S) and (T) will have surface 'positions' (text), and will also have hidden 'interests' (cognitive effects) and 'needs' (functions). The cognitive effects will be in terms of types of frame cued. It is the mediator's task to discover the array of needs and look for creative options (through concessions, offers and straight trade) to satisfy the interests and requirements of both sides. This leads directly to the idea of prioritorizing negotiable (and non-negotiable areas), and of course, each 'side' will also have different strengths and weaknesses. In fact, as Evan-Zohar, (1978:16) a cultural theorist, points out, "There can obviously be no equality [read 'equivalence'] between the various literary systems and types. These systems maintain *hierarchical* relations, which means some maintain a more central position than others, or that some are *primary* while others are *secondary*". Toury (1980:18) expands the polysystem theory, explaining that texts contain clusters of properties, meanings, and possibilities. All translations privilege certain properties/meanings at the expense of others.

As Theo Hermans (1999:110), one of the key players in translation studies today, points out in his volume, *Translation in Systems*, the "polysystem theory has benefited translation research by placing translation squarely in a larger field of cultural activity". This holistic or global approach to translation does not mean that a cultural mediator can disregard 'the text' itself. A successful mediator must be consciously aware of the importance of both text and context, which means both the words and the implied frames.

The next sections divide the discussion on text, context and translation into the three principle aspects of Universal Modelling: generalization, deletion and distortion.

7.2 The Meta-Model and Translation

The idea that one needs to understand the underlying intention of a writer to translate effectively has become a cornerstone of translation theory. Walter Benjamin (1968:77) in his 1923 treaty on translation said (emphasis in the original): "The task of the translator consists in finding that intended effect *[Intention]* upon the language into which he is translating which produces in it the echo of the original".

This aim, though, has been criticized for a number of reasons, including the fact that many writers are not entirely conscious of their intentions; and most of the time cannot even be asked about them.[3] However, intention, whether conscious or not, can be extracted from the text, as discussed in Chapter 6.3 (and in Katan 1996). To do this, a translator must be able to create a full linguistic representation of the text, which is where the Meta-Model can become a useful instrument. As Dilts (1983, V: 6) says, "The Meta-Model can provide substantial insight into the structure of thought and speech when applied to any personal, philosophical or political enquiry".

Nida (1976:71), as a Bible translator, has also been particularly interested in the structure of thought, and has been active in attempting to translate the thoughts of God as clearly and as closely as possible to the original. For this reason he adopted what he calls "an essentially deep structure approach to certain problems of exegesis", which we briefly touched upon in Chapter 5. However, one of Nida's reasons for applying a deep structure approach is based on the belief that at the full representation level the syntactic structures of various languages are similar. This belief has since been justly criticized (Gentzler 2001:47-50); and Chomsky (1965:30), in fact, has always warned that though there is a universal deep structure grammar, there is no necessary correspondence between languages:

> The existence of deep-seated formal universals ... implies that all languages are cut to the same pattern, but does not imply that there is any point by point correspondence between particular languages. It does not, for example, imply that there must be some reasonable procedure for translating between languages.

Our aim here does not, in fact, clash with this criticism because we are not looking for any linguistic correspondence between languages. What we are interested in is a speaker or writer and their message as meant within their particular construction of reality. Once we have understood the full extent of the message within its own reality we have the beginnings of a virtual translation. In fact, Gentzler (2001:47) does accept that:

> Whether one accepts Chomsky's beliefs on how the human mind is structured or not, his deep structures, postulated to contain all the necessary

---

[3] See, in particular, Dodds (1994:16-19) and his discussion of the question of author intention and the Intentional Fallacy.

syntactic as well as semantic information for a correct transformation into surface structure and interpretation, lend themselves well to the translation practitioner trying to represent an 'underlying' message in a second language.

This point is of great importance for the cultural mediator. Nida (1976:72) goes into more detail making two points in favour of investigating deeper structures with regard to the underlying message, both of which are particularly relevant today for those working cross-culturally.

First, Nida continues, one can more readily identify the semantic structures when investigating subsurface levels. This means that a translator will be in a position to determine more accurately the extent of equivalence and the need for supplementation or redistribution of semantic components. Second, on the deeper levels of structure, one can more easily determine the symbolic relations and their hermeneutic implications.

Yet, also, very importantly, Nida (ibid.:75) makes it clear that Chomsky's theory, or rather theories (standard, extended standard, generative semanticist), "involve certain important limitations" for translation. He makes two points here. First, that theories only account for propositional meaning, and not for the connotations, focus, emphasis, or foregrounding. Second, Nida also realizes that the theory depends on an ideal speaker and hearer, and as a result, on linguistic facts rather than actual contexts. He finishes his criticism of Chomsky with the following point: "Language cannot be discussed as though verbal communication occurs in a cultural vacuum".

Beekman and Callow (1974:169) also mention the importance of a deep structure approach to bring out the fullness of the text. They suggest a series of 'elicitation procedures', a rudimentary form of the Meta-Model, to be used in translation. They have in mind a language helper (a native source-language speaker). I would suggest here that translators, interpreters and others should use the Meta-Model themselves to consciously locate the deletions, distortions and generalizations in the source text. Mediators should also be conscious of their own modelling strategy in the production of the target text.

We will now look briefly at generalization, deletion and distortion in translation.

7.3 Generalization

Languages, as we have noted, categorize reality, when in reality there is no categorization. These unconscious generalized categories of everyday life are, of course, culture bound. Many of the categories overlap perfectly, others less so. The fact that languages categorize in different ways brings us to the first main area of Universal Modelling: differences in generalization. However, as the same modelling process is universal to all languages, so, further generalization can be performed by the mediator to reduce distortion (discussed in detail in Chapter 8).

In fact, Baker (1992:26) discusses the conscious use of this factor to improve translations when faced with non-equivalence, under the title "Translation by a more general word (superordinate)":

This is one of the commonest strategies for dealing with many types of non-equivalence, particularly in the area of propositional meaning. It works equally well in most, if not all, languages, since the hierarchical structure of semantic fields is not language-specific.

A step-by-step explanation of how to use this strategy is, as we have already mentioned, discussed in the following chapter.

7.4 Deletion

- implicit (from the text)
- hidden or absent (in the context of culture)
- addition/deletion

Beekman and Callow (1974:49) emphasize that surface structure deletions (implicit information) are also an important area to focus on:

> One of the problems that face a translator whose mother tongue is an Indo-European language is that of recognising the presence of implicit information in the original.

Though they limit their discussion to the Bible and to Indo-European languages, the same can be said for any translation into any language. The three areas translators should look at in their search for evidence of deleted material (according to Beekman and Callow) can be summarized as follows:

• **the immediate context**	of the original and translated texts: the same paragraph or an adjacent one;
• **the remote context**	elsewhere in the document, and in other related texts;
• **the cultural context**	the implicit information which lies outside the document, in the general situation which gave rise to the document, the circumstances of the SL writer and SL readers, their relationship, etc.

Mildred Larson (1984:42) uses a different taxonomy, belying a different approach to translation. For her, the immediate and remote context is 'implicit', whereas the cultural context is 'absent', as in the following adaptation:

Text:	Tony made the Queen's list
Implicit:	Tony Blair *compiled* Queen *Elizabeth II*'s *annual honours* list
Absent:	Tony Blair, Britain's first Labour prime minister in 19 years, and one of the youngest ever, promised wide-

> ranging reforms and a government of the people by the people. The New Year honours list was a "people's" or a "sirs for sirs" honours list. Half of the honours were suggested by the public, and many honours went to ordinary people, in particular teachers.

For a cultural mediator, both that which is implicit and absent is part of the message, and must be accounted for. We will use the term 'implicit' here to mean what can be made explicit from the text, and the term 'context of culture' for that which is absent from the text, but can be retrieved through implicature[4] or associative tie (Neubert and Shreve 1992:59).

Foreign news reporters are one category of 'translators' who constantly have both the implicit information and the context of culture in mind as they attempt to give their readers a fuller representation of events occurring abroad. We will now look at a number of examples showing how newspaper articles have made explicit what was either implicit or in the context of the source culture.

• *Implicit → Explicit (Addition)*

The extract below is a translation of a British *Guardian* article, which appeared in the Italian newspaper *La Voce*. By and large, the translation is extremely faithful to form. However, there are a number of implicit points that have been made explicit. In all cases, this strategy makes the frames available to the source-culture (SC) reader equally accessible to the target-culture (TC) reader.

The Guardian **Italy brainwashed** **by soft soap and hard sell**	*La Voce* *Lavaggio del cervello degli Italiani a base* *di soap-opera e marketing aggressivo*
If you remember **when J. R. died** then you remember a critical moment in the rise of Silvio Berlusconi. The triumph of image over substance is not a new lesson in the age of television politics. But the Berlusconi victory takes us further than any elsewhere in recent years toward sub-rational politics and toward the democracy that is anti-democratic because it is making its decisions in a world of dreams. This was, after all, the election in which	*Se vi ricorderete **quella puntata di Dallas in cui morì J.R.**, allora vi ricorderete anche uno dei momenti più critici di Berlusconi.* *Il trionfo dell'immagine sulla sostanza non è cosa nuova nell'era della politica televisiva – **aggiunge il giornale conservatore** – ma la vittoria di Berlusconi ci avvicina più di ogni altra cosa, negli ultimi anni, alla politica subliminale e alla democrazia che è antidemocratica perché prende le sue decisioni in un mondo dei sogni.* *Dopo tutto, queste dovevano essere le*

---

[4] The term 'implicature' was coined by Grice (1975) to mean the exophoric linking that a hearer needs to make an utterance relevant.

Italy was to rescue its political system and make its new start.	*elezioni destinate a segnare una nuova partenza per Italia.*
Instead, **it** has elected separatists, neo-fascists, and right-wing chancers under the leadership of an adventurer.	*Ed invece l'Italia ha eletto un gruppo di separatisti, neofascisti, avventurieri di destra guidati da un avventuriero.*

The abbreviation "J.R." was, at the time, well known in Britain but less so in Italy partly due to the spelling and pronunciation differences. Hence, the Italian translator made the Dallas TV serial frame much more explicit.

when J.R. died	*quella puntata di Dallas in cui morì J.R.*	that episode of Dallas in which J.R. died

The word "when" deletes much referential information which is easily accessible to a British audience. The clarification question is:

Question:	What does *when* refer to, exactly?
Clarification:	That episode of Dallas.

Further clarification ("which episode exactly?") would reveal the date of transmission or the episode number, which is not the focus of the text and is therefore unnecessary. This still leaves the identity of "J.R." implicit, but enables the TC readers to access the same frame (Dallas) with the same facility as the SC readers.

The next explication is *aggiunge il giornale conservatore*/"adds the Conservative newspaper". *The Guardian*, unfortunately, is not a Conservative paper, so a certain number of inappropriate implicatures will be accessed. Nevertheless, the translation makes the performative deletion clear:

Question:	*It is not a new lesson in the age of television politics*, according to whom?
Clarification:	a foreign (conservative/liberal) newspaper.

This explication now reminds the reader of the frame of interpretation, which is that this particular article is a translation of a foreign newspaper's viewpoint. For the same type of reason, the deleted referential index, "Italy", is made explicit in the translation to remind the reader that we are not talking about an "it", a foreign country, but about the reader's own country: Italy.

Instead, **it** has elected separatists	*Ed invece l'Italia ha eletto un gruppo di separatisti*	And instead Italy has elected a group of separatists

Question:	Who or what is *it* exactly?
Clarification:	Italy.

• *The Context of Culture*

The previous examples dealt with information that is implicit from the structure of the text. We mentioned earlier that a translator as cultural interpreter or mediator also needs to account for information that is implicit in the context of culture. We should also consider that the context of culture can be perceived at a number of different levels, from environment (e.g. institutions) to beliefs and values (cultural orientations) and identity. At the lowest level (environment), as Hatim and Mason show (1990:94), it is already fairly standard practice to add or delete according to the accessibility of the frame. They cite a *Guardian* translation of a *Le Monde* article. The translator, as mediator, has supplied the missing, or less accessible frame regarding Nouméa, while deleting the explicit reference to Australia, as this frame would already be more than implicit for the *Guardian* reader:

Le Monde	The Guardian
Les deux auteurs directs de l'attentat ... ont quitté Auckland ... l'un pour Nouméa, l'autre pour Sydney (Australie).	The two men who carried out the attack ... left Auckland ... one for Nouméa, **in the French Pacific territory of New Caledonia**, and the other for Sydney.

The following extracts show how a mediator has been aware of the readers' frames of reference. The first set of examples below illustrate how various 'translations' have mediated the culture gaps by adding information. The second set of examples to be discussed illustrates the opposite situation whereby, what is explicit in the source text may create unexpected and possibly undesired associations when translated into the target context of culture. In these cases, mediation is through omission or deletion.

Mediation through addition, or explication, may be made as above through unobtrusive manipulation of the text; with a comment outside the main body of the text, for example a footnote[5] or as an explicit note in the text, as below (emphasis added):

| «L'Italia? – si chiede Friedman-. È il prossimo Messico. Chiederle un parere economico è come chiedere al dottor Kevorkian (il "dottor Morte", N.D.R.) una cura per il mal di testa, te lo aggrava». *Corriere della Sera* (29/5/95) | "Italy?" wonders Friedman, "it's the next Mexico. Asking its opinion on economics is like asking Doctor Kevorkian (**"Doctor Death"**, ed.) to treat a headache. He'll make it worse for you". |

---

[5] Thompson (1982:30), in his article 'An Introduction to Implication for Translators', argues that information essential to the success of conversational implicatures should be included in the text and not in the footnotes. In practice, many clients are unhappy with any form of footnote.

The reference to *il dottor Morte* /'Doctor Death' is not culture specific, but gives readers enough encyclopaedic knowledge about Dr. Kevorkian to allow them to appreciate the simile. To use Newmark's (1981:85) terminology: object, image and sense, we have:

Object:	The Italian economy
Image:	Dr. Kevorkian

What is missing for the Italian readership is the sense, the point of similarity, showing in what particular aspects the object and the image are similar. The problem for the Italian reader is that the image is an unspecified referential index: "Who is *Dr. Kevorkian* specifically" (i.e. what aspect of the specific reference can provide an image pertinent to *the Italian economy*)? In answer to that question, the journalist has added *dottor Morte*. So we now have the link: death. With this link, the reader is able to process the information, and gain what Sperber and Wilson (1995:108-117) call 'a contextual effect'. The contextual effect is basically the effect on the listener or reader after having made a deduction through linking a new piece of information (in this case Friedman's comments) with an old piece of information (Dr. Kevorkian / *dottor Morte*). The effects may be strong or weak depending on the relevance of the text and the frames brought to mind.

Often, texts will make use of target culture frames to help the reader associate more closely with the depth of feeling engendered in the original. Thus, through target culture analogy, the source culture can be more fully understood:

I primi due candidati democratici eliminati, Kerrey e Harkin, erano entrambi senatori, dunque associati alla odiosa Washington, la «Roma» americana. *La Reppublica* (11/3/92)	The first two democratic candidates to be eliminated, Kerrey and Harkin, were both senators. So, they were both therefore associated with the detestable Washington, the American "Rome".

Here, immediate out-of-awareness feelings are generated with the metaphorical cue[6] *Roma* in the context of politics. A mediator's use of metaphor to help direct the reader should not be understated. As we have already noted, the use of indirect language can convey multiple meanings. In NLP, metaphor is just as important as the surgical clarity of the Meta-Model in opening up limited worlds. Where the Meta-Model aims to bring experience and meaning into consciousness, metaphorical (and other indirect) communication can unlock unconscious resources and

---

[6] For more on metaphors see Lakoff and Johnson (1980) and Sperber and Wilson (1995:231-37), who explain how linguistic cues access relevant frames and create heightened contextual effects for the hearer. With regard to translation, see Newmark (1981:84-96; 1988:104-113). Specifically for Italian-English, see Dodds (1994:169-77) and Scarpa (1989). For a collection of articles on *Cultural Metaphors* see Gannon 2001.

create new meanings. As O'Connor (2001:186) makes clear, "a good metaphor can be worth a thousand words and several pictures. Being able to use metaphor is a basis of good communication, writing, training, teaching and therapy" – and translation.

Notice, for example, how the English Guide to Venice manages to capture the vision of the Venetian *brìcole* through the addition of a simile.

Venezia, **Guide del Touring Club Italia** (1984:21)	*The Heritage Guide: Venice* (1999:27), (translated from the TCI)
E' infatti innanzitutto spazio prop-riamente urbano: "la più bella strada del mondo" – così già appariva al visitatore del sec. XV – è il lungo percorso dove i palazzi aprono direttamente sull'acqua rive d'ingresso e portoni, segnalati da **brìcole dipinte**, *logge e polifore, ...*	This is an exquisitely urban space – "the loveliest thoroughfare, I believe in the whole world," as a 15th-c. French visitor described it – a long water filled street, lined with palazzi, their entrances and portals and landing jetties opening directly out onto the water. Each palazzo is marked by **painted "brìcole," the bar-ber's pole-like mooring masts**, and fronted by loggias and mullioned windows.

Imagine how much would have been lost with the following 'correct' dictionary translation:

> Each *palazzo* is marked by **painted navigation poles**, and fronted by loggias and mullioned windows.

Below is an example of what Newmark (1988: 82-83) would call cultural equivalence, adopted here to provide the essential context for the focus of the Italian rewriting of the *Telegraph* article. The Italian journalist swapped ITV's breakfast morning show, *This Morning*, which would not cue any particularly meaningful frames in Italy, with *Meteo*, the Italian weather forecast programme. The inverted commas warn the reader, though, that *Meteo* is to be interpreted according to another frame, which is "Liverpool" and "British TV":

The Daily Telegraph	*Corriere della Sera*	Translation
Exposed Front Moves in from the West	«METEO» IN TV CON NUDO	"Meteo" on TV with a Nude
A STREAKER interrupted a television weather forecast when he boarded the huge floating map used by the This Morning programme Mark Roberts was completely naked as he came into view while Fred Talbot, the fore-caster, was predicting a warm sunny day. (3/5/95)	**Liverpool.** Mark Roberts il buontempone che ieri mattina ha inscenato un fuori prog-ramma a tinte boccaccesche sulla rete «Itv» è apparso in costume adamitico a milioni di telespettatori durante le pre-visioni del tempo. (3/5/95)	**Liverpool.** The easygoing Mark Roberts yesterday morning put in an unscheduled ribald appearance on ITV. He appeared in his birthday suit in front of millions of viewers during the weather forecast.

Other information, clear in the source context of culture is that *This Morning* is a popular ITV programme with a large audience. As the effect of streaking on television depends on how many people are watching, so the journalist felt it necessary to make this information explicit in the TL text (*milioni di telespettatori*/millions of viewers). Another change of focus is the Italian tendency to comment on the news: *a tinte boccaccesche*. Literally, this is "Boccaccio style" or "licentious". This should be compared to the more indirect but factual description in English of Mark Roberts' entrance: "while Fred Talbot ... was predicting a warm sunny day". This type of change in reporting for two different cultures will be investigated further in Part 3.

Returning to the use of target-culture frames to orient the reader, the relevant sense-link may be made as above, through an equivalent institution or, as below, through intertextuality and reference to another target-culture text (emphasis added):

> Even before the close of February, the Italian government is already well into **its own "annus horribilis"**. Mr Amato's political mentor and Socialist Party leader Bettino Craxi, finally resigned after an eighth cautionary warrant from judges in the Milan scandal. *The Guardian* (24/2/93)

The Guardian writer here attempted to convey to the British readership what was happening in Italian politics during its historic year of change. With only a few lines available, he decided to make use of the expression "annus horribilis". As in the previous extracts, this functions as a metaphor:

> Object: Italian politics
> Image: annus horribilis

First the reader accesses the frames relating to and around "annus horribilis" to create an image. In this case, these words were uttered by Queen Elizabeth II, as part of her speech to celebrate her 40th anniversary on the throne. It was, in fact, "the first unforgettable speech of her reign" (MacArthur 1993:488), and began with the following words:

> Nineteen ninety two is not a year I shall look back on with undiluted pleasure. In the words of one of my more sympathetic correspondents, it has turned out to be an 'annus horribilis'.

The reader, as with any metaphor, then associates the frames of interpretation brought to mind through "annus horribilis" with the theme of the article: the current situation in Italy. The most relevant frames regarding Britain would include the Royal Family's unpleasurable year of scandal, and the public questioning of the traditional system of royal privilege.

This mental image created by the reader through this use of word metaphor is extremely effective. As it tends to operate out-of-awareness, it influences the whole of the reader's thinking, and provides the framework for the more conscious interpretation of the Italian government's "annus horribilis". In fact, with only two words, the writer has been able to convey a great deal of what was happening in Italy:

Object:	Italian politics
Image:	annus horribilis
Sense:	scandal, upheaval, turmoil, public criticism...

A further approach is to create a totally imaginary 'as if' scene, with target culture institutions or personalities. The feelings generated from the image created are then transferred, as in the cases above, to the subject matter of the article in question. In this way, an otherwise impoverished frame can generate an improved contextual effect.

Below, the Italian reader could be expected to assume that if an ex-president is saying *addio alle armi*/farewell to arms,[7] his criticism must carry some weight. However, the full weight of Bush's words, *siete una piaga per la nostra nazione*/ "you are a scourge on our nation", will be lost by most readers, as they will not have the contextual knowledge accessible to the American readers. What is deleted for many an Italian reader is the cluster of Logical values and beliefs congruent with the identity "George Bush Sr." that would then provide the intended reader with a feeling of stupor as a result of reading the article.

The journalist, in this case, has first added a commentary to explain the meaning of the National Rifles Association in this context: *l'onnipotente lobby dei proprietari di fucili e pistole in America*/"the all-powerful lobby of gun and rifle owners". Second, it is extremely newsworthy that it is a former Republican president (and Bush in particular) to have uttered these words rather than a Democrat. This carries very strong contextual effects for the American reader. Once again, to trigger a similar level of feeling, the journalist has used target-culture personalities who can create the same level of contextual effects.

The personality chosen was the director and newscaster of one of Italy's main commercial TV stations, Emilio Fede. He is well known for his extreme anti-left opinions and for his public declaration of support for the right-wing[8] leader Silvio Berlusconi, who is also the owner of the TV station. Emilio Fede would certainly be front-page news if he were seen selling the ex-communist daily, *L'Unità*, on the streets. However, the journalist felt that it was necessary to further underline the newsworthiness of Bush's profound change of belief with another, similar, analogy. Armando Cossutta, historic leader of Italy's Neo-Communist Party, would also

---

[7] This is the title in both Italian and English of Ernest Hemingway's (1929) book, producing in itself strong contextual effects.

[8] The Italian press labels Berlusconi's party "centre-right", and Berlusconi describes himself as "centre". A *Corriere della Sera* report (16/1/95) complained about the American press' s description of *Il Polo per le Libertà* as a right-wing party. The left-wing coalition is also battling for the right to call themselves the "centre". See also Derek Boothman's (1983) article 'Problems of Translating Political Italian'.

be the last person to take Emilio Fede's place on the commercial *Tg4*/"the 4th Channel news", owned, as we have said, by Berlusconi. With these two target culture examples the Italian reader is more able to sense the importance of Bush's actions:

Bush addio alle armi con rabbia	Bush Farewell to Arms with Anger
Fuoco sui pistoleros d'America: «siete una piaga per la nostra nazione». *DAL NOSTRO INVIATO* *NEW YORK* – *L'ex presidente George Bush lascia la National Rifle Association, l'onnipotente lobby dei proprietari di fucili e pistole in America. In città suona come «Emilio Fede diffonde L'Unità in piazza» o «Armando Cossutta nuovo direttore del Tg4».* (12/05/95)	Bush Fires at America's gunslingers: "You're a scourge on our nation" FROM OUR OWN CORRESPONDENT. NEW YORK. Ex-President George Bush quit the National Rifle Association, the all-powerful American lobby of gun and rifle owners. Here, in Italy, this sounds like "Emilio Fede promotes sales of the communist L'Unità on the streets". or "Armando Cossutta new director of TG4 news".

The next article actually starts with 'home' news, with the target-culture personalities re-enacting the source-culture events. In this way, the most accessible frames are introduced first, thus immediately gratifying the reader and producing strong contextual effects:

A Prime Time Premier
"Good evening. After this morning's Fraud Squad raid on News International, the Prime Minister, Rupert Murdoch, is tonight meeting with his coalition partners, John Tyndall and the Reverend Ian Paisley". It is not easy to convey what it is like to live in Berlusconi's Italy – even the most outrageous parallels fall short of the mark. Silvio Berlusconi is not Rupert Murdoch: his power and influence in Italian society far exceeds that which Murdoch or anyone else has managed to establish in Britain. Umberto Bossi of the Northern league ... is a growling blustering, regional populist just like Ian Paisley. But he is crude to a degree that would horrify the Ulster cleric: the Northern League, he is fond of saying, 'has got a hard on'. The courteous, bespectacled and quietly dressed Gianfranco Fini of the National Alliance, the second biggest group in government, would seem to have nothing in common with the British National Party's John Tyndall. Except that he too leads a neo-fascist party, the Italian Social Movement (MSI), whose members account for about nine-tenths of the National Alliance's parliamentary representation. The *Guardian* Weekend, cover story (3/12/94)

It is not only *The Guardian* that has used the Rupert Murdoch/Silvio Berlusconi analogy to help the reader in accessing similar interpretative frames. The *Corriere della Sera* actually conflates the two names (emphasis added):

COME CAMBIERÀ LA MAPPA DEI MASS MEDIA INGLESI DOPO IL VARO DELLA NUOVA NORMATIVA ANTITRUST: ECCO L'ANGLO MAMMI'	HOW THE MAP OF THE BRITISH MASS MEDIA WILL CHANGE AFTER THE NEW ANTITRUST RULES ARE PASSED: HERE'S THE BRITISH "MAMMI" [LAW]
Rupert Murdoch ha riassunto i termini della battaglia che si sta scatenando. Il «Citizen Kane del villaggio globale» è uno dei potenziali sconfitti. ...	Rupert Murdoch has summed up the terms of the battle which is breaking out. The "Citizen Kane of the global village" is one of the potential losers. ...
La Mammi inglese, infatti, vieta agli editori di avere più di due canali della scuderia Itv.	The "British Mammi", in fact, prohibits publishers from owning more than two channels from the ITV stable.
«Non riuscirete a distruggermi», tuonò **Silvio Murdoch.**	"You won't destroy me", thunders Silvio Murdoch.
Parola di Rupert Murdoch. Intervistato dalla B.B.C. alla vigilia della legge antitrust, l'uomo che vuole costruire il più grande impero multimediale del mondo ha risposto alle accuse di monopolismo come se appena prima si fosse consultato con Arcore. I paragoni tra Berlusconi e Murdoch, ovviamente, sono impossibili viste le differenze di dimensione e di strategia. Ma i due imprenditori devono affrontare gli stessi problemi. A partire dal dover far convivere idee politiche di stampo conservatore con una grande sfiducia nella classe dirigente del proprio Paese. (29/5/95)	Strong words from Rupert Murdoch, interviewed on the BBC on the eve of the antitrust law. The man who wants to construct the greatest multimedia empire in the world was replying to accusations of monopoly as if he had just consulted with the Italian premier, Silvio Berlosconi. Comparisons between Berlusconi and Murdoch are obviously impossible given the differences in size and strategy. However, the two entrepreneurs are having to face the same problems. To begin with, they have to find a way to make their conservative political ideas fit with their distrust of their own country's ruling forces.

• *Explicit → Deletion*

All the above examples have added words to the texts to make what was implicit, or in the context of culture, accessible for the target text readers. At times, as we have hinted, the reverse should also take place. Though this method does little to increase knowledge of the source culture's way of being or doing, deletion is, at times, an extremely useful solution.

This is already the case for technical culture (which focuses on transferring the "what" i.e. the content from one language to another), localization being a case in point. With regard to formal culture (how content is transferred: appropriacy, form, style) biculturals understand the importance of deletion:

> Intelligent secretaries in North America know how to delete overtly compli-
> mentary statements from Latins, and to add appropriate expressions of greeting
> and friendship from their North American bosses. Otherwise, Latinos will
> think that American businessmen will be reluctant to do business with Latinos
> who appear to be too flattering and insincere.
> Nida (1997: 37)

It is, perhaps, telling that it is secretaries rather than translators that Nida is referring to. In Zeffirelli's film, "Tea with Mussolini", an Italian businessman dictates
a letter to be typed. The very English secretary (played by Joan Plowright) inter-
venes, corrects and reduces the dictated baroque Italian commercial letter to a short
prosaic typed note. Although the EU classes the two professions together, it is only
translators who have been harnessed to the norms of fidelity to the source text.

The main interest here is at the level of informal culture (why particular words
are chosen and the values that guide the choice). And it is here that translators are
even more afraid of making their mark and manipulating the text. Wierzbicka
(1992:31-35), though, does suggest manipulating the text when translating the Russian core value *duša* ('soul'). She points out (ibid.:63), that, as the "universe of
Anglo-Saxon culture often seems to be characterized by *bezdušie*, lack of *duša*", a
faithful translation leads to an oddness for the target text reader. This would make
Venuti happy, but not the reader. She gives the example below (ibid.:31, emphasis
added) to illustrate her point. It is from Robert Chandler's translation of Vasily
Grossman's (1980) novel *Zizn'i sud'ba*/"Life and Fate":

> I'm used to looking into people's eyes for symptoms of diseases – glaucoma,
> cataract. Now I can no longer look at people's eyes like that; what I see now
> is the reflection of the **soul**. A good **soul**, Vityenka! A sad, good-natured
> **soul**, defeated by violence, but at the same time triumphant over violence.
> A strong **soul**, Vitya!... Sometimes I think it's not so much me visiting the
> sick, as the other way round – that the people are a kind doctor who is
> healing my soul.

Her advice is to use other partial synonyms or eliminate some of the references
to *duša* altogether. One possible solution might be as follows:

> ... what I see now is the reflection of the soul. Ah! Vityenka's good! Sad,
> good-natured, defeated by violence, but at the same time triumphant over
> violence. A strong soul, Vitya!...

A cultural interpreter's decision with respect to recurrence of lexical items will
depend on many factors. The first task, though, is to be aware of their existence.[9]

---

[9] Dodds (1994:16-19; 44-45) discusses in depth the importance of repetition as part of his
discussion on the analysis of non-casual language. As a general principle, he believes that
repetitions should be rigorously maintained in translation.

Secondly, s/he will have to consider whether the recurrence opens important value frames (individual or cultural) or whether the recurrence is due to a culture's orientation to such rhetorical features as repetition. Simple behavioural rules regarding when and where it is appropriate to delete cannot be given. The mediator will need to juggle with a number of shifting frames at once, and it is only from the virtual text that a feel for the right set of TC words and co-occurrences will be generated. This will be discussed further in the section on "Chunking and Cultural Values" (Chapter 8.3.3).

However, on a cline of deletions, lexical items relating to values should be allowed to remain prominent compared with those relating to style. The problem for the mediator is to decide what is purely style and what relates to important deeper (cultural) values. Arabic, for example, has a very different style orientation compared to English. It is "a language that encourages hyperbole and elaborate verbal rhetoric spoken with great flourish" (Chesanow, in Brake *et al.* 1995:128). Hatim and Mason (1997:31-4) also note that Arabic has a higher threshold of tolerance for recurrence compared to English. As a purely stylistic feature, it would seem reasonable to reduce the oddness of the TC text by varying the lexis. That being said, the mediator will always need to check that the surface features are indeed only surface in meaning and do not open important frames. In fact, Hatim and Mason themselves, in agreement with "an informal survey of mother-tongue readers", were not satisfied with the translations into English. All agreed that Arabic lexical recurrence should have been retained in translation, and that deletion deleted important values too.

One area of informal culture where deletion can be particularly useful is highlighted by Baker (1992:234): "A translator may decide to omit or replace whole stretches of text which violate the reader's expectations of how a taboo subject should be handled". Piotr Kuhiwczak (1995:236) and Hervey *et al.* (2000:24-26) cite the following as an example of how a quasi-taboo subject has been mishandled. The example also highlights the cultural problems involved in attempting to retain the form of the message. It is an extract from a bilingual promotional label that came with a pair of ladies shoes (emphasis added, translation spelling as in the original):

Original Italian label	Official translation label
Complimenti! Lei ha scelto le calzature Blackpool realizzate con materiale di qualità superiore.	Compliments! You chosed the Blackpool shoes realized with materials of high quality.
*La pelle, accuratamente selezionata nei **macelli** specializzati, dopo una serie di processi di lavorazione viene resa più morbida e flessibile.*	The leather, carefully selected in the specialized **slaughter-houses**, after different proceeding of manufacture, becomes softier and supplier.

Apart from the lexico-grammatical problems, there are a number of cultural inappropriacies. First, though, we should correct the grammar:

> Compliments! You chose "Blackpool" shoes made with high quality materials. The leather has been carefully selected from specialized **slaughterhouses**; which, after a variety of treatment, has become softer and more supple.

The point to be stressed here, following Baker's discussion on taboo subjects, is the Anglo-American sensitivity to the treatment of animals. As Kuhiwczak and Hervey *et al.* note, the British and the Americans do not wish to be reminded that their shoes began life in a slaughterhouse.

We have already discussed the Anglo-American (PC) orientation towards increased sensitivity in language to vulnerable groups of people. Sensitivity to the plight of animals is just as strongly felt. In fact, in Britain, one of the fiercest post-war protest movements ever mounted was the violent and predominately middle-class protest, in 1995, against the live export of animals to the continent. The implication for cultural mediators is that the language arguments in favour of political correctness should apply just as strongly to animals. A more culturally appropriate translation, I suggest, would be as follows:

> Thank you for having chosen *Blackpool* shoes. They have been carefully made from the finest quality materials. The selected leather has been treated to make it soft and supple.
> *or*
> Your *Blackpool* shoes have been carefully made from the finest quality materials.

Needless to say, that while the brand name *Blackpool* may sound British for the Italian reader, and hence imply tradition, quality and class – *Blackpool*, for the British, stereotypically frames cheap seaside holidays, donkey rides and sticky sweets. Clearly, it is the mediator's task to make any changes in connotation known to the company.

Newmark (1993:69) is also in favour of deletion when the language may be taken as offensive. His article focuses on the English translation of a tourist brochure advertising the beach resort of Jesolo (near Venice). His article begins with an extract from the brochure itself:

> **JOLLITY IN JESOLO**
> 'We asked: Why Jesolo for your holidays?' [...] 'Because', the well-rounded beauty in the illustration replies, 'Jesolo can be reached so easily that my husband is able to come and see me every week-end, and each time he finds me more and more sun-tanned'. I assume this is a close translation of the Italian original, and, as it is sexist, the translator should have left out the reference to the husband and confined him/herself to Jesolo's accessibility and its warm weather.

Yet, we should note that Newmark's comment "as it is sexist" lacks a performative, and contains a value judgement. His implication is that his evaluation is a general universally shared rule. Michaela Wolf (1997:127) is not alone is claiming that translators need "profound cultural knowledge" before they can begin to evaluate another culture's ways. With this cultural knowledge, it would then be possible to understand the logic of this particular culture-bound behaviour. It would have revealed the fact that it is an Italian family tradition for those who can (home-employed wives and children) to escape from the summer heat and the humidity of the urban areas to the beach, and for those that can't (husbands mainly) to join them when they can – at the weekend.

Also, many people of both sexes, it transpires from the translation, enjoy the effects of the sun's rays. Jones (2003:112) has also learnt, after four years in Italy, that "here there's no bashfulness about wanting to look good. Tanning techniques are minutely discussed and dissected. A mountain tan, I learnt, has a different depth and tone to a beach tan". Objectively, this may well be dangerous for the skin but is not necessarily "wounding or demeaning to those whose sex, race, physical condition or circumstances leave them vulnerable to the raw power of words" (Bryson, 1994:425).

The decision to delete is often made by publishers. We have already noted the (American) publishers' deletion of politically incorrect words. Translators have also discovered exactly the same fate when translating children's stories for the American market. This use of deletion is to safeguard the publisher from any adverse publicity or possible legal action. At times, though, deletion can be a publisher's weapon to actually help sell a text. For example, Umberto Eco's *Il nome della rosa* was consciously abridged for the American market:[10]

> ... getting out the American edition required a bit of additional work mainly reducing the Latin content by about 10 per cent so as not to scare off the less-erudite reader. The 200,000 hardcover copies sold so far in the US indicate that this was probably a wise move.

However, neither Eco himself nor William Weaver, the translator, were involved.

7.5 Distortion

- Lexico-grammatical distortion
- Foregrounding
- Manipulation: gains and losses
- Translation shifts: changes
- Translator/Mediator as critical reader

---

[10] Sari Gilbert, 'A Medieval Rose takes Root' in *The Washington Post*, (9/10/1983, F1:6). See also the proceedings of the conference on the translation of *Il nome della rosa*, with the participation of Umberto Eco (eds. Avirovic and Dodds 1993). Two papers in particular focus on deletions: Chamosa and Santoyo (1993) and Katan (1993a).

Distortion in itself is neither good nor bad. It is a way of directing the addressee to
what the speaker or writer considers important. Distortion does not give us an objective picture of reality, but functions like a zoom lens allowing the reader to focus
on certain aspects, while leaving other aspects in the background.

There are a number of ways that a message can be distorted in communication.
First, languages differ in how their lexicogrammars show what is thematic, what is
in focus and what is emphasized. Larson (1984:420), and the Bible translator
Kathleen Callow (1974:49-69), among others, devote useful chapters to this surface
level distortion, using the term 'prominence'. Three important areas of difference
Larson emphasizes are as follows:

> - The grammatical and lexical signals indicating the main theme of a discourse.
> - The grammatical and lexical signals indicating background or supportive
>   material.
> - How focus and emphasis are signalled.

Distortion can occur through a faithful, literal translation and by making explicit
what was originally implicit. This can happen by focusing more attention on the
word itself in the TC. For example, the word "Batman" throughout the world brings
to mind the caped crime-fighter with or without his sidekick, Robin, and Gotham
City, as well as the Batman comics and films. However, the name "Batman" is
rarely translated. The article below taken from an Italian newspaper, however, offers a translation (emphasis added):

IL VECCHIO BATMAN VA IN PENSIONE	OLD BATMAN RETIRES
NEW YORK – Tempi duri per i supereroi: dopo la morte di Superman, anche Batman sta per uscire di scena. Tra pochi mesi andrà in pensione. Lo ha annunciato Dennis O'Neil, direttore editoriale della Dc-Comics, che pubblica le gesta dell'uomo pipistrello. "Batman – ha detto – lotta contro il criminale dal 1939. E' tempo che si riposi". (20/5/93)	NEW YORK. Hard times for the superhero. After the death of Superman, Batman too is about to leave the scene. In a few months he will retire. The announcement was made by Dennis O'Neil, the publishing director of DC Comics which publishes the feats of the bat man. "Batman", he said, "has been fighting crime since 1939. It's time he rested".

The word "Batman" is repeated three times, accessing the frames already mentioned.
It is also translated, focussing attention on the two separate elements: *uomo* +
pipistrello/"bat + man". Thus, the words themselves are the object of focus, bringing into the foreground frames that were in the SC background. In this case, the
reader is encouraged to focus on the fact that he, Batman, looks like and can move
like a bat. This foregrounding can be consciously used to heighten the contextual
effects in the target culture, as we shall see in 'Manipulation'.

• *Manipulation*

The example below reports the death of Roberto Calvi. He was the director of the
Ambrosiano bank; and the Vatican church was one of its clients. He was, in fact,
known as "God's banker". However, he only became known to the British at large
due to the fact that he died mysteriously in London after his bank went bankrupt. As
The Economist reported (emphasis added):

> The bank went under, and Calvi was found hanging – murdered, most people
> think – **beneath a bridge in London.**
> *The Economist* (20/2/93)

The Economist remarked that the mysterious death was probably a murder. But,
significantly – for Italians – the article did not name the bridge. The Italian press, on
the other hand, noted the symbolic significance of the name of the bridge: Blackfriars.

> *Ed ecco riemerge l'ombra del cadavere* Once again the shadow of the body of the
> *del banchiere dagli occhi di ghiaccio,* banker with the icy eyes re-emerges. He
> *trovato morto sotto il ponte dei Frati Neri* was found dead under the bridge of the
> *il 18 giugno 1982.* Black Friars on 18 June 1982.
> *Corriere della Sera* (02/04/93)

Twenty-one years after his death (31/03/03), a *Google* search gave 379 hits for
ponte dei Frati Neri/"bridge of the Black Friars", slightly fewer for "Blackfriars
bridge" (359 hits), and only 73 hits for "Black Friars" and "bridge". The vast majority of those hits were from the Italian press. The important point to mention is that
only one of the English reports explicitly noted the connotation of the name.

In present day English, 'Blackfriars Bridge' simply denotes one of the bridges
along the River Thames. It is a dead metaphor,[11] and brings to mind no obvious
extra frames. The translation into Italian, however, distorts the name of the bridge
by highlighting the two original names: black + friars/*frati + neri*. These two words
combine two separate frames for the general reader, resulting in new contextual
effects and a strong culture-bound myth: a negative/occult connotation (black) and
a Roman Catholic connotation (friars). [12]

So, the metaphor (*Frati Neri*) changes from dead to very much alive, in the
sense that it acts as a cue to open up a variety of frames. These two words, associated

---

[11] Newmark (1988:106) divides metaphor into original, recent, adapted, stock (common), cliché
and dead: "Dead metaphors, viz. metaphors where one is hardly conscious of the image".
[12] Blackfriars Bridge lies in the borough of Blackfriars, where the monastery of the former
Domenican order of monks was sited. The Domenicans were known as Black Friars because of
their black mantle. In fact, the translation into *Frati Neri* is etymologically incorrect as *Frati
Neri* are occult friars, not *Frati Domenicani*.

with the mysterious death of a Vatican banker and member of the Masonic Lodge, access Italian frames regarding fifty years of protected criminality under the very catholic umbrella of the Italian state.

The Italian translators/journalists took advantage of this translation possibility to convey their interpretation of the event with undoubted benefit for their reader. This form of distortion is an example of manipulation. If we denominalize this word we have 'to manipulate' (*CED*):

> 1. to handle or use, especially with some skill
> 2. to negotiate, control, or influence (something or someone) cleverly, skilfully, or deviously

Many theorists are clearly concerned about the possibility of deviousness in a translation. However, the very act of translating involves skilful manipulation as in definition one, and most of definition two. Deviousness can occur in any translation. Faithful translations can often be as devious as any conscious manipulation of the text. In fact, it was due to a literal translation that President Nixon was convinced that the Japanese were devious in their negotiations. The interpretation of the Japanese prime minister's words into English, though technically correct, led to an out-of-awareness misperception and misevaluation of the meaning. The result was a well-documented diplomatic fiasco.

Hence manipulation needs to be consciously understood and used, simply because it is part and parcel of the translation process – whether 'devious' or not. This principle has already been accepted in some quarters. The word itself began to appear in translation book titles, such as *The Manipulation of Literature* (Theo Hermans 1985) and André Lefevere's (1992) *Translation, Rewriting and the Manipulation of Literary Frame*.

Conscious manipulation of the text in recent times was first proposed by Anton Popovič (1970:78) who adopted the term 'shifts' in translation to show that losses, gains and changes are a necessary part of the translation process. Shoshana Blum-Kulka (1986) devoted her chapter to "shifts of cohesion and coherence in translation", and expressed the need to change the form to cohere with target-culture values. This was also discussed by Snell-Hornby (1988:23, emphasis added), who also described the rise of the 'Manipulation School': "their starting point is the exact opposite of that represented by the linguistically orientated school ...: not intended equivalence **but admitted manipulation**".

Bassnett (1991:30, emphasis in the original), too, is included under the Manipulation School umbrella. She wrote: "sameness cannot exist between two languages", and that once the goal of equivalent effect[13] is relinquished "it becomes possible to approach the question of *loss and gain* in the translation process". Bell (1991:6)

---

[13] The importance of the theories of equivalent effect and the problems associated with them are well documented in, for example, Nida (1964), Newmark (1981, 1988), Bassnett (1991), Ulrych (1992) and Gentzler (2001).

agreed with Bassnett, stating that equivalence is a "chimera". He went on to say that "Something is always lost (or, might one suggest, 'gained'?) in the process". "Gains" in translation, Bassnett continued (1991:30) "can at times enrich or clarify the SL text as a direct result of the translation process".

Gentzler (2001:199), commenting on his own (forthcoming) anthology of translations, closes with the following: "the contributions show how translation is always a partial [sic], with translations selecting certain elements – literary or ideological – to emphasize, thus demonstrating the partisan nature of their activity". In fact, as Holmes (1973:68) noted, different translators, however faithful to the source text will invariably produce their own and different renderings of almost any text. Any back-translations will further add to the differences, and, therefore: "To call this equivalence is perverse".

Rather than any search for equivalence we should return to Benjamin's main point. A cultural mediator, whether translator or interpreter, should concentrate on author intention or text function within a context of culture – and concentrate, in particular, on the facilitation of communication between original author and end receiver. So, rather than manipulation, it would be more useful to talk about the particular needs or objectives of the various parties involved (from original text author to commissioner, mediator and hypothesized reader). Susan Šarčević (2001: 49, emphasis in the original), noted for her work on legal translation, and the very real problems of translating EU law into Croatian, concludes one of her papers with the following remark: "the goal of translators of the *acquis* [Community law] should not be fidelity to *the* source text but fidelity to the single instrument [of law] and to one's own language".

Returning to the language of negotiation, it is clear that (small) concessions will be made in return for (large) returns that satisfy the more important needs of the parties. Hence, rather than 'manipulate' it would be more useful to define 'facilitate' and 'mediate':

facilitate:	to make easier; assist the progress of
mediate:	to resolve differences by mediation
	to be in a middle or intermediate position

While we are on the subject, having introduced the idea of the translator as a cultural interpreter, we should be clear about what 'interpreting' means:

interpret:	to clarify or explain the meaning of
	to construe the significance or intention of
	to convey or represent the spirit or meaning of

We shall now look briefly at how two literary translators have facilitated communication. In both cases they have resolved differences of perception and interpretation by making it easier for the target reader to appreciate the author's (probable) intention and the text function. In the first case, we have already noted how conscious deletion of *Il Nome della rosa*, was employed to reduce the cognitive effort of reading every passage in Latin boosting North American (and no doubt all English-speaking) sales. Clearly, though, as a text becomes more accessible, so the contextual effects are usually reduced. Yet, when the translator acts as a critical reader, increased accessibility can also mean increased contextual effect.

The example below (Katan 1993b) is a particular case in point. It is an extract from Shakespeare's *Troilus and Cressida*. Pandarus is telling Cressida that he thinks the beautiful Helen loves Troilus better than she does Paris. He continues:

Pand:	I think his smiling becomes him better than any man in all Phrygia.
Cress:	Oh! he smiles valiantly.
Pand:	Does he not?
Cress:	O! yes and 'twere a cloud in autumn.
Pand:	Why go to then.
	(Act I. II. 132-138)

The footnote to "a cloud in autumn", written by K. Palmer (1982:111), the editor of the Arden Shakespeare, is: "I do not understand this riposte". The result is that for Palmer, and presumably for many lay readers, there is little or no contextual effect. The relevance has been lost. The following translators, on the other hand, acting as critical readers have 'understood' this riposte.

Italian translation	Back translation	Translator
Sicuro, come una nuvola d'autunno.	Certainly, like an autumn cloud.	Mario Praz, 1940
Oh sì! e pare una nuvola d'autunno.	Oh yes! and it seems like an autumn cloud.	Demetrio Vittorini, 1990
Sì. Come una nuvola d'autunno.	Yes. Like an autumn cloud.	Cesare Lodovico, 1965
Sì, e in autunno ci sono le nuvole.	Yes, and in autumn there are clouds.	Luigi Squarzina, 1977

In all four cases, they have interpreted the text for the reader by adding a conjunction or link verb to the riposte. As a result, in Italian we now have an explicit ironic simile which can render an array of potential contextual effects:

Object:	Troilus' smile
Image:	clouds in autumn
Sense:	wet, unexciting, dismal...

We now know that Cressida is not particularly enthralled by Troilus' smile. In Squarzina's translation, "Yes, and in autumn there are clouds", Cressida's feeling of 'So what?' is even clearer.

Returning to *Il nome della rosa*, William Weaver's translation has been praised by some of the most important literary critics (reported in Katan 1993a:152-53). Yet, it is clear that he has distorted the original text. Apart from what has already been mentioned, in many small ways he has distorted the Englishness of Guglielmo/ *William*, so that he becomes even more "*Our* learned and ironic monk-detective" (*The New York Times* 5/6/1985, emphasis added) than in the original. One example will suffice:

Umberto Eco (1980:71)	Literal translation	William Weaver (Eco 1984:63)
[Ubertino:] *"Castiga la tua intelligenza, impara a piangere sulle piaghe del Signore, butta via i tuoi libri".*	[Ubertino:] Chastize your intelligence, learn to weep over the wounds of the Lord, throw away your books".	[Ubertino:] Mortify your intelligence, learn to weep over the wounds of the Lord, throw away your books".
"Tratterrò soltanto il tuo", sorrise Guglielmo. *"Sciocco di un inglese".*	**"I will** only **keep** yours", smiled William. "Foolish Englishman".	**"I will devote myself** only to yours," William smiled. "Foolish Englishman".

Weaver, here, has "improved" on William's original witticism, by overtranslating the verb *trattenere* ('to keep', 'to detain', 'to hold', 'to use', Picchi 2003) with "devote myself to", letting the reader fully enjoy Ubertino's reply. This ironic exaggeration fits in well with English style. Leech (1983:145-46) suggests that "The best safeguard against deceit is to make sure the utterance is so much at variance with context that no one could reasonably believe it to be 'the whole truth and nothing but the truth'". He continues by pointing out that "English speaking culture (particularly British?) gives prominence to the Maxim of Tact and the Irony Principle". Weaver's use of this prominence has certainly heightened the contextual effects for the target reader.

One final, and extreme, example of translating cross-culturally is illustrated in the following article. There was a very strong worded comment made in the *Corriere della Sera* (20/07/93) regarding a *Newsweek* report about the Italian military presence in Somalia in 1993. In fact, the headline ran:

ITALIA SOTTO ACCUSA: «INFORMAVA AIDID»	ITALY ACCUSED: "AIDID GIVEN THE TIP-OFF"
Intervista al ministro Fabbri: 'Sono solo nefandezze, ridicole e maldestre.	Interview with government minister Fabbri: "Just slanders, ridiculous and ham-fisted".
Durissimo attacco al nostro contingente dal settimanale "Newsweek" che parla di spionaggio a favore del generale e contro l'Onu.	*Newsweek*'s heavy attack on our contingent, and reports of spying for the General and against the UN.

> *ROMA. "Noi traditori, noi amici di Aidid? Noi che lo facciamo fuggire prima del bombardamento americano su Mogadiscio? Sono accuse ridicole, paradossali, talmente inconsistenti e gracili che si commentano da sole. Non vale nemmeno la pena di indignarsi". Fabio Fabbri, ministro della Difesa è perentorio. Legge l'articolo del prestigioso 'Newsweek' e trasecola. Le parole della corrispondenza sono dure come pietre.*
>
> *Puntano il dito contro il contingente italiano, reo di aver fatto scappare il leader somalo, proprio quando i soldati statu-nitensi lo avevano in pugno. "Il signore della guerra è riuscito a mettersi in salvo, solo perché gli italiani lo hanno avvertito. Altrimenti, a quest'ora sarebbe nostro prigioniero".*
>
> *L'accusa lanciata da 'Newsweek' è pesantissima. E infamante: «Gli italiani fanno spionaggio a favore del generale Aidid e contro le Nazione Unite».*

> ROME. "Us traitors, us friends of Aidid? Us, who let him escape before the American bombardment on Mogadiscio? These are ridiculous accusations, crazy, and so weak and unfounded that they speak for themselves. It's not even worth getting indignant about". Fabio Fabbri, Minister of Defence is blunt and to the point. He reads the article in the prestigious *Newsweek* and is dumbfounded. The words in the report are as hard as stone.
>
> The finger is pointed right at the Italian contingent, guilty of having allowed the Somali leader to get away just when the US soldiers had him in their hands. "The Warlord managed to get to safety only because the Italians had warned him; otherwise he would be our prisoner by now".
>
> The accusation hurled by *Newsweek* is scathing. It is slanderous: "The Italians are spying for General Aidid against the United Nations".

Most of the *Newsweek* article, however, does not focus on Italy, and the title itself is in terms of "a team effort". The extracts relevant to Italy and its action are reported below:

> ### THE PITFALLS OF PEACEKEEPING IN WAR-TORN SOMALIA, MAKING A MESS OF THINGS IS A TEAM EFFORT.
>
> [Aidid] may have been tipped off. A US-run surveillance network has more than once caught members of Italy's UN contingent warning Aidid about operations against his forces, three western sources told *Newsweek*. Did the Italians warn Aidid? "Draw your own conclusions", said a senior US official.

Distortion of the words is particularly noticeable here. The American text does not directly, *puntare il dito*/"point the finger" or *sparare a zero* (literally 'shoot point blank'). However, "draw your own conclusions" leaves the reader with only one relevant implicature to consider. The contextual effects within an Anglo-American frame are that Italy is being blamed for the incident, at least until there is any evidence to the contrary.

The Italian report is an extreme example of a translation shift, and the target translation bears little or no formal equivalence to the original article. However, the Italian journalist/translator has more than likely interpreted the illocutionary force of the article. So, through manipulation (or rather, mediation and facilitation) the Italian reader has the opportunity to respond to the illocutionary force as *Newsweek* and the senior US official intended.

The next chapter discusses translation shift under the umbrella term of 'chunking'.

Chapter 8. Chunking

The aim of this chapter is to:
* introduce the concept of chunking
* show how chunking can access frames
* give examples of chunking up, sideways and down
* give practical examples of chunking in translation:
  - to establish text function
  - for culture-bound lexis, behaviour and orientation
* discuss the mediator's translation/interpretation tasks according to Logical Level

8.1 Local Translating

Hönig (1991:87) noted that trainees: "love to learn and apply systemic language rules. But by applying these 'absolute' micro-strategic rules, they leave the mental reality of translating". Trainees (in particular first year) tend to translate like machines, according to absolute semantic equivalence and, like machines, translate at the level of technical culture. In fact, one area where machine translation is used successfully is for the translation of explicit or restricted language texts, such as legal contracts and weather bulletins. Wilss uses the term 'local' to describe this type of decoding and encoding translation, and 'global' to describe cognitive re-creation based on frame analysis.

The terms 'local' and 'global' come from Robert Sternberg's (1984:283) work on processing behaviour and intelligence. He claimed that "more-intelligent persons" tend to spend more time in "global (higher order) planning", a higher order processing which takes the wider context into account. Their "less-intelligent" colleagues, on the other hand, spend more time, like first-year translation trainees, on "local (lower order) planning".

The idea of local interpretation has also been put forward by Brown and Yule (1983:59). Their Principle of Local Interpretation is, however, universal. It "instructs the hearer not to construct a context any larger than he needs to arrive at an interpretation". This Principle is very close to Wilson and Sperber's (1988:140) Relevance Theory. They suggest that a partner's contribution will always aim at relevance, but that optimum relevance depends on the hearer being able to obtain "maximal cognitive effect for minimal processing effort". Both local and global processing strategies will follow these universal principles, but the results will be completely different. It is quite possible that local translating actually involves more cognitive effort than global translating.

A good example of local translating comes from one particular student translation of Kenneth Grahame's children's classic, *The Wind in the Willows*. All the characters in this story are animals, and all are simply called by their animal names, such as 'Mole', 'Ratty' and 'Toad'. An Italian student's draft translation of "Mole" was "La Talpa",[1] the Italian term for the burrowing animal. At a local level this is the correct translation. The Italian feminine gender *la* does not necessarily mean that the Mole in question is female. A male mole is also *la talpa*. The opening sentence in the original text tells us that the Mole in question is a male:

> The Mole had been working very hard all the morning, spring-cleaning **his** little home. First with brooms, then with dusters; then on ladders and steps and chairs, with a brush and a pail of whitewash; till **he** had dust in his throat and eyes, and splashes of whitewash all over **his** black fur, and an aching back and weary arms.

Many languages (including Italian) require that all adjectives, articles and pronouns follow the gender of the noun they precede and not the person they refer to as in English. By correctly following the lexico-grammatical rules of Italian, rather than interpreting at the global level, the Italian reader is left with a mental picture of a mole (feminine gender), cleaning the home (feminine gender). The reader relates this new information to the most relevant frames relating to 'spring-cleaning' and 'home', and naturally (in Italy, at least) pictures a female mole. This image is further confirmed as (Ms.) Mole continues spring-cleaning for the rest of the page. Indeed, it is not until the second page that the lexico-grammar allows Mole to be male: "'This is fine', **he** said to **him**self'".

At this point, the reader is left momentarily confused and has to make mental sartorial adjustments for the mole. There are two simple ways to avoid this particular problem: with the addition of an explicit cue or the deletion of the distorting element. In the first case, the addition of *signor*/'Mr' as the opening words would immediately open up the appropriate frame for the reader. The following 'Moles' could then be with the feminine article. Alternatively, by simply deleting the article, we have *talpa*/'mole', and the animal remains neuter until we have the explication on the second page.

This particular student's translation leaves no doubt that she had made no mental image of the story while translating, but was influenced by her mother-tongue lexico-grammar rules. This form of translation is a typical case of local processing. Similar strategies are adopted by intermediate second language students. They tend to process information according to the surface text, without taking the wider context or the meta-message into account.[2] It is this difference in the level of thinking which distinguishes a good translator or mediator from one who applies systemic language rules. Unfortunately, many trainees have learned to treat translation just like any other academic exercise, as a series of small chunks of information, regardless of the fact that translation practice books stress the need for global pre-reading. For example, C. Taylor (1990:193) states in capitals that "RE-READING of the

---

[1] I am grateful to Christopher Taylor for this example.
[2] See Katan (1989) for results of research into foreign language student use and understanding of messages and meta-messages.

text [is necessary] until the concepts are clear". Dodds (1994:49, emphasis in the original) says that "Reading the text means reading it *at least* three times". He also explains in detail what a translator should be looking for and doing during the various reading phases. Professional translators tend to opt for a more cyclical approach, and rarely ever read the text in its entirety. They get a feel for the virtual text through actual translation. Once they have a feel for the text, they will then return to the beginning and translate at professional speed.

Clearly, in all cases, attentive reading is a prerequisite to translation,[3] while Neubert and Shreve (1992:49) go further, talking about "reading for translation". We have, of course, already talked of the translator as 'critical reader'. However, although the necessary behaviour is clearly spelled out, there are few specific guidelines on how to read to access frames, which will, in turn, produce the overall picture and virtual translation. One procedure which can aid trainees in both accessing these frames and in understanding the meta-message is called 'chunking'. This procedure is also essential as a first step in mind shifting from one cultural reality to another.[4] As we briefly mentioned in Chapter 4.8, this is an essential prerequisite for a cultural mediator. More specifically, by consciously applying the chunking procedure, trainees should be able to move away from the direct one-to-one absolute semantic equivalence of Mole/*la talpa* towards a virtual text in which 'the Mole' and all other lexis will actually be visualized. Once the translator has visualized the scene s/he can begin to find the appropriate words to help the TC reader to see Mole/ *signor Talpa* as the author, Kenneth Grahame, would have intended.

8.2 Chunking

- Chunking Up
- Chunking Down
- Lateral Chunking

The term 'chunking' has been taken from computing, and basically means to change the size of a unit. A unit can be made bigger (chunking up) which means that as more comes into view so we move from the specific to the general, or from the part to the whole. Moving in the other direction, we chunk down from the general to the specific or from the whole to the parts.

In NLP, chunking has been developed to show two points (O'Connor and Seymour 1993:146-48). First, meaning not only depends on context or frame, but there is also a continuous cline of frames: from sub-atomic to universal. Second, this cline reveals how the language of the sensory-based real world is linked to general, vague and metaphorical concepts. We can link, for example, the sensory-based "To live or to die" to the more vague "To be or not to be" by chunking up to

---

[3] See, for example, Newmark (1988:21) and Bell (1991:161).
[4] See also Katan (2001b, 2002) for more on mind shifting.

higher levels. In this case we move from the Logical Level of Behaviour to an expression of Identity.

In terms of language and translation, cultural interpreters need to be able to chunk up and down to establish the wider and narrower frames of reference of the source text. Chunking down is necessary for componential analysis to better understand the semantic field of, for example, individual words. The Meta-Model is an example exercise in chunking down. Cultural mediation also requires the translator to be able to chunk up, above the individual and different cultures, to more generic, culture-inclusive frames. Finally, mediators must be able to chunk sideways to find comparable frames in the target culture, as the journalists in the previous chapter did.

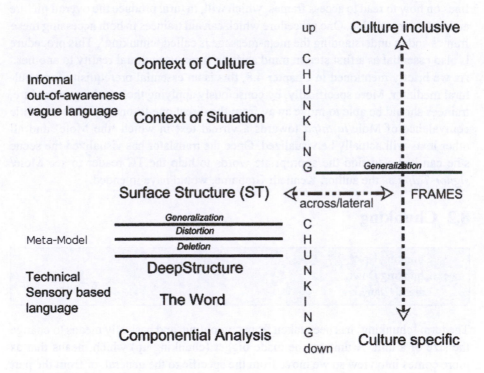

Figure 26. Chunking Overview

The process of moving from one level to another involves making associations. Mediators will need to exploit their bi-cultural competence to develop a feel for which associations or frames are the most appropriate in each particular context. As Neubert and Shreve (1992:61) mention: "Matching cultural frames is an extremely important and difficult translation task". The 'feel' for appropriacy or matching is accounted for by the Principle of Local Interpretation and Relevance Theory. This means that the first frames to come to mind will, in general, be those which are most relevant.

A number of translation theorists have suggested a chunking strategy. We mentioned earlier (in Chapter 7.2) that Baker proposed looking for a more general word (chunking up) to overcome the problem of non-equivalence. Newmark discusses the importance of chunking down, which he calls cultural componential analysis (1988:83). However, neither says how a trainee translator might be aided in acquiring this strategy.

NLP researchers are particularly interested in the 'how'. As we mentioned in Chapter 3, they have adapted Bateson's Logical Typing to make a model of human communication. One of the basic distinctions in learning that need to be noted is between the observable behaviour (knowledge 'what') and the not directly observable strategies (knowledge 'how').

The question NLP researchers tackled was: "How can we learn to chunk?" The answer lies in the use of a series of formulaic procedural questions. These questions access interrelated frames in a way similar to hypertext. Trainees who learn to apply these questions move away from the local word-for-word translation and are in a position to mediate between contexts of cultures.

• *Chunking Up*

Here we begin with the specific and move to the general. As an example, let us think of 'an armchair'. To step up to the next level, i.e. to a more general level, one would ask the question:

> What is (an armchair) an example of (in this context)?
> *Or alternatively:*
> What is (an armchair) part of (in this context)?
> What is (an armchair) a type of (in this context)?

A logical answer could be 'chair'. To move up to the next, more general, level, the same question is asked:

> What is (a chair) an example *or* part of *or* a type of?

In this particular case we arrive at 'furniture'. This is not the only answer, but in each case there will be a relevant link (in Sperber and Wilson's use of the term 'relevant'). If we are more interested in functional relationships the first chunk-up would be 'a seat', because an armchair functions as a seat. To chunk up again we ask: "*What is* a seat *an example of?*" Here, we could say 'support'. The more we chunk up, the more general the class, and at a certain point the generalization becomes so general that it becomes meaningless.

• *Chunking Down*

This is the reverse operation: from the general to the specific. The question to ask is:

> What is a specific example of furniture?"

This may lead us from furniture, to chair and armchair. We can descend further to a particular type of armchair, and contextualize the armchair geographically, finally down to a particular armchair in the living room. We can also chunk down to the micro level by looking at the constituents:

> What are the constituent elements of *the armchair in the living room?*
> What is *the armchair in the living room* made up of?

We would then talk of the material, the design and so on.

The hyponyms included also give the translator valuable information about what is *not* included, and hence translatability at that level. For example, if one were to say "I had breakfast", then what is included in the super ordinate (English) breakfast may well be very different from that on the Continent. The translator's virtual text will provide information on what gaps need to be filled when translating into any other language, e.g. with "English", "cooked" or simply "good" breakfast.

• *Lateral Chunking*

This is stepping sideways or laterally in much the same way as Edward De Bono's Lateral Thinking (1970). This procedure is particularly useful for cultural mediation, and provides the type of mental gymnastics or mind shifting required to change cultural frame. In chunking sideways, the mediator is looking for alternatives that can more readily access SC frames. The question to ask here is:

> What is another example of this class of things (in this context)?
> *or*
> What is at the same level as armchair?

Asking this question about 'armchair', we could get: dining-room chair, sofa, and so on. Chunking sideways from 'chair', we arrive at stool, table, etc.

Bell (1991:240-54) provides a procedural model of the process. Though he does not specify how the model could be practically applied, his listing of encyclopaedic entry relationships is very similar. (figure 27 below).

As can be seen from the NLP chunking arrows on the right, Bell has, in fact, separated two levels of chunking. Both above and below the level of the word in question one can chunk up, down or laterally. Bell distinguishes between two types of 'isa' (sic) meaning: either "is a" or "has". In the first case, 'isa' is a case of chunking up, as in "the tiger is a (member of) animal". In the second case, 'isa' (has as an example) is a case of chunking down. 'Has-as-parts' and 'applies-to' are also different examples of chunking below the word. As Bell points out, a property ('has-as-parts') is a defining characteristic, while quality ('applies to') is a variable association and will depend on the context.

The links can be made in a number of ways. What is important is that each time links are made, relevant concepts are being added providing a series of interlocking frames. It is this skill that actively goes on inside a professional translator's head and is an essential part of the global translation process. Trainees should practise chunking as a mental exercise in itself. Once students become consciously competent, the strategy can become internalized to become the unconscious strategy performed by professional translators, interpreters and other mediators. We will now look more specifically at how the chunking process may be applied to translation.

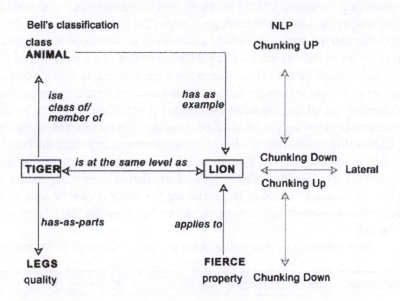

Figure 27. Bell's Procedural Model and NLP Chunking

8.3 Global Translation and Mediation

- Text Function
- The cline from Communicative to Semantic translation
- Culture-Bound Lexis
- Culture-Bound Behaviour
- Culture-Bound Value Orientations

• *Text Function*

When a reader reads, s/he brings a genre to mind. The closer the text being processed is to a known text type, the more fully it can be processed and a virtual translation be made. Chunking makes this procedure conscious. When trainees are faced with a text, however short, and this would include sentences used exclusively for grammar translation, they should chunk up asking the following question:

What is this text an example of?

This would clearly give an idea of the text type or genre, and access similar known texts. Bell (1991:171) points out that by accessing the genre or text type, sense can be made of the new text, while Carl James (1988) asserts that recognition of genre and its rules is the translator's most important task. Neubert and Shreve (1992:48) note that one of the telling findings of cognitive psychology is that "text comprehension only occurs when the comprehender actively conjectures or projects the semantic content contained in the text".

For many (e.g. Newmark 1981, 1988; Bell 1991), understanding of the text type is the principal key to translation strategy. Scarpa (2001:69) clearly states, "it will always be true that the approach to the translation of an article on astrophysics or even an essay on ethnolinguistics will be different to that of a translation of Dickens". Indeed, Riccardi (2002:115) suggests "to a great extent, technical texts must be translated or interpreted *semantically* and non-technical texts *communicatively*". The 'ill-formed' use of the universal quantifier ('it will always be true') and the modal operator of necessity ('texts must be translated') in these extracts should, of course, lead us to query the universality of these statements, as indeed the Functionalist translation scholars do. Yet, Katharina Reiss, one of the pioneers of the Skopos Functionalist theory also agrees that successful translation "seems dependent upon identifying the *source-text typologies*, including the text's appeal or aim, and reconstructing those elements in the receiving culture" (in Gentzler 2001:72, emphasis in the original).

As a further exercise in establishing genre students can chunk down and ask:

> **What are the constituent elements of this text?**

This will help in focusing on register and the other features that make the particular text under study an example of a particular text type. Lateral chunking would encourage trainees to consider other texts which would come under the same text-type heading.

The more this is done, the more students begin to get a feel for where the borders between one text type and another are. It also helps trainees to realize that a text-type label is often misleading, as a text will, in general, be polyfunctional (Vermeer 1978; Hatim and Mason 1990:141; Woodsworth 2002:131-32). A text, therefore, will not be bound by prescriptive norms that determine either a communicative or semantic translation. As Snell-Hornby (1988:31) states: "Blend-forms" rather than a rigid typology of texts "are part of the conceptual system and not the exception".

• *The Cline from Communicative to Semantic Translation*

As mentioned at the beginning of the chapter, a virtual translation is a useful metaphor for the vision a translator has of what the target text and its associated frames will be like. The cultural interpreter, faced with choices, will test the alternatives against the feelings s/he has related to the virtual text. Through chunking, the translator can decide whether to produce a more TC-oriented or SC-oriented translation. At the two ends of the cline we have the communicative and the semantic translation. The communicative translation, as expounded by Newmark (1981:39) is reader-centred, pragmatic and functionally oriented.

On the other hand, the semantic translation focuses on the original words of the author, remains faithful to them and ignores the real world of the target culture. In fact, Newmark (1988:46, emphasis added) mentions that the translator wishing to produce a semantic translation: "may translate less important words by culturally neutral third or functional terms but *not by cultural equivalents*". In this case the translator will chunk up from the specific SC to a more general, all embracing term. This term will tend to be less culture specific the more we chunk up.

If, instead, the translator wishes to produce a more TC-oriented translation, using (in Newmark's words) a cultural equivalent, then the translator will continue chunking. First it will be necessary to chunk laterally, to move away from the image of the source text. Then the translator will chunk down to move towards the sensory world of the target culture. The generally unconscious (out-of-awareness) operation is illustrated in the following (more technical) diagram:

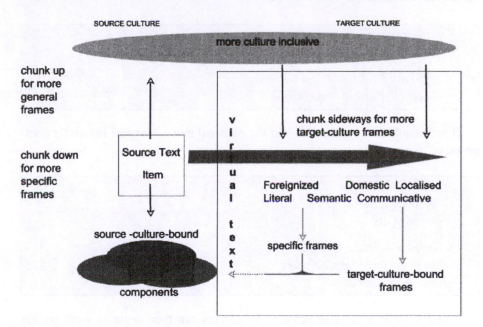

Figure 28. Chunking to Generate Choice

The last three sections of this chapter focus on how chunking can be used with regard to:

- culture-bound lexis
- culture-bound behaviour
- cultural orientations

The extracts are from a daily newspaper and from popular fiction. However, the principle remains the same, whatever the blend-form of text.

8.3.1 Culture-Bound Lexis

In Sue Townsend's (1985) popular work of fiction, *The Secret Diary of Adrian Mole Aged 13 3/4*, Adrian has a friend by the name of Maxwell House. The translator can chunk laterally, and quite legitimately simply borrow the name: "Maxwell House". This would, in general, be the most logical strategy with regard to personal names.

However, the fictional name here is not casual, and nor are the connotations. Christopher Taylor (1990:106-7) notes that the contraposition of Maxwell (first name) and House (surname) create a comic effect. Maxwell is a normal first name, yet the collocation with House accesses a totally different frame, that of instant or freeze-dried coffee. So, a translator, wishing to retain the comic effect will need to isolate the contributing factors by chunking up. We find, by chunking up, that "Maxwell House" is 'a member of' (the class of):

> • personal name
>   (name + surname)
>
> • brand of coffee
>   (*Maxwell House* instant coffee)

If we chunk down, we notice that the personal name *Maxwell House* 'is composed of' (connotes):

> • Name: *Maxwell*[5]
>   distinction, class (UK and US)
>   comedy (US)
>
> • *Maxwell + House* together:
>   is a brand name for a beverage
>   has a comic effect

The translator with these semantic constructs can then begin to work on the target culture. S/he will have a feel for what is needed from the variety of frames

---

[5] The following excerpt from a baby names' list gives a rough idea of the qualities of Maxwell (The TV series was only shown in America, though): "**origin:** Old English, **meaning:** from the influential man's well, **traits:** Maxwell strikes most people as a name for either a wealthy, quiet, older gentleman or a bungling, overconfident detective, like TV's Maxwell Smart". http://www.americanbaby.com/ab/ab/babynames/babyName.jhtml?babynameld=13661

More recently, well after Townsend's book was published, the word 'Maxwell' accessed another frame for the British: Robert Maxwell, the owner of the Mirror Group of Newspapers and embezzler of the Pension Funds. He made front-page news with his suicide, and the subsequent criminal investigations into his family's dealings.

making up the virtual text and will then open up, for example, Italian frames by asking an appropriate procedural question. In this case, the chunking down question to ask is: "what is an example in the Italian culture of a brand name of coffee, which could be read as a distinct name + surname, and create a comic effect?" An answer might well be *Illy Caffè*, Italy's most up-market brand of coffee.

This method would result in a domesticated or communicative (i.e. target culture oriented) translation. The virtual text, though, would tell us that Maxwell House is English, and that the whole context of culture is British. Clearly, having a friend called Illy Caffè would give him a continental flavour.

The natural step is then to ask, chunking sideways: "What is at the same level as Maxwell House and Illy Caffè?", i.e., what would create a comic effect for the target reader, but at the same time would remain source text oriented? An inspired answer was "Teo Lipton" (Corbolante 1987). For an Italian, Lipton Tea, or rather *Tè Lipton* is synonymous with Anglo-Saxon culture. The advertising of the product in Italy is also deliberately comic: an American speaking Italian with a strong mid-Atlantic accent.

The diagram below shows the principal stages in chunking:

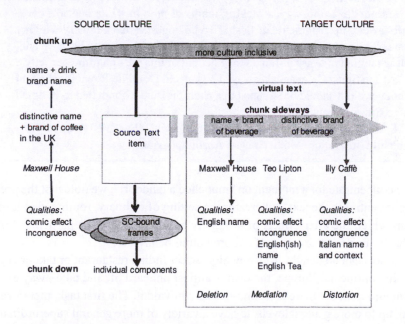

Figure 29. Translating and Chunking: Maxwell House

8.3.2 Culture-bound Behaviour

The following is an extract from *The Guardian* (22/03/93), which gives an account of a terrorist attack in Belfast in 1993. The journalist gives a little background to the scene after the bomb attack (emphasis added):

BOMB BLASTS HOLE IN TOWN'S SENSE OF CONTENTMENT

Erland Clouston finds Warrington's citizens confused, resentful and wondering why they were chosen to suffer a second IRA atrocity.

"Got any ID?" The squat shadow guarding the gates of Warrington's Territorial army barracks warily studied the plastic card in the magnesium glare of a road called, of all things, O'Leary Street.

Was he nervous? The caretaker shrugged. "Now and then," he admitted. He was an ex-professional soldier. He knew a bit about bombs and violence. Half a mile away, uptown civilian Warrington was in an emotional daze, shaken rigid at the hole punched in the easy-going contentment of a community previously famous only for its breweries, its soap factory, and its Rugby League team.

A notice on the door of the Postern Gate Tavern, just around the corner from the first Bridge Street bomb, announced "In respect for the dead and the injured we shall not be opening this evening". Yet Gaffer's Bier Keller, 50 yards nearer the explosion, was packed. "It's a form of defiance, isn't it?" a brunette in a black cocktail dress declared over the blare of disco music.

A bit further down Bridge Street, HGV driver Mark James munched a tandoori in a doorway, watching teams of men in white overalls carefully sweep up fragments of flesh. "To be honest, I had a big cry with my mates," said 34-year-old Mark. "I don't think the troops should be in Ireland, but what kind of sense of fun do they get out of this? It's an effing atrocity".

At the Spicy Chicken takeaway, 17-year-old Dominic Reynolds thought whoever did it should be strapped to a chair that had a bomb tied to it, timed to go off in an hour.

"That's too quick," snorted a female colleague. "Bastards. A three-year-old child, just before Mother's Day. Absolutely sick".

If we concentrate for a moment on "munched a tandoori", we note that the predicate is not central to the text, but creates the setting of ordinary, routine, day-to-day life from which the after-effects of a tragedy are witnessed. This particular 'ordinary life' though is an example of culture bound behaviour.

A tandoori can be bought from any high-street Indian restaurant or take-away in Britain. In continental Europe, the dish is almost unheard of, and take-away eating is still uncommon. So, there is no one-to-one equivalent. The first task, therefore, is to chunk up to more general levels, to have a variety of more general superordinates. (See figure 30)

Having established a variety of superordinates, we translate those that seem most promising, and then begin to chunk down in the target language (in this case, Italian), till we find the expression that best fits both the virtual text and the original array of feelings and reactions to the SC text. It may be that the translator will wish to chunk down further to a more sensory-based concept, to let the target reader fully savour this contraposition of daily life and tragedy. (See figure 31)

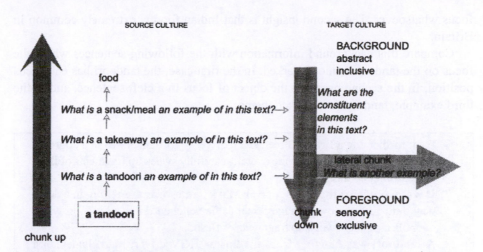

Figure 30. Chunking Questions

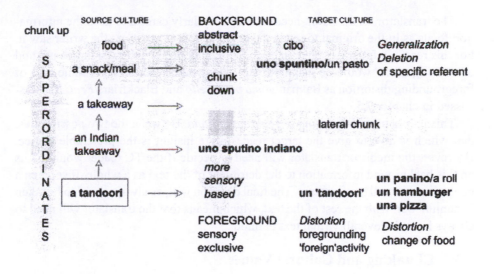

Figure 31. Translating and Chunking: Tandoori

The (domesticated) target culture snacks will, in general, be disregarded for two reasons. First, the frame is an eyewitness report of what was seen – and neither a hamburger, *panino*/a filled roll, nor a *pizza* was seen. In these cases, generalization is better than distortion.

Second, if it has been decided to translate this piece (whether for trainee practice or for eventual publication) then, one of the aims of the translator as cultural mediator will be to help the reader gain an insight into another culture. One insight is already implicitly given, that eating in the streets is a normal activity. The 'munched a tandoori' is simply part of everyday life, with no foregrounding or information focus whatsoever. The second insight is that Indian food is extremely common in Britain.

Compare this background information with the following sentences where the focus on the tandoori is more marked. In the first case, the tandoori has end focus position. In the second case it is the object of focus in a cleft sentence, and in the third example, tandoori is a marked theme:

> 1. A bit further down Bridge Street, HGV driver Mark James was in a doorway watching teams of men in white overalls carefully sweep up fragments of flesh as he **munched a tandoori.**
> 2. **It was a tandoori that HGV driver Mark James was munching** in a doorway a bit further down Bridge Street as he watched teams of men in white overalls carefully sweep up fragments of flesh.
> 3. **A tandoori was hanging from his lips** as HGV driver, Mark James, in a doorway a bit further down Bridge Street, watched teams of men in white overalls carefully sweep up fragments of flesh.

The translator, as mediator, needs to be particularly careful to keep the information focus as in the original to retain the construction of reality as the writer saw it. For this reason a fuller explanation, such as "a tandoori, which is an Indian method of cooking meat" would be inappropriate. This would lead us to the same area of foregrounding distortion as Batman/*uomo pipistrello* and Blackfriars/*Frati Neri* discussed in chapter 7.5.

This leaves us with *spuntino* or *spuntino indiano*. Between the two possibilities, that which is able to give the target reader more insight is the preferable choice. However, the mediator/translator will need to decide if the TC reader would focus on this background information to the detriment of the text as a whole. If so, then a generalization will be necessary. The final decision will, as always, need to be taken in conjunction with the rest of the text, which means that the translator will need to always have the overall virtual text in mind.

8.3.3 Chunking and Cultural Values

We have already noted Newmark's (1993:69) problem reading of a "close translation". If we apply a Logical Levels analysis, it becomes clear that mono-cultural TC readers will always interpret and evaluate according to their own hidden, out-of-awareness value system. (See figure 32)

So, we can see, an unmediated translation will logically lead the reader to an ethnocentric set of values. This is hardly surprising if we take the Attribution Theory and Logical Levels Theory into account. Readers can only tolerate just so much difference. Any more difference and they (we all) become ethnocentric. The translator as mediator needs either to be conscious of his/her own tolerance limits and deal with them (see Chapter 12) or already be in a (meta) position to direct the reader to a comparable frame.

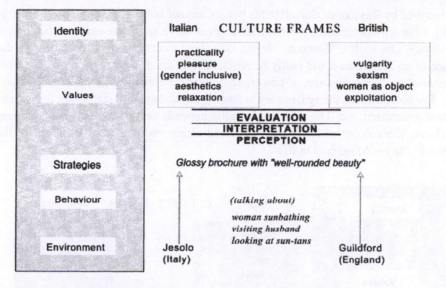

Context of Situation: Tourist reading a holiday pamphlet advertising a summer resort

Figure 32. Translating without Mediating Values: suntan

For another example of cultural values (and how to mediate them) we return to the American writer, Tom Wolfe, and his chronicling of life in New York (1990). Not unusually, there are many references to the price of things (emphasis in the original):

> [Sherman McCoy]: "Once you had lived in a $2.6 million apartment on Park Avenue – it was impossible to live in a $1 million apartment! Naturally, there was no way to explain this to a living soul. Unless you were a complete fool, you couldn't even make the words come out of your mouth. Nevertheless – *it was so*! It was ... an impossibility!"
>
> He [Sherman McCoy] sat with his $650 New and Lingwood shoes pulled up against the cold white bowl of the toilet and the newspaper rustling in his trembling hands, envisioning Campbell, her eyes brimming with tears, leaving the marbled entry hall, on the tenth floor for the last time, commencing her descent into the lower depths.

The dollars, on a technical level can be translated into any other currency with no problem whatsoever. But in what frame are we going to understand $650 shoes? An American, within his or her own cultural frame is likely to find the question strange. It is natural (for an American) to talk about the price of things; and, if it is at all possible to attach a price to something, as approximate as it may be, that price will surely be mentioned.

For other cultures this is not so. This is part of the out-of-awareness culture Hall cited in his Triad of Culture. A French reader's reaction to this use of money is well described by Raymonde Carroll in his book *Cultural Misunderstandings* (1988:128-29), which was originally written with an even more apt title *Evidences Invisibles*: "Money", he writes, "Someone should talk about money. For a French person, the face of an American could easily be replaced by a dollar sign. A sign of 'incurable materialism', of arrogance, of power, of 'vulgar', unrefined pleasure".

For an American though, money is simply a useful symbol signifying the type of shoe, apartment, etc. The underlying value depends on the context. Here, dollars indicate the amount of effort, sacrifice, and ultimately success that Sherman, the hero in the book, has had in life.

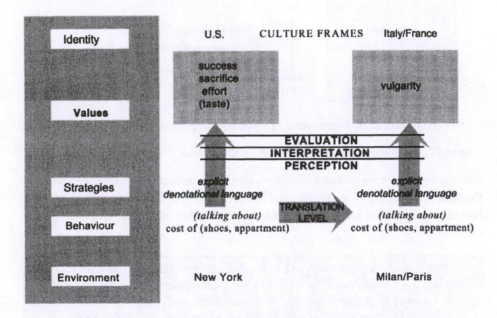

Figure 33. Translating without Mediating Values: money

As we can see, a direct translation leads the reader to a different set of values, and hence distorts the writer's intention. This is an example of the danger of a faithful translation, and highlights one of the problems of 'foreignizing' a text. The idea of 'foreignizing' a translation to *prevent* ethnocentrism comes from Lawrence Venuti (1995b:4). He defines the concept as follows: "Foreignizing ... means taking the reader over to the foreign culture, making him or her see the (cultural and linguistic) differences. ... A foreignizing strategy seeks to evoke a sense of the foreign".

However, in this case by leaving the foreign money as money, the translation will only *strengthen* the ethnocentric view that all American eyes are made up of Donald Duck dollars. As some pointed out during the debate with Venuti on the subject (Schäffner 1995:32): "what is intended to be a non-ethnocentric ... translation ... can be read as being extremely ethnocentric" (Douglas Robinson), and "literalism is not always a good way of being non-ethnocentric" (Baker). Robinson and Baker give three examples of seemingly non-ethnocentric translations:

Language	Faithful translation	Interpretation
Mexican	Like water for chocolate	Meaningless in English, and 'perpetuates a stereotype, a quaint, picturesque, Hispanic mind or mentality'
Spanish	The world is a handkerchief	'perpetuate[s] condescending, first world stereotypes about a third world culture'
Arabic (from the 1st Gulf War)	The mother of all battles	'a literal translation from Arabic which provided a convenient stereotype'

This means chunking up to those core values underlying the symbol (money) in America.

Essentially the translator will need to be aware of the SC frame from within which s/he can interpret 'money'. That being done, the translator will look for a sign, or criterial equivalent, in the TC which fits the overall virtual text and which relates to this particular value frame. The words 'luxury' and 'designer' in Italian or in French would both act as a cue to accessing the same value frames as the American 'money'.

The chunking procedure to mediate the evaluation of money is explained in the following diagram. The chunking-up tells us the general values that the shoes and the apartment are a member of. Lateral chunking takes us to the TC frame. Then we chunk down, in Italian or French in this case, to specific examples (criterial equivalents) which satisfy these values:

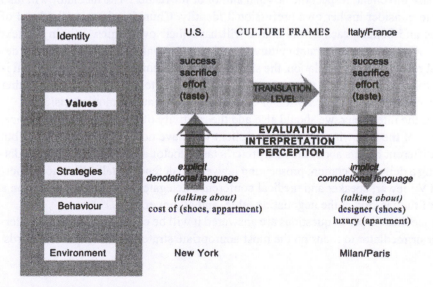

Figure 34. Chunking to Mediate Values

A cultural mediator can now help the TC reader to access the same values (success, effort and taste) by substituting the sum of money with "luxury", "desirable" or "designer". We now have (back translated):

> [Sherman McCoy]: "Once you had lived in **a luxury** apartment on Park Avenue – it was impossible to live in a **merely desirable** apartment! Naturally, there was no way to explain this to a living soul. Unless you were a complete fool, you couldn't even make the words come out of your mouth. Nevertheless – *it was so*! It was ... an impossibility!"
>
> He [Sherman McCoy] sat with his New and Lingwood **designer** shoes pulled up against the cold white bowl of the toilet and the newspaper rustling in his trembling hands, envisioning Campbell, her eyes brimming with tears, leaving the marbled entry hall, on the tenth floor for the last time, commencing her descent into the lower depths.

8.3.4 The Logical Levels of a Mediator's Task

To conclude Part 2 on Translation and Mediation, we can begin to clarify the mediator's task. In line with the Functionalist theory of translating I would say that the most important question to ask when called on to translate or interpret is "what is going on?" This question can be asked at every level of the Logical Levels Model. One can chunk up from the Environment or down from Identity to get more information, all of which will then be fed into the virtual text.

The mediator should also be able to note where or at which level there is more "going on" or, where there is more at stake. Chunking laterally, what is more apparent: the context of situation or that of culture? Will it be more important, for example, to please the client, respect the original author or the reader? The mediator will also have to consider his/her own professional identity. Chunking down to the level of values and beliefs, each of the above will have their own ethics. Within the text itself, what are the important culture-bound or other values? What is/was the declared reason for the translation, the skopos (the communicative goal)? If the goal is not explicit then it will be the mediator's responsibility to make it so, through either enquiry and insistence on a brief, or by making visible autonomous decisions.

For the interpreter, we should also add the relativity of appropriate performance. In each of the following situations the client will have not only differing needs but also different beliefs about the interpreter's task: doctor and economic migrant discussing a delicate operation; prosecuting lawyer and defendant; talk-show host, guest and TV viewer; speaker and medical conference delegates; supplier and buyer on a tour of the factory, at the negotiating table, and at dinner.

Once these types of questions are answered it will be easier for the cultural interpreter or mediator to focus on the most appropriate strategies and choice of words.

LEVEL	What is going on?	within the culture	in the context of situation
Identity *Informs*	Who is involved in this 'going on'?	National, ethnic, gender, religious, class, role	The author, the text, the mediator, reader, commissioner/client
Values Beliefs *Informs*	Why are these things going on?	The hierarchy of preferred value-orientations Beliefs about identity and about what is 'right' or 'standard'	The intentions, the skopos the message, the presuppositions
Strategies *Informs*	How are these things going on?	General, spoken/written, styles, habits, customs appropriacy, rules	Pragmatics: the illocutionary force house rules, individual style, register, discourse
Behaviour	What is it that is going on?	Individual acts, actions	The choice of words: The visible text The locution
Interacts with **Environment**	Where and When is this going on?	Environment (physical, political, social), period, people, setting, artefacts, intertextual links	The lexico-grammatical resources, the genre

Figure 35. The Mediator's Task by Logical Level

Part 3 will focus on the array of possible orientations that make up value clusters. The more sets of values the mediator is aware of, the more able he or she will be to infer meaning behind behaviour in any context.

Part 3. The Array of Frames
   Communication Orientations

Edward Sapir's (1994:119) lecture notes focused on the needs for the future. He was very interested to know what it was that motivated certain cultural configurations, or rather patterns of behaviour:

> We must therefore discover the leading motivations for these configurations – the master idea of culture. These leading motivations constitute the culture in an anthropological sense. They are the fundamental dynamic concepts involved in the notion of cultural patterns. Nothing in behaviour, cultural or otherwise, can be understood except as seen as in reference to these configurations.

Edward Hall (1990:184) had the same questions in mind:

> Some time in the future, a long, long time from now when culture is more completely explored, there will be the equivalent of musical scores that can be learned, for each type of man or woman in different types of jobs and relationships, for time, space, work, and play ... What are the sets, isolates, and patterns that differentiate their lives ...?

Part 3 looks at some of the leading motivations, and investigates some of the sets, isolates and patterns. The term used principally in this Part will be 'orientation'. What is of particular interest is how these orientations act as frames in which the transmission and reception of messages are interpreted, and also how cultures vary in what aspects of reality are considered.

Chapter 9 discusses orientations in general, comparing them with values, norms and cultural myths.

Chapters 10, 11 and 12 focus on the two most consistently relevant orientations for translation: communication and action, and show how they affect preferred listening, speaking and writing styles. The chapters also contain a brief description of how the other orientations also affect language across cultures.

Chapter 9. Cultural Orientations

The aim of this chapter is to:
- discuss cultural myths:
  – the myths cultures have about themselves
  – the myths cultures have about others
- introduce a taxonomy of orientations

9.1 Cultural Myths

- English cultural icons
- Norms v Values
- Examples of national stereotypes

Rollo May, in his book *The Cry for Myth* (1991:6), follows Barthes (1993) in suggesting that there are two modes of communication: myth and rationalistic language. Myth, according to May, "orients people to reality, transmits societal values, and helps the members of the society find a sense of identity. Myths give significance to our existence and unify our societies". This type of myth is culture itself, as explained also by Schneider (1976:203):

> Where norms tell the actor how to play the scene, culture tells the actor how the scene is set and what it all means. Where norms tell the actor how to behave in the presence of ghosts, gods, and human beings, culture tells the actors what ghosts, gods, and human beings are and what they are all about.

Kramsch (1993:235, 207) points out that most people do not realize that meaning is based on a "social construction of cultural myths". The heroes, for example, that Hofstede talks about (Chapter 2) are often part of a culture's myths – what a society tells itself and believes about itself:

> On the reality of facts and events that constitute a nation's history and culture is superimposed a cultural imagination that is no less real. This cultural imagination or public consciousness has been formed by centuries of literary texts and other artistic productions, as well as by certain public discourse in the press and other media.

The influence of the press and other media in framing meaning, or spinning, should not be understated. 'Spinning', according to *Time* magazine, "means describing a reality that suits your purposes. Whether it resembles the reality we all share is an issue that doesn't even arise". [1] The second part of that definition is a spin in itself, and is a perfect example of mythical thinking, riddled with Meta-Model violations.[2] Susan Pierce (unpublished), a sociologist from Gettysburg college, notes that even the difference between a slightly differently spun early and late edition of a particular *New York Times* article resulted in two different national collective memories of the same event.

The idea of myth, as mentioned earlier, was first made popular by Barthes in 1957 in his volume *Mythologies*. His understanding of myth is much wider (1993:109): "Myth is a type of speech". This myth is metalanguage, the language used to speak about what is perceived: "it points out and it notifies, it makes us understand something and it imposes it on us" (ibid.:117). Quite how much we are influenced by myths can be seen from any investigation of the collective memory.

---

[1] www.time.com/time/poy2000/mag/spin.html
[2] 'Reality' is a nominalization; 'we all' contains a universal quantifier, but the 'we' is not inclusive – and we are left to imagine which members of the population are included; e.g., patriotic, educated Liberal White Anglo-Saxon Protestant American adults (WASPS). "Share" is unspecified; in what way, how, to what level are we supposed to share the perception, interpretation and evaluation of what is actually really going on? And so on.

We rely on our memory to tell us what is true or normal. Logically, though, what is in our memory will always be a deletion, distortion and generalization of reality, regardless of the level of social or ideological spinning.

With regard to myths in collective memory *The Daily Telegraph* (04/10/95) asked readers to name a dozen cultural icons which characterized Englishness. Clearly, *Telegraph* readers will have their own culture (definitely HAP rather than LAP, and politically centre-right). It is Britain's best selling quality paper, with over one million readers, and is therefore representative of a HAP culture. What is more interesting, though, is that for the vast majority of the one million readers the top five icons mentioned have very little to do with their actual life in England.

Reader Cultural Icons	Social Reality
• fish and chips	Non-English take-aways are much more popular such as Chinese, Indian, hamburgers and the ubiquitous kebab.
• cricket on the village green	A minority sport, played on an ever dwindling number of village greens.
• pubs – usually with low ceilings and/or warm beer	These are still popular, though the 'local' is unlikely to have low ceilings. Cold lager, ice beer, wine, etc., outsell warm British beer.
• church bells	Heard more in sleepy villages than in town. The number of churches open is at an all time low.
• the Last Night of the Proms	A British, rather than English institution, epitomizing nostalgia for a once powerful Britain. The last song of the last night is: "Rule Britannia".

In most of the cases the images evoked have much more to do with a distorted memory of an idealized reality. 'Reality' is also another nominalization (in this case a de-adjectival noun) as is 'life', and so a clearer question would be "for whom are the above icons real?" or "Who actually lives with, or among, these icons?" The answer is a tiny minority of the population still living in what remains of upper-middle class rural England (except for the fish and chips). The majority of the people (including *Telegraph* readers), whatever their class, live in towns. One real urban event ritual played out every Saturday night, and affecting many more people, is described below in an article by Theodore Dalrymple only two weeks after *The Telegraph* survey:

It is when you see the English enjoying themselves that you realize the futility of life ... Is this a city without mirrors? The girls in their cheap and flimsy finery (I mean cheap in the aesthetic, not the financial sense), who shiver in the cold as they trip along. How the Italians would despise and laugh at them. Many of the boys, especially those with shaven heads, look angry with an unfocused, non-specific anger which might erupt if you were to look at them a

> fraction too long in the eye ... There is vomit in the gutters already (the whole
> city smells of fried takeaway food) and a pool of as yet uncongealed blood
> next to a broken bottle of Budweiser ...There is trouble on the dance floor
> and the doormen move in with surprising agility ... A body-building type is
> emphatically escorted off the premises out into the relatively fresh air. I fol-
> low him outside where a drunk girl with fat legs in cream satin culottes is
> being carried over the road by her boyfriend, draped over his shoulder like a
> sack. She looks sea-sick; soon she will want to vomit and then she will know
> that she has had a really good night out.
> *The Sunday Times* (22/10/95:3.3a)

This is a picture of a different England, and much closer to the Lower Autonomy Professional culture discussed in Chapters 4 and 7. However, many of the LAPs, and even more of the HAPs – who may eat Chinese or Indian, live in a town, drink canned Bud or wine, and get drunk on a Saturday night – still cherish the thought of rural England. Many of these myths will, of course, be related to actual past practice and are then romanticized. As a result, the beliefs behind the behaviour of playing cricket, listening to church bells, etc. remain in the collective imagination if not in the collective practice.

Trompenaars and Hampden-Turner (1997:32) give a very practical example of this paradox, differentiating between what he calls values and culture-bound norms. Both are part of our imprinting, but norms are the practical rules guiding actual behaviour, whereas value-laden beliefs are ideals which we allow to be overridden by more pragmatic norms:

> For instance, in one culture people might agree with the value [read belief]:
> 'Hard work is essential to a prosperous society'; yet the behavioural norm
> sanctioned by the group may be: 'Do not work harder than the other mem-
> bers of the group because then we would all be expected to do more and
> would end up worse off'. Here the norm differs from the value [or rather,
> belief].

Trompenaars, in fact, confuses beliefs with core values. The value 'work' is still satisfied in the new norm, but is part of a constellation of values that will also contain the more valued 'collective good' and 'prosperity'. To a large extent though, norms represent the intersection or habitus between desired values, based on historical response to perceived needs, and the behaviour linked to the external environment of the present. Environments (like hairstyles) can change quickly along with behaviours (e.g. global entertainment pursuits). The driving motivations (core values, meta-programs) dictating *how* the behaviour is to be framed will already be fossilized. Though they do not change, they do accommodate new behaviours and environments.

Values, then, may refer to past fossilized norms. The important point to be underlined here, though, is that our sense of identity also includes icons which have never had anything to do with our own lives – except as spectators. Most readers in

The Daily Telegraph poll mentioned, for example, at least three from the following list as being a part of the English identity. Yet the majority will never have had any direct involvement with any of these English people or events for pragmatic normative reasons (status, cost, time, other interests). Television, of course, has brought many of these icons into our homes. What is important for identity is not what we directly participate in, but what lies in the collective memory, the myth:

• The Queen	• Henley	• Trooping the Colour	• The Chelsea Flower Show
• The Queen Mother	• The Boat Race	• Remembrance Day	• Crufts
• Carols from Kings College, Cambridge	• Wimbledon	• Aintree	

Kramsch (1993:208) notes that what a culture believes about itself will override any evidence to the contrary. She gives a salient example about her compatriots (ibid.:207): "The French individualists? Any trip to Paris will show the visitor how conformist the French can be in dress and fashion. And yet, everyone believes that 'il n'y a pas plus individualiste que le Français'. That myth is tenacious".

This example of self-created and self-perpetuating myths, could equally apply to the Italians. They also believe in their creativity and individual taste – and in particular when it comes to fashion. However, a *Sunday Times* fashion report (29/12/91:3, 3) suggests that the Italians (seen through British eyes) are even more collectivist and conservative than their French cousins: "The Italian look is the most classic and easy to wear. The Milanese are smart but never outrageous, more relaxed than the French, although they do all wear the same thing" (see also Jones, 2003:112).

Kramsch suggests that after having distorted perceptions of our own culture, for example through the media and the collective memory, we then compound the distortion by perceiving a second culture through the distorted perception of ourselves. Each ring around "real culture" in figure 36 takes us further from what is real, and more into the realms of myth. Intercultural dialogue doubles the myth-creating potential. Cultural interpreters mediating these two rings of distortion will need, in turn, to 'right' some of the distortion to allow the communication to develop as intended (see figure 36).

Hence, as Kramsch shows, the German image of America is partly an anti-image of itself: desolation and alienation, as seen for example in Wim Wender's vision of America. This is a particularly important point for translation. As Venuti (1995b:47) says: "...since all translation is fundamentally domestication and is really initiated in the domestic culture, there is, therefore, a fundamental ethnocentric impulse in all translation". Translations are commissioned according to whether they fit in to the target culture's (distorted, generalized and deleted) perception of the source culture. In this way, the ethnocentric perception of the other culture is strengthened, and further domesticized.

It is extremely difficult, as we have already mentioned, to perceive another culture, except through our own ethnocentric map of the world. Bromhead's view of Britain, which can only perceive other cultures in terms of British dominant values is a case in point. If we move to continental Europe and the United States, there is still the myth of the Englishman with his bowler and umbrella, tea at four, and so on. For those who have never been there, England is a place of nobility and tradition.

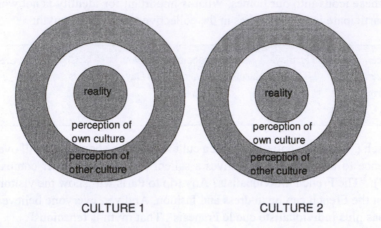

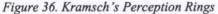

CULTURE 1   CULTURE 2

Figure 36. Kramsch's Perception Rings

This is not surprising, as most day-to-day news about the country abroad is in terms of the Royal Family, nobility, and prestige events. The worldwide concern over the death of Princess Diana was a perfect example. It is still difficult to imagine a Theodore Dalrymple type article attracting any space at all in a foreign newspaper. What fascinates is what is believed to be quintessentially English. Most countries, for example, no longer have a monarchy or nobility (at least formally), so the view of Britain is, to an extent, seen through the image these countries have of themselves: a republic, a 'cycling' monarchy, and so on.

Alfredo Castelli, mentioned earlier, notes exactly the same with regard to Europe and its love of American western comics:

> Europeans never got tired of western comics as has happened in the U.S. Italy, in particular, produces the world's best-selling Western strip Tex (500,000 copies monthly)…The explanation is simple: we tend to want (and to mythicyze) what we don't own, and in Europe there is nothing comparable to the Western epics.[3]

Not only *Tex* but every other locally produced 'American' cartoon strip is created according to "the iron rule" of comic writing. Alfredo Castelli (ibid.), who created *Martin Mystère/Martin Mystery* continues: "Though many of his adventures are set in Italy, Mystère 'is' American and 'lives' in Washington Mews N.Y, where he has been a lecturer more than once".[4] Castelli explains that this allows the

---

[3] http:/www.bvzm.com/english/conferenzaeng.html.
[4]In fact, Italian fans of this particular French named hero rang the doorbell of 3 Washington

local European reader to identify with the character (in terms of personality) while at the same time accept situations that at home wouldn't be possible: "we can *pretend* to believe, for instance, that in America, a university professor like Martin Mystère can become famous and maybe rich; were the professor Italian, it would seem rather unrealistic, as we *do* know the problems that afflict our school system (probably the same as in American schools, but we can pretend not to know them)".

In the same vein, literary rewritings:

> ... are of crucial social and cultural relevance because they determine the 'image' of a literary work when direct access to that work is limited or non-existent. Maria Tymoczko (1995) [argues] that the selection of texts and the particular mode of representation create an image which readers across the world take metonymically for that culture as a whole. (Hermans 1999:128)

Hence, the local (young) reader is likely to generalize the distorted interpretation of America as a country where academics are rich and famous to the rule that all professionals are rich and famous.

As Barthes (1993:124-25) noted, once something is taken out of its original logical world, and translated into (or for) a new world it becomes the object of mythicization. He explains how response to the built environment varies according to context. As a tourist wandering through the Basque country, he says, "I do not feel personally concerned" about the architecture. An individual house "does not call out to me, it does not provoke me into naming it. He simply notices that each house will reflect a common style, and will be part of a wider system with its own history. At home in Paris, though, on seeing "a natty white chalet" at the end of "the rue Gambetta or the rue Jean-Jaurès" (i.e. on seeing a 'translation' of the original) he feels obliged to mythicize it: "I feel as if I were personally receiving an imperious injunction to name this object a Basque chalet: or even better, to see it as the very essence of *basquity*", even though (as he notes), there is little that is actually Basque left: "the barn, the outside stairs, the dove-cote, etc. – has been dropped; there remains only a brief order, not to be disputed". The few idealized features are immediately, and indisputably, distorted and generalized into his own culture-bound map of the world, and then evaluated against a French, Parisian or other non-Basque world.

Continuing with Italy, we can investigate the way in which news about England is actually portrayed through the media. First, the Italian press tends to stereotype English behaviour in terms of understatement, composure and so forth. An example is the following Italian newspaper headline focusing on Major Rose's English self-composure during a sniper attack when in Sarajevo:

The examples below (all taken from quality papers or weeklies) actually use

---

Mews looking for the American hero. Alfredo Castelli wrote to the real resident apologizing: "The real resident – a Mr. Claxton, working for NYU – was very kind with me, and answered that, indeed he was surprised by the strange pilgrimage to his home, still stranger as the pilgrims were Italians". http://www.bvzm.com/english/conferenzaeng.html

Un cecchino spara contro Rose. L'inglese non si scompone «Non si uccide così un generale». *Corriere della Sera* (20/05/94)	A sniper shoots at Rose. The Englishman is unruffled: "That's not how you kill a general".

English words to heighten what they perceive is not part of their culture:

   The advertising in Italy of British products is, naturally, selective. The whiskey

ROMA *– sul registro dei visitatori ha scritto semplicemente «Charles», senza nessuno dei titoli che pure gli spet-terebbero.* **Understatement***, la chiamano in inglese. Ovvero quella straordinaria capacità di smorzare i toni che distingue il vero* **gentleman** *da un qualunque nuovo ricco.* *Corriere della Sera* (27/03/92)	**ROME** – in the visitor's book he simply wrote "Charles", without any of the titles he had the right to use. **Understatement**, that's what they call it in English. It is that extraordinary capacity to reduce the pomp which distinguishes a real **gentleman** from any ordinary *nouveau riche.*

ANCHE IL «SIR» IN LISTA DI ATTESA *Panorama* (3/3/92)	"SIRS" ARE ALSO ON THE WAITING LIST [meaning that nobility in England also has to wait its turn when booking for restaurants]

PUB DESERTI PER LA GUERRA IN TV *Ma a volte prevale lo* **"humor"***:[5] un negozio vende maschere antigas per cani. A Bond Street le* **ladies** *che si incontrano a fare lo* **shopping** *si vestono come la regina con molto colore blu ...* *Corriere della Sera* (24/1/91)	PUBS DESERTED DUE TO THE WAR ON TV But at times "humour" prevails: a shop sells gas masks for dogs. In Bond Street the ladies who meet to go **shopping** are dressed like the queen with a lot of blue...

A TU PER TU CON LA REGINA *... il segretario del Quirinale Sergio Berlinguer, legato all'* **establishment** *attraverso la moglie Liza [non può mettere] piede nel salottino dove invece possono entrare liberamente i cani* **corgi***, golosi dei biscotti di cioccolata che saranno serviti alla regina e al presidente [Cossiga] insieme al tè* **Earl Grey***, ai*	FACE TO FACE WITH THE QUEEN ... the Italian President's secretary, Sergio Berlinguer, linked to the **establishment** through his wife Liza [is not allowed to put] his foot in the drawing room, whereas the **corgi** dogs can freely enter, greedy for chocolate biscuits which will be served to the queen and to the president [Cossiga] together with **Earl Grey** tea, cucumber and

---

[5] Note the American spelling of humour.

> | | |
> |---|---|
> | *sandwich al cetriolo, al salmone affumicato, ai pasticcini alla panna. Prima e dopo il tête-à-tête con Cossiga la regina sarà occupatissima: per seguire alla televisione la champion stakes, corsa a siepi all'ippodromo di Cheltenham e per esaminare con il Cancelliere dello Scacchiere il budget.*
Panorama (3/3/92) | smoked salmon **sandwiches**, and cream cakes. The queen will be extremely busy both before and after the tête-à-tête with Cossiga: watching the **Champion Stakes**, the hurdles at the **Cheltenham** race track, on TV and examining the **budget** with the Chancellor of the Exchequer. |

is for refined people with exquisite taste. The cars are exclusive: Range Rover and Jaguar. The tea is Twinings, which gives the impression of a population of public school boys drilled in conformity, sobriety and tradition. This particular brand is actually drunk by a small minority of the population, even fewer of whom would be sure of the pronunciation without reading the label.

On the other side of the Channel, it is the British who believe Italians to be the traditionalists, particularly when it comes to food. Notice, for example, how the stereotype has been used effectively by *The Daily Telegraph*, to attract readers to take part in a competition to watch the 1990 World Cup competition in Italy:

> **PASTA CRUISE ITALY FOR DE PASTA AND DE FOOTBALL**

The popular image is also denoted by the lack of variety of food metaphors to describe someone of Italian origin, as noted by Irving Allen in his publication *The Language of Conflict* (1983:59): meatball, spag, spaghetti, spaghetti-bender, spaghetti-legs, macaroni. Yet, the Italians might also note that it is the British who (traditionally) believe in "meat and two veg", who go abroad to find (and relish) restaurants in Spain, Majorca, Crete, Corfu, and a host of other British holiday haunts specializing in:

> **TEA JUST LIKE MUM MAKES IT**

> **ALL DAY BACON AND EGG BREAKFASTS**

All countries retain elaborate rituals, which they tend to note only in other countries. The Italians, for example, note the elaborate ritual concerning, for example, the Christmas event in Britain precisely because the Italian equivalent for the 25th December is not so detailed:

> **Constituent elements for 25th December:**
> **UK and Italy**: The Christmas tree, nativity scene, holly and missletoe, midnight mass; Father Christmas, chimney, a good lunch, presents
> **UK**: carol singing, the Christmas stocking, The Queen's speech at 3 p.m., the

> Christmas lunch (turkey, stuffing, Christmas cake, Christmas pudding, flambé, money, mince pies). Anything else, as an advert for plump Christmas turkeys states, "just isn't Christmas".

Clearly, many individuals and groups have other 'variant' rituals, which equally form part of the same culture. Also, Ritchie (1981:223) points out that "what a people believe themselves to be is not invalidated by lack of performance in keeping with the belief". We will now turn to what lies behind the beliefs cultures hold, and what motivates people within their cultures to behave in their various patterned ways.

9.2 Cultural Orientations

In this section we distinguish between general orientations, also known as learning styles, and culturally formed orientations.

• *Orientations*

> • Meta-programs
> • Chunk Size
> • Separate shapes – Single picture

The word 'orientation' is another case of a nominalization (in this case, a de-verbal noun), suggesting a frozen state. The verb 'to orient' means "to adjust or align oneself according to surroundings or circumstances" (CED 1991). People, in fact, tend to orient their way of doing things consistently over a wide range of circumstances, according to their character or personality. In NLP, these orientations are called 'meta-programs': "perceptual filters that we habitually act on" (O'Connor and Seymour 1993:149). Orientations tend to be consistent, but this is not always the case (emphasis in the original):

> Metaprograms are systematic and habitual, and we do not usually question them if they serve us reasonably well. The patterns may be the same across contexts, but few people are *consistently* habitual, so metaprograms are likely to change with a change of context. What holds our attention in a work environment may be different from what we pay attention to at home.

In Chapter 4.7, we noted that much of our imprinting is fully developed by the end of school-age. Likewise, meta-programs, and hence personality, are relatively fixed by that stage. But, as O'Connor and Seymour mention above, our orienting can change across contexts.

It is our orientations which govern *how* perception is generalized, distorted and deleted. A well-known example of how an orientation distorts reality is as follows:

a bottle that has been opened and drunk from, can either be perceived as being half empty or as half full. Our perception of it has little to do with that actual bottle and the quantity of liquid inside (reality). Perception is distorted to fit in to the way we orient ourselves to the world in general. Our perception of the contents ultimately has to do with who we are. In this case, optimists or pessimists.

One of the orientation meta-programs suggested in NLP regards chunk size. Chunk size has already been introduced during the discussion on local and global translation styles. The polar-opposites of chunk size are the generalities (the context) or the details (the individual words themselves). This chunking orientation has an important place in Gestalt therapy, and is now understood to be a major factor in learning.

To see how we normally and unconsciously chunk, we can look at the following example. The diagram can be perceived in at least four different ways, depending on this local/global orientation.

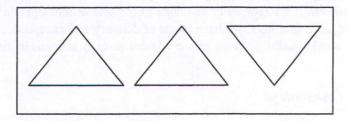

Figure 37. Testing Orientation: Local or Global?

Example descriptions of this diagram are as follows:
1. there are three separate shapes
2. there are some triangles, one upside down, in a picture
3. there is a picture with two identical triangles and one upside down
4. there is a (single) picture of triangles

All four answers are correct, just like the bottle being half-full or half-empty. This sorting of information comes under a variety of names[6] depending on the field and the application. The terms below come from Gestalt psychology, cognitive psychology and linguistics. Apart from 'sorting' and 'mismatching' which is only to be seen in NLP literature, the other terms now tend to be used across all disciplines:

Separate Shapes	Single Picture
• field independence	field dependence
• sorting for different	sorting for same
• mismatching	matching
• deductive	inductive
• specific	general

---

[6] See also Laura Gran's (1989:94) study on brain hemisphere function for a further list of names.

• local/part	global
• analytic	synthetic
• atomist	holistic

Response number one shows a definite orientation towards the left hand column (separate shapes) while number two begins to notice the differences first, and then focuses on the picture. Answer three, instead, begins at the right, focusing on "a single picture" and then moves to the left. Finally, response four focuses exclusively on the whole: the gestalt. "Gestalt" actually means an organized configuration or pattern of meaning.

It should always be remembered that the idea of polarization is a convenient model (deleting, generalizing and distorting the far more complicated reality), and that any orientation is, as the word suggests, no more than a tendency towards one way of perceiving the world. Creating taxonomy of these orientations is necessarily limiting. However, if we remember that none of the orientations operate in isolation, and that, as in grammar, we have levels of delicacy and exceptions, then we can begin to build a useful grammar primer of what actually happens in the context of culture.

• *Cultural Orientations*

| • Kluckhohn's Value Orientations |
| • Hofstede's Four Dimensions |
| • Brake's Ten Orientations |

• *The Cultural Iceberg*

A cultural orientation is a shared meta-program: a culture's tendency towards a particular way of perceiving. The orientation or meta-program influences how reality is modelled, i.e. which aspects are to be generalized, distorted and deleted. An orientation is based on a number of complex and interrelated (and sometimes conflicting) values, which, as we have seen, are also in dynamic relation with a number of other factors. At the heart lie the fixed and totally-out-of-awareness core values. Figure 38 illustrates the relation between values and orientations.

There are relatively few core values. These generate a number of more context-defined values, (see figure 38 overleaf). A cluster or set of these specific values will result in a certain orientation towards or away from a particular way of perceiving, interpreting and behaving in a number of contexts. Reality, then, within a specific culture will be distorted, generalized and deleted to suit the cultural orientation.

Many authors (and disciplines) have come up with a taxonomy of cultural orientations. Florence Kluckhohn (Kluckhohn and Strodtbeck 1961:341) coined the term 'value orientation', and defined them as follows:

> Value orientations are complex but definitely patterned (rank-ordered) principles, resulting from the transactional interplay of three analytically

distinguishable elements of the evaluative process – the cognitive, the affective, and the directive elements – which give order and direction to the
ever-flowing stream of human acts and thoughts as these relate to the solution of 'common human' problems.

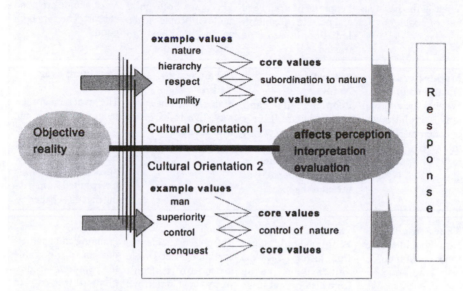

Figure 38. Cultural Orientations

She (ibid.:10-20) suggested that there were five basic problems or concerns common to all human groups, and also mentioned a sixth common human problem, the
conception of space, but admitted that the orientation had "not been worked out
sufficiently well to be included":

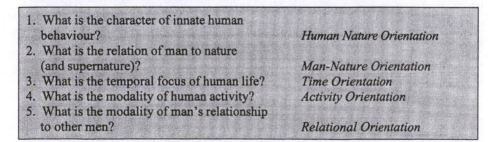

1. What is the character of innate human
   behaviour? *Human Nature Orientation*
2. What is the relation of man to nature
   (and supernature)? *Man-Nature Orientation*
3. What is the temporal focus of human life? *Time Orientation*
4. What is the modality of human activity? *Activity Orientation*
5. What is the modality of man's relationship
   to other men? *Relational Orientation*

For each of these questions there are three possible responses that constitute a
culture's (dominant or variant) value orientations (see table in page 232).

It should be pointed out that every culture and every individual will, in theory,
have access to every orientation, but will tend to favour the use of one orientation
over the others, and conversely will have difficulty in comprehending the other
orientations. A cultural mediator, on the other hand, should have almost equal access to all orientations. This may of course result in disorientation through too much
choice, as we shall see in Part 4.

Concerns/ Orientations	Possible responses based on core out-of-awareness beliefs		
Human Nature What is the basic nature of people?	**Evil** People ae basically bad and need to be controlled. People can't be trusted.	**Mixed** There are both good and evil people in the world. you have to check people out.	**Good** Most people are good at heart. They are born good.
Man-Nature Relationship What is the appropriate relationship between man and nature?	**Subordinate to Nature** People really can't change nature. Life is largely determined by external forces, such as fate and genetics. What happens was meant to happen.	**Harmony with Nature** Man should, in every way, live in harmony with nature.	**Dominant over Nature** The great human challenge to conquer and control nature. Everything from air conditioning to the "green revolution" has resulted from having met this challenge.
Time Sense How should we best think about time?	**Past** People should learn from history, draw the values they live by from history, and strive to continue past traditions into the future.	**Present** The present moment is everything. Let's make the most of it. Don't worry about tomorrow: enjoy today.	**Future** Planning and goal setting make it possible for people to accomplish miracles, to change and grow. A little sacrifice today will bring a better tomorrow.
Activity What is the best mode of activity?	**Being** It's enough to just "be". It's not necessary to accomplish great things in life to feel your life has been worthwhile.	**Becoming** The main purpose for being placed on this earth is for one's own inner development.	**Doing** If people work hard and apply themselves fully, their efforts will be rewarded. What a person accomplishes is a measure of his or her worth.
Social Relations What is the best form of social organization?	**Hierarchical** There is a natural order to relations, some people are born to lead, others are followers. Decisions should be made by those in charge.	**Collateral** The best way to be organized is as a group, where everyone shares in the decision process. It is important not to make important decisions alone.	**Individual** All people should have equal rights, and each should have complete control over one's own destiny. When we have to make a decision as a group it should be "one person one vote".

Trompenaars and Hampden-Turner (1997) follows Kluckhohn's dimensions adding a further two taken from Talcott Parsons' (1982) 'five pattern variables'. Hofstede

(1991) has four orientations, which he terms 'dimensions', adapted from the sociologist Alex Inkeles and the psychologist Daniel Levinson (Inkeles and Levinson 1969:447), who suggested four issues which qualified as common basic problems world-wide:

Inkeles and Levinson	Hofstede
1. relationship to authority	Power Distance
2. concept of self, in particular:	
a. the relationship between the individual and society	Individualism/Collectivism
b. the individual's concept of masculinity and femininity	Masculinity/Femininity
3. ways of dealing with conflicts including the control of aggression and the expression of feelings	Uncertainty Avoidance

Brake *et al.* (1995:39) have ten orientations, an amalgamation of Kluckhohn, Talcott Parsons, Hofstede and Hall.[7] Their taxonomy is the most comprehensive in the literature (to date), and forms the framework for the following sections. At this point we should look at the cultural iceberg (see Chapter 2.4.) once again:

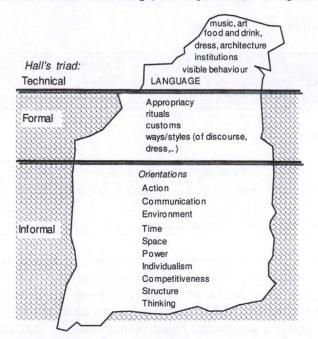

Figure 39. Brake's Iceberg of Cultural Orientations

---

[7] Brake *et al.* have integrated other authors too, but those of most interest here are the five orientations introduced by Kluckhohn (Kluckhohn and Strodtbeck 1961); Hall's (1982, 1983, 1990) time, space and contexting, and Hofstede's (1991) four dimensions.

Each of the items below the waterline is a cultural orientation. In the following chapter we will focus our attention on two cultural orientations which automatically influence the way we use language to communicate: the orientations towards action and communication.

The other orientations directly influence behaviour, and hence communication in a wider sense. A short explanation of these orientations, and the possible options according to Brake *et al.* (1995) is given below, both to give the reader an idea of the array of possible combinations, and also because a number of these orientations will be referred to in our discussion on action and communication orientations. Where there is a significant difference in labelling, the authors responsible have been shown.

9.3 A Taxonomy of Orientations[8]

The first two orientations are discussed in detail in Chapter 10.

- *Action*

Brake et al.	Hofstede	Trompenaars
• be/do	masculine/feminine	affective/neutral

- *Communication*

Hall	Trompenaars
• High Context Communication	Diffuse
• Low Context Communication	Specific

- *Environment*

Brake et al.	Trompenaars	NLP
• control	inner-directed (internal)	proactive
• harmony		
• constraint	outer-directed (external)	reactive

If we accept that cultures are animate agents for a moment, we can then say that they vary in their perception of the environment: some may feel that they can control the environment, as in "Just Do It" discussed in Chapter 5.4, and feel in charge of their own destiny. Others, at the opposite end of the cline, will believe that the environment – including supernatural forces, destiny and luck – has a measure of control over them (*Che sarà sarà, Inshalla*).

---

[8] For more details on indicators of orientations and statistics regarding a culture's orientation see, in particular, Hofstede (1991); Hampden-Turner and Trompenaars (1993); Trompenaars and Hampden-Turner (1997).

The United States is a prime example of a control orientation, from its insistence on air-conditioning to the conquering of space and "the buck stops here". Southern Europe, on the other hand is closer to a constraint orientation, with people more willing to accept the importance of *force majeur* and acts of God.

A third perception of the environment is the dominant Native-American and Eastern orientation, which is to operate in harmony with real or perceived environmental forces. The following extract from "Isho: the vigyana bhairava tantra[9] offers us a glimpse of how the two polar orientations differ in their fundamental perception of what really happened:

> When Hillary reached to the highest peak of the Himalayas, Mount Everest, all of the Western world reported it as a conquering – a conquering of Everest. Only in a Zen monastery in Japan, on a wall newspaper, it was written, "Everest has been befriended" – not conquered! This is the difference – "Everest has been befriended"; now humanity has become friendly with it. Everest has allowed Hillary to come to it. It was not a conquering. The very word 'conquer' is vulgar, violent. To think in terms of conquering shows aggressiveness. Everest has received Hillary, welcomed him, and now humanity has become friendly; now the chasm is bridged. Now we are not unacquainted. One of us has been received by Everest. Now Everest has become part of human consciousness. This is a bridging.

• *Time*

Brake et al		Hall	NLP	Trompenaars	Kluckhohn
• single-focus	fixed	monochronic	through time	sequential	Past/Present/Future
• multi-focus	fluid	polychronic	in time	synchronic	

• *Monochronic/Polychronic Time*

Hall (1983) devotes most of his book to the cultural understanding of time. Monochronic time cultures perceive time as the frame. The focus is on the task rather than the relationship; and schedules are important and adhered to. According to Tannen (1992) and Pease and Pease (2001) men in general are more task oriented than women. With regard to national cultures, rather than gender, Northern Europeans and Americans also tend towards this orientation. Those with this orientation would consider it rude to interrupt a meeting, client or phone call to attend to another person. The word "interrupt" is itself a monochronic word.

Polychronic or multi-focus cultures, on the other hand, place greater emphasis on the relationship, and multi-tasking. Tasks will be completed according to relationship needs rather than time needs. In a bank, serving only one person, and not

---

[9] http://www.oTantra.net/VBTv2/chapter03.html

answering the phone or another important person would be considered rude. Mediterranean, Arab, South American and Asian cultures tend towards this orientation.

• *Fluid/Fixed Time*

Fixed time cultures perceive time technically. A minute is sixty seconds: "Time is money", and can be spent, used and wasted. "On time" means technically 'on time', and apologies are expected between 1 and 5 minutes after, depending how close to fixed time the culture is. Time management, 'Just in Time' and 'Time and Motion' studies work well in these cultures. American, German and Swiss cultures are particularly conscious of technical time.

Fluid time defines punctuality with more flexibility. *Subito* in Italian technically means "immediately". It is the standard reply given by those in the service industry when being asked for service. The informal meaning is "I'll be with you when I have finished what I'm doing". In fluid-time cultures, delays are expected and tolerated. A meeting can start fifteen to thirty minutes late depending on the culture without undue tension being created. Those with a fixed-time orientation have difficulty in comprehending the Italian informal but institutionalized *quarto d'ora accademico* / "the university fifteen minute sliding start" much loved by Italian academics and students alike. It is always useful to check which time is being talked about: e.g. "German time", "Italian academic time", "Neapolitan time", "Milan time", and so on.

> **From Spanish Abroad, Inc.**[10]
>
> The fabled Mexican attitude toward time – 'manana, 'manana,...' – has probably become legendary simply from comparison with the USA. But it's still true. Especially outside the big cities, that the urgency Europeans and North Americans are used to is often lacking. Most Mexicans value *simpathia* (congeniality) over promptness. If something is really worth doing, it gets done. If not, it can wait. Life should not be a succession of pressures and deadlines. According to many Mexicans, life in the 'businesslike' cultures has been desympathized. You may come away from Mexico convinced that the Mexicans are right!

• *Past/Present/Future*

Past-oriented cultures emphasize tradition. Any change tends to take place over a long period and in relation to the past. The historical context is paramount to understanding the present, and history itself is highly valued. This is certainly true of Italy with many of its road names recording an event or personality in history. Television interviews (both in Britain and in Italy) tend to concentrate on the background of the subject in question, much to the irritation of the American guest who wants to talk about 'now'.

---

[10] http://www.spanishabroad.com/mexico/country_guide/mex_society.htm

Present-oriented cultures, such as America, emphasize the here and now. "History is bunk", said Henry T. Ford. The future also is not so important: "time waits for no man"; "take care of today and tomorrow will take care of itself". Long-term planning tends to be in terms of five to ten years at maximum (Hall 1990:141).

Future-oriented societies can plan ahead to the next generation. Japanese business plans take account of the past and can plan for the next hundred years in "the eternal cycle" (Adler 1991:30-1; Hampden-Turner and Trompenaars 1997:138; Brake *et al*. 1995:52). Italy also has a future orientation in terms of relationships. Once formed they are expected to be long term, with dues and favours to be repaid over a long period.

The terms "enduring" and "infinite" need to be interpreted against these orientations. President Bush's use before the 2nd Gulf War is discussed below (in *The Denver Post* 28/11/01) in terms of everything but enduring or infinite. To a large extent both the past and the future are deleted, and for many will only go to strengthen negative stereotyping:

TO SPIN OR NOT TO SPIN

Rick Jacobs, principal and owner of Monigle Associates, corporate identity and branding consultants in Denver, says names like 'Infinite Justice' and 'Enduring Freedom' are really more like 'brands'.

His company, by the way, just unveiled a new logo for Fort Lewis College in Durango, hoping to change its reputation as 'Fort Leisure'. One of the problems with the college's old logo is that it showed beckoning mountains in the background with a book in the foreground. A closed book.

This is the sort of stuff Monigle does for its 800 clients, 95 percent of whom are outside Colorado. So Jacobs knows his brands.

'I was a bit surprised at how they're using branding principles in order to rally the troops, if you will', Jacobs said.

There is, of course, the example of 'Desert Storm', the brand name for the 1991 Gulf War. It seemed to catch on.

'I think we saw in Desert Storm the value of being able to define something with terms that allow people to rally behind it. It's a very interesting use of branding', Jacobs said.

'Something like "Enduring Freedom" doesn't have as much of an action associated with it. 'Desert Storm' clearly is action-oriented, and it sends very powerful, visual signals to people. But that's what it was. That was an appropriate name for that kind of an engagement.

'"Enduring Freedom" seems more long-term than a storm, and I think the nature of this engagement is going to be exactly that. This is likely not going to be a huge front where we send in massive troops, but a long-term, precise, very surgical kind of operation that is going to go for years'.

It takes a completely different orientation to approach the subject as Arundhati Roy does. Here, we have an orientation which focuses on everything *but* the present:

> Could it be that the stygian anger that led to the attacks has its taproot not in American freedom and democracy, but in the US government's record of commitment and support to exactly the opposite things – to military and economic terrorism, insurgency, military dictatorship, religious bigotry and unimaginable genocide (outside America)? It must be hard for ordinary Americans, so recently bereaved, to look up at the world with their eyes full of tears and encounter what might appear to them to be indifference. It isn't indifference. It's just augury. An absence of surprise. The tired wisdom of knowing that what goes around eventually comes around … But war is looming large. Whatever remains to be said must be said quickly. Before America places itself at the helm of the "international coalition against terror", before it invites (and coerces) countries to actively participate in its almost godlike mission – called "Operation Infinite Justice" until it was pointed out that this could be seen as an insult to Muslims, who believe that only Allah can mete out infinite justice, and was renamed "Operation Enduring Freedom".

• *Space*

• Private/Public	Individual privacy v more public use of space
• Distance/Proximity	Preference for distance/low physical contact v. proximity/ high physical contact
Trompenaars:	
• Specific orientation	Open access to personal life space; but access, position and authority etc., segregated according to context
• Diffuse orientation	Selected entry to individual's private life space, but relationship, position, authority, etc., crosses contexts

The Japanese have an orientation towards public space and distance, with open-plan offices, and small communal living quarters, but very little physical contact (public/distance). In comparison, an American or European house or office will tend towards the private, and higher levels of proximity are tolerated (private/proximity). We have already mentioned (in Chapter 4.1) Hall's appropriate distances for white North Americans when discussing culture at the level of environment. Typical appropriate distances for Southern Europe and South America will be closer – and will be perceived as much too close for the British.

> The British are notoriously poor 'touchers' compared with other cultures. One study by Nancy Henley ('Body Politics') counted the number of touches between pairs chatting in cafes during a one hour sitting. The results: in Puerto Rico there were on average 180 instances of touch, in London, none. [11]

---

[11] http://www.globalideasbank.org/TouchHealth.html

• *Diffuse/Specific*

Space can also be perceived as psychological (Trompenaars and Hampden-Turner 1997:73-76). The degree to which individuals let others into their life (psychological space) tends to change with culture. Americans tend to the specific. New acquaintances become intimate friends over a relatively short period of time. However, this relationship (including both entitlements and obligations) is specific to a particular activity or sector.

A diffuse life space orientation, on the other hand, has a relatively guarded approach to acquaintances. However, once a relationship has been formed (whether business or personal), entry, including entitlements and obligations is expected to all areas of private space. Germany is a prime example of this system, and Italy also tends towards this system. The meaning of the word "friend" and the expected reciprocal rights and the duties will vary according to cultural orientation. The word itself should not be translated but mediated. Trompenaars and Hampden-Turner (1997:83) write about a personal experience in the U.S.A:

> ...the British author had been introduced at a reception following a graduation ceremony as Dr. Hampden-Turner, but at a party for much the same people a few hours later as Charles Hampden-Turner. He had also been introduced as "I want you to meet my very good friend Charles... (what's your surname?).

• *Power*

Brake et al.	Hofstede	Trompenaars
Hierarchy	High Power Distance	Ascription
Equality	Low Power Distance	Achievement

In all societies there is power. It can be distributed evenly, with an attempt to reduce the degree of visible status. Alternatively, hierarchy and visible status can be emphasized. Italy is a relatively high power distance country, while Northern Europe, Britain and the States in particular tend to emphasize low power distance. South America, Asia, and (to a lesser extent) Southern Europe tend to respect high power distance. The importance of 'respect' when addressing a person, address rituals, and the degree of HAP or LAP type language most of the citizens have, are indications of a culture's power distance orientation.

In a similar way, Trompenaars and Hampden-Turner distinguish between cultures that tend to accord status according to 'who' someone is (according to family, background or title) and those cultures oriented towards awarding status to proven results (achievement) regardless of background. Clearly a professional's obligations are also culture-bound here: to the people who employ you (ascription) or to the task (achievement), as Trompenaars and Hampden-Turner (1997:109-10) explain:

> ...it often becomes clear that the translator from an ascriptive culture be-
> haves "unprofessionally" according to the standards of achieving cultures.
> According to British, German, North American, Scandinavian and Dutch val-
> ues, the translator is an achiever like any other participant and the height of
> his or her achievement should be to give an accurate, unbiased account of
> what was said in one language to those speaking the other language. The
> translator is supposed to be neutral, a black box serving the interests of mod-
> ern language comprehension, not the interests of either party who may seek
> to distort meanings for their own ends.
>
> In other cultures, however, the translator is doing something else. A Japa-
> nese translator, for example, will often take a minute or two more to "translate"
> an English sentence 15 seconds long. And there is often extensive colloquy
> between the translator and the team he or she serves about what the opposite
> team just said. The translator on the Japanese side is an interpreter, not sim-
> ply of language but of gesture, meaning and context. His role is to support his
> own team and possibly even to protect them from confrontational conduct by
> the western negotiators.

• *Individualism*

Brake et al.	*NLP*
Individualism	(tend to) Internal + Independent/Proximity
Collectivism	(tend to) External + Co-operative

Japan is the most well-known "we", collective, oriented culture. However, Southern European (such as Turkey and Greece), Central and South American countries
are even more collective, relying on tight social networks for most communication.
America leads the "I", "do your own thing" cultures on all individualism indexes,
while Northern Europe (such as Italy and France) are also heavily individualist.
Differences between these countries occur most on the universalistic/particularist
orientations.

•*Particularism*

Trompenaars	*Hofstede*
Universalism	Truth
Particularism	Virtue

Universalist codes are universally applicable. There is a tendency to generalize
laws and procedures, and to apply them universally. American mass-production,
McDonald's, sneakers (as we have seen in Chapter 4.1) and Henry Ford's "You can
have any colour you like as long as it's black" symbolize the desire for universalism.
Particularist cultures, such as those on the Russian subcontinent, Asia, Central and

South America, and Southern Europe plus France and Italy, do not reduce situations to simplistic rules. These cultures emphasize difference, uniqueness and exceptions, from food and restaurants to the application of parking fines and queuing. We have already mentioned the universalist American difficulty in understanding the particularist Mexican approach to speeding offences in Chapter 2.3.

George Orwell noted how it is possible to be particularist in a politically collectivist society in his political satire *Animal Farm*: "All animals are equal, but some animals are more equal than others" (see also Hofstede 1991:161). This orientation nurtures the patronage system, which can work for the good of the collective society as in Japan, or for a particular group or family as in Italy (see also Mead 1994:111-37 and Gannon 2001:126). This means that the translation of the term 'democracy', for example, needs to be contextualized (see also Lewis 2000:131). Francesco Rossi does so in his 1963 film *Le Mani Sulla Città/*'Hands Over the City', an investigation into the collapse of a block of flats. Jones, in his *The Dark Heart of Italy* describes the plot to explain Italy today, perceived, understandably enough from a universalist orientation, as corrupt:

> [The Christian Democratic] party get rich by assigning building contracts to *Mafiosi*, who in return guarantee the politicians their votes ... As far as the law goes, *tutto è in regola*, everything is 'by the book'. The [illegal construction of the flats] has been legalized. The commission of enquiry can reach no conclusion. Politics is reduced to the buying and selling of votes made possible by the vast amounts of money slashing around by the construction business. Besieged by angry women, the mayor unfolds huge notes and passes them around. Looking over his shoulder he smiles and says 'Consigliere, see how democracy works?'

• *Competitiveness*

Brake et al.	Hofstede	NLP
Competitive	Masculine	Proactive + Independent + Self Sorting style: (material) things
Cooperative	Feminine	(Reactive) + Co-operative + Others Sorting Style: people

Competitive cultures privilege the more masculine character. There are winners and losers, people "live to work", workaholics are respected, and material success is a high motivator. Cooperative cultures, on the other hand, work together as interdependent teams, "work to live" and place a higher value on the quality of life. Japan, Germany, Italy and the Anglo-American countries are all competitive cultures. High-cooperative cultures include the Scandinavian countries, Spain and a number of South American countries. As Hofstede (1991:90, emphasis in the original) explains, this orientation affects the interpretation and evaluation of terms such as 'average' and 'best':

> Experience in teaching abroad and discussions with teachers from different countries have led me to conclude that in [...] the more masculine cultures like the U.S.A. the *best* students are the norm. Parents in these countries expect their children to try and match the best. The 'best boy in class' in the Netherlands is a somewhat ridiculous figure.

• *Structure*

Brake et al.	Hofstede	NLP
Order	Strong Uncertainty Avoidance	Procedures
Flexibility	Weak Uncertainty Avoidance	Options

The future is an unknown factor for all cultures, and day-to-day life can also present people with the unknown. The degree to which a culture feels threatened or uncomfortable with ambiguity, uncertainty or change, is an indication of its orientation towards order or flexibility. Japan, Greece, Italy and Germany have a strong orientation towards order, and tend to avoid ambiguity or change in all things. Hence change tends to come about through destabilization and revolution. In Italy, though the appearance of structure is highly valued, its particularist orientation ensures that the orientation towards order is never fully achieved.

The Anglo-American countries have a relatively high toleration for uncertainty and change. According to Hofstede (1991:113), Great Britain is the most unperturbed of that group, and rates forty-eighth out of the fifty-three countries surveyed in terms of "the extent to which members of a culture feel threatened by uncertain or unknown situations". Singapore, at number fifty-three, has the highest toleration. These cultures have less need for detailed rules which attempt to define all situations. Flexibility (except for time itself), choice and options are valued. To a certain extent this orientation explains the reasons why the Italian equivalents of "No Smoking" or "Thank you for not smoking" notices are the more detailed and legally structured:

DIVIETO DI FUMARE
Ai sensi della Legge n. 584 del 11.11.1975 è severamente vietato fumare; i trasgressori sono soggetti all'applicazione delle previste Sanzioni Amministrative.

SMOKING IS FORBIDDEN
Pursuant to regulation no. 584, 11/11/1975, smoking is severely forbidden. Those in breach will be subject to the relevant Administrative Sanctions

• *Thinking*

Brake et al.	NLP	Hall	Trompenaars
Deductive	Match / Similarities / Large Chunks	HCC	
Inductive	Mismatch / Differences / Small Chunks	LCC	
Linear	Specific	Monochronic	Specific
Systemic	General	Polychronic	Diffuse

• *Deductive/Inductive*

Alternative labelling for deductive/inductive has already been given at the beginning of the chapter. Deductive thinking orientations focus on theories, logic and principles. This is very true of Germany and France, and to a lesser extent Italy. Situations are classified according to already existing theories. Inductive cultures are more pragmatic and specific, starting from empirical observation. Facts and statistics are highly valued. The United States and Britain are particularly inductive.

• *Linear/Systemic*

Linear-oriented cultures will dissect problems into logical and precise sequences, look for detail, precision and minute cause and effect, such as the McDonald's itemization of the service counter routine. Systemic, on the other hand is holistic, and tends to look at the full picture, the background and relationships with other parts of even bigger pictures. Explanations will be less in terms of statistics and logic; but rather in connections, feelings and similes. Italy tends towards the systemic, while Japan is a clear example of the most systemically oriented culture.

Many have already noted how communication patterns between men and women differ. Any popular book on the subject will tell you that it is not necessary to go abroad to encounter difference: men tend to be linear while women tend be systemic – and the results of these different orientations to reality are known to us all.

> Even today we still need translators. Men and women seldom mean the same things when they use the same words. For example, when a woman says "I feel like you *never* listen", she does not expect the word *never* to be taken literally. Using the word *never* is just a way of expressing the frustration she is feeling at the moment. It is not to be taken as factual information.
> To fully express their feelings, women assume poetic license and use various superlatives, metaphors and generalizations. Men mistakenly take these expressions literally. (Gray 1993:60)
> A woman's superior sensory equipment picks up and analyses [verbal and non-verbal] information and her brain's ability to rapidly transfer between hemispheres makes her more proficient at integrating and deciphering ... This is why most men have difficulty lying to a woman face-to-face. But as most women know, lying to a man face-to-face is comparatively easy, as he does not have the necessary sensitivity ... most men, if they're going to lie to a woman, would be far better off doing it over the phone, or with the lights off, and a blanket over their heads. (Pease and Pease 2001:29)

Chapter 10. Contexting

The aim of this chapter is to:
- introduce Edward T. Hall's Theory of Contexting in communication
- discuss the links between contexting and left/right brain distinctions
- illustrate a number of the language behaviour differences as a result of contexting differences
- show the relevance of contexting for a cultural interpreter/mediator involved in translation and interpreting transactional situations

10.1 High and Low Context

Communication			Possible cultural priorities	
Hall	*Trompenaars*	*Simons et al.*		
• HCC	Diffuse	loosely knit	Relationship	what is understood
				the context of the message
				the meta-message
• LCC	Specific	tightly woven	Task	what is said
				the text of the message

One of the guiding orientations, which perhaps could be termed a meta-orientation, is 'contexting'. This term was coined by Hall in 1976 (1989:85-128) and further discussed in 1983 (59-77). The basic concept is that individuals, groups, and cultures (and at different times) have differing priorities with regard to how much information (text) needs to be made explicit for communication to take place.

The words 'text' and 'context' have particular meanings here. Context is "stored information", and as such is very close to Halliday's (Halliday and Hasan 1989:47) "non-verbal environment of a text" which is made up of "the context of situation and the wider context of culture". In terms of communication, according to Hall (1983:61), it is "the amount of information the other person can be expected to possess on a given subject", while the text is "transmitted information".

Both Halliday and Hall, among many others, agree that communication entails both text and context. Gregory Bateson's comment (as cited by Ting-Toomey 1985:83) is clear and to the point: "All communication necessitates context and ... without context there is no meaning".

Halliday suggests that the context of situation is "the total environment in which a text unfolds" (Halliday and Hasan 1989:5, 36) but then goes on to say: "In the normal course of life, all day and every day, when we are interacting with others through language ... we are making inferences from the situation to the text, and from the text to the situation". It seems that here Halliday is concentrating on the immediate context of the text within a single frame of culture. Hall's context though, is explicitly both the context of situation and the context of culture, i.e. it includes the beliefs and values that determine the behaviour to be interpreted.

Clearly, also, in any communication, the speaker and listener will have their own perception of the context. The more these perceptions are shared the more possible it will be, as Halliday suggests (Halliday and Hasan 1989:5), to use them as a framework for hypothesizing what is going to be said. Sperber and Wilson (1995:15) also understand 'context' in terms of perception rather than reality. They suggest that it is "the set of premises used in interpreting an utterance" and that it is "a psychological construct, a subset of the hearer's assumptions about the world. It is these assumptions, of course, rather than the actual state of the world, that affect the interpretation of an utterance".

Halliday (Halliday and Hasan 1989:12-14; also Taylor Torsello 1992), on the other hand, sees context of situation as a tangible construct (visible and audible). The description is in terms of a simple conceptual framework of three headings:

the field	what is happening
the tenor	who are taking part
the mode	what part the language is playing

Problems in understanding, through translation or otherwise, arise from the fact that assumptions about the world differ. Widdowson (1979:138) shows the importance of sharing mutual assumptions in successful communication with this well-known conversation exchange:

> A: doorbell!!
> B: I'm in the bath.
> A: Ok.

Both parties 'know' that "I'm in the bath" did not mean what was textually said. As a result, the meta-message is successfully communicated through what is already shared. In another situation, between two other people who do not know each other, less can be assumed to be understood; and the conversation might be as follows:[1]

> (*phone rings*)
> A: George?
> B: Yes?
> A: Look, I'm a little tied up at the moment – do you think you could answer it and ask them to phone back in 10 minutes?
> B: Sure. Where is it?
> (*phone stops ringing*)
> A: Never mind.

---

[1] See also Scollon and Scollon (2001:76-82) and their discussion on meta-communication and unclear reference.

Interlocutors in each communication event will, usually out-of-awareness, arrange themselves and others along the context scale. We tend to believe we know how much needs to be said and explained to have our message understood the way we meant. Whether or not this is true, as we cannot mind read, is usually difficult to objectively judge. In cross-cultural communication, the scope for error is even larger.

There are, then, two aspects to communication (text and context), each represented by a triangle:

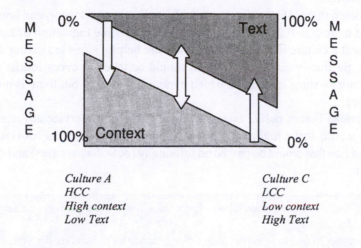

Culture A
HCC
High context
Low Text

Culture C
LCC
Low context
High Text

Figure 40. Hall's Triangles

At one theoretical extreme, all the information that is to be conveyed is made visible, or explicit, in the 'text' triangle. While at the other extreme, no text is necessary as all the information is implicit, i.e. it is contained in the 'context' triangle. The diagram, adapted from Hall (1983:61), shows how both triangles operate together in a cline to form the message. He explains that, "as context is lost, information must be added if meaning is to remain constant".

Hall suggests that contexting is a fundamental aspect of culture; and also that members of a culture will have a shared bias, either towards communication through the text or the context. This will be their guiding principle in all decisions to be made. However, as we have already noted in the introduction, orientations *can* change according to situation. Following other authors, we will refer to a High Context Communication orientation as 'HCC' and a preference for text as a Low Context Communication orientation or 'LCC'.

Hall's contexting theory is "begging to be connected" (Vincent-Marrelli 1989:473) to a language based theory of communication. In her paper is a clear indication of how the theory can prove fruitful in understanding Anglo-Italian cross-cultural miscommunication.[2] George Simons *et al.* (1993) have also made extensive

---

[2] See also Katan (1994).

use of this HCC/LCC polarity in their volume on cross-cultural business management. They also suggest that all cultural orientations depend on this meta-orientation,
which they relate to two principle types of culture: 'loosely knit' and 'tightly woven'. The metaphors relate to the adaptability of a loosely knit fabric, which has yet
to take on a final form and can be stretched without damage. This is compared with
a dense, interwoven, more solid fabric – and more resistant to change. We begin to
see parallels here with the uncertainty avoidance orientation: either towards structure or flexibility.

How much written information is available for the foreign visitor, and how much
will need to be obtained from a local informer is a possible indication of how high
or low context a culture is. In New York, there are helpful signs indicating the best
time and angle from which a photograph should be taken at every tourist site. In
Cairo there are no signs telling you which pyramid is which – but there is no short-
age of guides.

On American Forces radio,[3] there are a variety of public service adverts giving
advice that would strike higher context communication cultures as 'obvious', i.e.
the sort of advice that would be passed on informally (out-of-awareness) and through
observation:

> - It's a dog's life, so please don't stroke us while we are eating, or chase us
>   around the garden.
> - Remember, those nice exotic house plants could be poisonous for your little
>   ones.
> - Eating too fast is not only bad for your diet; it is also bad for your digestion.
> - Oil and grease on linoleum floors can be dangerous. It's just an accident wait-
>   ing to happen.
> - Spend quality time with your family. **You** can make a difference.
> - When it comes to choosing a life-mate, be sure to check with your best friend.

Universities vary their welcome to new students according to how text-based
they are. The British and the American have "Freshers' Week"[4] and "Orientation"
respectively. During this time, administrative, academic and student organizations
battle for the time to formally and technically explain and entertain. In Italy, and
other Mediterranean countries, the explaining and the entertaining is very much
more informal and unplanned. Students are informed through the grapevine.

Some British universities, being older, are more 'tightly woven', and therefore
less explicit in their dissemination of information. Two Americans, Bill Bryson and
Stuart Franklin noted the inaccessibility of the culture for an outsider at one of the
Oxford colleges:

---

[3] Heard on ZFM, American forces Radio (1995-6)
[4] The term "fresher" is British English; "freshman" is the less PC American term.

> Waiting for a professor one day, I passed the time by glancing through [the bulletin board announcements]. 'Master's Handshaking will take place in the Dining Room of the Master's Lodgings. Please wait in the passage outside,' said one. Another, more cryptically, announced: 'Lagrangian Mechanics – Saturday 11 a.m'. A third stated: 'RFC 1st and 2nd XV practice Thurs. 2 p.m'. Perhaps 50 such notices were pinned to the board, all dealing with some important component of college life, and it occurred to me, as I stood there idly looking them over, that I couldn't truly understand a single one. It is a feeling you soon grow used to in Oxford. *National Geographic* (November 1995:120)

Other universities, in higher context communication cultures, do not even use bulletin boards; and students are expected 'to know' through the informal network of personal contact where and when lessons are, and in particular when and where changes have been made. In an HCC, tightly woven culture, the participants are expected to share more of the larger context – whether or not this is actually the case.

Identity, in tightly woven cultures, is closely related to social position. People take their place within a pre-formed, stable and interwoven network where change is unusual. Japan would be a case in point. Trompenaars (1997:102-119) uses the term 'achievement' and 'ascription' orientations to explain cultures' options in according status. An LCC culture will tend to accord status to the person who merits the position through proven capability in the field and through election. Particularly important is a written CV. In an HCC culture you already need to be known for who you are. Long-term contacts and networking become increasingly important – paper qualifications less so.

So, HCC cultures are not immediately oriented to the newcomer (though the guest will be very well looked after). The United States, on the other hand, is a prime example of a 'loosely knit' society, accepting newcomers into its social fabric. The successful newcomers will also have an orientation to low uncertainty avoidance and the ability to change identity. They quickly become, for example, ethnic Black, Afro- or Chinese- American. In this melting pot there is space (both physical and mental) for change.

Many authors have also likened the LCC and HCC differences in terms of rooting systems. Some cultures have more solid and interwoven roots, while others, with a shallow root system can be uprooted without creating great disturbance. Remarks made (reported below) by two ministers (one British and one Italian) on the problem of unemployment reflect this presence or lack of a deep root system.

In each case the ministers' reaction to unemployment is totally 'natural'. In Britain, in the aftermath of the 1981 Brixton riots, Norman Tebbit, the then Secretary of State for Employment, made the "infamous assertion that 'My father didn't riot but got on his bike to look for work. 'Get on your bike' became the moral imperative of conservatism":[5]

---

[5] Quoted from "The Silent Takeover Global Capitalism and the Death of Democracy" in www.thirdworldtraveler.com/Global_Economy/ Silent_Takeover%20_Part1.html

> SOME CONSIDERATIONS ON POLITICAL IDEOLOGY AND THE BRITISH SEARCH FOR
> PROSPERITY FOR ALL ITS CITIZENS
> **4.4** Labour market flexibility. The Conservative government believed that
> insecurity in the workplace motivates the workforce. The government resisted
> all measures to give part-timers the same rights as full timers or to introduce
> a minimum wage in the belief that these measures would cost jobs. The argu-
> ment used is 'low pay or no pay'. If work is not available you should simply
> 'Get on your bike' to find it. There is no such thing as 'a job for life'. [6]

Not only is this idea firmly accepted by the Conservative party (and to a large extent
by the general populace) but the expression "get on your bike" has now come into
the language, and into recent dictionaries (e.g. *Longman* 1992).

Tiziano Treu, the Italian Employment minister in Berlusconi's centre-right government (1995), had a very different point of view when talking about the chronic
unemployment situation in Southern Italy:

[...] è naturale che i ragazzi, specie se diplomati o laureati, piuttosto che spostarsi preferiscono attendere qualche opportunità nella zona in cui hanno le loro radici. *Corriere della Sera* (3/5/95)	It's natural that young people, particularly those with college or university qualifi- cations, would prefer to wait for an opportunity in their own area where they have roots, rather than move.

The fact that a culture is more HCC or LCC will also mean, according to Hall,
that there will also be other related text/context orientations. Victor (1992) and
Simons *et al.* (1993) have produced lists of typical (and simplified rather than actual) features of these two different orientations. With some adaptations, they are
outlined below:

Low context operating mode	**High context operating mode**
More loosely knit	More tightly woven
shallow rooted	deep rooted
Emphasis placed on:	*Emphasis placed on:*
• text	context
• facts	relationship/feelings
• directness	indirectness
• consistency	flexibility (in meaning)
• substance	(social/personal) appearance
• rules	circumstances
• monochronic	polychronic

---

[6] John Baillie of Park Lane College, Leeds, United Kingdom, 1997. Contribution to the
EDUVINET "Living Conditions of EU Citizen", http://www.eduvinet.de/eduvinet/uk005.htm

If we take two different cultures, such as Italy and Britain, and compare them on the above lists, it is clear that they can be associated more with one list than with another. Italy would tend to operate on a more tightly woven, high context basis, while the British would tend to operate on a more loosely-knit, low context basis. Comparing Britain and the United States, it would seem that the US is even further down the cline towards low context. We should also remember that the operating mode favoured will, as we have already mentioned, depend on many variables: culture, sub-culture, gender, class, age, situation, and, of course, individual personality.

That being said, there are some useful generalizations that can be made (always couched in the positive, to reflect prioritized cultural values). If we think about the way the British and the Italians regard fashion, food and furniture, it is clear that the British are lower context, attaching more value to functionality, whereas Italy places a higher value on design, taste and aesthetics.

With regard to appearance, we have already mentioned the English city without mirrors: "The girls in their cheap and flimsy finery ... How the Italians would despise and laugh at them". Another article, published a year earlier, echoes the same thoughts. The article (*The Sunday Times* 18/12/94, 6:5) has an LCC title "Face Facts" and discusses the case of a woman who had been described as "ugly" by a policeman. The verbalization of 'ugly' flouts PC norms (discussed in Chapter 5.3). The article, in fact, begins by discussing the public outcry which resulted from the police officer's ill-advised description. The article then moves on to look at Britain as a whole (emphasis in original):

> Britain *does* look a mess, particularly compared to our EC neighbours. The average Italian waiter would not dream of working in anything other than starched white coat and bow tie. The average Italian banker is kitted out in immaculate tweed and has perfectly manicured fingernails – as does the local fruit seller and probably newsagent too. I've lived in Milan. I remember feeling obliged to look neat and tidy for the plumber/telephone man/cleaner.

Using the Meta-Model we can immediately note the use of the modal necessity: 'to feel obliged'. The values that lie behind that statement are steeped in a culture which values individual freedom (an orientation towards self). An Italian would tend to value in-group norms. It would, therefore, be 'normal' to dress neatly and tidily in public groups (an orientation towards others).

The culture-bound aspects of the normality are hidden in the deletion of the performatives of words such as *rispetto* / "respect" or *normale* / "normal", and in the nominalization of *in ordine* / "neat and tidy". The full representation (hidden to most speakers) would be as shown in figure 41.

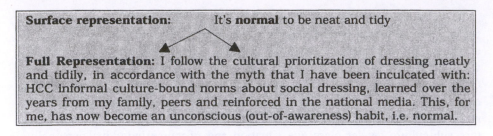

Surface representation: It's **normal** to be neat and tidy

Full Representation: I follow the cultural prioritization of dressing neatly and tidily, in accordance with the myth that I have been inculcated with: HCC informal culture-bound norms about social dressing, learned over the years from my family, peers and reinforced in the national media. This, for me, has now become an unconscious (out-of-awareness) habit, i.e. normal.

Figure 41. Full Representation of Italian "normal"

What is hidden in the English remark is as follows:

Surface representation: I remember feeling **obliged** to be neat and tidy

Full Representation: I follow the cultural prioritization of dressing in accordance with LCC culture-bound norms regarding individual practicality in accordance with the myth that I have been inculcated with: LCC informal culture-bound rules about social dressing, learned over the years from my family, peers and reinforced in the national media. This, for me, has now become an unconscious (out-of-awareness) habit, i.e. normal.
I have also mind read other (Italian) group behaviour not only as a limit to my world but also as an obligation to conform, which I have decided to accept at a behavioural level to satisfy other important values such as universalism, group acceptance and harmony. However, there is conflict between my behaviour and my strong individualist values.

Figure 42. Full Representation of English "obliged"

The two cultures, British and Italian, not only disagree on the importance or cultural prioritization of being "neat and tidy", but there is also disagreement over the criterial equivalence, i.e. what has to happen for the neat and tidiness value to be met. We have already seen how 'casual clothes' need to be contextualized before we can fully understand what is being talked about. Also, what is 'tidy' for one culture (and, of course, generation) will not necessarily meet the criterial equivalence of another. Hofstede (1991:118) notes a related culture-bound concept, that of 'dirt', or as he calls it "matter out-of-place". He points out that what is dirty or clean is also an extremely relative concept: "The Italian *mammas* and nannies see dirt and danger in the piazza where the American grandparents see none".

However, the Americans, British and Italians are in complete agreement that the Japanese have an exaggerated sense of dirt. The Italian fruit seller and newsagent may have "perfectly manicured nails", but the Japanese train, taxi and bus drivers, for example, wear starched white gloves. Their gloves, in harmony with the rest of their immaculate uniforms, are expected to remain clean all day.

What counts as neat and tidy in Singapore is also very different generally from accepted Western 'civilized' attitudes. Fines for litter dropping in Singapore are taken seriously, and laws requiring houses to be repainted are also a sign of the culture's perception, interpretation and evaluation of dirt. As a result, both the Japanese and the Singaporeans tend to perceive the West in much the same way as the West sees a developing country, i.e. as a dirty place. Dirt, as we have said, is a relative concept, and each culture is happy with its own understanding of the concept. There will always be cultures that exaggerate, and cultures that do not come up to our standard. And so every culture positions itself on a cline, convinced that its position is the correct one. This is the heart of the belief that the map or myth is reality.

The following contexting cline comes from a business article adapted by Victor (1992:143). Hall's theory, in fact, has been developed, like much anthropological theory more in the very pragmatic field of business management than in any other field. It should also be pointed out that unlike the other orientations mentioned in the previous chapter, this particular cline is not based on any published statistics:

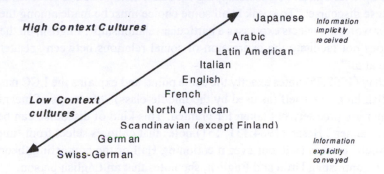

Figure 43. Context Ranking of Cultures

The highest context communication culture is the Japanese, which fits our stereotype of their inscrutable culture, where silence is more valued than the word. At the other end of the cline is the Swiss-German where the stereotype of exacting precision and detailed information fits their LCC position.

An extreme example of a low context character comes from Charles Dickens' *Hard Times* (1987). The schoolmaster, Thomas Gradgrind is presented to the reader with these words:

> Now what I want is Facts. Teach these boys and girls nothing but facts. Facts alone are wanted in life. Plant nothing else, and root out everything else. You can only form the minds of reasoning animals upon Facts: nothing else will ever be of any service to them. Thomas Gradgrind, sir. A man of realities. A man of fact and calculations. A man who proceeds upon the principle that two plus two are four, and nothing over, and who is not to be talked into allowing anything else.

Thomas Gradgrind, as we can see from the cline, will be appreciated by cultures lower down the ranking scale. In fact, he has problems enough in England, and with this orientation should not be sent to a teaching post in Japan.

Returning now to an earlier discussion on language and culture, we can now look at the relationship between the use of the lexico-grammar and the contexting theory. We will look first at the English language, and then at British and American differences in the use of English.

10.2 English – The Language of Strangers

The English language itself, as a lexico-grammatical system, is decidedly LCC in comparison with many other languages. The language is well-adapted to explication, and less suitable for the signalling of pre-established social relationships, as Mühlhäusler and Harré (1990:32-33) note. They point out that in Japanese, the language itself obliges speakers to pronounce themselves on one of the four levels of relationship with others. Membershipping the relationship itself is an essential part of Japanese discourse: "To speak at all some choice must be made among the four. Whatever word one selects expresses a particular relationship". English, on the other hand "does not facilitate the expression of social relations between speakers and audience at all".

Halliday (1992:75) notes exactly the same point, and explains the LCC nature of the English language itself (as used by the middle-class): "the ways of meaning of the listener are precisely not taken for granted. This kind of discourse can be spoken to a stranger". Hasan (1984:131, 151) notes that cultures select from 'implicit' and 'explicit' options (without ever mentioning Hall or the contexting theory). In her study, contrasting Urdu and English, she notes that an English person:

> could not speak as implicitly as the Urdu speaker, even if he tried – the system of his language will not permit him to do so ... We can claim without hesitation that the dominant semantic style in Urdu is the implicit one ...

Urdu, spoken by eighty-five million people in Pakistan, North and central India and Bangladesh is an example of a language spoken by a tightly woven group. According to both Halliday and Hasan, speakers of this language will tend to select the implicit option, not only for lexico-grammatical reasons, but also because the context of situation will not have changed in time and there are strong relations between events.

Concluding her research on the high level of assumptions made by Urdu speakers, and the expectation that the addressee (whether total stranger or not) will implicitly know, Hasan (1984:153) makes a strong case for the tightly woven/loosely structured hypothesis: "the Urdu speaker's world must be a fairly-well regulated place in which persons, objects and processes have well-defined positions with reference to each other, and the speakers know the details".

• *American and British English*
We now turn to differences in standard usage of the same lexico-grammatical sys-

tem: English. The two national standards under discussion are British and American, which many have noted can actually seem like a different language:

> We have really everything in common with America nowadays, except, of course, language. Oscar Wilde, c. 1881-82, in Richard Ellmann. *Oscar Wilde* (1988)
>
> When I speak my native tongue [U.S. English] in its utmost purity in England, an Englishman can't understand me at all. Mark Twain, *The Stolen White Elephant* (1882)
>
> The American I have heard up to the present is a tongue as distinct from English as Patagonian. Rudyard Kipling, *From Sea to Sea* (1889)
>
> England and America are two countries separated by the same language. George Bernard Shaw, *Reader's Digest* (Nov. 1942)
>
> Britain speaks the world's most popular language – so do the Americans, up to a point. *The Economist* (20/10/90)

At the heart of these quoted differences is not so much the lexico-grammar but the greater orientation in the United States to LCC, and hence towards textual explication. John Dodds (1989:12), Canadian-English, notes how the logical mathematical design of the American urban grid system automatically entails greater clarity: "instead of saying (as an American would) something like 'up two blocks, then take a right and it's three blocks along', he (the Englishman) said keep following this road for about half a mile, turn right, and then its the third turning on the left".

The American technical rather than rough calculation was noted by Sapir, and recorded in his lecture notes (1994:33):

> Only in American culture could the phrase 'fifty-fifty' have evolved, for only here do we find such willingness to measure intangibles; expression must be quantitative. There is pretence of extreme objectivity, of objective control of situations, which cannot be tangibly measured.

This reminds us of the McDonald's technical itemizing of the service encounter, and we should also remember that concepts such as Management by Objectives (MBO), time and motion studies, *The One Minute Manager* and Procedural Re-Engineering are a product of a low context culture – and less popular in the UK than in the US.

The British, unwritten, 'gentleman's agreement' is not part of the American way, according to Victor (1992:150). In America, a written signed agreement is the preferred way of doing business. A popular and possibly true story is the successful case brought against the Dé Longhi Company in America, regarding a microwave oven. The written instructions did *not* include an explicit warning against using the microwave for drying pet animals. What is certainly true is the following:

> **YOU HAVE BEEN WARNED**
>
> The fear of being sued for millions of dollars under America's sweeping prod-
> uct liability laws is producing some absurd warning signs. Following a $2.7m
> (£1.8m) fine awarded to a scalded customer, McDonald's serves its coffee in
> mugs stamped with the bright red words "Caution HOT!" Starbucks, Ameri-
> ca's top café chain, says more graciously: "Careful, the beverage you are
> about to enjoy is extremely hot".
>
> Toymakers are obliged to remind parents they are buying toys. Kiddies'
> plastic construction hats are not, they are told, intended to protect their off-
> spring from falling masonry. A Batman costume comes with the following
> advice: "For play only. Mask and chest plate are not protective. Cape does
> not enable user to fly". *The Sunday Times* (09/03/97)

Note, by the way, the same Meta-Motel violation ("Toymakers are obliged"), which
points to the tolerance limits of the writer.

The fact that the American variety of the language is more LCC than the British
is partly explained by the history of the American people and the geography of the
country. In 1620, 102 Pilgrim Fathers left a relatively homogeneous, highly developed and inflexible culture for a new land. Some of these adventurous pioneers
survived, and others began to arrive in the following years to this new found land.

Bryson (1994:35), in his publication on America and the American language,
makes the following comment which we can immediately relate to the more tightly
woven/more loosely knit categorization of cultures (emphasis added): "Gradually,
out of this inchoate mass a country began to emerge – *loosely structured*, governed
from abroad, populated by an unlikely mix of refugees, idealists, slaves and con-
victs, but a country nonetheless".

The Founding Fathers, faced with a new (continental) environment were obliged
to invent new names for the new plants and animals they encountered. As can be
seen from the list they are all compounds taken from existing words:

> jointworm, glowworm, eggplant, canvasback, copperhead, rattlesnake,
> bluegrass, backtrack, bobcat, catfish, bluejay, bullfrog, sapsucker, timberland,
> underbrush.

However, not only was the natural environment named by joining known monosyl-
labic words together, but some of the known, man-made environment was also
renamed, as we have already seen in Chapter 5.3.

What is particularly relevant for our discussion here is Bryson's (ibid.:26) comment on the reasons why this approach was so common: "These new terms had the
virtue of directness and instant comprehensibility – useful qualities in a land whose
populace included increasingly large numbers of non-native speakers – which their
British counterparts often lacked".

The birth of America as an independent country is also marked by a high degree of text. The third U.S. President, Thomas Jefferson, was the chief drafter of the Declaration of Independence. In a letter he wrote to fellow American Henry Lee he spelled out the underlying importance of explicit rather than implicit communication. His priorities are clear as he explains why the Declaration of Independence was written: "to place before mankind the common sense of the subject, in terms so plain and firm as to command their assent".

Within the Declaration of Independence is an explicit meta-message, a declaration of why the declaration is being made (emphasis added):

> When in the course of human events, it becomes necessary for one people to dissolve the political bands which have connected them with another, and to assume, among the powers of the earth, the separate and equal station to which the Laws of Nature and of Nature's God entitle them, *a decent respect to the opinions of mankind requires that they should declare the causes which impel them the separation.*

The need to explain in text and "in a language that everyone can understand" (ibid.:50) demonstrates an orientation to Universalism and Equality – both of which remain at the heart of American core orientations.

10.3 Contexting and the Brain

> * Hall's Contexting Theory and Hemispherical Preference
> * Hampden-Turner and Hemispherical Cooperation
> * Grinder's Taxonomy of Skills
> * Lateralization and Translation Strategies

Hall (1983:60) postulates that these two basic distinctions (HCC and LCC) relate very closely to the brain and its division into left and right hemispheres. Though most brain specialists and psychologists feel that this division is far too simple, there is some evidence to support this hypothesis. The left cerebral hemisphere is to a large extent regarded as being responsible for 'text': language production, facts, logic, and "precise sequencing in space and in time" (Stein 1988:132).

The right hemisphere, on the other hand, is largely responsible for relationships, the non-verbal, the holistic and patterns. These constitute the frame within which the transmission of text takes place. The right hemisphere is also involved in language production, but its influence is not on the text itself but on the frame of interpretation (E. Ross 1988:188-89): "evidence has been gathered in the last decade to show that the right hemisphere (has) a major role in modulating attitudes and emotion". More recent research (cited in Obler and Gjerlow 1999) simply confirms the above.

Clearly, like Hall's triangle halves, the two hemispheres working together create meaning, and also, as hypothesized by Hall, "there is continuous competition between the two hemispheres for the level of control" (Stein 1988:133). According to one textbook on the brain (The Diagram Group 1982:291), "Theory has it that left brain hemispheres inspired our Western, strongly verbal, scientific culture, while right brain hemispheres produced the artistic, mystic cultures of the East". Not only – the great gender divide – according to Pease and Pease (2001:41-69) is also due to separately developed hemispheres. They cite neurological research confirming the following:

> - A woman's brain has a thicker corpus callosum (bridging the two hemispheres)
> - A women has up to 30 % more connections between left and right hemispheres
> - Men's brains are more compartmentalized: e.g., men's speech is located predominantly in the left hemisphere whereas women have many locations for speech
> - Women have more right brain activity, except for spatial skills

Charles Hampden-Turner produced *Maps of the Mind* (1981:86-89). In this book, he gives much space to 'The Mind-Splitters', and links 25 major philosophical theories to the left-right split. He also suggests that Chomsky's surface structure is left hemisphere, while the deep-structure is right hemisphere. Paul Watzlawick (1993:14) of the Mental Research Institute in Palo Alto agrees. His book, *The Language of Change*, is devoted to communication problems and hemisphere differentiation. What emerges from the research he cites is that the full representation of "experiences of our inner world" lies in the right hemisphere while, in his words, "grammar, syntax and semantics" are organized in the left hemisphere.

However, at the same time Hampden-Turner (1981:88) adds a warning:

> By the same token it would be an error to conceive of the two hemispheres as containing homunculi, i.e. little musicians dancing in the right, mathematicians wrangling in the left. Rather, both hemispheres show some activity almost all the time. They merely process information differently and in varying levels of intensive intensity.

Michael Grinder (1989:40), brother of one of the NLP founders, and National Director of NLP in Education in the United States, suggests that individuals develop different communication skills depending on their hemisphere development. His taxonomy of skills (and that of Pease and Pease 2001:49) is very similar to those presented for low and high context modes:

Modes of consciousness	
Left hemisphere	**Right Hemisphere**
• verbal	non-verbal
– symbols	– spatial relationships
– language (words)	– shapes/patterns; melody
– phonetics	– visualization

• logical	intuitive, creative
• sequential	random
• linear/lineal	holistic/spatial
– locating details	– the big picture
• reality-based	fantasy-oriented
• facts	feelings/ emotions
• temporal	non-temporal

Watzlawick (1993:33, 35), reporting others, notes that "the hemispheres are much less differentiated in childhood than in later life". He suggests that eventual dominance will depend on parent reinforcement.[7] This is very possibly the basis of how cultures have developed. A problem will be perceived in the environment as requiring either a right or left hemisphere type of solution. Hence: "The hemisphere for which a certain outcome is more important will take the initiative and determine the problem-solving behaviour".

• *Lateralization and Translation Strategies*
We can now also see how the teaching, or at least the presentation, of translation theory has changed over the past thirty years in terms of learning style and hemisphere preference. The decoding-encoding model, for example, focused on the surface or deeper structures of the text, whereas now the emphasis is very much on heuristic processes and frames.

The differences in approach are a reflection of analytical and holistic thinking styles. The decoding, analyzing and recoding approach is very LCC oriented, with a high priority placed on 'the text' and the source language words. The more recent approach is HCC in orientation. The emphasis now has shifted to the context and the relationships between the words in the text and other frames.

We also mentioned, in Chapter 8.1, that trainee translators and interpreters tend to process locally rather than globally. Franco Fabbro (1989:79-80), who has worked on trainee interpreters, has been able to demonstrate experimentally that the trainees begin their university career left brain oriented, processing text, field dependent, and analyzing small chunks of speech. Grinder (1989:2) points out that this is not particularly surprising. The education system in North America (and I would include the West in general) has, he says, a "propensity to the left hemispheric way of thinking". Fortunately, Fabbro also discovered that by the time the trainees reach their final year, the right hemisphere is just as active.

We can now link this to lateralization. Cultural interpreters and mediators will be both left and right brain oriented to enable them to both analyze and create frames. Laura Gran (Gran and Dodds 1989:95), talking specifically about interpreting makes the same point: "Obviously, the interpretation process also

---

[7] See, however, Pease and Pease (2001:52) summary of 'natural' hemisphere development in children.

presupposes the activation of both logical and intuitive skills. It is my conviction that there is a lot to be learned about how to develop these two different abilities".

• *Summary*

To sum up, all cultures will be on a cline with a tendency towards giving priority either to the left hemisphere, the text, or to the right hemisphere, the context. When communicating, most people in all cultures intuitively and unconsciously calculate what constitutes a message, and therefore what is already shared and what need not be mentioned. How the message is then transmitted, and how much through the text or through the context is also an agreed principle within a culture.

Again we must stress that this is a general organizing principle, and as we go into more detail we will find that cultures vary their text/context priorities according to context of situation. The next chapter focuses on contexting with regard to culture-bound use of language and how this can affect translation.

Chapter 11. Transactional Communication

The aim of this chapter is to:
- discuss HCC and LCC culture preferred communication styles
- develop KISS/KILC communication styles
- give practical examples of spoken and written differences
- discuss the importance of clarity

11.1 Transactional and Interactional Communication

The context of situation will influence the appropriacy of communication style within cultures. A purely transactional situation based entirely on the transmission of facts, such as a catalogue of screw sizes, a price list or invoice is hardly likely to engage the reader at a personal level – whatever the culture. Clearly, a request, an invitation, a refusal and any form of negotiation involves engagement at a more personal level, as does all phatic communication. Invariably, native speakers and writers will adapt their style according to the context. It must be stressed, of course, that these contexts are never totally clear-cut, and like text-typologies, appear in blend forms. In communication there are 2 levels at which contexting takes place. We have already mentioned the play off between expressed information and shared (background, contextual) information. The second level of contexting has to do with the text itself. How much text needs to be written or spoken "to express information"? American-English guides stress the 'KISS principle': keep it short and simple, or 'the C-B-S style': clarity, brevity and sincerity. The British English equivalents are to be found in the language of the writer Jonathan Swift: "Proper words in proper places make the true definition of style", or Sir Ernest Gowers: "Be short, be simple, be human".

An alternative (more diffuse) approach values completeness of expression. This could be termed "KILC": keep it long and complete. A KILCy approach is also a preferred Anglo-American style when the situation of context is judged as interactional. The idealized preferred speaking and writing styles may be classified as follows:[1]

COMMUNICATION	GB preferred style LCC	ALTERNATIVE preferred style HCC
TRANSACTIONAL	**KISS (clarity)** • low information load • clarity • reader friendly • synthetic	**KILC (completeness)** • high information load • completeness • writer friendly (expert / non-expert) • detailed

---

[1] See also handout No. 11 from Trickey and Ewington's (2003) Trainer's Manual, which includes more detailed (idealized) differences between English, French, German and Italian.

	• single task logic • relevant facts in text • inductive • black and white photo	• multi-task logic • situation explained in text • deductive • oil painting

INTERACTIONAL	**KILC (completeness)**
	• invitation/request +
	  politeness in text
	• indirect
	• avoidance of negative
	  answers, so neutral style
		KISS (clarity)
		• invitation/request in text;
		  politeness in context.
		• direct
		• personal feelings not
		  placed above the whole
		  situation (i.e. no special
		  allowance for personal
		  feelings)

The following sections focus principally on transactional communication as the context of situation, while Chapter 12 has interactional communication as its focus. Most of the examples will relate to translating *into* the preferred English style.

11.2 Medium

Medium   spoken
            written
            visual
HCC/LCC Examples
• Contracts: agreements
• Typical expressions
• House buying
• Advertising

Higher context communication cultures will tend to prefer more personal communication (e.g. face-to-face, telephone) and will be more drawn to the visual. LCC cultures, on the other hand, will tend to prefer written explicit information (letters, memos, emails, meeting agendas, and so on).[2] Both Sifianou (1989) and Hall (1982:40) note that the British tend to use the phone mainly for "actual business or emergencies" and for transactional communication. The Greeks, on the other hand, being more HCC, use the telephone for much phatic (interactional) communication, and to replace the fact that they cannot make the same number of personal visits that their HCC culture would necessitate. Interestingly, though hardly surprisingly, the topics discussed by women and men on the telephone in Britain (Telewest survey reported in Pease and Pease 2001:143) fall into the same HCC/LCC divide:

---

[2] See, for example, Priscilla Rogers' study on the impact of context on managerial writing in Victor (1992:143).

	Men	Women	
Friends	30%	50%	¦HCC
Sex/relationships	18%	22%	¦
			¦
Work	25%	11%	¦LCC
Sports	16%	2%	¦
Other	11%	12%	¦

Below are a number of practical examples highlighting contexting differences that would require cultural mediation.

11.2.1 Contracts

Whether one prefers to use the phone or send an email indicates the preferred approach towards communication. Surveys show that HCC countries have a higher mobile phone and a lower internet use compared to LCC (Anglo and north European) countries:[3]

	Mobile phone (verbal)	internet penetration (written)	(communication)
Finland	86%	52%	
Norway	85%	54%	
Italy	84%	33 %	HCC
UK	79%	57%	
Netherlands	75%	58%	
Greece	75%	12%	HCC
Denmark	74%	60%	
Portugal	73%	11%	HCC
Sweden	73%	65%	
Ireland	73%	40%	
Spain	67%	12%	HCC
Germany	75%	39%	
France	62%	26%	HCC

How binding the communication is depends also on a culture's preference regarding medium. This is particularly important during the drawing up and the signing of agreements and contracts – a 'purely' transactional form of communication.

Interpreters need to be particularly aware of the culture-bound differences in the finality of the written or the spoken word. One example is the meaning of "signing

---

[3] Statistics not strictly comparable: culled from a number of survey sites using different parameters and not all including latest (2002) results; including www. Nua.com's 2002 Global Internet Trends report on Internet access and penetration, www.Eroscom.de and OECD reports.

an agreement". This signifies the end of the negotiation for the Americans, while it is only a "way station" (Brake *et al.* 1995:41) for the Arabs.

In other countries, company negotiators feel they have the right to change the written agreement if the interlocutors change; or rather, the contract's validity is tied to the makers of that contract – as can happen in Italy. At the other end of the scale, Germans, for example, would not consider it automatically necessary to make a new contract simply because the people who were involved in drawing up or signing the original contract had been substituted. A contract for an LCC culture is with an impersonal organization, not with the person.

Hampden-Turner and Trompenaars (1993:123-24) describe how a written Australian-Japanese sugar agreement teetered during 1976-77. After the agreement was duly signed, the context changed: world oil prices quadrupled and the world price of sugar dramatically fell. The Japanese people, consequently, had to pay well over the world price for their sugar. As a result, the Japanese government immediately asked for a renegotiation of the terms on the grounds that mutual benefit to all parties required it. The *Japan Economic Newspaper* wrote: "It is true that a contract is a contract, but when customers are in a predicament, we believe that assistance is routinely extended to customers from a long-term viewpoint, even in Australia". According to the authors, the LCC Australians considered the Japanese to be "seemingly indifferent to the small print" and saw no reason to renegotiate.

Equally, a spoken contract or rather a gentleman's agreement will be more or less adhered to depending on the culture-bound understanding of its importance. As we have already noted with regard to British and American English, an LCC culture will feel less bound by a verbal promise of intent than a higher context communication culture.

• *Typical Expressions*

Clearly, these different ways of giving information and interpreting agreements have to be mediated by the interpreter. Below is a list of expressions to listen for, which indicate a particularly LCC operating mode:

> I wasn't given the full facts.
> We need a complete report/detailed plan.
> I'd like it in writing.
> I'll expect the draft proposals by next week.
> Can we have a written agenda?

On the other end of the contexting scale we have these types of expressions:

> A verbal promise.
> I give you my word.
> My word is my bond.
> I thought/expected you to know.
> We can work out the details as we go along.
> Everybody already knows what's what.

The implications for negotiation-interpreters are enormous. Translating the content-based discussion from LCC English for a higher context communication culture may well be perceived as impeding the progress (read 'relationship building') of the negotiation.

On the other hand, the English, and even more the Americans or Germans are going to feel frustrated at not being given all the information. They will feel that the other side is working to some 'hidden agenda', which to an extent will be true. A highly text oriented culture will rarely be happy with a lack of information, whereas a high context culture is more likely to understand that first, information is implicit in the context, and second, information comes after the relationship.

The term 'organization' can also be understood in HCC or LCC terms. All countries have a form of organized crime. The mafia in Chicago went by the name of "the syndicate", which conjures up a more technical organization compared to the more HCC "octopus" / *la piovra* or "Our Thing"/*La Cosa Nostra*. We could, in fact, imagine two different ways of conveying the same 'contract', depending on one's contexting priorities:

HCC:	Zio Giulio let it be known that he didn't like Roberto's face.
LCC:	Lucky Luciano ordered Quick Finger Joe to waste Larry the Lad.

However, Francesco Straniero Sergio (1998) points out that labelling Americans as LCC explicit is simplistic: "[Katan] does not consider the fact that the FBI and the DEA, for example, understand perfectly the implications and the connotations (the context of culture) of organized crime in Italy. They have even coined their own acronym: LCN (La Cosa Nostra)".

In reply I would say that the FBI acronym is, in fact, a perfect example of an LCC explicit technical mentality. Naturally, in the same way as the map-makers have to make symbols to represent reality, so the LCC cultures tend to specialize in acronyms. When President Clinton was elected, the term FOB (Friend of Bill) became a commonly used term to show disapproval, or at least make explicit, the HCC, particularist way in which political relationships and communication channels can form. The British (politicians and press) began to copy the idea later with MOB (mate of Blair). These are further examples, along with DINKY, TGIF and Nimby,[4] of a typical LCC pattern: making informal routines of life (to use Hall's expression) technical.

However, paradoxically, it is also true that, as more precise information is added to the model so the language itself becomes more coded due to the universal modelling needs of deletion. The technically codified language (as in this particular sentence) will appear HCC to those who are not party to the context – due mainly to the LCC KISSy rather than KILCy orientation.

---

[4] DINKY: 'Double income no kids yet'; Nimby: 'Not in my back yard', referring to those who protest about road and other developments taking place in their neighbourhood: TGIF: 'Thank God it's Friday'.

11.2.2 House Buying

The buying and selling of a house in the U.K. follows a set procedure, involving a large volume of text information. To attract the buyer there is always an information sheet. The sheet can (and usually does) extend to 3 or 4 sides. The contract between the buyer and seller with the estate agent is always written, and specifically states responsibilities, rights and exclusions. The surveyor's report is a lengthy, costly, but necessary business in house buying in Britain.

None of the above activities is part of the traditional approach to house buying in Italy. When information is given, it tends to be given orally. Hence, perception and interpretation of the following utterance will be culture-bound:

Statement in English	Equivalent statement in Italian
I went to the Estate Agent on Saturday and he **gave** me the details of the house.	*Sabato sono andato dall'agente immobiliare e mi **ha dato** le informazioni sulla casa.*

The two sentences appear to be equivalent, but we should immediately notice the unspecified verb "give"/*dare*. In both cases there is deletion. Using the Meta-Model we ask the question:

How did the estate agent give the details?

It should immediately become clear that the presupposition behind 'how' is different. In English, the full representational form would include LCC written details, while the presupposition behind the surface structure in Italian is a more HCC, particularist and synthetic verbal rendering of the information:

LCC meaning of 'give'	HCC meaning of *dare*/'give'
He handed me the written sale particulars of the house for me to read.	*Mi ha **spiegato** com'è la casa.* He told me what the house was like.

Below is a typical extract from an English Estate Agent information sheet describing the house for sale:

PRICE: £149.950 FREEHOLD
We are delighted to receive instructions to sell this spacious versatile Victorian home offered for sale in good decorative condition throughout. The property is ideally situated close to all amenities with local shops and railway station just a short walk away. Other benefits include a private garage to the rear with further off-road parking facility and a private rear garden. The accommodation briefly comprises: reception hall, lounge with fur-

ther sitting area, dining room, luxury appointed kitchen/breakfast room, three bedrooms, with study and large Victorian bathroom.

Berkhamsted has good facilities and offers various shopping facilities including Waitrose, Tesco and Boots; the mainline railway station serves the commuter and there is schooling for all age groups in both the state and private sectors. Leisure is catered for by a new sports centre and local golf courses and equestrian establishment. The M1 at Hemel Hemspstead and M25 at Kings Langley provide access to London and the North. The new A41 bypass is now open.

Accommodation comprises –

brick built covered entrance porch with tiled floor and outside light. Step up to half glazed front door with brass accessories leading into the...

Reception Hall

stripped pine doors to reception areas, spindle staircase to first floor, high skirtings, double radiator, coving to ceiling, coat hanging area, electric meter cupboard, telephone point (subject to BT regulations).

Dual aspect 26' 3 x 12' 8. Divided naturally into:

sitting room two areas with front room having attractive gas fire with brass surround, marble insert and hearth with solid pine surround sash bay window to front aspect, double radiator, telephone point, TV point, coving to ceiling, high skirting. Square arch leading to...

The description extends for another two pages. The Italian preference is, as already stated for personal communication. Written particulars, where available, have yet to take on this LCC approach. On one occasion on asking for details regarding the size of the house, the Italian estate agent replied: *Mah, è grande, anzi grandissima/* "Well, it's big. No, actually, it's really big". It is, of course, quite possible that the estate agent had correctly sized up the needs of his clients, and had given them more useful information at that moment than four pages of detailed print. Nevertheless, a client expecting 'text' is not going to be easily satisfied with the above comment.

11.3 Author/Addressee Orientation

Orientation	Language	Strategy	Priority
Author/Speaker towards self	expressive high information load completeness	KILC	the relationship rhetorical skills/rich style the author authority production power distance
Addressee/Listener towards other	factual low information load 'reader friendly' clarity	KISS	the task simplicity the addressee comprehension equality

This section covers differences in how information is viewed and transmitted. In particular three areas will be discussed:

- clarity
- information load
- facts

The basic distinction in all three cases, in NLP terms, is between two meta-programs, towards 'self' and towards 'other'. In this particular case, with regard to the transmission and reception of a message, priority can either be given to the production and full expression (self) or to the reception and understanding (other). The sub-orientations that follow will illustrate more clearly the difference in practice between these two culture-bound orientations.

11.3.1 Clarity v Completeness

In 1943, Ernest Gowers, a distinguished civil servant, was asked by the British Treasury to write a guide to writing, as a contribution to what the civil service was doing to improve official English. Fifty years later, Italian minister Sabino Cassesse was asked to chair a governmental committee charged with a similar remit (Tosi 2001:100). Gowers' *The Complete Plain Words*, first published in 1948, has been consistently revised, is still required reading in government departments, and "has exercised a large and salutary influence on official and much other English". The Italian *Codice di Stile delle comunicazioni scritte ad uso delle amministrazioni pubbliche. Proposta e materiali di studio*, or rather "A Written Communication Style Code for Public Administration Use: a Proposal and Study Material" is a perfect KILCy equivalent. However, here, the equivalence ends. It has been published, but has yet to exercise much influence. The KISSiness of the English publication is as clear as is the Italian KILCiness (which we will return to when discussing interactional communication).

Gowers (1976:14) began his pithy prologue with the following:

> Writing is the instrument for conveying ideas from one mind to another; the writer's job is to make his reader apprehend his meaning readily and precisely. ... when he knows what he means, and says it in a way that is clear to him, is it always clear to his reader? If not, he has not been getting on with the job.

The Economist Pocket Style Guide (Grimond 1986, introduction) is another popular publication, and provides a typical example of the practical reader-oriented advice that is given in the British style guides:

The first requirement of *The Economist* is that it should be readily understandable. Clarity of writing usually follows clarity of thought. So think what you

> want to say, then say it as simply as possible. Keep in mind George Orwell's six elementary rules ("Politics and the English Language", 1946):
> 1) Never use a METAPHOR, simile or other figure of speech, which you are used to seeing in print.
> 2) Never use a long word where a SHORT WORD will do.
> 3) If it is possible to cut out a word, always cut it out.
> 4) Never use the passive when you can use the ACTIVE.
> 5) Never use a FOREIGN PHRASE, a scientific word or a JARGON word if you can think of an everyday English equivalent.
> 6) Break any of these rules sooner than say anything outright barbarous.

More recently, *The Open University* (1993:2, 4) also published a style guide, which we have already noted in Chapter 5.3. Not only does it discuss Political Correctness in detail (a clear indication of an orientation to equality or low power distance) but it also emphasizes simplicity and clarity. It is principally designed for its own academic course writers, but is also intended "for everyone producing written or audiovisual materials – from memos to publicity materials – on behalf of any University, for any purpose".

It adds the following points to *The Economist*'s style guide (emphasis in original):

> Try to make your style as simple as possible, so that your meaning is as plain as possible. That way you will be less likely to discourage people, and they will be able to read faster, enjoy more, understand better and remember longer. The important thing is to keep your readers in mind and imagine you are *talking* to them. This will help you to write in a natural, friendly, conversational style. Here are some ideas:
> * Use 'I' or 'we' and address your reader as 'you', so long as this doesn't involve making false generalizations.
> * See if it could be appropriate to use contractions as you would in speech (for example I'm, can't, that's).
> * Give examples from real life to illustrate your meaning (anything that's given a human touch is likely to be more interesting and easier to remember).
> * Try to avoid a mismatch between the reader's ability and the style of writing.
> * The level of difficulty of course material should be appropriate to the particular stage of the student's learning.

The importance of this orientation should not be understated. The impression, as the OU themselves state, is that these rules are for "everyone", for "any University" and "for any purpose". Application of the Meta-Model (Chapter 6.4) on generalizations should heighten awareness of the linguistic violations, which hide a culture-bound map of the world:

> * Absolutely everyone, any university, any purpose, always?

This orientation is not, in fact, universal. Though it is universal to those whose world privileges the principles of Greek classical literature or the "Utilitarian Discourse System" as discussed in Scollon and Scollon (2001:110-26). Newmark (in Séguinot 1995:80), for example, is convinced that though there may be different styles of academic writing (e.g. Anglo-Saxon versus the Germanic style) there is a "far more universal question of good writing versus this clouded kind of writing that you often get in academic articles". This statement is another Meta-Model violation. It is a value judgment. There is a missing performative, so unfortunately we do not know who is taking responsibility, or performing, this particular judgement. The clarification question to ask is as follows:

> • *Good writing* according to whom and according to which set of cultural-bound values?

The answer[5] clearly illustrates the limits of the speaker's world: 'Good' writing according to Greek classical literature. This particular 'good' writing frame values (according to the *CED*, emphasis added) beauty of form, good taste, **restraint** and **clarity**. The emphasized words illustrate that "good", in this case, is measured against "restraint and clarity". It is never possible then to ever judge "clarity" against any other, higher, value. It is, according to some, *the* universal value. This value, however, is in net contrast with more HCC Asian discourse (Scollon and Scollon 2001:151): "For example, Japanese culture places a very high value on the communication of subtle aspects of feeling and relationship and a much lower value on the communication of information".

Italian, which is also a more author, or speaker-oriented culture, does not value 'clarity' so highly either (see Katan 2000). John Denton (1988:243), English, notes that "The obscurity of much Italian media has come in for a great deal of criticism by distinguished Italian linguists, such as Tullio De Mauro and others both in the press ... and in broadcasting". More recently there has been some move in the direction of LCC factual transparency and clarity. The *Repubblica* newspaper (14/12/95) reported that a group of individuals had for the first time begun the arduous task of changing the language of the civil service, which is:

oscura, astruso, spesso minacciosa nei riguardi del cittadino ... la voce della Pubblica Amministrazione non si è mai interrogata su quanto potesse risultare chiara ai suoi destinatari, e cioè a noi ... Ora, in un momento di eccellente disordine, qualcosa accenna a cambiare.	... obscure, abstruse and often threatening towards the public ... The Italian civil service has never asked itself how clear it is to its addressees, that is, us ... but now in a moment of supreme chaos something is beginning to change.

Tosi (2001:91-105) in his chapter on Italian bureaucracy adds the following warning:

---

[5] This is a paraphrase of Newmark's answer during a personal conversation in Trieste, 1997.

> ...the motivation to introduce the reform involves much broader political is-
> sues reflecting the ideological orientation of any government that may be in
> favour of such a change, or indeed against it.

As culture is a dynamic process (Chapter 2.3) cultures can, and indeed do, change
their behaviour even within an opposing ideology. In Italy, though, the orientation
to hierarchy will ensure that the reform measures will be taken up relatively slowly.
As Tosi (ibid.:97) points out, "The status of the civil service or the local authorities
would be diminished if ordinary situations were to be discussed in ordinary language". There has long been resigned acceptance *within* the local context of culture.
The favoured solution by the uninstructed reader is, of course, avoidance. Where
this strategy is not possible, either personal contacts within the system or paid specialists are employed to mediate between the specialist language of bureaucracy
and the language of the people.

Italy, though, is now part of a supranational administration and is increasingly
more engaged in communication with non-Italians, both through immigration and
through globalization. Hence, 'clarity' and an orientation towards equality is becoming more pressing for practical reasons. These reasons hinge round two
interrelated points. First, clarity is the Western business and administration standard. It is true that Hampden-Turner and Trompenaars (1993), for example, also see
potentials for the HCC Japanese model for the 21st century, but for the moment it is
transparency and clarity that is lubricating global communication and business.

The second reason is based on the theory of logical contexting: in an era of
increasing intercultural communication, as a general principle, first encounters are
going to be more successful if conducted in an LCC style. Importantly, it is not
whether one orientation is 'good' or not, but whether or not a particular orientation
(e.g., author or addressee) is more appropriate for a particular group of interlocutors
in a particular context (time and place).

We now return to the Anglo-American value on 'clarity' and look at how this
affects translation strategy (into English). One example, illustrating the difference
in approach between Italian and English, picked almost at random, is the following
extract from a best-selling CD-ROM pack on Giotto, aimed at the general public,
and in particular at the teenage market:

> *LE FIGURE E LO SPAZIO*
> *le figure sono sempre rigorosamente volumetriche, più vicine al rigore*
> *spaziale della scultura che alle estenuate cadenze melodiche medio-bizantine.*

A literal translation into English would be:

> FIGURES AND SPACE
> figures are always rigorously volumetric, closer to the spatial rigours of sculp-
> ture than to the extenuating melodic rhythms of the Middle Byzantine.

The language is poetic, intended to induce a feeling rather than information. The facts are not clear. To translate this text into English (once it has been established that this is not a piece of poetry), we should look for the information, highlight it, and reduce the context to a minimum so that the textual information can shine through. We should always remember that this is the strategy for translating from high to low context language cultures. It is not so necessary the other way round – though the reader might appreciate it:

> FIGURES AND SPACE
> the figures have a disciplined geometry, closer to sculpture than to the sweeping curves of Middle Byzantine.

Professional translators may find that their translations will be 'improved' (according to cultural orientation) by external mother-tongue proofreaders. One particular example[6] is given below. The translation was from an Italian instruction and guarantee booklet for an espresso machine, and the 'corrections' were made by mother-tongue English readers. Most of the corrections involve shifting from an orientation towards completeness to that of simplicity, thus improving clarity:

Original Translation	Correction
top quality espresso coffee machine	top quality espresso machine
thank you for your preference	thank you for choosing Saeco
The machine has been devised for domestic use and is not indicated for continuous professional use	The machine has been designed for domestic use only
Avoid direct skin contact with hot components	Avoid direct contact with hot components
The machine voltage has been set upon manufacturing	The machine voltage has been set at the factory
Remove the filter holder and empty it of grounds	Remove and empty the filter holder
In case an extension cord is used, check that it is adequate	In case an extension cord is used, be certain that it meets or exceeds all safety standards
Never immerse the machine into water and do not introduce it in a dish washer	Never immerse the machine into water
We recommend you to clean the water tank daily and to fill it	Clean and fill the water tank daily

---

[6] Claudia Calistri (1996) professional translator, personal communication.

Follow in all cases the manufacturer's in- structions	Follow the instructions
These instructions cannot include every possible and thinkable use of the machine	These instructions cannot anticipate every possible use of the machine
Moreover, we point out that these instruc- tions are not part of any previous or existing agreement or legal contract and they do not change their substance	Moreover, these instructions are not part of any previous or existing agreement or legal contract

The very first correction has denominalized the original literal translation, re-sulting (as we have noted during the discussion of the Meta-Model) in a clearer message. The only correction to go against the KISS principle regards the extension cord. However, the proofreader has again showed his or her preference for a more reader-oriented style. S/he has (unconsciously) applied the LCC Meta-Model clari-fication tool and has made explicit "adequate for what/according to whom?"

11.3.2 Information Load

An essential feature of the KISS principle is the sensitivity to information load. Larson explains (1984:438):

> The information load is related to the speed at which new information is in-troduced, and to the amount of new information which the language normally incorporates in particular constructions. Some languages introduce informa-tion slowly. Others use complicated noun phrases which allow for information to be introduced more rapidly.

I have adapted the concept here, focusing on high or low information load at the discourse rather than lexico-grammatical level.

The goal of a cultural mediator will be to vary the information load according to text function and target culture, taking into account the information level in the original. The translators of the Bible, being particularly concerned with the effec-tive transmission of the message, have long noted the importance of cultural differences in information load.

Thomas Headland (1981), for example, explains the problems involved in trans-lating the South American Casiguran Dumagat New Testament. A more accurate revised translation had been prepared, but was not appreciated by the target audi-ence. According to Headland, the reasons were to be found in the difference in orientation to information rate causing information overload and communication problems. The Bible translators in this particular case had not taken account of the particularly low information load preferences of the Casiguran Dumagat readers.

A similar problem occurred in translating the Bible for another South American people, the Guaraní of Paraguay. The Bible translators had decided that a more 'idiomatic approach' (i.e. more explicit rather than allusive) was needed to clarify the message. However, as Robert Dooley (1989:52) notes:

> The 'idiomatic approach' translation was effectively rejected and much implicit information that had been made explicit in the text [in the revised translation] was relegated to a footnote, a picture, the glossary or eliminated altogether. Such implicit information, when it was made explicit in the text, came to be viewed as 'explanation' of the text per se.

However, information load differences not only concern 'primitive tribes' but all language cultures.

11.4 Formal/Informal Communication

This section investigates formality in the language from the point of view of cultural orientation. Within cultures, the choice between formal or informal language will, clearly, be guided by the context of situation. If we compare genres across cultures and note a relatively high level of formality in comparison with, for example, English, this may well indicate a culture's orientation towards Structure. This is the case in Germany. It may also be the result of a culture's focus on Power Distance (Italy, for example), and the need to formalize in language the distance between interlocutors.

If we speak about an author/addressee orientation, then an orientation towards the addressee would generally require more informal language, while an orientation towards the author can result in a more formal language.

11.4.1 Formality/Informality in the Text

At the level of text, the preference for formal or informal can be broken down into the following:

Orientation toward...	
Formal	*Informal*
long sentences	short sentences
coordinating conjunctions	full stops
formal register	informal register
text or author oriented	listener or reader oriented
nominal style	verbal style
impersonal	personal
3rd person singular	1st/2nd person singular
exclusive 'we'	inclusive 'we'
Adapted from Musacchio (1995)	

Many authors agree that there is a tendency for British, and even more American, English to favour informal language compared to other European languages, such as Italian,[7] French and German.

Severgnini (1992:251) notes, in his book *L'inglese: Lezioni semiserie/*"English: Semi-Serious Lessons", that Italian tends to *costruzioni barocche/*"baroque constructions" and that these constructions do not travel. He points out that in both Britain and in North America serious problems will arise if translated rather than adapted. As far as KISSy cultures are concerned, Larson (1984:438) points out that "long sentences and complicated grammatical constructions make it harder for the reader to follow what is being said".

11.4.2 Distancing Devices

These are linguistic devices, which increase the distance between author and addressee. Interpreter and Englishman David Snelling (1992:39) singles out the Portuguese *é essential que/*"it is essential that" and explains that impersonal structures of this kind are much less frequently used in English. These distancing devices are also common in Italian and German:

Distancing device in Italian/German	Appropriate English
Is it possible to use the telephone?	May/Could/Can I use the phone?
It is essential that this is read	You must/should/ought to read this
This is how it is done	This is how we do it/you should do it

Informative texts in English (and even more in American) prefer to address the reader personally:

Original Italian	Translation	Original English
Il ferro da stiro Braun è dotato di un sistema autopulente; ...	The Braun iron is equipped with a self-cleaning system.	**Your** Braun steam iron is equipped with a self-cleaning system.

1.*DESCRIZIONE DELL'APPARECCHIO*	1. DESCRIPTION OF THE MACHINE	1. YOUR MACHINE
La macchina per caffè Saeco Magic Espresso è indicata per preparare 1 o 2 tazze di caffè ed è dotata di un tubo orientabile per l'erogazione del vapore e dell'acqua calda.	The Saeco Magic Espresso Coffee machine is designed to prepare 1 or 2 cups of coffee and is furnished with a flexible tube for the supply of steam and hot water.	Your Magic Espresso machine can make 1 or 2 cups of coffee and has a flexible tube for steam and hot water.

---

[7] "Indeed, [Italian] often appears to be more formal than English and this again suggests that the translator be alert for the question of register" (Taylor 1990:125). "Works of criticism in Italian, for instance, tend to be rather more elaborate both syntactically and lexically than their English counterparts" (Ulrych, 1992:135). In Italy a more formal style is normally used here [compared

The mediation shifts in the second extract can be summarized as follows:

1. KILC to KISS
2. Verbalise
3. Change 3rd to 2nd person
4. Reduce information load
5. Focus on 'What does the reader need to know?' and foreground "What does X do?"

For more formal writing, such as for academic journals, the impersonal will be the preferred form in Italian.[8] In English there will be a greater preference towards the personal, though, as in this book, there is still a tendency to use 'we' instead of 'I'. In American English, the first person singular is a logical consequence of the culture's orientation to personal transparency:

Original Italian	Literal Translation	Original English
In questo articolo saranno illustrate le due diversi teorie.	In this article will be illustrated the two different theories.	In this article I/we would like to illustrate the two different theories.

More than anything else, in English (both American and British), there will generally be an option regarding formality depending on the subject, the type of journal and its audience. For example, a similar article discussing "Law, Food and Geometry" written by the same two British authors in two British journals *Mathematical Spectrum* and *Philosophical Transcripts of The Royal Society London* resulted in two very different styles. The first has a magazine style, and is essentially directed at students and teachers of mathematics in schools, colleges and universities. The second is directed at professionals, mathematicians and chemists.

> Specific migration is also dealt with in Article 4, which includes: [...]. The specific migration limits in the list set out in Annex II are expressed in mg/kg [...]. Many readers may suppose that we have miscopied the last sentence, but that is not so; others may be laughing! As we show below, it is ludicrous. In the next two sections, we give some simple calculations to expose some of the serious faults in these regulations.

> It is important to prove this contention, namely that the scientific base of migration research has been too narrow, till now at least. Evidence is easy to find, and two examples are discussed in detail in the two appendices. Appendix A demonstrates that an existing Directive does not provide the protection to the consumer that is its intention. A major reason is that the package size

---

to English], unless it is a work designed for an extremely wide audience (Musacchio, 1995:100, personal trans.).

[8] For a detailed analysis of English/Italian formal writing see Scarpa (2001).

> and shape are totally ignored; additionally the directive makes some implicit, but erroneous, assumptions about basic science. Appendix B points out some of the serious errors ...

However, translation into English does not always mean a shift from formal to informal. As Ian Mason (1994:24) points out, Sigmund Freud's essays were translated from a standard and "subjective" German into a "more clinical, more scientific, and less subjective" Latinized English. Mason continues:

> [The translator] strove to render the target text more abstract, more learned, and more scientific in order that it would appeal to the Anglo-American medical/scientific community and thus win acceptance for a set of ideas which, in the original, stemmed from a different European humanist tradition.

Clearly, here, the overriding cultural orientation differences are between the (relatively informal) humanities and the (more formal) medical/scientific community.

11.4.3 Formality in Titles

Titles distinguish people by sex, marital status, educational qualifications and status. The Americans and Australians (see Wierzbicka 1986a) are the most informal, dispensing with most titles, and even abbreviating peoples' names. In general, the higher the context orientation the more important the title because it ascribes status. However, LCC cultures (such as Germany) may also appreciate titles because they clearly categorize and define people's roles.

Britain, which is relatively HCC in relation to America, has a greater 'respect' for titles and full names, as the following extract from Tom Wolfe's novel clearly shows. Peter Fallows (British English) is at his desk at work, and reacts to appropriate American levels of language informality with regard to the use of titles. The scene is, appropriately, New York (emphasis in the original):

> Peter Fallows kept his head down and lifted one hand, as if to say, 'Please! This call cannot be interrupted'. "Hello Pete, said Goldman. *Pete!* he said, and not very cheerily either. *Pete!* The very sound set Fallow's teeth on edge. This ... appalling ... Yank ... familiarity! and cuteness. The Yanks! – with their Arnies and Buddies and Hanks and ... *Petes*".

Trompenaars and Hampden-Turner (1997:72) suggest that the American propensity to use diminutives is due to the shifting and temporary nature of relationships, and the need to re-socialize several times in a lifetime. Wierzbicka (1986a:352) gives a taxonomy of Australian abbreviations and suggests that each class of abbreviations "reflects a characteristic Australian attitude" such as the desire for informality, anti-intellectualism and verbal affection.

The individual use of titles will not only depend on the relative cultural orientations of the two interlocutors, but also on the context of situation, such as perceived so-cial (or power) distance, the relationship and whether or not any other listeners are present. Hence, the same person may well have been called with the following titles during the course of a long day:[9]

> Your Royal Highness
> the Princess of Wales
> Princess Diana
> Lady Di
> Diana
> Di
> Squidgy

The most important point is that formal oriented cultures will value titles, and will require their use more than informal oriented cultures do. Hence, it will not always be appropriate for an American to introduce himself as follows: "Hi! My names Charles Edwards, I'm CEO, but just call me Chuck and we'll all get along fine". It should be the role of the cultural interpreter to inform people of the possi-ble misinterpretation of such 'friendly' overtures. Scollon and Scollon (2001:57-58) write "When someone addresses you as Mr Schneider and you answer back, 'Juan,' whatever your intentions might be, ... we hear one person taking a higher position over the other". They also point out how difficult it is to arrive at a mutually satis-factory naming ritual, even when both parties are culturally sensitive. The answer to this type of problem lies in the conscious use of rapport skills, well described in the NLP literature.

The Anglo-American use of titles will be based on the formality of the immedi-ate context (as in the Diana example). This should be compared with diffuse cultures that prefer to ascribe status irrespective of context, such as the German. As Trompenaars and Hampden-Turner (1997:82) point out, "Herr Doktor Muller is Herr Doktor Muller at his university, at the butcher's and at the garage; his wife is also Frau Doktor Muller in the market, at the local school and wherever she goes". This is particularly true in the South of Germany and in Austria, where it is also possible to hear the chemists' wife being called Frau Apotheke, literally "Mrs Chemist".

Formality in German dictates the use of both academic and professional titles. However, as already mentioned, this is not a result of Power Distance, but of the need for defined Structure: clarity in the procedure. Hence the status is well defined in the title: Univ.-Prof. Dr. Horst W. Drescher. Drescher has a university degree (Dr.) and is a university professor. Italians also have a high respect for titles, though wives do not carry the husband's title; and professors do not state whether or not

---

[9] Princess Diana lost her "Highness" title as a result of her divorce, which further illustrates the importance of context of situation. With her death there have been calls for a reinstatement of the title; a sign that – for some – the context of situation has significantly changed again.

they are school or university professors nor do we know whether or not they have a degree. People should already know. Similarly, the unstated Italian procedure of starting university life at 'a quarter past' is clearly stated in Germany. A conference starting at "09.00 on the dot" is explicitly written as "09.00 s.t.", whereas if it is to start 15 minutes later the text will read "09.00 c.t.".[10]

When translating between formal and informal cultures, mediators will need to delete many of the normal terms of address. In fact, most of the Italian status titles, shown in the following table, necessary when addressing a person of that status in a formal setting, will be translated by the all-encompassing "Mr/Mrs/Ms." or by first and last name. For example, the president of a Chamber of Commerce in Italy would be greeted by his staff in the morning with a "*Buongiorno signor Presidente*". On his arrival to England, he would be greeted by name: "Good morning Mr. Donaggio". Clearly, on arrival to more formal countries, his British counterpart would be addressed as "Mr. President".[11]

Term of Address	Translation Gloss	Status
Cavaliere	horse rider	knight (equivalent to a British OBE)
Magnifico	magnificence	university rector
Presidente	president	president/chair of an organisation
Avvocato	lawyer	lawyer
Ingegnere	engineer	engineer
Professore	professor	school teacher
		university lecturer/professor
Dottore/ssa	doctor	graduate

To reduce cross-cultural problems a number of people carry two business cards; one for a formal and one for an informal culture. With regard to the use of business cards and translation, Mead (1990:153) suggests:

> Try to have your cards translated and printed before you leave your own country. You may be expected to present cards as soon as you meet your opposite number when landing at the airport. If necessary, seek the advice of the other country's embassy or chamber of commerce on where to find an efficient translator and printer. Have your title translated in terms of an appropriate equivalent rank in the other culture.

11.5 Example Texts

In this section we will examine a number of text types, all of which focus on giving information. In each case, the main translation issue is cultural orientation.

---

[10] s.t.: *sin tempore*; c.t.: *con tempore*.
[11] For a discussion of the translation of Nelson Mandela's non-hierarchical naming into Italian see Katan 1996.

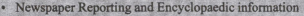

- Newspaper Reporting and Encyclopaedic information
- Informative Texts
- Price and Technical Information

11.5.1 Newspaper Reporting and Encyclopaedic Knowledge

Below, we look at an example of Italian, American and British news reporting. The *Corriere della Sera* was compared with *The Washington Post* and *The Independent* for factual references in articles relating to the same event on the same day: the attempted Russian coup in 1993 (Katan 1998). The journalists from thee three papers write for the same socio-economic group of readers, yet the re-presentation of the essential elements of the coup is markedly different. The research focused on the analysis of the extrinsic features (Downing and Locke 1992:459): "those factors realized by the qualifier, (which) identify an entity by something outside it, or add supplementary information".

The reason for choosing the presence or lack of extrinsic features is that they are a clear indication of the contexting bias of a text and hence of the target reader. The following is a list of the principal actors and places, and their related extrinsic features as first mentioned in articles on the attempted coup in Moscow, October 3rd 1993:

Corriere della Sera	Translation	*The Independent*	*The Washington Post*
Boris Eltsin	Boris Yeltsin	President Boris Yeltsin	President Boris Yeltsin
La Casa Bianca	The White House	the White House	The parliament, known here as the White House
sostenitori di Rutskoi e Khasbulatov	supporters of Rutskoi and Khasbulatov	supporters of the Soviet-era parliament, the (pro-Rutskoi) fighters	hard-line rebels
Alexander Rutskoi, che incita alla rivolta	Alexander Rutskoi, who is inciting the revolt	Their leaders, Vice President Alexander Rutskoi and Speaker Ruslan Khasbulatov	Alexander Rutskoi, the self proclaimed 'president' leading the anti-Yeltsin forces
l'assalto ... alla televisione	the assault ... on the television	the Otskankino television centre	state television complex/the television station in Northeast Moscow.
l'assalto ... alla Tass	the assault ... on the Tass	the offices of Itar-Tass news agency	The Russian Tass news agency

As can be seen, there is a much higher qualification in both *The Independent* and *The Washington Post* compared to the *Corriere della Sera*. So, as we would expect from relatively LCC cultures, both the British and American reader is given more factual information in the text than their Italian counterpart. There are a number of possible reasons.

First, the Italian readers, as members of a higher context communication culture, may be expected to have a wider encyclopaedic knowledge gained from other sources. Alternatively, at a meta-level the explicit dissemination of factual information is not what is expected or needed. In fact, the Italian journalist and writer Beppe Severgnini who has spent part of his career in England, notes:

Il disagio davanti alla precisione delle risposte americane (gli italiani non sempre domandano per sapere; spesso domandano per parlare). Il fastidio per la precisione nord europea. (*Corriere della Sera* 15/11/95).	The unease felt with American replies – Italians don't always ask questions to know something; they frequently ask questions so that they can speak. The annoying Northern European precision.

As we shall see more clearly there is another more HCC cultural priority in operation, systemic thinking, which focuses on the wider situation, and the implications.

11.5.2 Informative Texts

The second example focuses on the implicitness of information in HCC cultures, and the need for explicit information in English. Below is an extract from a circular sent by the organizing committee to speakers at an international conference:

Gli speaker possono restare 7 giorni presso l'albergo.	The speakers can stay for 7 days in the hotel.

The Italian is implicitly clear (to an Italian audience). Equivalent clarity in English requires explicit disambiguation:

Implicit in Italian...	To be made explicit for LCC readers, and to reduce miscommunication
from a separate brochure	the dates of the conference, and hence the maximum number of nights a conference speaker can stay
from encyclopaedic knowledge	single, rather double, room only
from knowledge of conference administration procedure	paid by conference organiser, not by delegate

Good style in English would be as follows:

> Single room accommodation for speakers will be paid by the conference organizers for a maximum of 6 nights between 7th and 16th July.

With regard to the dissemination of information, recent changes in the issuing and punching of rail tickets in Italy has, unusually, led to an explanatory leaflet published in four languages. It was also noted[12] that the informative leaflets and television campaign began to be seen only after a handsome 18 billion old lire (approx. € 9 million) had been collected by the railway inspectors in fines.

However, apart from the delay in preparing the leaflet, the information was not particularly clear (from an LCC point of view), due to the KILCY Italian orientation towards hierarchy and structure. The orientation towards structure places a priority on the listing of all possibilities, such as a complete set of rules and regulations, to reduce any ambiguity in the text and to cover all eventualities. Any translation attentive to form will make the Anglo-American orientation to simplicity difficult to follow, as the following official translation shows:

Original Italian	Literal Translation	Official translation
Ecco a Voi un ufficio informazione sui biglietti ferroviari, che sembra un dépliant.	Here you are, an information office about railway tickets, which appears to be a leaflet.	Just for you, a ticket office that looks like a leaflet.
BIGLIETTI FS DI CORSA SEMPLICE	SINGLE TICKETS	FS SINGLE TICKETS
I biglietti possono essere utilizzati entro due mesi dal giorno di emissione, questo compreso, salvo diverse disposizioni tariffarie.	The tickets can be used for up to two months from the date of issue, this [date] included, except for different tariff regulations.	These tickets can be used for up to two months from the date of issue inclusive. Different periods and conditions may be based on other tariff regulations.
I biglietti per essere validi devono essere convalidati prima della partenza del treno utilizzando le apposite macchine obliteratrici o rivolgendosi prima della partenza, di propria iniziativa, al personale del treno, previo pagamento del diritto di esazione (Lire 10.000).	The tickets to be valid must be consolidated before the departure of the train using the placed-for-that-purpose punch machines or by addressing oneself, of one's own initiative, to the staff of the train, subject to the payment of the right of levy (Lire 10,000).	Tickets are only valid if they are stamped prior to train departure by means of the appropriate ticket-stamping machines or if passengers, of their own initiative, pay a charge of Lire 10,000 to the train staff before departure.

---

[12] *Corriere della Sera*, 17/12/95

In caso di mancanza o inagibilità delle obliteratrici, il viaggiatore può ottenere la convalida del biglietto rivolgendosi prima della partenza alla biglietteria FS oppure, di propria iniziativa, al personale del treno senza dover corrispondere il diritto di esazione.	In the event of the lack or unusability of the machines the traveller can obtain a validation of the ticket addressing him/herself before departure at the FS ticket office or, of his/her own accord, to the train staff without having to pay the right of levy.	In the event of the machine being out of order or unavailable, passengers can validate their tickets at the FS ticket office, or else by asking the train staff of their own initiative without having to pay any extra charge.
La mancata o errata convalida determina l'applicazione della penalità di Lire 30.000 e del diritto di esazione di L. 10.000.	**The missing or incorrect validation will result in the application of a penalty of Lire 30.000 and a Lire 10.000 right of levy.**	Otherwise, besides the charge of Lire 10.000, a fine of Lire 30.000 will be imposed.

Apart from the translation errors (ticket-stamping machine rather than ticket-punch), the official translation lacks clarity in these first three paragraphs. The Anglo-American audience (and more importantly anybody else who does not speak Italian) will be looking for the facts, and what to do. A more LCC style fact-sheet, with an orientation towards the reader, would look something like this:

ITALIAN RAIL TICKETS: WHAT YOU NEED TO KNOW	
SINGLE TICKETS	**If I don't punch?** Inform the ticket inspector on the train and pay €5.00 excess.
Validity: Unpunched, 2 months, unless otherwise specified.	*or* Risk paying excess + €15.00 fine.
What to do: Punch ticket in the platform ticket-punch. These are yellow, and are conspicuously placed near the platforms.	**And if there's no ticket-punch?** Validate ticket at the ticket office. *or* Inform the ticket inspector on the train. No excess payable.

11.5.3 Advertising

The advertising of goods and services in theory is transactional communication. In practice, the function is not the dissemination of information but the desire to influence, particularly at the level of personal values and beliefs. Here we will investigate how culture and orientations affect advertising text and also a number of other aspects a mediator should be aware of when translating this genre.

Many translation theorists have already noted that translating for the advertising industry across cultures means distorting the surface message to successfully retain the hidden. Bassnett (1991:28-9), for example, noted that Scotch and Martini advertising in Britain and Italy presented the same values but in reverse to achieve the same effect. The marketing of whiskey in Britain focuses on age, maturity, quality and the discerning taste of the buyer. Martini advertising emphasizes the fashionable status of the product and the beautiful people who drink it. In Italy, Martini has been the traditional drink, emphasized maturity in taste and intellect of the buyer. Whiskey is the fashionable product, the perfect gift at glamorous thirty-something parties: *Chivas Regal. Il più regalato dei whisky*/"Chivas Whiskey. The whiskey most given as a gift". As a result, Martini in Italy has recently recruited a thirty-something Hollywood name (George Clooney) to give voice to the current slogan, *No Martini? No party*.

Séguinot (1995:63) emphasizes the importance for a translator to consider, and be an expert in, positioning and pricing strategies: "To isolate the marketing strategy for translation it helps to view the text as a directed reading of the visuals. Will the target population identify with the representation of the user of the product?" Clearly, the visuals may have to change totally as above. Where the visuals remain the same, the text will need to be manipulated until it is congruent at each Logical Level:

Identity:	Can the TC identify with the product through the text?
Beliefs/Values:	What are the myths/values in the original text? Can they be transferred? What clashes might there be with TC?
Strategies:	Are the graphics appropriate? Is the text organized appropriately? To what extent does it fit TC generic norms? Are there any inappropriate text connotations? Does the overall image flaunt any cultural norms?
Behaviour:	Are there any traditions, taboos to take into account?
Environment:	Is there any legislation that might affect the marketing of the product in the TC? Where physically will the text be printed? Where will it be read, by who, and when?

If we think of British advertising, perhaps the most striking feature is the words. Some have already made their way into dictionaries of modern quotations (which themselves fulfil the needs of LCC cultures):

> Catch phrases such as Kiam's [Remington shaver: "I liked it so much, I bought the company"] have proved so effective, UK advertisers alone now spend £ 15bn (approx. € 22bn) a year hammering home messages such as "the future's Orange" or "men can't help acting on Impulse". Arguably, it all began with a slogan so powerful it is still familiar to children more than 85 years later. That

was Lord Kitchener persuading millions of Britons to enlist for the First World War with the stirring poster "Your Country Needs You". Author Fay Weldon provided possibly the most famous catchphrase of the 1960s, transforming life for the Eggs Marketing Board with the effective "go to work on an egg". It was the decade of "only the crumbliest, flakiest chocolate", "shhh...you know who", "beanz meaning Heinz". But the heyday of the British advertising slogan came in the 1970s. This was the decade of Heineken's "refreshes the part other beers cannot reach", Martini's "anytime, anyplace, anywhere", and the "naughty but nice" slogan for cream cakes, coined by author Salman Rushdie, then a humble advertising copywriter. In 1974 came the TV debut of toy martians advertising Cadbury's instant mashed potato, with their catchphrase "for mash get Smash". This ad got so much fanmail the agency behind it had to prepare special literature to send out in reply. In 1999 it was voted advert of the century by a panel of industry experts, for its creativity and effectiveness.

Creatives of the 1970s also came up with one of the earliest examples of sexual innuendo in advertising, with Harmony Hairspray's "Is she or isn't she?" In the 1980s pop or classical tunes were used so successfully that the music almost became, in some instances, the slogan. Many still find it difficult to hear Puccini without trilling "Just one Cornetto, give it to me – delicious ice cream, from Italy". The 1990s was the decade of "Papa! Nicole!", "Ambassador, you're spoiling us", and knowing when you've been Tangoed. But it was also the decade when advertisers came under severe scrutiny for increased levels of sexual innuendo. Cars came to a screeching halt across the country with the 1994 Playtex Wonderbra campaign featuring Eva Herzigova's cleavage and the slogan "Hello Boys".

Other Favourite slogans (sent in by readers):

A pinta milka day	Milk
Unzip a banana	Bananas
Roses grow on you	Roses
Trebor Mints are a minty bit stronger	Mints
Things Go Better with Coke/It's the Real Thing	Coca Cola
Don't say I didn't warn you!	Thompson's Waterseal
It does exactly what it says on the tin.	Ronseal
Real men do it in a Jiffy.	Australian condoms
There is more than one way to slice it	Spam
The Milky Bars are on me!	milk chocolate bar
Wassssuuuuuuppp!!!	Beer
lipsmakin, thirst quenchin, …	Pepsi
What We Want is Watney's	Beer
Ah! Bisto	Gravy
They asked me how I knew, it was	Blue Esso Petrol
Don't leave home without it/ Your flexible friend	Amex Credit card (news.bbc.co.uk/1/hi/uk/ 1357091.stm)

Not only is the text important, but knowledge of the intertextuality is vital for understanding. Greg Myers (1994:5), an American professor of Linguistics at

Lancaster University, notes in his publication *Words in Ads*:

> When I moved from Texas to Britain I found it impossible to understand
> most bill-boards ... This is not because the words in American and British
> English are so different, taken in their isolated, dictionary meaning but be-
> cause the ads typically drew on daily uses of language I had not yet
> encountered.

One particular strategy is to relate one advertising slogan to another, thus height-
ening the effect for those who already know the previous campaign. Nike's "Just
Do It" has engendered a number of copies, including a Thomas Cook travel organization reply: "Don't Just Do It. Thomas Cook It" and a (less inspired) anti-smoking
campaign "Just Don't Smoke". Finally, one highly successful advertising campaign
featured nothing but a huge "Z" on a plain black background. To understand this
particular message, the reader would need not only to know about "Zero tolerance",[13]
but also that "Z" was the intertextual cue.

   This emphasis on the text and intertextuality in advertising is not necessarily
pan-cultural. Séguinot (1995:64) cites Kaynak's handbook and guide to advertising, which illustrates the tendency for France and Japan to prefer style and visuals
to text and argumentation. As higher context communication cultures, this is exactly what we would expect. The Gaelic word for battle-cry, 'slogan', has no
equivalent in the Romance languages, and did not enter the Italian language until
the 1930s. Anna and Giulio Lepschy (1988:16), in their study of the Italian language, note that although "some ads strive to be memorable by their unusual
expressions", they "mostly popularize rather than innovate". Alternatively, an advert will try to impress itself "more surreptitiously, through a smooth, colourless
message presenting itself as artless rather than drawing attention to its structure".

   However, a study by Arturo Tosi (2001:161-87) shows that the choice of text
has now become just as important in Italy as it is in Britain. His findings show that
advertising in Italy is moving closer behaviourally to the British (global?) model,
though Italy's underlying values ensure that advertising strategies remain different.
Clear differences are to be found, for example, in the use of British, American and
Italianized English, and in the continuing non-PC connotations (ibid.:182) in Italian advertising. One Italian publicity campaign that did draw world attention was
Oliviero Toscani's pictures for Benetton: they are not remembered for the slogan,
and do not even focus on the product.

   With regard to contexting and translation for advertising, the default tendency is
that, for most products, an LCC culture is going to expect more attention paid to the
text both in terms of eye-catching wordplay and in terms of factual information. An
HCC culture will focus more on the overall picture and the aesthetics or feelings
created by the advert.

---

[13] A form of policing that allows no crime to be overlooked. Came into use in the USA in the
1980s. Since used in other countries.

• *Price and Technical Information*

The discussion of cost can be perceived either as an aid to clarity and transparency or as an invasion of privacy and a threat to a particularist relationship. Price is mentioned less readily in the text in HCC countries. Differences abound from advertising to the cost of a meal (written menus are only standard in LCC countries). A typical mis-contexted question is as follows (low context question – high context answer):[14]

LCC: "Did you ask how much you'd get for the job?"
HCC: "No, sono una signora" [No, I'm a lady].

The following adverts give an idea of the difference in information focus and load when (in theory) the function is dissemination of information. The English adverts focus on the price and the technical information, all of which can be objectively checked and used to compare with other products:

CANDY AV800 Washing Machine

- **800 rpm spin speed**   ONLY £10.57 PER MONTH
- **3 phasetimer**   SAVE £ 110.00
- **18 programmes**   NOW £279.99
- **Eco system saves water,**   WAS £ 389.99
  energy and detergent.

**3 YEAR AGREEMENT.

Deposit	**£28.00**
Amount of credit	**£251.99**
Charge for credit	**£128.52**
Total amount payable	**£408.51**
34.2% APR	

33% Off! 'FOGARTY' DUCK FEATHER AND DOWN DUVETS.

Individual duvets, 9.0 tog for spring/autumn use and
a lighter 4.5 tog one for summer, join together for comfort all year round.
SIZES: Single, Double and King size
TOG RATINGS: 4.5 AND 9.0 = 13.5 TOG MAXIMUM

These examples illustrate the clarity of an LCC approach, with reader-friendly technical information and cost to potential buyers clear. The emphasis is usually on saving money. Séguinot (1995:64) notes that in many cultures (such as the East) price is a taboo word, and so advertisements in HCC cultures tend to be more coy on price (except for the new technologies). In Italy, potential buyers can be attracted by stating the fact that the buyer might have to pay (an unspecified amount) more –

---

[14] Personal conversation with an Italian university lecturer.

as the following advert for a washing machine illustrates:

Original Italian advertisement	Translation
Scegliere la migliore lavatrice non è più un mistero da iniziati.	Choosing the best washing machine is no longer a mystery for those who aren't in the-know.
LA QUALITÀ SI RIVELA SOLO A CHI TOCCA: **Tanto di più, spendendo poco di più**	QUALITY SHOWS ITSELF ONLY TO THOSE WHO ARE READY FOR IT: **So much more, spending just a little more**

Also, where technical information is given, it tends (according to an LCC view) to "blind with science" rather than give information the customer can use to compare it with other products, such as comparable tog[15] ratings:

Tecni-Dry asciutto anche nelle condizioni più avventurose.	Tecni-Dry **dry even in the most adventurous conditions**
Tecni-Dry **protegge dal freddo e dall'umidità esterna.**	Tecni-Dry **protects from the cold and from outside humidity.**
Scamosciati e bordura impermeabilizzati, membrana Sympatex, Imbottitura a cellula aperta, fodera Microdry.	**Oil-tanned and waterproofed edging, Sympatex membrane, open cell filling, Microdry lining**
IN VENDITA PRESSO I MIGLIORI NEGOZI DI ARTICOLI SPORTIVI	ON SALE AT THE BEST SPORTS SHOPS

The information appears technical "to stimulate credibility and persuasion" (Tosi 2001:162), just like the English adverts; yet application of the Meta-Model will illustrate that much objective information has been deleted. What exactly, for example, is 'Tecni-dry', 'Sympatex' and 'Microdry'? And how, and to what level exactly do they protect against the cold and the humidity? The result in both cases is an impression of particular expertise, which illustrates the Italian tendency to high power distance and particularism, i.e. "our products cannot be compared with other products".

---

[15] "Tog: An official measurement that shows how warm a blanket or quilt is; used in British English" (*Cobuild* 1995).

Chapter 12. Interactional Communication

The aim of this chapter is to:
* investigate Contexting in terms of Interactional Communication
  (Be v Do; Direct v Indirect communication; the verbalization of emotion)
* discuss British indirectness
* investigate how culture affects newspaper reporting
* conclude with a tentative model of the context of culture

12.1 Expressive/Instrumental Communication

So far, we have looked primarily at the transmission of information (transactional communication). In this chapter we will investigate how cultures orient themselves with regard to more interpersonal (interactional) communication. For many cultures, the very fact that the communication event is interpersonal warrants an affective response. For other cultures, particularly the more LCC, interpersonal does not necessarily mean affective. These countries Trompenaars terms "neutrals". The more HCC cultures will be more sensitive to communication that affects 'face'. These two facets of communication, transactional and interactional, are the communicative equivalents of Hall's technical and informal (out-of-awareness) culture. Although we shall be linking the discussion to verbal language, we should bear in mind that this is only a part of interpersonal communication.

Orientation	Language	Possible cultural priorities
Expressive:	affective	'how' something is said.
		subjectivity; immediate expression of personal feelings.
		appreciation of emotion; body language important.
		wide voice and intonation range.
Instrumental:	neutral	'what' is said.
		objectivity, precision.
		control: of feelings, body language, voice.

12.1.1 Facts/Feelings

Cultures vary in their orientation towards expressive or instrumental communication according to their HCC or LCC orientation. Orientation can be inclined towards feelings or facts, the person or the issue. Expressive cultures are happy wearing their heart on their sleeve (not a common English expression), whereas instrumental cultures believe more in self-control.

More expressive cultures (Japan included) will tend to highlight feelings and relationships rather than facts; and do so, also, through heightened non-verbal communication. On the other hand, instrumental cultures, such as Germany, Britain and the USA, tend to put a priority on explaining the facts, the issues rather than focusing on the human, interpersonal element. What is said is placed above how. Displays of emotion are considered embarrassing; and losing control is perceived negatively. However, as we shall see, American, for example, allows for much more expression in certain situations than the British would consider appropriate.

We should also remember that use of verbal expression may be raised to an art form, with extensive use of expressive language for rhetorical effect rather than for the expression of feelings. This is very much the case in the Arab world, as discussed in Chapter 7, and to a lesser extent in Latin America. At the other extreme is a culture such as Japanese which values silence in much the same way as expression may be valued by other cultures. Their proverbs speak, as it were, for themselves:

> Only a dead fish has an open mouth.
> The mouth is the source of all calamities.
> Who gossips to you will gossip of you.

Cultures also compartmentalize their acceptance of expression according to public and private space. Clearly, in a private context, much more expression is appropriate. However, what is considered 'private' and 'public' is, in itself, a culture-bound orientation.

12.1.2 The Verbalization of Emotion

Western society is a predominantly verbal culture, yet there is a great deal of difference regarding what is to be verbalized. An abundance of British English expressions highlight the importance of non-verbalization:

> Children should be seen but not heard.
> Keep a stiff upper lip.
> Bite the bullet.
> Big boys don't cry.
> Self-control.
> (Don't be a) Whinge-bag

All these expression refer to the internalization of feelings. Trompenaars and Hampden-Turner (1997:69-70) compiled a questionnaire asking participants how they would behave if they felt upset about something at work. The question was would they express their feelings openly? The results show the percentage of respondents who would keep their feelings to themselves. Note, in particular the difference between Spain, the US/UK and Japan. (The results are the percent who said they would *not* express their feelings):

Egypt	18
Spain	19

Italy	33
France	34
Germany	35
Norway	39
USA	43
UK	45
Netherlands	46
Singapore	48
Hong Kong	64
Indonesia	55
Japan	74

The extent to which open expression is or is not part of 'normal' daily activity will depend a great deal on the HAP/LAP divide and also on the context of situation. The expression 'road rage', for example, has entered the British vocabulary to describe motorists' uncontrolled anger against fellow motorists, leading spectacularly to murder in 1995. So far, there appears to be no 'office rage' equivalent. The important difference, though, between instrumental and affective cultures, is that verbalization of emotion in British society takes place *after* breaking point and is a sign of communication breakdown. In cultures that tolerate or approve of expressivity in communication, the verbalization of emotion does not signify any form of breakdown. Instead, verbalization is an indication of present state of mind. Communication is generally expected to continue with appropriate verbalization from the interlocutor.

12.1.3 Under/Overstatement

Orientation	Language	Possible cultural priorities
overstatement	hyperbole	visibility of speaker and feelings, full expression of meaning, spotlight on speaker. understatement perceived as: sign of weakness.
understatement	litotes	speaker modesty, listener to construct full meaning. overstatement perceived as: sign of conceit.

Hofstede (1991:79) recounts how he failed a job interview due to his cultural orientation towards understatement. The American interviewers were expecting candidates to express themselves in a way he, as a Dutchman, found exaggerated:

> American applicants, to Dutch eyes, oversell themselves. Their CVs are worded in superlatives, mentioning every degree, grade, award, and membership to demonstrate their outstanding qualities. During the interview they try to behave assertively, promising things they are very unlikely to realise

– like learning the local language.

    Dutch applicants in American eyes undersell themselves. They write modest and usually short CVs ... They are careful not to be seen as braggarts...

Understatement is also a typically British orientation. Its full effect can only be attained through contextual implicature, and is typically favoured in interactional situations, much to the annoyance of more expressive interlocutors. A more expressive culture, such as the United States, tends to presume that everything that needs to be said – should be said. The British or Dutch, on the other hand, presume that the less said – the better.

    Within their own cultures, interviewers, and others, know how to interpret the degree of expression in the communication. The problem only starts in crosscultural communication. There is a clear case here of the need to increase or decrease the expressivity in the same way as we would convert from the higher number Fahrenheit to the lower Centigrade to talk about the same temperature.

    Newmark (1988:14) suggests the following scale of 'emotional tone' to describe the same piece of music. This gives us an example of how the same feelings could be verbalized according to one's orientation to under- or over- statement:

Term	expressivity	example language
Intense	profuse use of intensifiers	absolutely wonderfully inspired
Warm		gentle, soft, heart-warming melodies
Factual	cool	a significant piece of music
Understatement	cold	not an undignified piece

The United States and Britain embarked on noticeably different clean-up campaigns – the American was expressive, while the British as always was low key. The Italian campaign slogan was also expressive, aiming to affect the reader on a more personal level.

American	British	Italian	Translation
Keep America Beautiful	Keep Britain Tidy	Tieni pulito il *tuo* paese	Keep *your* country clean

The same direct and particularly emotive Italian style is to be found on cigarette packets. The difference between the British and the Italian medical warnings is another good example of the expressive and instrumental styles – both of which are appropriate for their culture-bound audiences:

Italian	Translation	British
PROTEGGETE I BAMBINI NON FATE RESPIRARE LORO IL VOSTRO FUMO	PROTECT THE CHILDREN DON'T LET THEM BREATHE YOUR SMOKE	TOBACCO SERIOUSLY DAMAGES HEALTH SMOKING CAUSES CANCER

Where there could be space for the expression of emotion in a text, HCC cultures will tend to use more expressive language. This may, actually, then render a text more informal, as the example from Ulrych (1992:74-75) illustrates:

Italian	Back translation	English
È mancata serenamente la nostra dolcissima mamma ...	Our sweetest mummy passed away peacefully ...	SMYTHE – On September 30th Denise Crowther, aged 79 years, beloved wife of the late Henry, much loved mother of Angela Jones ...

Italian not only allows for more emotivity in informative texts but also in vocative texts[1] such as in newspaper headlines. In fact, according to Stefano Ondelli (1995), Italian regularly has more dramatic newspaper headlines than the equivalent British. Italian also uses many more expressive modifiers than English or German.

According to Wierzbicka (1986b:288), "In Italian, it is very common to reduplicate adjectives, adverbs, and adverbial expressions – roughly speaking, for expressive purposes". She suggests that most reduplications would be rendered in English (she does not differentiate between British and American) by the intensifier 'very':

bella bella	very beautiful
duro duro	very hard
zitto zitto	very quiet(ly)
adagio adagio	very slowly

She also gives examples of translations that have opted for alternative expressions, but rarely reduplication:

Italian	Literal translation	English
due occhi, neri neri anch'essi ...	two eyes, black black too	a pair of eyes – jet black too.
e me ne vo diritto diritto a casa mia	and (I'll) go straight straight back home.	...and (I'll) go straight off back home.
Appena appena da poter passare	just just [enough] to let us pass.	just enough to let us pass.
Quasi quasi gli chiedevo scusa io	Almost almost I asked forgiveness myself.	I'd almost have got to the point of asking forgiveness myself.
subito subito	immediately immediately	straightaway

---

[1] Newmark's (1981:13) adaptation of Bühler's statement of the functions of language is: Informative, Vocative and Expressive. "Vocative" is persuasive, or emotive language intended to affect the reader, "so that he gets the message".

Bene, bene, parleremo!	Ok, ok we'll talk!	Very well, we'll have our talk.
Vedrà, vedrà	He'll see, he'll see.	He'll see – he'll just see.
Parla, parla!	Speak, speak!	Go on, speak out!

The point that Wierzbicka makes is that the first lexical item is often an approximation for an expressive culture, and the repetition is necessary to underline that what has been said is really true – not just natural exuberance. There is, as it were, a lot of expression on the language market. Therefore, as in inflation, the value of the individual unit of expressive currency is reduced. To bring the expression up to its 'pre-inflationary' or rather instrumental value one has to add a number of lexical noughts, and therefore reduplicate. As a recent advert in Italian for butter had it: *Non è burro qualsiasi. E' burro burro!/*"It's not just any old butter: it's butter butter!", or rather, the real thing.

Wierzbicka also mentions the use of the absolute superlative. Here again, for an instrumental culture we have a case of inflation. Literally, the meaning of *generosissimo/dolcissimo/bellissimo* is "most generous", "sweetest" (as in the epitaph cited earlier) and "most beautiful". However, these words will not always be used by an expressive culture to show accuracy or sincerity (as with reduplication) – but emotion: positive or negative. For the English, an expression such as "most generous" tends to reflect the quality of generosity rather than the intensity of the emotion.

Snelling (1992:45, 46) notes a more general phenomenon throughout the Romance languages, that of "cumulative rhetorical style ... the repetition of adjectives of similar or even identical meaning to reinforce a rhetorical effect". He gives one extreme example from Portuguese:

| *Temos uma só língua antiga, evoluída, rica, expressiva, versátil.* |
| We have a unique language, ancient, evolved, rich, expressive [and] versatile. |

As he says, "six adjectives are simply too much for English ears. English will generally prefer one single intensive adjective or at most two". His suggested translation is as follows:

| The ancient language we share has evolved maintaining its expressivity and versatility. |

Below are further Portuguese to English examples:

Portuguese	Literal translation	Preferred English
un páis próspero e poderoso	a rich and powerful country	a thriving country
difícil e complexa	difficult and complex	complicated

um ambiente propício e collaborate	a collaborative and propitious atmosphere	propitious atmosphere
longa e rica experiência política	a long and rich political experience	mature political experience

A cultural mediator needs first to check that the cumulative rhetorical style or reduplication is not performing chiefly a poetic function. S/he then must membership the interlocutor's cultural orientation, and from there decide whether the reduplication or absolute adjective signifies sincerity, accuracy, or emotive comment.

So, depending on the context 'pianissimo' (in terms of speed) could be translated as:

more instrumental	extremely	
⇓	really	
⇓	terribly/awfully	slowly
more expressive	beautifully	

12.1.4 Self Expression

Self Expression	Language	Possible cultural priorities	Example
high	associated	personal information and personal opinions preferred	"I want you to know that I ..."
low	disassociated	objective information depersonalized opinions preferred	"It seems to be the case that ..."

This (sub) orientation relates to the degree of personal involvement a culture prefers to hear expressed. This orientation helps distinguish one of the main differences between the British and the American style of English. Self-expression is the natural behaviour for those who value clarity and public space over indirectness and private space in interpersonal communication. We will look briefly at two example comparisons, both of which focus on written discourse: British/American and French/Anglo-Saxon.

• *British and American English*
There is a great difference here between American and British English. Henry Widdowson (1990:13), English professor of linguistics, points out the culture-boundness of self-expression in his enigmatic comment on American inspired 'whole person' teaching, which encourages students to get in touch with their feelings: "If people learn by caring and sharing and linking hands in Southern California, it does not follow they will learn by similar therapeutic techniques in

Thailand and Tanzania". Nor, do we presume, following Widdowson's orientation, in Taunton or Teddington, England.

An American religious commentator (an improbably named Walt Baby Love) on a religious phone-in on American Forces Radio station, ZFM (14/01/96) replied to a caller with the following words: "I loved talking to you, and I love your thought-processes". An equivalent British commentator would feel the need to depersonalize the level of emotion, and say: "It's been nice talking to you, and I appreciate your reasoning".

The difference between British and American is evident in written discourse too. Judith DeLozier (1995:5), an American psychotherapist, and NLP co-founder, has lived and worked in the heart of the 'caring and sharing' California, in Santa Cruz. Her verbal style is distinctly self-expressive American, and distinctly inappropriate for a British instrumental oriented audience. This is an extract from an article, an edited transcript of the highly personalized talk she gave to an NLP group in Paddington, London – a very long way from California (emphasis added):

> Thank you **for taking time out of your busy lives** to be here tonight. What this group is doing here really does remind me of how NLP started in the first place. There are not many places I've been in the world where the community spirit of NLP is creating what you are creating here. And that is **a really wonderful thing** and you all do yourselves proud; **it makes me want to cry** because this is what I want to see happening.
>
> I was asked to write something for a brochure and I want to read it to you: "The discipline known as NLP began, before it had a name, with an interdisciplinary group of people ... We were motivated by a shared curiosity about how we know, about how we learn, how we communicate, and how we change. And how we can influence the process of change in a well-formed, ecological way. The patterns of NLP were not imparted to us, but unfolded in our learning".
>
> **I want you to be aware** of **just how special what you are doing is**. That you can get together on a regular basis and unfold knowledge in this group. Because it really is about unfolding knowledge in a group of people coming from different models of the world. **So, bravo to you. I will carry this around the world and let them know what you are doing here** ...

Before a mediator is to translate this text for a more instrumental audience, two points need to be borne in mind: the casual or non-casual use of language, and the target audience expectations. The first question is: "is the language standard American, or is it being used by this particular author in a particular way to achieve a particular effect on the intended audience?" The more standard the language the more we edit for another culture.

The second point is: "who was and is the target audience?" In this case, there was an oral presentation to a group of fellow NLPers (albeit British), whose professional culture (psychology) would include an orientation to expression. The speech was then published to be read in an international journal. The mediator, in creating the virtual text, will equally need a model reader. This idealized reader may well accept this form of expressive language in an oral presentation, but would not expect, or appreciate, the same words written in an international professional journal. The original author would lose credibility as a professional.

• *French/Anglo-Saxon*

Blaise Pascal started his professional life as a mathematician and physicist, highly text oriented, in search of technical explanations for the universe. He then had a mystical experience and became a theologian. He is known to the scientific world for his calculation of coefficients of a binomial expansion and for his work in fluid mechanics. In the rest of the world he is known for his *Pensées sur la religion,* a high-context poetical essay on human nature. From that essay came the well-known aphorism:

> *Le coeur a ses raisons que la râison*   The heart has its reasons which
> *ne connaît point.*   reason knows nothing of.
> *Pensées,* iv. 277

However, the fact that one can apply reason to the heart shows that Pascal, as Bateson (1972:138-39) notes, "no doubt thought of the reasons of the heart as a body of logic or computation as precise and complex as the reasons of consciousness". What is of interest for a cultural interpreter is that in academic writing, the French (following Pascal) are even more instrumental than what would be considered appropriate for the Anglo-Saxons. Bateson, an Englishman, continues:

> I have noticed that Anglo-Saxon anthropologists sometimes misunderstand the writings of Claude Lévi Strauss for precisely this reason [i.e. giving the heart logical reasons]. They say he emphasises too much the intellect and ignores the 'feelings'. The truth is that he assumes that the heart has precise algorithms.

Where British English is too 'cold' for American academic or professional discourse, so can French discourse be for the British and the Americans.

On the other hand, the French are traditionally thought of as being more expressive than the English or the Dutch. Bateson (ibid.:10-11), in one of a series of imaginary conversations with his daughter, discusses the following question: "Daddy, why do Frenchmen wave their arms about ... when they talk?" She interprets this non-verbal behaviour as meaning 'silly' and 'excited'. This apparent paradox (cold rationality and excitement) is also noted by Hall (1990:109). In giving advice to his fellow Americans about cultural differences he notes that "The French can be coldly intellectual and cerebral in their approach to literature, art and science, and this is a paradox – they show emotion in their speech and most often in their non-verbal communication".

Snelling (1992:28-29) also notes that the French are an exception, preferring to personalize their mother country in a way that the rest of Europe would not. Two examples he gives are as follows:

Background	Example	Translation
Pompidou's announcement of the death of General de Gaulle	*La France est veuve*	France is widowed
French farmer protest slo-gan, 1992	*Ne vous attaquez pas aux mamelles de la France*	Don't attack the bosoms of France

12.1.5 Involvement

Tannen (1992:196) suggests another orientation closely related to expressive/instrumental, and that is a 'high involvement' or 'high considerateness' conversation pattern. Scollon and Scollon (2001:46) use the terms 'involvement' and 'independence'. These are spoken language orientations towards either the speaker or the listener. There is a clear link between these two orientations and the author/addressee orientation. Deana Levine and Mara Adelman (1993:66) categorize those from a high involvement culture as people who:

- talk more
- interrupt more
- expect to be interrupted
- talk more loudly at times
- talk more quickly

They quote Tannen as categorizing the following cultures as high involvement:

Russian
Italian
Greek
Spanish
South American
Arab
African

Within each country there are clear divides. Levine and Adelman (ibid.:67) mention the high involvement New Yorkers and the relatively high considerate Californians. The same type of divide exists between Southern and Northern Italy, Britain, Germany, and many other countries.

• *Turn-taking*
Listener or speaker orientation will dictate the length and overlap or pauses be-

tween speakers. As Trompenaars and Hampden-Turner (1997:74) says, "Western society has a predominantly verbal culture" and therefore leaves little space for silence or pauses (Finland being the obvious exception). However, there are a variety of turn-taking style possibilities. Trompenaars has produced an idealized diagram of three different styles according to three different cultures he terms: Anglo-Saxon, Latin and Oriental. In each case there are two interlocutors (A and B), and the lines indicate talk-length. The (ideal) Anglo-Saxon verbal interaction is without conversation overlaps (as exemplified by the Latin style) or silent periods (Oriental):[2]

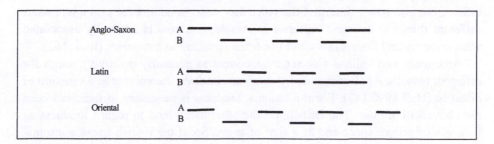

Figure 44. Trompenaars' Idealized Turn-Taking Styles

Statistics provided by John Graham, and quoted by Adler (1991:210) illustrate the differences between Japanese, American and Brazilian negotiators:

Behaviour/Tactic	Japanese	Americans	Brazilians
Silent periods (No. of periods greater than 10 seconds/30 mins.)	5.5	3.5	0
Conversational overlaps (Number per 10 mins.)	12.6	10.3	28.6

The Brazilians are more verbal, and overlap more, than either the Japanese or the Americans. Tannen (1992) also notes a significant difference between men and women with regard to conversation overlaps or interruptions. She suggests that men interrupt to gain power and respect, and their interruptions tend to be on the lines of "Yes, but ...". Women, on the other hand, tend to interrupt more cooperatively, and more often, for a shorter space of time, to demonstrate their agreement and involvement.

• *Voice*

Voice quality, the overall impression that a listener obtains of a speaker's voice (including loudness and intonation patterns) is closely related to expressive and instrumental orientation. In general, a wider variety of tones will be deemed appropriate in a highly expressive culture. An instrumental culture, on the other hand, is

---

[2] See also Adler (1991:211) for a similar graph.

likely to feel that the speaker is not in control or not being serious. Again, the point made by Mead (1990:162):

> A voice feature that is stereotyped positive in one culture may strike the outsider very differently. The listener reacts in terms of his or her own cultural preferences, and hence is in danger of stereotyping the speaker on the basis of voice.

So, interpreters need to be aware not only of their own voice and its potential effects, but also how to interpret the voice they hear. Loudness for example, means different things to different cultures. In Arabic, loudness is generally associated with sincerity and forcefulness, but not when speaking to a superior (ibid.:162).

Americans and Italians also regard loudness as generally positive, though for different reasons. As already noted, Americans increase the volume as a function of distance (Hall 1990:142). For the Italians, loudness is necessary to gain and keep the conversation floor. The British, on the other hand, tend to regard loudness as invasion of private space and as a sign of anger. So, if the British speak appropriately for their culture, their softer style of speaking may be interpreted as a lack of confidence or conviction by a more expressive culture.

The differences clearly become more important during negotiations where it is vital that the right degree of conviction is received as intended. This means that the interpreter must be in a position to modulate voice according to culture – and even more to individual interlocutor. The following figure is an idealized graph, produced by Trompenaars and Hampden-Turner (1997:75), which gives a simplified idea of typical tone patterns for three language types he distinguishes as: Anglo-Saxon, Latin and Oriental:

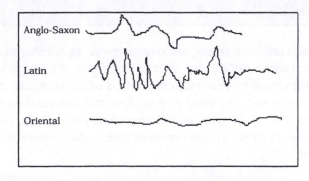

Figure 45. Trompenaars and Hampden-Turner's Idealized Tone of Voice

The authors relate these graphs to the cultures as follows:

> For some (instrumental) societies, ups and downs in speech suggest that the speaker is not serious. But in most Latin societies this 'exaggerated' way of communicating shows that you have your heart in the matter. Oriental societies tend to have a much more monotonous style: self controlled, it shows

respect. Frequently, the higher the position a person holds the lower and flatter the voice.

This is closely related to how much emotion a culture accepts is appropriate to express. The Southern European cultures are freer to express feelings directly, and one of the ways of achieving this is through loudness. The equivalent loudness in English suggests a much deeper level of emotion; and there is the very real danger of the interlocutors misinterpreting their respective meta-messages.

Loudness in an expressive culture can also be understood in terms of Bateson's (1972:179) research on 'play', a term he used to describe monkeys who "engaged in an interactive sequence of which the unit actions or signals [are] similar to but not the same as those of combat". Expressive cultures know that the frame of interpretation is 'play', whereas for cultures that are more instrumental the loudness may be interpreted as combat. This helps to explain the problem in translating the Italian *discussione* into English. Dictionaries give the following possibilities:

discussion
heated discussion
argument
to have words with
a fight

The perception will first be governed by context of situation:

discussione	**discussion/argument/fight**
A: *Abbiamo avuto una seria discussione, ma alla fine abbiamo raggiunto un accordo*	We had a serious discussion, but at the end we reached an agreement.
B: *Abbiamo avuto una seria discussione – alla fine sono volati i pugni.*	We had a bad argument/fight – by the end fists were flying.

The context of culture adds an extra interpretative frame. What counts as routine discussion in an expressive culture with raised voices, overlapping turn-taking, is often perceived first as an argument, and then as a sign that there is a breakdown in communication, as with 'road rage' for example.

For the British, this type of discussion/argument (open demonstration of feelings) is harder to settle and has longer term consequences compared to the Italian or other expressive cultures.[3] For a more expressive culture, this is not the case. Instead, a discussion/argument may well be a healthy part of the cooperative communication event. As Levine and Adelman (1993:66) note, "Many 'high

---

[3] Mead actually devotes a chapter to 'Dispute' (1994: 225-50), in which he discusses the meaning, interpretation and tolerance of open conflict in business and across cultures.

involvement' speakers enjoy arguments and might even think that others are not interested if they are not ready to engage in a heated discussion".

12.1.6 Non-Verbal Language

Non-verbal language is a very large subject, and still not fully catalogued. Some writers on communication glibly report that non-verbal language accounts for any-thing between sixty-five and ninety-three percent of the message (Mead 1994:190; O'Connor and Seymour 1993:17; Pease 1984:9). An interpreter, in particular, needs to be aware that, like any other aspect of communication, the non-verbal signals have different meanings, and are more or less appropriate in different cultures. See also Jane Kellett's (1995) findings on non-verbal performance of interpreters.

Hatim and Mason (1990:71), for example, note that the non-verbal expression of emotion, such as crying, can make or break presidential careers, depending on the culture. The Egyptian president Nasser cried and "strengthened his political hand". On the other hand, the American presential canditate (1970), Senator Edward Muskie cried and "it effectively ended his political hopes". More recently ex-prime minister Margaret Thatcher cried, and it was the final sign of defeat and the end of an era. Expressive oriented cultures tend to encourage spontaneous non-verbal re-actions and value them positively, while instrumental cultures value the stiff – non moving – upper lip.

Some of the meaning of any message is non-verbal, but, as we have mentioned, the non-verbal signs do not always have the same meaning. Also, some cultures will be very much more attentive to the non-verbal signs. An HCC culture, such as Japan will be more attuned to the smallest of non-verbal signals, most of which are out of a Westerner's awareness. The Japanese 'inscrutable smile', the *warai*, for example is in reality one of many non-verbal facial gestures that carry meaning (Japan Travel Bureau 1991:177). Mediators need to be able to pick up these com-municative acts and change the channel of communication from, for example, Oriental visual to cushioned Western verbal.

The subject as we have said is large, and outside the scope of this book. More detailed information should be sought from a guide[4] specializing in one particular culture.

12.2 Direct and Indirect Communication

Orientation strategy	Language (verbal and non)	Possible cultural priority
Indirect:	modal, hypothetical softeners, silence,	conflict avoidance, face-saving, harmony,

---

[4] Allan Pease (1984) has a practical and informative guide focussing principally on the Anglo cultures: *Body Language*. Edward T. Hall's *The Hidden Dimension* (1982) is still a classic guide to cross-cultural proxemics, and his other books all contain references to cross-cultural non-

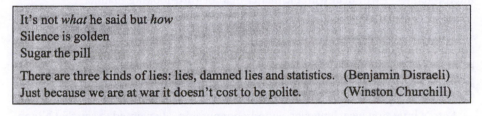

	indirect eye-contact	tact and diplomacy, avoidance of (visible) power distance
Direct:	declarative	acceptance of conflict,
	imperative	acceptance of power distance,
	raised voices	clarity
	direct eye-contact	immediacy

12.2.1 Indirectness and Miscommunication

Cultures favouring indirect communication strategies would fully understand comments such as:

> It's not *what* he said but *how*
> Silence is golden
> Sugar the pill
>
> There are three kinds of lies: lies, damned lies and statistics. (Benjamin Disraeli)
> Just because we are at war it doesn't cost to be polite.   (Winston Churchill)

At the other end of the scale an LCC culture will generally favour clear, unambiguous and explicit communication. These cultures would agree with:

> Call a spade a spade
> Don't beat about the bush
> Get to the point
> Straight talking
> 'Just Do It'
> WYSIWYG (What you see is what you get)
> *La clarté est la politesse de l'homme de lettres*/Clarity is the politeness of the man of letters. (Jules Renard, *Journal,* 1892)

This is perhaps one of the clearest examples of cultural orientations affecting language and communication. An LCC way of thinking follows the logic that if something is said, then the person making the utterance must follow the maxims of cooperation, as articulated by H. P. Grice (1975:46-47). Grice's Cooperative Maxims are as follows:

- The Maxim of Quantity   give as much information as needed.
- The Maxim of Quality   speak truthfully.
- The Maxim of Relevance   say things that are relevant.
- The Maxim of Manner   say things clearly and briefly.

---

verbal (mis)communication. The Japan Travel Bureau, as mentioned above, gives a clear guide to some of the more salient aspects of Japanese non-verbal behaviour.

Though these maxims allow for flouting of the rules, an LCC approach is to treat the text as containing appropriate quantity, quality, relevance and manner – when the context is that of cooperation. However, it is clear that Grice's Maxims do not operate in the same way across cultures.[5] We have already mentioned the American misreading of Japanese meaning during our discussion of manipulation of the text in chapter 7. We will now analyze the incident from the point of view of different cultural orientations.

President Nixon was in Japan to discuss trade and the Okinawan islands with Prime Minister Sato. In the middle of negotiations (also bound by cultural frames) Nixon had conceded the islands to Japan. He therefore asked that Japan might provide some concessions regarding import quotas to the United States. The interpreter duly translated the request. Sato's reply was "*zensho shimasu*", which was literally interpreted as "I will deal with the matter in a forward-looking manner".

Nixon later discovered that Sato had done absolutely nothing to stem the flow of imports into America. The American President was convinced that Sato had flouted the maxim of quality, and in the words of Masaomi Kondo (1990:59), "Nixon felt betrayed and thought all Japanese politicians liars and utterly untrustworthy". Nixon's response was then to inflict as much political and economic damage as he could on Japan.

Sato's intention was, however, entirely honourable. He wanted to say that Nixon was an honoured guest, and did not wish to offend him. A fellow Japanese would have understood the indirect nature of this communication in much the same way as an Anglo-American would understand the following example supplied by Grice (1975:52). On being asked by a student to give him a reference for a university post in Philosophy, his tutor wrote: "Dear Sir, Mr. X's command of English is excellent, and his attendance at tutorials has been regular". The implication is that the student has no command of philosophy.

Returning to Sato's reply, a more understandable flouting of Grice's maxims would also have been in terms of quantity, for example: "We would not wish to spoil your stay here". Nixon may well have got upset, but at least the intention would have been faithfully carried, and Nixon would not have felt betrayed. This would be in line with our earlier discussion on manipulation and cultural interpreting in Chapter 7.2.

In English, it is possible to flout the maxim of quality, which states that the contribution should not include what you know to be false nor what you have no evidence for. Flouting is common when part of a counter-argument: "Citing an opponent's thesis, rebutting this and substantiating the point of the rebuttal" (Hatim and Mason 1997:127). The following sentence is a particularly interesting example, a "lopsided" counter-argument where "the counter proposition is anticipated by using an explicit concessive":

> "No doubt I am biased, but it was the most cruel, evil face I have ever set eyes on". (*Cobuild* 1995)

---

[5] See, e.g., Palmer (1996:191-94); Blum-Kulka (1997:4); Hatim and Mason (1997:140).

Both aspects of the maxim are flouted here. First, regarding evidence, the assertion that "it was the most cruel, evil face ..." is a Meta-Model violation. There is no objective evidence for the value judgement, and there is no evidence to demonstrate the implicit generalization that a particular face, ever or always, signifies "evil" or "cruelty", both of which, incidentally, are nominalizations. Second, the speaker is also saying something, which others may believe but he clearly does not: "No doubt I am biased". Hatim and Mason (ibid.:139-41) point out that this use of counter-argument in Arabic (a high Power Distance culture) can be understood by the addressee as a speaker's loss of Power in that space is conceded to the addressee's point of view. This clearly goes against the needs of a high author orientation culture and hence is not only rarely used but also has a very different interpretation.

In English, the maxim of quality can also be violated to relay irony. A well-known example comes from Shakespeare's *Julius Caesar* (iii.ii. 85-105). Mark Anthony speaks to the Romans after Caesar's assassination by Brutus. The moment Mark Anthony refers to Brutus as an "honourable man" it is clear his message is the opposite. Walt Disney used exactly the same technique in *Robin Hood*. The narrator tells us "The Sheriff of Nottingham is an honourable man". The Anglo-American teeny-tot audience is left in no doubt about the irony of the remark. However, this flouting of the maxim of quality may not work in translation due to what Hatim and Mason (ibid.:140) call "socio-cultural factors such as the attitude to truth". For HCC cultures, truth is not in the word itself. They point out that if one wishes to translate irony into Arabic it should be done through flouting the maxim of quantity rather than quality. Mark Anthony does repeat the same words five times, so readers will pick up the irony either through violations of quality or quantity. On the other hand, as our narrator in *Robin Hood* does not flout the maxim of quantity, the dubbing or subtitling of it into Arabic would need further embellishment.[6] Hatim and Mason give an example of the kind of embellishment necessary to carry the same level of irony as the KISSy English original:

Flouting the Maxim of Quality to produce irony in English	Cultural interpretation: Flouting the Maxim of Quantity to produce irony in Arabic
Since these facts are facts, Balfour must then go on to the next part of his argument ...	Since these are flawless and totally unblemished facts, Balfour finds it incumbent on himself to proceed and invite us to sample the next part of his argument...

---

[6] Subtitling and dubbing leave less space for mediation for technical reasons, so embellishment is, in fact, usually out of the question. See Taylor (2002:154).The translation into Italian *l'onorevole sceriffo di Nottingham* loses the irony totally. The solution is to find a more direct and clear statement, such as *il poco onorevole sceriffo di Nottingham* / "the not very honourable ...". If necessary "Nottingham" could be deleted, and reinserted elsewhere. This approach would have helped the listener understand the basic character of the sheriff.

The flouting of the maxim of manner (say things clearly and briefly) is a particularly culture-bound maxim. Its use in Anglo-American discourse, though, is restricted to KISSy transactional discourse. That being said, in comparison, many HCC cultures can be even KILCier in interactional discourse than the Anglos. Chinese scholar Robert Kapp (1983:20-21) points out that "The indirection that permeates Chinese speech even in translation, can be particularly disconcerting to Americans".

As Grice's Cooperative Maxims do not function in the same way across cultures, the translation, whether it be oral or written, will have to be mediated to allow the interlocutors to cooperate, and to be seen to cooperate, exactly as far as they wish to. This means, at the very least, that mediators must be able to context their interlocutors so that they are able to put the right interpretative frame to the statement. Kapp gives some ideas on HCC Chinese and mediated translation for Americans:

Statement (faithful translation from HCC Chinese)	Usually means (for an LCC American)
Maybe I will come with you.	I'm coming.
Perhaps it's too far for you to walk.	There's no way I'll let you walk.
It is inconvenient.	It is impossible.

Englehorn (1991:115-16) illustrates a cline of possible 'nos' from an Asian culture with their interpretative frames (see also Mead 1994:171). In response to a Westerner's question: "Has my business proposal been accepted?", an Asian businessman might give these responses:

Possible Asian responses	"Has my business proposal been accepted?" ... Interpretative frame for an LCC culture
If everything proceeds as planned, the proposals will be approved.	*The conditional yes.*
Have you submitted a copy of your proposal to the Ministry of Electronics?	*The counter question – the question is avoided.*
Your question is difficult to answer.	*The question is criticized.*
We cannot answer this question at this time.	*The question is refused.*
Will you be staying longer than you originally planned.	*The tangential answer.*
Yes your approval looks likely, but...	*The "yes but..." reply. However, the meaning here is more negative than in English. It probably means: "it might not be approved."*
You will know shortly.	*The answer will be delayed.*

• The Meaning of 'Yes'

The standard translation of the Japanese *hai* is "yes". However, this direct sounding "yes" does not necessarily signify direct affirmation. Ferraro (1994:52), in his *Cultural Dimension of International Business*, points out that "the Japanese in everyday conversation frequently use the term *hai* ('yes') to convey not agreement necessarily, but rather they understand what is being said".

This difference in meaning also exists between Italian and English. The example below is between an English person and an Italian speaking in English:

A: (English)	Thank you for your presentation – it was very clear.
B: (Italian)	Yes.

The English interlocutors are likely to interpret the response as totally self-centred and conceited. Agreeing to praise is not positively valued. Acceptable responses for an English interlocutor would need some self-effacing KILCy comment to downtone the effect of the praise. However, the Italian meaning of "yes" here was "I hear you and am ready to listen". Tannen (1992) notes that this is also one of the uses of "yes" among North American women.[7] The female use of "yes" is a more phatic, rapport based meaning than for men, who expect "yes" to mean agreement – as can be clearly understood from the following example.

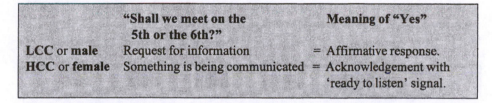

	"Shall we meet on the 5th or the 6th?"	**Meaning of "Yes"**
LCC or male	Request for information	= Affirmative response.
HCC or female	Something is being communicated	= Acknowledgement with 'ready to listen' signal.

Intonation clearly has a particularly strong effect on meaning here, but is outside the scope of this book.[8]

• *The Meaning of 'Thank You'*

Not only is the direct or indirect response to a compliment culture-bound, but the decision to reply at all is culturally determined. Kramsch (1993:8) notes that complimenting in American obliges a reply. The example she gives is "I like your accent – Oh, thank you". She points out that there is no pressure in French to say *merci*: "On the contrary a *merci* in French would be perceived in this instance as inappropriate and even conceited".

• *The Meaning of 'No'*

Adler (1991:207) has compiled a table of "verbal behaviour tactics" comparing various cultures. A flat "no" is to be heard in all negotiations, but the frequency is

---

[7] See also Maltx and Borker's (1992:171) article on interpretation of minimum response. They point out that 'mm' is a phatic 'I'm listening' signal for women and an 'I agree' signal for men.
[8] See, for example, Taylor Torsello (1992:67-143) for a detailed account of intonation and communication, and Hatim and Mason (1997) for discussion on intonation and interpreting.

noticeably different. Below is an extract from the table showing the relative frequency of "nos" per half-hour in negotiations:

Japanese	American	Brazilian
8.4	9	84.7

As can be seen, the gap between the Brazilian and the Japanese/American is
huge. The meaning of "no" in each case is culture-bound. Accepted practice for
LCC cultures is, according to Gricean theory, "to say what you mean". In a relatively HCC culture, the words themselves have less meaning than the context. Some
HCC cultures (Japanese, for instance) use few words. Others (such as Brazilian)
use many, but with variable meaning. In all cases, the full meaning can only be
gleaned from the context. We have already noted that a Japanese priority is harmony, and that therefore "no" is an extremely strong statement, signalling the
proximity of breakdown in the negotiation. Brazil, on the other hand, having a more
direct form of communication will more freely say "no" as a spontaneous expression of feeling. The expression is not intended to affect the outcome of the negotiation
greatly. The Italian approach is also much more direct.

Negotiations are carried out according to a set of (usually) unwritten rules, with
a set number of phases to be followed in order, each phase being marked by particular language. The Anglo-American model ideally follows a seven-point scheme:

1. Relationship Building Period
2. Agreeing a Procedure
3. Exchanging Information
4. Questioning, Checking and Clarifying
5. Generating and Evaluating Opinions
6. Bidding and Bargaining
7. Settling and Concluding

In theory, and often in fact, negotiators will not need to say a direct "no" until
stage 6. According to the model, at stage 5 (generating and evaluating opinions),
the conditional is used, e.g. "How would you feel if we increased the offer by about
2%". The answer would be in terms of "That wouldn't really help matters much" or
"That might help a little". And so, by stage 6, the limits and possibilities are already
clear and much of what is to be negotiated will have already been discussed. The
"nos" at this stage will then relate very closely to the real final limits in the negotiation: 'the walk away'.

The Mediterranean and South American system, on the other hand, is to begin
with a direct indication of where heavy negotiating is expected ("no") and then
concede the minimum possible. In this model the "nos" are negotiable. For an
LCC culture negotiator, if the "nos" become negotiable, the other party may be
interpreted as being untrustworthy, unreliable, and in the end, not a person to do
business with.

• *The Meaning of "Meeting"*

The word "meeting" is translated into Italian by *riunione*. Yet the two things tend to be very different. The Anglo-American approach is very much based on a written agenda outlining the issues, which will be discussed by all. The object will be to decide on a number of issues. The chair will control the meeting; check "it does not get out of hand"; encourage people "to get to the point" and "be objective". This is a classic (albeit idealized) example of a meeting in an instrumental oriented culture.

A meeting in an expressive culture will not put a high priority on a written (and limiting) agenda or on the role of the chair, because its purpose is more of a creative re-union to generate ideas and express feelings. Real decisions of the day may have already been made. The meeting is very much a chance to meet and express opinions; and it fulfils important rapport needs.

Though Italy is a relatively expressive culture, this would also be glossing over the fact that the further North one goes, the less this orientation is apparent. It is also true that in business, many companies have formally adopted the Anglo-American (instrumental) model for meetings. Nevertheless, as Hall ((1982) 1990) explains, it is the informal or out-of-awareness and cultural, rather than the formal and corporate, values that will determine the actual conduct in a meeting. There is also, fortunately, sufficient overlap between an instrumental and an expressive interpretation of a meeting for international meetings to take place with only limited mutual frustration. The subsections below will help isolate some of the key differences between cultures that share either an instrumental or an expressive orientation.

12.2.2 British Indirectness

Wierzbicka (1986b) notes the preponderance of (direct) imperatives in Italian compared to English, and suggests that the English indirectness is related to core British values of freedom, respect for privacy, principles of negative politeness and not wishing to impose.[9] Scollon and Scollon (2001) call this form of politeness 'independence', which emphasizes individuality and the right not to be completely dominated by other group or social values (the context). The Italian values, on the other hand, will be towards satisfying self-expression (author orientation) and towards satisfying more contextual rather than textual value orientations. This alternative aspect of politeness as we have seen is called 'involvement'.

Many of the typically British values are captured in the following article by a British expatriate in Italy.[10] He is clearly outraged at the Italian context-based culture, which has neither privacy nor an LCC 'WYSIWG'[11] as a cultural priority. He devotes the first five paragraphs of his article to giving the background to his particular problem. The background concerns the conflicts of interest between hunters and anti-hunters. He realizes, with bitterness, that his newly bought house and land

---

[9] The English use of the imperative is restricted to transactional instructions and directions for the benefit of the addressee. Otherwise, the imperative, in an interactional context, is a sign of extreme urgency or lack of politeness.

[10] Barry Unsworth, *The Observer* Magazine, 21/11/93.

[11] WYSIWYG: What you see is what you get.

forms part of a regular hunters' route. He now realizes, with even more bitterness, that he had not looked for the wider context when negotiating, believing as he did in the value of the written text for the complete picture: "[the hunters' rights were] something naturally not known to us when we were negotiating to buy the house".

The problem now, as the author mentions, "lies in discovering what remedy is available to us". He believes that his values are shared not only by his audience, but are standard world-values. In fact, these values simply limit his world. They are made clear in the following extract: "No use trying the voice of reason. No good pointing out that we have a right to privacy". What is particularly interesting about this article, apart from his culture-bound beliefs which he believes are universal truths, is the degree of indirect language he uses to express his feelings:

> We really would rather not have people tramping about on our land shooting
> at anything that moves, that we would prefer them to go somewhere else to
> do it, if do it they must.

This indirect use of language is learned, and indeed taught at a very early age. Vincent-Marrelli (1989) notes that Italian children are noticeably 'less polite' than their English counterparts, tending to prefer direct forms where their English counterparts would use more indirect forms and a higher frequency of 'thank you'.

We have already mentioned that nursery schools in Italy teach polite forms not used in Britain, such as *Buon appetito*. In Britain, on the other hand children are taught indirect request and denial forms, and are expected to use them at an early age. In Italy, this form of politeness is not a priority. Hence, communication breakdown and the end of a beautiful friendship can occur at the age of two and a half:

A: (English) Could I have a go on my bicycle, please?
B: (bilingual but not bi-cultural Anglo-Italian): No.
A: (exit crying)

Clearly this does not mean that the English cannot say or cope with a bare-faced "no", but as Tannen says (1985:205), "There are cultural differences with respect to how and what type of indirectness is expected in particular settings". Let us return to the example "Tell me". It can be appropriate in both English and Italian to use the imperative as an opening request for information, as in the following extract from 'The Dead', one of the short stories in the *Dubliners* by James Joyce. Gabriel, a middle-aged friend of the family is about to start a conversation with the teenage Lily (translation by Anne and Adriano Lami 1933):

– **Tell me**, Lily, he said in a friendly tone, do you still go to school? – O no, sir, she answered. I'm done with schooling this year and more.	– ***Dimmi***, *Lily, – disse in tono amichevole, – vai ancora a scuola?* – *Oh no, signore, – rispose. – È già più di un anno che ho lasciato la scuola.*

However, to translate *dimmi* with "tell me" would not be appropriate to indicate

"I'm listening":

– *Signorina, – chiese.*	'Signorina' he asked.
– *Dimmi.*	*'Yes?' [not 'Tell me]*
– *Perché piange?*	'Why are you crying?'
– *Perché sono sfortunata in amore.*	'Because I'm crossed in love.'
– *Ah!*	'Ah!'

Italo Calvino, *Pesci grossi, pesci piccoli*, trans. Archibold Colquhoun:

This explains the typically British negative reaction to the perceived overuse of the direct Italian *Dimmi*/"Tell me", which we used as an example of culture-bound misinterpretation in Chapter 5. The British hear the imperative as a coercive, a face threatening act. Much ethnic conflict in Britain is fostered through the misinterpretation of direct language, and intonation adopted, for example, by the Indian communities. Also, as Hatim and Mason (1997:81) point out, "Crucially, it should be added that the seriousness of an FTA (face threatening act) is a cultural variable; it cannot be assumed that that the same act would carry the same weight in different socio-cultural settings".

It is not only the British who interpret directness in interpersonal language as negative. Below is a classic example of misattribution (Hatim and Mason ibid.). The request for onions, below, made by a Moroccan man in Amsterdam would have been appropriate in Italian. However, the Dutch stallholder reacted as his British counterpart would have:

Culture	Original comment in Dutch	Back translation
Moroccan	*Ik moet een kilo uien*	I must have one kilo of onions.
Dutch	*Zoiets vragen we hier beleefd*	Such a thing we ask here politely.

One point worth mentioning about indirect speech acts is that, as Dressler (1992:14) notes, "indirectness does not always increase politeness". What it does do is make explicit in the text what is already implicit in the context for higher context communication cultures. Figure 46 in page 312 shows the LCC situation (on the left), where the context frame contains little information as to how to interpret the text. On the right, the HCC context frame supplies much of the information necessary as to how the text should be interpreted.

• *Cushioning*

This term[12] is a useful metaphor for the mental process. The speech act ("Send this fax") will need to be softened by a series of verbal 'cushions' according to

---

[12] 'Cushioning' was coined by Tim Johns at Birmingham University, and developed by David

culture as figure 47 demonstrates. The number of cushions will depend on a culture's orientation (or sensitivity) towards the text and towards indirect communication:

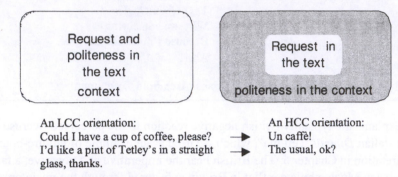

An LCC orientation: An HCC orientation:
Could I have a cup of coffee, please? →   Un caffè!
I'd like a pint of Tetley's in a straight → The usual, ok?
glass, thanks.

Figure 46. Contexting Politeness

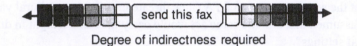

Degree of indirectness required

Figure 47. Cushioning a Request

The appropriate degree of indirectness *within* each culture will depend on six non-cultural factors:

	More cushioning normal when:	No cushioning could mean:
• level of acquaintance between the interlocutors.	low	old friends
• The social roles and perceived power distance.	other in higher position	same level
• The delicacy of the request or subject matter.	delicate	routine/impersonal
• The social context.	formal/public	informal/private
• The urgency.	no (apparent) urgency	emergency
• The present level of rapport	good rapport	breakdown of rapport/ anger

Cultural interpreters will need, as always, to context their interlocutors and be aware of the degree of indirectness required. Below is an idealized 'equivalence'

Trickey of TCO-International. See also Leech (1983:107) on Tact Maxim and illocutionary force of requests; and Brown and Levinson's (1987) positive and negative politeness. The British would tend to negative (non-imposing) politeness. See also Scarpa (2001:150-52) on English hedging, use of 'should/may', etc. in technical texts.

chart between (British) English and Italian for interlocutors in a formal relationship (such as head of department and personal assistant). The formality in Italian is encoded in the grammar through the use of the third person singular. English does not have an equivalent stable grammatical encoding nor is 'formality' such an important orientation as in Italy. Instead, there is an array of grammatical (modals, conditionals) and lexical (e.g. "please") options; and, due to the British English orientation towards indirectness in interpersonal communication, there are more KILCy cushions to choose from:

English	Italian 'equivalent'	Literal meaning	
Send this fax, please.	*Mi spedisca questo fax.*	Send this fax.	3rd person singular (formal, polite, imperative)
Can you send this fax?	*Mi può spedire questo fax?*	Can one send this fax?	3rd person singular (formal, polite, present)
Could you send this fax?	*Mi spedisca questo fax, per favore(?)*	Send this fax, please (?)	Questioning intonation, 3rd person singular (formal, polite, imperative)
I wonder if I could ask you to send this fax?	*Mi potrebbe spedire questo fax?*	Could you send this fax?	Questioning intonation, 3rd person singular (formal, polite, conditional)
I was wondering if I could ask you to send this fax?	*Mi potrebbe spedire questo fax?*	Could you send this fax?	Questioning intonation, 3rd person singular (formal, polite, conditional)
I wondered if I could ask you to send this fax?			
Do you think I could possibly ask you to send this fax?			
If it's not too much trouble, do you think I could ask you to send this fax?			
Fred, um, if you're not doing anything, I was wondering if I could ask you to do something for me. You see, I've got a train to catch, and …			

Direct and indirect cultural orientation not only relates to requests and invitations but to the whole subject of tact and diplomacy in communication. According to Leech (1983:109), the Tact Maxim is of extreme importance for the "English-speaking society":

> Minimise cost to h [hearer], and ... maximise the benefit to h. It means, for example, that in proposing some action beneficial to h, s [speaker] should bias the illocution towards a positive outcome by restricting h's opportunity of saying 'No'.

On the other hand, for a higher context communication culture the tact and diplomacy is more firmly encoded in the context, and so verbal tact is not necessarily such a priority.

An outline of strategies for converting culturally appropriate direct statements into culturally appropriate tactful and diplomatic statements is given below (from Goodale 1987):

Tact and diplomacy strategies

1. If you use *would, could* or *should* you make what you say more tentative.
2. If you present your views as a question rather than a statement they become less dogmatic.
3. If you use a grammatical negative (adding *n't*) you make a suggestion more open and therefore more negotiable, e.g. *Wouldn't it be better if we ...*
4. Using an introductory phrase prepares your listener for your message, e.g. *I hope you don't mind my/me being perfectly frank here ...*
5. By adding *I'm afraid* you show you recognize the unhelpfulness of your comment.
6. If you use words which qualify or restrict what you say you make your position more flexible, e.g. *a bit difficult, a slight problem.*
7. Using *not* with a positive word instead of the obvious negative word softens the impact of disagreement, e.g. *It's not very convenient, I'm not very happy about this.*
8. If you use a comparative (*better, more convenient*) you soften your message, e.g. *Wouldn't 3 o'clock be more convenient?*
9. By using the continuous form (*I was wondering*) instead of the simple form (*I wondered*) it makes the suggestion/request more flexible.
10. The use of the 2nd conditional allows you to show the potential negative consequences of a proposal without rejecting it totally; you focus on the fact that it is possible but, in your opinion improbable owing to the consequences, e.g. *If I were to come to Cannes this week it would create some problems.*

Severgnini (1992:220-21, personal trans.) notes this particularly British orientation with some semi-serious examples of his own:

> In a restaurant in Bristol, for example, it's totally unacceptable to literally translate the type of conversation that you might have in a restaurant in Bolo-

gna. If you say, "I want to change my table," staring right into the waiter's eyes, you will convince everyone present that you are a public danger to society. The best approach is to say "I am afraid this table is not entirely convenient."

He continues with other semi-serious appropriate translations:

English	Italian equivalent	Translation
Your English is somewhat unnatural	*Il tuo inglese è spaventoso*	Your English is frightening.
I agree up to a point	*Che stupidaggine!*	What stupidity!
(How are you?): I'm a bit tired	*Sono a pezzi!*	I'm in pieces/exhausted.
(How are you?): Not too bad	*In punto di morte*	On death's door.
She's not very tall	*È una ragazza bassa!*	She's a short girl.
She's not very nice	*È antipatica*	She's unpleasant.
(in matters of love): I don't object to you I rather fancy you in fact	*Amore, amore folle* [13]	I'm in love, in fact, I'm madly in love

In other words, as ably put by Severgnini (ibid.:221):

Resta il fatto che gli inglesi non sempre vogliono dire quello che dicono, e quasi mai dicono quello che vogliono dire.	The fact remains that the English don't always want to say what they do say, and hardly ever say what they actually want to say.

12.3 The Action Orientation

Action Orientation	Language	Possible Cultural Priorities
Being	describes a scene	Relationship, affiliation, quality of life, involvement.
	Static: nominal	The context
	Existential processes	Status through ascription.
Diffuse		People and activities together, 'be' + 'do' together, less marked differentiation between public and private life space.
		***

---

[13] Severgnini takes these last two examples from George Mikes, *How To Be an Alien*.

Doing	describes the event, close-up on the action.	Task, motivation by accomplishment, involved.
	Material processes	Status through achievement.
Specific		Segregation of people and activities, 'be' + 'do' separate, more marked differentiation between public and private life space.

12.3.1 Be and Do Orientations

The Action Orientation can tend either towards action, 'doing', or towards a state, 'being'. These 'being' and 'doing' orientations correspond to cultures that are tightly woven or loosely knit. An HCC orientation is by definition already tightly woven as most of the information is mainly in the context. Its members grow up modelling the pre-set patterns. An LCC culture, on the other hand, is still developing. Following this argument it seems reasonable to suggest that this HCC non-action and LCC action might also permeate the language. We have already mentioned, for example, that nominalization is more common in Italian (HCC) than in English (LCC).

The 'being' orientation operates at the level of identity: you are what you do. The 'doing' orientation clearly separates the level of behaviour from the level of identity: you are *and* you do. Highly 'doing' oriented cultures, such as the United States and Germany have little problem separating facts and personal feelings. They can criticize the action without necessarily any implication that the person's identity is under attack. All that is involved is the criticism of behaviour. The difference in the way ex-president Bill Clinton and Italian premier Silvio Berlusconi reacted while under investigation is a case in point. The American did his best not to mention the affair in public, and responded to questions from the prosecution. The Italian openly talked to the press about his feelings regarding the trial, and in particular towards the investigating magistrates - while preferring not to answer factual questions from the prosecution.

At the 'being' end of the cline, any criticism of behaviour is automatically understood as a criticism at the level of identity, i.e. it is taken personally. In these cultures, it will be difficult to have objective text-based feedback. Trompenaars and Hampden-Turner (1997:71) relate a story of an LCC (Dutch) and two HCC (Italian) interlocutors at a meeting. The HCC interlocutors, according to their LCC counterpart, had got "over-excited" as a result of having been told that "the idea is crazy". The Italian reaction was, of course, quite understandable. To call 'the idea' crazy is to call the creator of the idea crazy.

An LCC interlocutor, on the other hand, will perceive the event in terms of 'emotional neutrality', to use Trompenaars' term. In this particular case, the LCC norm has been breached. Anger, delight and intensity are all regarded as "unprofessional" in the context of a meeting for an LCC instrumental culture. So, here, the Italians will be regarded as having "lost their cool" whereas the Italians will regard their more LCC counterparts as emotionally dead, "cold fish", or untrustworthy because they hide their feelings behind a mask.

For some cultures, as we mentioned at the beginning of this chapter, interpersonal communication is necessarily affective. The reason for this is that there is a strong private/public space divide. The Americans can be very personal in public because they have a large public space; hence, it is rare that their relatively small private space is affected. The British, on the other hand, who value privacy above openness, need to protect themselves from interpersonal behaviour or language because it affects their larger private domain.

Cultures with a strong private space attempt to avoid direct confrontation, but they do so in different ways. Highly LCC cultures, of course, rarely take criticism at the level of identity, and so have little need to avoid verbalizing criticism. The Dutch and the Germans, for example, as Trompenaars points out, tend to treat criticism not as confrontation at the level of identity, but as feedback for improvement at the level of behaviour. Southern Europeans and the Asian cultures, on the other hand, faced with the possibility of losing face, tend to avoid direct negative feedback by not stating it. On the contrary, where possible they would like to be seen complimenting rather than criticizing.

As we have already noted, the British culture tends to an indirect orientation particularly for any interactional communication that might lead to a negative reaction; and, not by chance, the English language has an elaborate system for verbalizing politeness. A similar system of cushioning is available to deal with direct criticism. With this system it is possible, through language, to criticize the action and not the person. In this way, it is possible to satisfy both the 'being' (you are what you do) and the 'doing' (you are and you do) at the same time.

As can be seen from the box below, a linguistic marker cushions the criticism. It serves two functions. First the marker explicitly addresses the person before discussing the behaviour, reassuring him or her that politeness to the person is being respected. Second, it serves as a warning for the addressee to be prepared for the criticism. This satisfies the strong private/public space aspect of British culture. Then issue can be taken with the behaviour (or, if needs must, with the person).

INTERPERSONAL FRAME	
Polite to the person	**Criticize the behaviour**
+ve to the being orientation	*-ve to the doing orientation*
With (the greatest of) respect	
Frankly	the idea is crazy
To be frank	
To be honest	
I'm afraid	

For a more fully 'being' oriented culture the person and the issue are one. The difference between private and public is much more relative (or is 'diffused' rather than 'specific'). Therefore, at best it does not make sense to be positive and negative in the same breath: one should be either positive or negative. A more evaluative HCC, 'being' oriented view of the above (Italian for example) would be that the English politeness system is hypocritical (Severgnini 1992:220):

L'inglese è una lingua deliziosamente ipocrita, e non costringe chi la parla alla imbarazzante franchezza all'italiano.	The English language is deliciously hypocritical. It doesn't oblige those who speak it to any of the embarrassing Italian frankness.

As can be seen, this stereotype of the English is simply the result of distorted processing of perceived behaviour through a different cultural orientation. From an HCC (direct, expressive) viewpoint, lack of emotion, long-winded politeness strategies, and pedantry with regard to detail are clearly negative attributes. For LCC cultures, emotional outbursts and difficulties in giving facts, or keeping to them, are equally interpreted negatively. People with these cultural orientations will be regarded as unreliable, as not saying what they mean and, through non-disclosure of the facts, working to a hidden agenda.

12.3.2 Grammatical 'Be' and 'Do'

This section concludes part three and will present a tentative model of the context of culture, linking language and cultural orientation. It aims specifically to show how the same reality is reconstructed by different mental maps and how the HCC/LCC orientation can be linked to language. We have already mentioned that language is a surface representation of the model or mental map and that "grammar construes reality" (Halliday 1992:65). Hasan (1984:106) takes the argument one step further purporting

> that there is a culture-specific semiotic style [which] is to say that there is a congruence, a parallelism between verbal and non-verbal behaviour, both of which are informed by the same set of beliefs, values and attitudes.

She also suggests that there should "exist some organizing principle" which will ensure that congruence. As we have suggested, this organizing principle is to be found in the theory of Logical Levels (Chapter 3.2); and through the strict relation between dominant hemisphere and value clusters which favour text or context. Let's look at this in a little more detail and discuss how the orientation at the level of values, in particular, influences the choice in process transitivity.

We return to the newspaper coverage of the attempted coup in Moscow as represented by the American *The Washington Post* (*WP*), and the Italian *Corriere della Sera* (*CdS*). Below is a comparison of the most important headlines from the *WP* and the *CdS* between October 4th and 7th 1993:

October	*The Washington Post*	*Corriere della Sera*	Translation
4	TROOPS CLOSE IN ON YELTSIN FOES AS BATTLE RAGES AT PARLIAMENT	*BATTAGLIA A MOSCA, MORTI PER LE STRADE*	BATTLE IN MOSCOW, THE DEAD ON THE STREETS
5	ARMY SHELLFIRE CRUSHES MOSCOW REVOLT; DOZENS KILLED IN ASSAULT ON PARLIAMENT	*MASSACRO A MOSCA, VINCE ELTSIN*	MASSACRE IN MOSCOW, YELTSIN WINS
6	YELTSIN TIGHTENS GRIP, FIRES RIVAL OFFICIALS	*RUSSIA, IL GIORNO DEL CASTIGO*	RUSSIA, THE DAY OF PUNISHMENT
7	YELTSIN LIFTS CENSORSHIP, VOWS TO HOLD DECEMBER ELECTIONS	*ELTSIN AI RIBELLI «SARETE PUNITI»*	YELTSIN TO REBELS "YOU'LL BE PUNISHED"

In terms of orientation towards 'being' or 'doing' we could say that: *WP* shows us a film with close-ups while the *CdS* gives us a wider picture of the situation, and involves feelings. This could well be an isolated case, but it does coincide with the general HCC/LCC division as (implicitly) described by Tannen (1993b:14-56). She noted significant differences between North American (LCC) and Greek (HCC) subjects' oral accounts of the same film. The Americans, on being asked about the film described the actual events of the film; while the Greeks produced elaborate stories with additional events, and detailed accounts, of the motives and feelings of the characters.

Stella Ting-Toomey (1985:78) discusses how different cultures interpret conflictual events, such as a negotiation impasse or, as in this case, an attempted coup. In her discussion she suggests:

Individuals in LCCs are more likely to perceive the causes of conflict as instrumental rather than expressive in nature.

Individuals in HCCs:
1. are more likely to perceive the causes (or more importantly, they tend to focus on the process) of conflict as expressive rather than instrumental in nature.
2. would have a much more difficult time in objectively separating the conflict event from the affective domain

Of course, Ting-Toomey's understanding of 'objectively' is from an instrumental LCC perspective, also confirmed through her "difficult time" value judgement.

Scollon and Scollon (2001:106-34) point out that (all) Westerners unconsciously resort to Utilitarian discourse in professional contexts; and that "Utilitarian discourse forms *should appear* to give nothing but information, that they *should appear* to be making no attempt to influence the listener or the reader except through his or her exercise of rational judgment".

Seen through Asian eyes, the Utilitarian discourse form, as practised by the quality Anglo-American press, may well be seen as devious and underhand. These writers, according to the Asians, are simply hiding their message or intention behind a facade of carefully selected 'facts'.[14] Hatim and Mason (1997:127-36) note that Arab speakers prefer the consciously subjective 'lopsided' argument. With the 'lopsided' approach, the writer makes his/her beliefs explicit. They suggest (ibid.:135) that any translation from English to Arabic (which does not make the original author's bias clear) "needs to make sure that the thesis to be opposed ... is rendered in a way that reflects the attitude of the source text producer towards what could be implied by the facts ..." In short, the mediator should make the (hidden) meta-message more explicit; otherwise, author intention will be lost in the translation

As we already mentioned at the end of Chapter 7, when discussing Manipulation in translation, this is exactly what the *Corriere della Sera* did in 'translating' the comments made in the *Newsweek* article:

Newsweek	Corriere della Sera (translated)
Did the Italians warn Aidid? "Draw your own conclusions", said a senior US official.	The accusation hurled by Newsweek is scathing. It is slanderous: "The Italians are spying for General Aidid against the United Nations".

• *Linguistic analysis*

Returning to the newspaper headlines, we notice that the *CdS* has a clear affective orientation, while the *WP* is more instrumental in its headline account. However, if we wish to study how language can reflect the 'being'/'doing' polar orientation, we should start at the level of clause. As Jay L. Lemke says (1989:37), "Every clause constructs some representation of the material and social world". Downing and Locke (1992:110) are even more unequivocal: "The clause is the most significant grammatical unit, since it permits us to encode, both semantically and syntactically, our mental picture of the physical world or reality and the worlds of our imagination".

In this mental picture, clauses represent "patterns of experience" (Halliday

---

[14] This is the area of Critical Discourse Analysts, which does not pretend to be a "dispassionate and objective social science, but ... engaged and committed" (Fairclough and Wodak 1997:258). See also Katan (1996) for non-native reader problems in following hidden persuasive discourse due to the out-of-awareness frame cueing of intertextual links.

1994:107), and the central part of this pattern is termed 'the process', i.e. the verb (Downing and Locke 1992:110). According to Halliday (1994:108) there are three principle aspects which make up "a coherent theory of experience".

First we have the outer world. In terms of the Logical Levels Model, this is the environment and observable behaviour. The second aspect is internal reaction (reflection, awareness, and generalization), which relates to strategies and beliefs. Thirdly, fragments of experience are related to others. Halliday uses the terms 'classification' and 'identification', which clearly relates to the level of identity.

Although Halliday does not put these processes in any particular order of importance, following the Logical Levels Model, there are clear logical differences of level between external observable behaviour, internal reaction (beliefs) and attribution (identity).

The three main process categories as identified by Halliday, with their associated Logical Levels, are as follows:

Logical Level	Process	Exponent
Behaviour	Material (the doing)	Jill texted Jack
Capabilities	Mental (the sensing)	Jill loved Jack
Values/Beliefs	" "	Jack wasn't convinced
Identity	Relational (the being)	Jack wasn't Jill's

Halliday also categorizes three sub-categories.[15]

Verbal	(related to material and mental)	Jill asked him to marry her
Behavioural	(related to material and mental)	Jack staggered backwards when he read the message
Existential	(related to relational)	There was no wedding

Of the three main categories, we can immediately see that experience can be categorized in terms of what the *situation* is, and how it relates to other aspects of reality (the context): "Jack wasn't convinced", "Jack wasn't Jill's" and "There was no wedding". Alternatively, we can categorize according to what *happened* (the text): "Jill texted Jack", "Jill asked him to marry her" and "Jack staggered backwards".

Returning to the newspaper headlines, we can now focus on the process strategies to study the patterns that underlie the construction of reality.[16] We can immediately note that the *WP* focuses on the material:

WP	Material processes	close in on, crush, kill, tighten, fire, rage

---

[15] For a full discussion on transitivity and analysis see Halliday (1976b; 1994), and Taylor Torsello (1992:260-304), particularly for the difficulties involved in analysis.

[16] For a bibliography of authors using process strategies to analyse newspaper reporting see Katan (1998).

The *CdS* reporter witnessed the same event, but saw *una battaglia*/"a battle" and *morti*/"dead bodies". The action here is implicit, and the implicit processes in these minor clauses are in both cases the verb *essere*/"be", a relational process. On day two, there is one material process. On the last day of the front page news the *CdS* chose a material process and an ellipted verbal: *Eltsin (dice) ai ribelli «sarete puniti»*/"Yeltsin [says] to the rebels 'You will be punished'". The complete list is as follows:

Paper	Processes	Italian	Back translation
CdS:	Material	*vincere, punire*	win, lose
	Verbal	[*dice*]	[says]
	Relational	[*È*] *il giorno*	[It's] the day
		[*C'è*] *una battaglia*	[There's] a battle
		[*Ci sono*] *morti*	[There are] dead bodies
		[*C'è stato*] *un massacro*	[There has been] a massacre

Whatever the surface reason (space, style, etc.) both papers chose from a similar system of resources, i.e. the *WP could have* deleted the processes or chosen relational processes, and the *CdS could have* opted for material processes in the most eye-catching headlines. In both cases they did not: a definite choice was made.

The effect in either case is in some ways very similar. In both cases drama is created: in one case there is close-up video action, concentrating on 'doing'; in the other case we have a wider picture, the situation, the 'being' – and the drama is created through the lexis rather than through the process. So, the Anglo-American audience reads a dynamically reconstructed action-packed film with close-ups. The Italian reconstruction on the other hand, is a richer but more static series of still photographs or even paintings.

This finding is not restricted to the headlines but to the articles themselves. The survey, which also included a British newspaper, *The Independent*, showed that the Italian regularly opted for relational processes over and above the British and American newspapers, with the American selecting the most material processes:

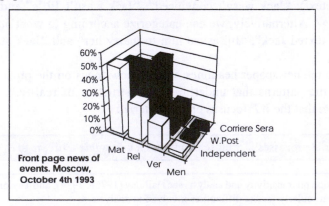

Mat = Material; Rel = Relational; Ver = Verbal; Men = Mental
Figure 48. News Reporting and Transitivity Choices

According to Lemke (1991:26), and to use his terminology, there should be a difference in transitivity between an article with a dynamic perspective – "what-could-be-being-meant", and one with a synoptic perspective – "what-evidently-must-have-been-meant". What he means is that there should be more material verbs in the news (as-it-is-happening) report and more relational verbs in the leader or editorials, as they would focus on the relationship *between* events rather than *on* events themselves.

However, as we can see from the following chart, the *CdS* variation in the use of relational processes is slight. The real difference is between the Anglo-American and the Italian:

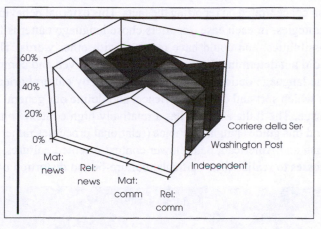

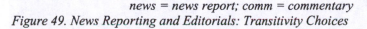

news = news report; comm = commentary
Figure 49. News Reporting and Editorials: Transitivity Choices

It does seem, then, that the selection of process will depend first on a particular culture's cluster of values (its cultural orientations), and then only second, on the function of the language – in this case an editorial or a news report.

Hence, language choice is first made at the level of cultural orientation, which, according to the Logical Level Theory then informs the next level down – the semantic level. As a result, semantic style, as exemplified by transitivity and process types will select predominantly relational processes if there is an HCC orientation, and material if there is an LCC orientation. As Lemke (ibid.:28) states, "It is not only the context of situation, but also context of culture that is dynamically implicated in a semantic view of text production".

Translators, in particular, should be aware of process types as they translate. When they have the choice they should favour the relational when translating into an HCC language, and material when translating for the LCC, to fit their translation into the local behavioural style. This is particularly important within the environment of newspaper reporting of reality.

• *Towards a Context of Culture*
We are now in a position to sketch in a number of "the leading motivations" (Sapir 1994:119) and the "sets, isolates, and patterns that differentiate ... lives" (Hall

1990:184). In short, we have the beginnings of a context of culture that combines Hall's contexting, Halliday's processes and NLP Logical Levels. The Logical Levels diagram below illustrates the different choices to be made at each Logical Level according to culture in the context of newspaper reporting. The United States and Great Britain are on the left, while Italy is to the right. The basic level for the context of culture is the Environment – in this case the attempted coup in Moscow.

Each culture operates on, and reacts to, its own environment through behaviour. In some respects the behaviour is similar. All three cultures reported the event on the front pages of their papers, gave information and commented. However, the Italian gave more of the background, the context and the feelings, while the American and British concentrated on reporting the facts. This external behaviour is guided by internal strategies. In each case, reporters chose language patterns from a large system of possibilities, and could have reported with other words. The language system itself did not determine the way reality was perceived and communicated.

Instead, the language options selected were guided by cultural orientations: the sets of values which sort and orient experience, and define our general approach to a particular issue. The Italian culture has a relatively high context communication orientation, and this guides language choice (relational processes rather than material). The British and American, being lower context oriented cultures, select more material processes to realize their particular culture-bound distortion of reality:

Figure 50. Towards a Context of Culture

12.4 Conclusion

I began this book by asking, "What is the culture factor?" Culture, in fact, is not a factor but rather the framework (the context) within which all communication takes place. Culture will affect the interpretation or translation according to Logical Level. Each level is logically linked in a hierarchy, though only one level will be the object of attention at any one time. Hall's Triad suggests that the context of culture becomes more important as we move from technical to out-of-awareness uses of language.

The cultural interpreter or mediator will need to understand how culture in general operates and must be able to frame a particular communication within its context of culture. Then, as mediator, he or she will need to disassociate from that frame and mindshift or chunk to a virtual text that will guide choice when creating a new text for the addressee.

The cultural orientations are filters that help individuals orient themselves in society. They provide individuals with a way of interpreting the environment and guide visible behaviour that is congruent with other members of the same culture. Misperception, misinterpretation and mistranslation can easily result when these out-of-awareness orientations are not taken into consideration.

The map individuals make of the world is a local (culture-bound) map and is not a good guide to understanding texts produced by other cultures. Hence, the heart of the mediator's task is not to translate texts but to translate cultures, and help strangers give new texts welcome.

Part four illustrates the developmental stages a trainee translator or interpreter will pass through before becoming a cultural interpreter or mediator.

Part 4. Intercultural Competence
     On Becoming a Cultural Interpreter and
     Mediator

Chapter 13 contains the Developmental Model of Intercultural Sensitivity (DMIS) adapted for translators and interpreters. There are two main reasons for introducing the model. First, it is a useful way of understanding how beliefs about translation, and comments made by translation scholars themselves, can make more sense once framed in one of the stages. Second, the introduction of culture for translators and interpreters can be more usefully organized in accordance with trainees' levels of intercultural sensitivity. When the teaching matches these levels, it will be easier for the students to make the cognitive changes necessary for a translator or interpreter to attain intercultural competence, and hence function as a mediator.

Chapter 13. On Becoming a Mediator

The aim of this chapter is to
- introduce the DMIS model
- frame translation beliefs, strategies and behaviour according the model
- outline a development programme for training in 'translating cultures'

13.1 The Developmental Model of Intercultural Sensitivity (DMIS)

In this final part I wish to explore the various idealized stages a translator can pass through in his or her personal growth from student to professional and from translator[1] to intercultural mediator. I suggest, following Robinson (1997:231), that using a model of these stages can help sensitize translators and interpreters to intercultural communication in general, and in particular, can help in ordering conflicting beliefs about the translator's role, his/her translation strategies as well as in the teaching of culture itself.

The Developmental Model of Intercultural Sensitivity presented[2] (DMIS) highlights aspects of cultural blindness and distortion, and shows how, for example, a translator's belief towards the task of translating a text for a new local culture can change over time. More importantly, the model predicts a change of identity as the translator moves from personal local reaction to global sensitivity. A fundamental aspect of the model is linked to a change in the 'natural' core belief in ethnocentrism, i.e. superiority or centrality of one language-culture over another – towards that of ethnorelativity, the belief in mediation between text, reader and context of culture.

Culture, as I have stressed, is what is 'normal'. Beliefs, also, whether they be about other cultures or about appropriate translation strategies, have a habit of

---

[1] Though, most of the examples will focus on the translator, the same steps will be followed by the interpreter.

[2] The DMIS is just one of many similar developmental models. The subject is covered in more depth in Katan 2001b.

being interpreted as truths – and thus tend to be thought of as being timeless. Though beliefs tend to be thought of as withstanding time, very few do. In reality, as both the model and common sense suggest, beliefs about the world do change over time in response to a variety of factors, though rational argument is very rarely one of them. The change, or passage, has more to do with the change in an individual's cognitive environment, which can then help in opening up options towards the interpretation of the surrounding reality (see Dilts 1990).

The single most important aspect of culture, following this theory, is that one's own understanding of the world is necessarily a limited mental map or model of the world, and entails an equally limited understanding of 'the other'. Milton Bennett's (1993) DMIS model charts the change in reaction to 'the other' in an idealized cline over a period of six stages. Each stage may be likened to part of a rite of passage in the sense that, each stage represents a change in fundamental beliefs about self and others. The significant stages are as follows:

> THE ETHNOCENTRIC STAGES
> 1. denial
> 2. defence
> 3. minimization
> THE ETHNORELATIVE STAGES
> 4. acceptance
> 5. adaptation
> 6. integration

I have actually combined two models here to allow for an important reversal in the cline, which does not, though, affect the stages. The 'W' graph below is taken from Levine and Adelman (1993:41), while the added numbers refer back to the Bennett model:

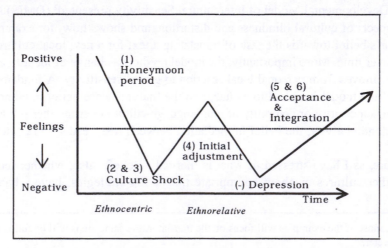

Figure 51. From Culture Shock to Acculturation

13.2 The Six Stages

Stage 1: Denial

Honeymoon

Initial reaction to 'the other' begins as if the 'other' did not exist as a separate world, though Bennett (1998:34) is also careful to note that, "oppressed people may navigate the development of intercultural sensitivity differently from those in the dominant group". Cues taken from reality, as I have mentioned, are interpreted according to an individual or locally shared model of the world, which is, at this stage, believed to be "central to all reality" (Bennett 1993:30). Levine and Adelman's 'honeymoon' refers to what it is that attracts in a second language or culture. On honeymoon, on a dream holiday, or just even away from home, everything can seem brighter, better and tastier. The positive reasons for going abroad are confirmed. We concentrate on what we expect (distortion), and much of what is actually different is filtered out (deletion), in the same way as cultural myths are created. Honeymoons last until reality sets in and we began to perceive that 'the other' is also 'different' in ways that test our tolerance.

Blindness

The honeymoon attraction, though, as Hymes notes (in Katan 2001b:288) is not always part of one's first contact with 'the other'. Bennett's model, in fact, begins simply with cognitive naivety. In his model, at this stage, there is simply no response to the other, as the differences are simply not, to use Sperber and Wilson's (1995:42) term, 'manifest'. Denial is deletion from our map of the world. Cultural differences are simply not accounted for, in the same way that a woman in an all male group may be treated as "one of the boys". Not many men, though, would appreciate being treated as "one of the girls".

This blindness may lead people to maintain wide categories for cultural difference, such as "all Chinese look the same". The Welsh, the Scottish and the Irish are not "English", nor are Canadians American, though they are all loosely included as such by many foreigners, including the English themselves. Bennett terms this form of parochialism as a 'benign stereotype'.

Separation, following Bennett (1993:33) is "the intentional erection of physical or social barriers to create distance from cultural difference as a means of maintaining a state of denial". Extreme examples were the apartheid (ethnic segregation) policies in South Africa, and the original *ghetto* in Venice where the Jewish people were settled.

More informally, Chinatowns and other ethnic groupings are a phenomenon everywhere, making it possible to live in the same town, without ever having to meet people from different cultures. When meeting does occur, 'denial' can still effectively take place, as E. M. Forster's ((1924) 1966:39) *Passage to India* cogently illustrates. In the opening pages of the novel, Dr. Aziz, a young Indian doctor arrives in a hired *tonga* outside the house of one of his patients, a British officer. He only meets the officer's servant and a discussion ensues as to the whereabouts of the officer (emphasis in the original):

> While they argued, the people came out. Both were ladies. Aziz lifted his hat. The first, who was in evening dress, glanced at the Indian and turned instinctively away. "Mrs. Lesley, it *is* a tonga", she cried. "Ours?" enquired the second, also seeing Aziz, and doing likewise. "Take the gifts the gods provide, anyhow", she screeched, and both jumped in. "O Tonga wallah, club, club. Why doesn't the fool go?" "Go; I will pay you tomorrow", said Aziz to the driver; and as they went off he called courteously: "You are most welcome, ladies". They did not reply, being full of their own affairs. So it had come, the usual thing – just as Mahamoud Ali said. The inevitable snub – his bow ignored, his carriage taken.

In practice there are no competent translators at this level. We have translation students (to whom we will return) and incompetent professionals. The latter translate robotically, word-for-word, creating illegible instructions, comic relief for tourists in hotels and restaurants or disastrous advertising campaigns, as we have seen. In all these cases the reader is effectively denied, ignored or snubbed.

Stage 2: Defence

"What is Different is Dangerous"
This is the title of Hofstede's (1991:109) chapter on orientation to perceived difference, and is the first response to "Culture Shock": "the emotional reactions to the disorientation that occur when one is immersed in an unfamiliar culture and is deprived of familiar cues" (Paige, 1993:2). R. Michael Paige, Professor of International and Intercultural Education at the University of Minnesota, points out that this term was first coined by Cora DuBois in 1951 and popularized after Kal Oberg's 1960 article 'Cultural Shock: Adjustments to New Cultural Environments'.[3] This subjective distortion of reality happens to all of us in varying degrees when we are affected by unexpected behaviour in a different culture.

It is at this stage we can no longer deny the fact that differences exist; and we react to the real gap between our expected world and the world we are dealing with. The most natural reaction to difference in others' behaviour, discourse patterns and value systems is to defend our own, particularly because the threat is felt at the level of core beliefs regarding what is 'right', 'normal' and 'correct'. This response is logically ethnocentric, the feeling being that *my* model of the world is *the* model of the world, and hence, any other model is not only wrong but is also a destabilizing threat.

Logically, then, the first defensive reaction tends to be one of Denigration, which

---

[3] See Paige (1993) for full bibliography.

allows 'the other' to be reclassified as a threat to our survival (such as the Jews, Zionism or Palestinians depending on the viewpoint). Alternatively, denigration allows us to reclassify peoples as sub-human or animal, which makes ethnic cleansing more palatable.

Superiority

This level of intercultural development "emphasizes the positive evaluation of one's own cultural status" (Bennett 1993:37), and is the form of ethnocentric defence that many translator scholars and practitioners work from. Very often, the feeling of superiority is benign towards other cultures, and is backed by logical arguments of 'progress', 'development', with the implicit assumption that evolution following one's own culture path is the best path for all cultures. For instance, a language education project in Hungary, supported by the World Bank in 1995, was entitled 'Catching up with Europe'. This title along with 'underdeveloped', 'less developed' and 'developing' countries, suggests that there is but one target in development, and the West is the only model. This level of ethnocentrism accepts that cultures are different, but expects them to adapt according to the superior model. An example of this comes from Newmark's (1993:69) comments regarding the 'sexist' translation of a tourist brochure, discussed earlier.

Reversal

An interesting 'option' in the intercultural sensitivity model is the phenomenon of 'reversal'. This still revolves around superiority, but in reverse. It is the "denigration of one's own culture and an attendant assumption of the superiority of a different culture" (Bennett 1993:39). Dropouts, for example, represent a move away from their host culture. The reasons may be manifold, but generally involve "a disavowal of all [C1] values and an embracing of unchanging [C2] values" (ibid.:40). Alternative subcultures, the hippie movement and New Age, for example, reject dominant western competitive orientation in favour of cooperative, or Eastern values.

In translation, Venuti (1995a:291) describes himself "a nomad in my own country, a runaway from the mother-tongue". He explains why (1998:10): "it is this evocation of the foreign that attracts me [...]. This preference stems partly from a political agenda that is broadly democratic: an opposition to the global hegemony of English". In fact, both Venuti and Newmark wish to redress inequality and to intervene to help the more vulnerable through translation; they also, however, both view 'the other' from a Defensive position. The Critical Discourse Analysts would also be at this level.

Stage 3: Minimization

Bennett divides minimizations into physical and transcendent universalism. Physical minimization is based on biological and ethological considerations that beneath the thin veneer of civilization we are all the same. Though this is true, our out-of-awareness responses tend to relate to how we have been civilized.

The second minimization is transcendent universalism. A religious truth states "we are all God's children". Whether or not the children of Allah, Buddha or any other divinity wish to be included is usually not considered. There tends to be a belief in a single guiding plan for the universe – and, as Bennett (1993:44) succinctly points out (emphasis in original):

> The principle or supernatural force assumed to overlie cultural difference is invariably derived from one's own worldview. I have yet to hear anyone at this stage say, "There is a single truth in the universe and it is *not* what I believe.

Danila Seleskovich, "a brilliant interpreter" (Newmark 1988:6), stated: "Everything said in one language can be expressed in another – on condition that the two languages belong to cultures that have reached a comparable degree of development". This type of comment is indicative of this final ethnocentric stage in Bennett's model, and is the last to preserve the centrality of one's own worldview. It overtly acknowledges cultural differences, but suggests that these are (superficial) details not to be confused with general universal similarities to which all people (and their texts) adhere.[4] Chesterman (1997a:58), for example, states that Grice's Maxims "must evidently be interpreted with respect to particular cultures", but then goes onto say: "but I do not think that this detracts from their universal applicability". He is even clearer on the Minimalists' "Golden Rule" (Bennett 1993:41): "I will stick my neck out and claim that clarity will survive as an ethical linguistic value long after the postmodernist textual anarchists are dead and buried" (Chesterman 1997b:150). Newmark says much the same (in Schäffner and Kelly-Holmes 1995:80).

Beliefs like these propagate and become self-fulfilling norms, which, as Chesterman himself realizes (1997a:6), become more real than reality itself. One particular entrenched universal norm in the translating habitus is that meaning can be "transferred" from one language to another, and that meaning is immanent in the text. This norm, as already noted, is actually unconsciously encoded at the European Union: translating and interpreting = copying.

Stage 4: Acceptance

According to the DMIS, this next stage "represents a major conceptual shift from reliance on absolute, dualistic principles of some sort to an acknowledgement of non-absolute relativity" (Bennett 1993:45). This is where the translator begins to perceive that his/her ethnocentric model of the world is not the only one, and that text-based copying, though possible, will not communicate the same message across cultures. The translator's model of the world is now framed to include local contexts of situation and culture.

---

[4] For an alternative view see Katan and Straniero Sergio 2001:224-25 and Pym 2000:186.

Respect for Behaviour Difference

At this first ethnorelative stage, people "begin to recognize differences in communication style" (ibid.:45). As Nida (1997:37) puts it: "Many translators believe that if they take care of the words and grammar, the discourse will take care of itself, but this concept results from an insufficient understanding of the role of discourse structures in interlingual communication".

This is clearly then the first stage at which translators accept the importance of context and marks the beginnings of the 'cultural turn' (Bassnett and Lefevre 1990:11). Kondo, as mentioned earlier, is extremely aware of the context of culture and frames of interpretation yet, is aware of the constraints engendered by the established norms of interpreting. In the end, though, he yields to the text-oriented norm: "interpreters can work essentially only with what has been expressed" (ibid.:63). Nida (ibid.), on the other hand, suggests manipulating the text, not in favour of a universal or superior rule, but simply in respect of the different ways in which language triggers responses in others: "When in Rome, do as the Romans". Yet, according to Bennett, this level of Acceptance is also one of indirection and experimentation – leading also to indecision. Which communication style do we adopt, for example, at an international meeting. How should Beowolf be translated for the twenty-first century? Translators (rather than Nida's bicultural secretaries) will not yet have "developed ethnorelative principles for taking action" (Bennett 1998:28). Interestingly, the skopos theory, seems to fit very well into this stage: "The [skopos] theory does not state what the principle is...The skopos theory merely states that the translator should be aware that some goal exists ... The important point is that a given source text does not have one correct or best translation only" (Vermeer 2000:228). As Bennett (1993:54) puts it "judgment is paralyzed by a plethora of equally valuable alternatives".

Respect for Value Difference (or Depression)

During the ethnocentric stages, translators on the developmental path to intercultural sensitivity still believe that their own personal or locally shared hierarchy of values is the only valid system across all cultures. Yet, as Bennett (ibid.:49) points out, "relativity of cultural values is central to intercultural difference. At this stage of development, there is the acceptance of the different worldview assumptions that underlie cultural variation in behaviour". It should also be remembered that this understanding of the logical relationship between other-behaviour and other-value system is essential if a translator wishes to consider reader uptake.

No less importantly, as Levine and Adelman (1993) indicate, understanding the behavioural differences, such as those outlined by Nida, without understanding the different belief and value systems will, in the end, result in stress and also depression for the sojourner. The stress will result from the evaluation of Culture 2 behaviour, using Culture 1 values, which then creates internal conflict.

The many writers, who write about countries, often profess their passion for the particular culture's different way of doing things, yet cannot perceive, let alone respect, the different logical values supporting the different behaviour. What they are actually responding to is a conflict with their own value system; for example, criticism of the obscurity of Italian or the hypocrisy of politeness of English.

At the Acceptance stage, the translator is attempting to enlarge his or her own culture-bound map of the world, rather than construct a separate map to model the 'other' system. With a separate model to work with, translators will be in the position to make their own moral, professional, ethical and translation decisions, which means that they need to be capable of taking multiple positions.

Stage 5: Adaptation

At this stage "new skills appropriate to different world views are acquired as an *additive* process" (Bennett 1993:52). What Bennett (1998:28) underlines at this stage is that people can "use knowledge to intentionally shift into a different frame of reference".

The 'cultural turn' marked a series of reference shifts. Focus shifted from formal fidelity to the original text, to "The Death of the Author" (Barthes, 1977; Arrojo 1997) and interest in reader response. It marked the beginning of a discussion on the translator's status, and in particular, the translator's (in)visibility (Venuti 1995a, 1998). This entailed a new belief regarding the translator's task, as Snell-Hornby (1988:23) highlights: "the starting point is the exact opposite of that represented by the linguistically orientated school ... not intended equivalence but admitted manipulation".

Bennett divides adaptation into two levels. The first level is empathy, which means being able to attempt to understand by imagining the other's frame of interpretation. This is the stage where the translator or interpreter is able to automatically construct a virtual text, based on a number of 'others': client, publisher, readers, and so on.

The second stage is pluralism, which means actually being able to reference or access alternative maps of the world (source and target contexts of culture). This is the cultural equivalence of bilingualism. Identity remains paramount with core-beliefs remaining intact. However, just as in the change of role during the day from conference interpreter or proofreader to mother, or from sales director to weekend mountaineer, different aspects of identity will come to the fore. Many people unconsciously adapt successfully to two particular cultural roles, such as women who are successful in business.

One particularly example, bizarre for most of us, is that of the Prince of Swaziland who was able to combine two cultures (Swazi and Western diplomatic protocol) in different ways during the same day. He was host for an official ceremony of the 13th United World Colleges Annual Council.[5] The main business of the day was discussion of the accounts and the next year's budget. He emerged gracefully from his Rolls-Royce in full tribal dress. Later that evening he changed to a more Western style, appearing for the official United World Colleges gala dinner in an

---

[5] I am grateful to Giovanna Ferrara, who was at the conference in 1995 for this example.

immaculate dinner suit – and he gave his speech in the English he had learned at Oxford University. His four wives sat comfortably with him at the high table, while his four concubines sat at lower tables.

Pluralism

At this second level of Adaptation the translator satisfies "the requirement that understanding of difference must derive from actual experience *within* that cultural frame" (Bennett 1993:55). And it is at this stage that a translator can be said to be bicultural, with a minimum of two maps in one mind. Hermans' discussion of polysystem theory shows how translators (in academia at least) are now much more prepared to look beyond the text to the system or system of systems it is part of. As he says (1999:110), "it has benefited translation research by placing translation squarely in a larger field of cultural activity". But, as he rightly claims, this field is still vague and abstract. Also, as Bochner points out (1981:12), knowing more than one culture is a necessary, but not a sufficient condition for cultural mediation, which is the next stage. What the translator still needs is a belief system which is ready to exploit specific translation competency skills (see Pym forthcoming) at the level of global perception rather than local reaction.

Stage 6: Integration

At this stage, "One does not have culture; one engages in it" (Bennett 1993:52). Translators, as mediators, "see their identities as including many cultural options, any of which can be exercised in any context, by choice at a certain stage" (ibid.:60).

Contextual Evaluation

The first level of integration is where "one attains the ability to analyze and evaluate situations from one or more cultural perspectives ... the outcome of this action is a judgment of relative goodness that is specific to some identified context (ibid.:61). A translator is not only able to mindshift and associate with both the source text and the virtual target text but is also able to take a third perceptual position (Katan and Straniero Sergio 2001:220-21; Katan 2001b), which is disassociated from both cultures. In this meta-position, translators are "conscious of themselves as choosers of alternatives" (Bennett 1993:62), which fits with Pym's (forthcoming) discussion of competence: "the translation competence that interests us is thus a process of choosing between viable alternatives".

In Bennett's model, there is a definite identity change here. The translator is now a cultural interpreter or mediator and has a supra-cultural mission: to improve crosscultural cooperation, and build trust and understanding between communities. Translators are no longer paralyzed by cultural relativity but can make decisions regarding any text, according to what Pym (2000:190) calls "an ethics of contextualized human relations rather than a barrage of abstract universal rules". This, possibly surprisingly, is also the essence of four out of five of Newmark's Five Purposes of translation (1993:57-8). The fifth, by the way, concerns language teaching.

Constructive Marginality

Bennett, himself, places the cultural mediator at this level. The person, here, has a meta-map of the world, over and above any culture-bound maps. A person at this level has no specific cultural identity, and there are no unquestioned assumptions. As the title implies, marginality brings with it isolation. A mediator, at this level, may help negotiate others' cultural differences, but will have few of his or her own to share.

13.3 The Translator Student

We can use Bennett's model to raise awareness of the centrality of one's own beliefs regarding cultural difference, and to benchmark students in terms of intercultural competency.

Bennett *et al.* (1999) suggest that the teaching of intercultural competence can begin at Stage 1 of the development model, though the focus should be on support rather than challenge. A particularly interesting feature of the Bennett approach to intercultural competency is the practice of delaying experiential methods until the students are developmentally ready. In fact, the authors suggest introducing intercultural awareness through emphasis on similarities rather than on difference. They suggest dividing learners up as follows:

Language level	Likely intercultural awareness level	Focus
Novice:	Level 1: Denial and Defence	cultural similarities, support worldview
Intermediate:	Level 2: Minimization	exploring perception, acceptance, self awareness exercise
Advanced:	Level 3: Adaptation and Integration	experiential learning, cultural contrasts, value systems

Level 1: *Denial and Defence*

In my own experience as a teacher, the vast majority of first year students behave as 'outsiders' and expect similarity rather than difference, even though they are at an advanced (Threshold Level and beyond) level linguistically. Hence, almost every single student is either at a honeymoon/denial stage or in Defence. In the former case they are usually attracted to the language (as in 'langue' rather than 'parole') or to the literature. In the latter case, the students tend to still have an idealized vision of the culture tempered by actual contact (such as a student exchange). Invariably, the contact will have resulted in some form of culture shock and negative perception of some aspect of the environment or behaviour. Typical negative beliefs Italian students arrive at the University with are the following:

Food: British food is not only bad, greasy, but eaten on the streets (bad manners) or in isolation at home, often straight from the microwave (rather than cooked, and with the family).

Drink: English coffee tastes like dishwater (this includes the watery espresso, etc.); the British (men, women and teenagers) drink alcohol to get drunk on a regular basis.

Dirt: British houses are exceedingly dirty. The general standard of hygiene is extremely low (e.g. no bidet). Carpeted floors trap dirt and provide home for infectious diseases.

Behaviour: The British are cold, distant and hypocritical (their politeness strategies mean that they rarely say what they think); they are pedants (and leave no space for particular, human, circumstances); mentally slow and naïve.

Though these differences are 'small', difference is more insidious the more hidden it is. The assumption of sameness is a Stage 1 error in the DMIS. It is only when there is an acceptance that cultural differences exist that one can begin to address them; and as every woman and man knows it is the pattern of repeated small differences in communication which cause the most miscommunication. Culture shock is particularly difficult to deal with at this early stage of intercultural development, as students are not yet ready to accept that their models of the world are limited. Logically, they will also be convinced that intercultural communication has little to do with translation training.

Bennett *et al*. suggest that students be given more support and reassurance at this stage; so students should begin with similarities between languages and cultures. Any differences illustrated should be at the level of environment and hence non-threatening: geographical place names, institutions, and so on (see also Dodds and Katan 1996:125-26). The students can then move on to a comparison of behaviour, such as traditions. Again, these are non-threatening differences between cultures. Students can be made more aware of difference and outsider reading by providing two translations of the same text: one translation for insiders and one for outsiders. The compensation strategies (additions, glosses, translation couplets, and so on) can usefully be taught at this level (see Chapter 8).

In terms of intercultural training, the students can be made aware of the relative "do's, don'ts and taboos". This is particularly useful for students of dialogue interpreting, who will be concerned with face-to-face communication. These activities help raise awareness and curiosity, and more importantly an understanding that different is different, and not necessarily dangerous.

Level 2: *Minimization to Acceptance*

At this stage, students are aware that both learning language and how to translate means thinking about insiders and outsiders, and also means going beyond the dictionary. Here students are ready to learn about discourse, and investigate genre across cultures. They learn that there is not just one good or appropriate or normal style. The Internet, here, provides a wealth of material which the students can collect as dossiers. An analysis of their dossiers will bring the discourse patterns to light, which can then be compared. Students at this stage should be able to model native-writer writing styles and be able to shift between appropriate ST and TT register style.

Along with communication style, students will now be ready to learn about 'face' and politeness norms across cultures. They will also now be open to learn from cultural simulations and culture shock exercises. These are extremely useful in showing the student that normal behaviour is culture-bound, and that communication across languages and cultures means separating perception, interpretation and evaluation. The brainstorming and feedback from these sessions are extremely enlightening for students, especially if linked to the Meta-Model tools necessary to re-attribute their evaluations (see Katan 1989 and forthcoming). Finally, these exercises will help the student become a more critical reader of the ST and consequently more mindful of the consequences of writing the TT.

Level 3: *Adaptation and Integration*

At this level, students are ready to explore the underlying values and beliefs that make the different communication strategies so logical. They are extremely aware of the limits of their own world, including their own toleration limits. The word "normal" is now used with caution. Students begin to explore different translatorial beliefs and strengthen their own meta-cultural set of mediational convictions. They practice the theories of the day (communicative/semantic, domestication/ foreignization, localization, mediational …), and learn to appreciate the ideologies that support the various translation strategies proposed. Translations are retranslated according to the conflicting theories and then discussed in terms of utility, relevance, hegemony, intercultural ethics, and so on.

The student at this level will also have explored 'the grammar of culture' discussed in Part 3, and will start identifying how the cluster of national, cultural and individual value orientations form a synaesthesia of beliefs in context. They can then beginning using mediating strategies to reduce the value gaps (see also Katan:1999).

Students here will be ready to move beyond superiority or reversal to a higher meta-level of intercultural and mediational competency (Katan 2001b:303). In the same way, as competent mediators, they will have learned to rise above the divisive either/or, faithful/free and master/servant debates, to see translation as a potentially powerful opportunity in bringing individuals and cultures closer to understanding and respecting each others' ways.

Bibliography

Abelson, Robert and John Black (1986) 'Introduction', in *Knowledge Structures,* J. Galambos, R. Abelson and J. Black (eds), Hillside, NJ: Lawrence Erlbaum, 1-18.

Adler, Nancy J. (1991) *International Dimensions of Organizational Behavior*, Boston: PWS-Kent.

Aitchinson, Jean (1989) *The Articulate Mammal: An Introduction to Psycholinguistics*, 3rd ed, London: Unwin.

Aixela, Javier Franco (1996) 'Culture Specific Items in Translation', in *Translation, Power and Subversion*, R. Alvarez and M. C. Vidal (eds), Clevedon-Philadelphia-Adelaide: Multilingual Matters, 52-78.

Allen, Irving L. (1983) *The Language of Conflict*, New York: Columbia University Press.

Arijoki, Carol (1993) 'Foreign Language Awareness in the Business Community', in *Language and Culture Bridges to International Trade, Proceedings of ENCoDe 5th International Seminar* 4-6 February 1993, Lancaster, Lancaster Business School: University of Central Lancashire, 13-33.

Arrojo, Rosemary (1997) 'The "Death" of the Author and the Limits of the Translator's Visibility', in *Translation as Intercultural Communication*, M. Snell-Hornby, Z. Jettmarové and K. Kaindl (eds), Amsterdam and Philadelphia: Benjamins, 21-32.

Artemeva, Natasha (1998) 'The Writing Consultant as Cultural Interpreter: Bridging Cultural Perspectives on the Genre of the Periodic Engineering Report' *Technical Communication Quarterly*, Vol 7, 3, 285-299.

Asher, Ronald E. (ed) (1994) *The Encyclopaedia of Language and Linguistics,* 10 vols, Oxford: Pergamon.

Aston, Guy (ed) (1988) *Negotiating Service: Studies in the Discourse of Bookshop Encounters*, Bologna: CLEUB.

Austin, J. L. (1962) *How to Do Things with Words*, Oxford: Clarendon Press.

Avirovič, Ljiljana and John Dodds (eds) (1993) *Umberto Eco, Claudio Magris: autori e traduttori a confronto*, Atti del Convegno Internazionale Trieste, 27-28 Novembre 1989, Udine: Campanotto Editore.

Baker, Mona (1992) *In Other Words: A Coursebook on Translation*, London: Routledge.

------ (1996) 'Linguistics and Cultural Studies: Complementary or Competing Paradigms in Translation Studies?', in *Übersetzungswissenschaft im Umbruch: Festschrift für Wolfram Wilss*, Angelika Lauer, Heidrun Gerzymisch-Arbogast, Johann Haller and Erich Steiner (eds), Tübingen: Gunter Narr, 9-19.

Bandler, Richard and John Grinder (1975) *The Structure of Magic I*, Palo Alto, CA: Science and Behavior Books.

Barthes, Roland ([1964]1967) *Elements of Semiology*, trans. Annette Lavers and Colin Smith, London: Jonathan Cape.

------ (1977) *Image, Music, Text*, ed and trans. Stephen Heath, New York: Hill and Wang.

------ (1993) *Mythologies*, trans. Annett Lavers, London: Vintage.

Bartlett, Frederic C. (1932) *Remembering: A Study in Experimental and Social Psychology*, Cambridge: Cambridge University Press.

Bassnett, Susan (1991) *Translation Studies*, London: Routledge.

------ (ed) (1997) *Studying British Culture: An Introduction*, London: Routledge.

------and Lefevre Andre (1990) 'Proust's Grandmother and the Thousand and One Nights:

The "Cultural Turn" in Translation Studies', in *Translation, History and Culture*, S. Bassnett and A. Lefevre (eds), London: Routledge, 1-13.

Bateson, Gregory (1972) *Steps to an Ecology of Mind*, New York: Ballantine Books.

------ (1975) 'Introduction', in *The Structure of Magic I*, R. Bandler and J. Grinder (eds), Palo Alto, CA: Science and Behavior Books, ix-xi.

------ (1988) *Mind and Nature: A Necessary Unity*, New York: Bantam Doubleday Dell.

Beekman, John and John Callow (1974) *Translating the Word of God*, Grand Rapids, MI: Zondervan.

Bell, Roger T. (1991) *Translation and Translating*, Harlow, Essex: Longman.

Benjamin, Walter (1968) 'The Task of the Translator', in *Illuminations*, trans. Harry Zohn, and H. Arendt (ed), New York: Harcourt, Brace and Jovanoch, 69-82.

Bennett, Milton J. (1993) 'Towards Ethnorelativism: A Developmental Model of Intercultural Sensitivity', in *Education for the Intercultural Experience*, Michael R. Paige (ed), Yarmouth, Maine: Intercultural Press, 22-73.

------ (1998) 'Intercultural Communication: A Current Perspective', in *Basic Concepts of Intercultural Communication: Selected Readings*, M. J. Bennett (ed), Yarmouth, MA: Intercultural Press Inc., 1-34.

------ and Allen Walter (1999) 'Developing Culture in the Language Classroom', in *Culture as the Core: Integrating Culture into the Language Curriculum*, R. M. Paige, D. Lange and Y. A. Yershova (eds), Working Paper 15, University of Minnesota, Minnesota: Center for Advanced Research in Language Acquisition, 13-46.

Bernstein, Basil (1972) 'A Sociolinguistic Approach to Socialization: with some References to Educability', in *Directions in Sociolinguistics: The Ethnography of Communication*, J. J. Gumperz and D. Hymes (eds), New York: Holt, Rinehart and Winston, 465-497.

Berry, Margaret (1989) *An Introduction to Systemic Linguistics 1: Structures and Systems*, Nottingham, Department of English Studies: University of Nottingham.

Biagi, Enzo (1995) *'I' come Italiani*, Milan: Fabbri Editori.

Bishop, Nancy (1992) 'A Typology of Causatives, Pragmatically Speaking', in *Language in Context: Essays for Robert E. Longacre*, Shin Ja J. Hwang and W.R. Merrifield (eds), Arlington: The Summer Institute of Linguistics and The University of Texas at Arlington, 295-304.

Blakemore, Diane (1992) *Understanding Utterances*, London: Blackwell.

Bloomfield, Leonard ([1933]1984) *Language*, Chicago: The University of Chicago Press.

Blum-Kulka, Shoshana (1986) 'Shifts of Cohesion and Coherence in Translation', in *Interlingual and Intercultural Communication: Discourse and Cognition in Translation and Second Language Acquisition Studies*, S. Blum-Kulka and J. House (eds), Tübingen: Gunter Narr, 17-35.

------ (1997) 'Discourse Pragmatics', in *Discourse as Social Interaction*, Teun A. Van Dijk (ed), London: Sage, 38-63.

Boas, Franz ([1911]1986) 'Language and Thought', in *Culture Bound: Bridging the Cultural Gap in Language Teaching*, J. M. Valdes (ed), Cambridge: Cambridge University Press, 5-7.

Bochner, Stephen (ed) (1981) *The Mediating Person: Bridges Between Cultures*, Cambridge: Schenkman.

Boothman, Derek (1983) 'Problems of Translating Political Italian', in *The Incorporated Linguist* 22(4): 179-182.

Bourdieu, Pierre (1990) *In Other Words: Essays Towards a Reflexive Sociology*, trans. Matthew Adamson, Stanford: Stanford University Press.

Brake, Terence, Danielle Medina-Walker and Thomas Walker (1995) *Doing Business Internationally: The Guide to Cross-Cultural Success*, Burr Ridge, IL: Irwin.

Brislin, Richard (1981) *Cross-Cultural Encounters*, Needham Heights, MA: Allyn and Bacon.

------ (1993) *Understanding Culture's Influence on Behavior*, Orlando, FL: Harcourt Brace.

Bromhead, Peter (1985) *Life in Modern Britain*, Harlow: Longman.

Brown, Gillian and George Yule (1983) *Discourse Analysis*, Cambridge: Cambridge University Press.

Brown, Penelope and Stephen Levinson (1987) *Politeness: Some Universals in Language Usage*, Studies in Interactional Sociolinguistics 4, Cambridge: Cambridge University Press.

Bryson, Bill (1991) *Mother Tongue: The English Language*, London: Penguin Books.

------ (1994) *Made in America*, London: Martin Secker and Warburg.

Caliumi, Grazia (ed) (1993) *Shakespeare e la sua eredità*, Atti del XV Convegno dell'Assocazione Italiana di Anglistica, Parma, 22-24 Ottobre 1992, Parma: Edizioni Zara.

Callow, Kathleen (1974) *Discourse Considerations in Translating the Word of God*, Grand Rapids, MI: Zondervan.

Candlin, Christopher (1990) 'General Editor's Preface', in *Discourse and the Translator*, B. Hatim and I. Mason (eds), Harlow, Essex: Longman, vii-x.

Carmichael L., H. P. Hogan and A. A. Walter (1932) 'An Experimental Study of the Effect of Language on Visually Perceived Form', *Journal of Experimental Psychology* 15: 73-86.

Carroll, Lewis (1981) *Alice's Adventures in Wonderland and Through the Looking Glass*, New York: Bantam Books.

Carroll, Raymonde (1988) *Cultural Misunderstandings: The French-American Experience*, Chicago: University of Chicago Press.

CED (1991) *Collins English Dictionary*, Glasgow: HarperCollins (3rd ed).

Chamosa, J. L. and J. C. Santoyo (1993) 'Dall'italiano all'inglese: scelte motivate e immotivate di 100 soppressioni' in *The Name of the Rose, Umberto Eco, Claudio Magris: autori e traduttori a confronto*, Atti del Convegno Internazionale Trieste, 27-28 Novembre 1989, L. Avirovic and John Dodds (eds), Udine: Campanotto Editore, 141-148.

Channell, Joanna (1994) *Vague Language*, Oxford: Oxford University Press.

Chesterman, Anthony (1997a) *Memes of Translation: The Spread of Ideas in Translation Theory*, Amsterdam and Philadelphia: John Benjamins.

------ (1997b) 'Ethics of Translation', in *Translation as Intercultural Communication*, M. Snell-Hornby, Z. Jettmarové and K. Kaindl (eds), Amsterdam and Philadelphia: Benjamins, 147-160.

Chomsky, Noam (1965) *Aspects of the Theory of Syntax*, Cambridge, Mass: MIT.

CID (1995) *Collins Italian Dictionary*, Glasgow: HarperCollins (1st ed.).

Cobuild (1995) *Collins Cobuild English Dictionary*, Glasgow: HarperCollins.

Corbolante, Licia (1987) *La traduzione di un successo umoristico 'culture bound'. The Growing Pains of Adrian Mole di Sue Townsend.* Unpublished Degree Thesis, Trieste: SSLMIT, University of Trieste.

Crystal, David (1987) *The Cambridge Encyclopedia of Language*, Cambridge: Cambridge University Press.

Curti, Lidia, Laura Di Michele, Frank Thomas and Marina Vitale (eds) (1989) *Il muro del linguaggio: conflitto e tragedia*, Atti del X Congresso Nazionale, AIA, Sorrento, Ottobre 1987, Naples: Società Editrice Intercontinentale Gallo.

DTI (1994) *Business Language Strategies*, National Languages for Export Campaign, London: Overseas Trade Services, DTI.

------ (1994) *Trading across Cultures*, National Languages for Export Campaign, London: Overseas Trade Services, DTI.

------ (1994) *Translating and Interpreting*, National Languages for Export Campaign, London: Overseas Trade Services, DTI.

De Bono, Edward (1970) *Lateral Thinking*, New York: Harper and Roy.

DeLozier, Judith (1995) 'Mastery, New Coding, and Systemic NLP', in *NLP World* 2(1): 5-19.

Denton, John (1988) 'A Contrastive Textual Analysis of Co-Referential Paraphrases in English and Italian Lexical Cohesion and the Problem of Translation', in *Metamorfosi: Traduzione/Tradizione*, E. Glass, F. Marroni, G. Micks and C. Pagetti (eds), Pescara: Clua editore, 243-250.

Diaz-Guerrero, Rogelio and Lorand B. Szalay (1991) *Understanding Mexicans and Americans: Cultural Perspectives in Conflict*, New York: Plenum Press.

Dickens, Charles (1987) *Hard Times*, Harmondsworth, Middlesex: Penguin.

Dilts, Robert (1983) *Applications of Neuro-Linguistic Programming*, Cupertino CA: Meta Publications.

------ (1990) *Changing Belief Systems with NLP*, Cupertino, CA: Meta Publications.

------, John Grinder, Richard Bandler, Leslie Cameron-Bandler and Judith DeLozier (1980) *Neuro-Linguistic Programming, Vol. I*, Cupertino (CA): Meta Publications.

Dodds, John M. (1989) 'Transatlantic Tropes Compared and Contrasted', in *Aspects of English: Miscellaneous Papers for English Teachers and Specialists*, J. M. Dodds (ed), Udine: Campanotto Editore, 11-18.

------ (1994) *Aspects of Literary Text Analysis and Translation Criticism*, Udine: Campanotto Editore.

------ and David Katan (1996) 'Cultural Proficiency Training for Translators and Interpreters: The X Factor', in *Proceedings of Eurolinguauni – 2*, Moscow: University of Moscow, 123-131.

Dooley, Robert. A. (1989) 'Style and Acceptability: The Guaranì New Testament', *Notes on Translation* 3 (1): 49-57.

Downing, Angela and Philip Locke (1992) *A University Course in English Grammar*, London: Prentice Hall.

Dressler, Wolfgang U. (1992) 'Marked and Unmarked Text Strategies within Semiotically Based NATURAL Textlinguistics', in *Language in Context: Essays for Robert E. Longacre*, Shin Ja, J. Hwang and R. Merrifield (eds), Arlington: The Summer Institute of Linguistics and The University of Texas at Arlington, 5-17.

Eco, Umberto (1980) *Il nome della Rosa*, Milan: Bompiani.

------ (1984) *The Name of the Rose*, London: Pan.

Ellmann, Richard (1988) *Oscar Wilde*, New York: Random House.

Encyclopedia Britannica (2000) Millennium Edition (CD-ROM): Encyclopedia Britannica.

Englehorn, Christopher (1991) *When Business East Meets Business West: The Guide to Practice and Protocol in the Pacific Rim*, New York: Riley.

Eriksen, Thomas Hylland and Finn Sivert Nielsen (2001) *A History of Anthropology*, London: Pluto Press.

Even-Zohar, Itamar (1978) 'Papers in Historical Poetics', in *Papers on Poetics and Semiotics*, B. Hrushovski and I. Even-Zohar (eds) Vol. 8, Tel Aviv: University Publishing Projects.

Fabbro, Franco (1989) 'Neurobiological Aspects of Bilingualism and Polyglossia', in *The Theoretical and Practical Aspects of Teaching Conference Interpretation*, L. Gran and J.M. Dodds (eds), Udine: Campanotto Editore, 71-82.

Fairclough, Norman (1989) *Language and Power*, Harlow, Essex: Longman.

------ and Ruth Wodak (1997) 'Critical Discourse Analysis', in *Discourse as Social Action* T. A. van Dijk (ed), London: Sage, 258-284.

Falinski, Josef (1989) *An English Grammar*, Florence: Valmartina Editore.

Farb, Peter (1973) *Word Play: What Happens When People Talk*, New York: Knopf.

Favaron, Roberta (2002) *L'interprete ai raggi X: interpretazione in campo medico in Australia, la gestione dell'interazione da parte dell'interprete*, University dissertation deposited at Scuola Superiore di Lingue Moderne per Interpreti e Traduttori, University of Trieste, Trieste.

Fawcett, Peter (1998) 'Ideology and Translation', in *The Encyclopedia of Translation Studies*, M. Baker (ed), London/ New York: Routledge, 106-111.

Ferraro, Gary P. (1994) *The Cultural Dimension of International Business*, Prentice Hall: New Jersey.

Fillmore, Charles J. (1977) 'Scenes and Frames in Semantics', in *Linguistic Structures Processing*, Antonio Zampolli (ed), Amsterdam: Benjamins, 55-81.

Forster, Edward Morgan ([1924] 1966) *Passage to India*, Harmondsworth: Penguin Books.

Forster Fowler, Roger (1977) *Linguistics and the Novel*, London: Methuen.

Gannon, Martin J. (2001) (ed) *Cultural Metaphors: Readings, Research Translations, and Commentary*, Thousand Oaks, CA/London: Sage Publications.

Gavioli, Laura (1993) 'Achieving Roles in Service Encounters', in *Shakespeare e la sua eredità*, Atti del XV Convegno dell'Assocazione Italiana di Anglistica, Parma, 22-24 Ottobre 1992, G. Caliumi (ed), Parma: Edizioni Zara, 379-392.

Gentzler, Edwin (2001) *Contemporary Translation Theories*, Clevedon: Multilingual Matters.

Goffman, Erving (1974) *Frame Analysis*, New York: Harper and Row.

Goodale, Malcolm (1987) *The Language of Meetings*, Hove: Language Teaching Publications.

Gottlieb, Henrik (1997) 'Quality Revisited: The Rendering of English Idioms in Danish Television Subtitles Printed Translations', in *Text Typology and Translation*, Anna Trosborg (ed), Amsterdam/Philadelphia: John Benjamins, 309-338.

Gowers, Ernest (1976) *The Complete Plain Words*; revised B. Fraser, Harmondsworth, Middlesex: Penguin Books.

Gran, Laura (1989) 'Interdisciplinary Research on Cerebral Assymetries: Significance and Prospects for the Teaching of Interpretation', in *The Theoretical and Practical Aspects of Teaching Conference Interpretation*, Laura Gran and John Dodds (eds), Udine: Campanotto editore, 93-100.

------ and John Dodds (eds) (1989) *The Theoretical and Practical Aspects of Teaching Conference Interpretation*, Udine: Campanotto Editore.

Gray, John (1993) *Men are From Mars, Women Are from Venus*, London: Thorsons.

Grice, H. P. (1975) 'Logic and Conversation', in *Syntax and Semantics, Vol. 3: Speech Acts*, P. Cole and J. L. Morgan (eds), New York: Academic Press, 41-58.

Grimond, John (1986) *The Economist Pocket Style Book*, London: The Economist Publications.

Grinder, Michael (1989) *Righting the Educational Conveyer Belt*, Portland, Oregon: Metamorphous Press.

Guirdham, Maureen (1990) *Interpersonal Skills at Work*, Hemel Hempstead, Herts: Prentice Hall.

Gumperz, John J. (1977) 'Sociocultural Knowledge in Conversational Inference', in *28th Annual Round Table Monograph Series on Language and Linguistics*, Norman Fairclough (ed), Washington, DC: Georgetown University Press, 98-106.

------ (1982) *Discourse Strategies*, Cambridge: Cambridge University Press.

Hale, Nikola (1996) '"Sciences-Po" Meets the Bible Belt: Bi-cultural Team-building', in *Proceedings of the 8th ENCoDe Conference: Communicative Ability and Cultural Awareness: A Key to International Corporate Success*, 28 February – 1 March 1996, Nice: GroupeEd, HEC.

Hall, Edward T. (1976/1989) *Beyond Culture*, New York: Doubleday.

------ (1982) *The Hidden Dimension*, New York: Doubleday.

------ (1983) *The Dance of Life*, New York: Doubleday.

------ (1990) *The Silent Language*, New York: Doubleday.

------ and Mildred Reed Hall (1989) *Understanding Cultural Differences,* Yarmouth, Maine: Intercultural Press.

Halliday, Michael A. K. (1968) 'Language and Experience', *Educational Review* 20(2): 95-106.

------ (1976a) 'Systemic Grammar', in *Halliday: System and Function in Language*, G. R. Kress (ed), London: Oxford University Press, 3-6.

------ (1976b) 'The Teacher Taught the Student English: An Essay in Applied Linguistics', in *The Second LACUS Forum* 1975, P. A. Reach (ed), Columbia, SC: Hornbeam, 344-349.

------ (1987) 'Spoken and Written Modes of Meaning', in Comprehending Oral and Written Language, R. Horrowitz and R. Samuels (eds), San Diego: Academic Press, 55-81.

------ (1992) 'New Ways of Meaning', in *Thirty Years of Linguistic Evolution*, M. Pütz (ed), Philadelphia: John Benjamins, 59-95.

------ (1994) *An Introduction to Functional Grammar,* 2nd ed., London: Edward Arnold.

------ and Ruqaiya Hasan (1976) *Cohesion in English*, London: Longman.

------ and Ruqaiya Hasan (1989) *Language, Context, and Text: Aspects of Language in a Social-Semiotic Perspective*, Oxford: Oxford University Press.

Hampden-Turner, Charles (1981) *Maps of the Mind: Charts and Concepts of the Mind and Its Labyrinths*, New York, Collier Books: Macmillan.

------ and Fons Trompenaars (1993) *The Seven Cultures of Capitalism*, London: Piatkus.

Harper, John (1993) 'Cross-National Mergers and Joint Ventures: The Cross-Cultural Issues and Role of Training', in *Proceedings of the 8th ENCoDe Conference: Communicative Ability and Cultural Awareness: A Key to International Corporate*

Success, 28 February – 1 March 1996, Nice: GroupeEd HEC, 75-82.

Harris, Philip R. and Robert T. Moran (1991) *Managing Cultural Differences*, Houston, Texas: Gulf Publishing Company.

Hasan, Ruqaiya (1984) 'Ways of Saying: Ways of Meaning', in *The Semiotics of Culture and Language, Vol. 1: Language as a Social Semiotic*, R. P. Fawcett, M. A. K. Halliday, S. M. Lamb and A. Makkai (eds), London: Frances Pinter, 105-162.

------ (1989) 'Semantic Variation and Sociolinguistics', *Australian Journal of Linguistics* 9:221-275.

------ (1991) 'Questions as a Mode of Learning in Everyday Talk', in *Proceedings of the Second International Conference of Language Education: Interaction and Development*, M. McCausland and Thao Lê (eds), Launceston: University of Tasmania, 70-119.

------ (1992) 'Rationality in Everyday Talk from Process to System', in *Directions in Corpus Linguistics*, J. Svatvik (ed), Berlin: Mouton de Gruyter, 257-307.

Hatim, Basil and Ian Mason (1990) *Discourse and the Translator*, Harlow, Essex: Longman.

------ and Ian Mason (1997) *The Translator as Communicator*, London, Routledge.

Headland, Thomas (1981) 'Information Rate, Information Overload and Communication Problems in the Casiguran Dumagat New Testament', *Notes on Translation* 83:18-27.

Heider, Fritz (1958) *The Psychology of Interpersonal Relations*, New York: Wiley.

Hermans, Theo (1985) (ed) *The Manipulation of Literature: Studies in Literary Translation*, New York: St. Martins Press.

------ (1999) *Translation in Systems*, Manchester: St. Jerome.

Hervey, Sándor, Ian Higgins, Stella Cragie and Patrizia Gambarotta (2000) *Thinking Italian Translation. A Course in Translation Method: Italian to English*, London: Routledge.

Hewson, Lance and Jacky Martin (1991*) Redefining Translation: The Variational Approach*, London: Routledge.

Hofstede, Geert (1991) *Cultures and Organizations: Software of the Mind*, London: McGraw-Hill.

Holmes, James S. (1973-4) 'On Matching and Making Maps: From a Translator's Notebook', *Delta* 16 (4): 67-82.

------ (1988) *Translated! Papers on Literary Translation and Translation Studies*, Approaches to Translation Studies 7, Amsterdam: Rodopi.

Hönig, Hans, G. (1991) 'Holmes' "Mapping Theory" and the Landscape of Mental Translation Processes', in *Translation Studies: The State of the Art. Proceedings of the First James. S. Holmes Symposium on Translation Studies*, K. M. Van Leuven-Zwart and Ton Naaijkens (eds), Amsterdam: Rodopi. 77-89.

Humphrey, Janice H. and Bob J. Alcorn (1996) *So You Want To Be an Interpreter: An Introduction to Sign Language Interpreting*, Amarillo, Texas: H and H Publishers.

Huxley, Aldous ([1932]1955) *Brave New World*, London: Penguin Books.

Hwang, Shin Ja J. and William R. Merrifield (eds) (1992) *Language in Context: Essays for Robert E. Longacre*, Arlington: The Summer Institute of Linguistics and The University of Texas at Arlington.

Hymes, Dell (1974) *Foundations in Sociolinguistics: An Ethnographic Approach*,

Philadelphia: University of Pennsylvania Press.

Inkeles Alex and Daniel J. Levinson (1969) 'National Character: The Study of Model Personality and Sociocultural Systems', in *The Handbook of Social Psychology*, 2nd ed., Vol. 4, G. Lindsey and E. Aronson (eds*)*, Reading, MA.: Addison-Wesley.

International, Dr. (ed) (2002) *Developing International Software*, 2nd ed., Portland OR: Microsoft Press

Italy: The Rough Guide (1990) London: Harrap-Columbus.

Ivir, Vladimir (1987) 'Procedures and Strategies for the Translation of Culture', in *Translation across Cultures*, G. Toury (ed), New Delhi: Bahri Publications, 48-60.

Jakobson, Roman (1959) 'On Linguistic Aspects of Translation', in *On Translation*, R. A. Bower (ed), New York: Oxford University Press, 232-39.

James, Carl (1988) 'Genre Analysis and the Translator', *Target* 1(1): 29-41.

Japan Travel Bureau (1991) *"Salary Man" in Japan*, The Japan Travel Bureau, Japan: Japan Travel Bureau Inc.

Jones, Tobias (2003) *The Dark Heart of Italy*, London: Faber and Faber.

Joyce, James (1933) *Gente di Dublino*, trans. Anne and Adriano Lami, Milan: Corbaccio.

Kapp, Robert (1983) *Communicating with the Chinese*, Chicago: Intercultural Press.

Katan, David (1989) 'From Yes to No: A Lesson in How to Avoid Conflict', in *Il muro del linguaggio; conflitto e tragedia*, Atti del X Congresso Nazionale, AIA, Sorrento, Ottobre 1987, L. Curti, L. Di Michele, T. Frank and M. Vitale (eds) Napoli: Società Editrice Intercontinentale, Gallo. 553-564.

------ (1993a) 'The English Translation of *Il nome della rosa* and the Cultural Filter', in *Umberto Eco, Claudio Magris: autori e traduttori a confronto*, L. Avirovič and J.M. Dodds (eds), Udine: Campanotto editore, 149-165.

------ (1993b) 'Conversational Implicatures and Translation Implications in Troilus and Cressida', in *Shakespeare e la sua eredità*, Atti del XV Convegno dell'Assocazione Italiana di Anglistica, Parma, 22-24 Ottobre 1992, Caliumi Grazia (ed), Parma: Edizioni Zara. 347-355.

------ (1994) 'Learning about Culture', in *Atti del Seminario Regionale per formatori del PSLS 'Strategie di apprendimento'*, M. G. Moro and P. Pellicioli (eds), Mestre: IRRSAE del Veneto, 79-97.

------ (1996a) 'The Translator as Cultural Mediator', in *Quaderno: Programma Sociologia Internazionale, Sezione Relazione Internazionali*, 96 – 2, 1-11.

------ (1996b) 'Deedes and Misdeedes: The Culture Bound Nature of Interpreting Meaning', in *Aspects of English 2*, C. J. Taylor (ed), Udine: Campanotto Editore, 121-140.

------ (1998) 'Contexting Culture: Culture-bound Interpretation of Events in and between the Anglo(-)American and Italian Press', in *British/American Variation in Language, Theory and Methodology*, C. Taylor Torsello, L. Haarman, and L. Gavioli (eds), CLEUB, Bologna, 141-155.

------ (1999) '"What is it That's Going on Here": Mediating Cultural Frames in Translation', *Textus* II, S. Bassnett, R.M. Bollettieri Bosinelli, and M. Ulrych (eds), 409-426.

------ (2000) 'Language Transfer: What Gets Distorted or Deleted in Translation', *Mostovi* 7, Delozier (ed): 29-37.

------ (2001a) 'Cueing the Picture: Contexts and Strategies in Translating Dialect Poetry from the Carnic Alps', in *Miscellanea numero speciale traduzione poetica e dintorni*, Dipartimento di scienza del linguaggio, dell'interpretazione e della traduzione,

Università di Trieste, Trieste, 158-180.

------ (2001b) 'When Difference is not Dangerous: Modelling Intercultural Competence for Business', *Textus* XIV, Giuseppina Cortese and Dell Hymes (eds), 2, 287-306.

------ (2002) 'Mediating the Point of Refraction and Playing with the Perlocutionary Effect: A Translator's Choice?', in *Critical Studies: Vol. 20, Cultural Studies, Interdisciplinarity and Translation*, Stefan Herbrechter (ed), Amsterdam/New York: Ridolphi, 177-195.

------ (forthcoming) 'The English are All Cold Fish: The Reattribution Generator and the Creation of Alternative Models of Meaning'.

------ and Francesco Straniero Sergio (2001) 'Look Who's Talking: The Ethics of Entertainment in Talk Show Interpreting', in *The Translator: The Return to Ethics*, Anthony Pym (ed), Special Issue, 2001: 2, 213-238.

Kellett, Jane (1965) 'Video-Aided Testing of Student Delivery and Presentation in Consecutive Interpretation', *The Interpreters Newsletter* 6: 43-66.

Kipling, Rudyard ([1902]1966) *Just So Stories,* New York: Airmont.

Kluckhohn, Florence Rockwood and Fred L. Strodtbeck (1961) *Variations in Value Orientations* , Evanston (IL): Row, Peterson.

Knapp-Potthof, Annelie and Karlfried Knapp (1981) 'The Man (or Woman) in the Middle: Discoursal Aspects of Non-Professional Interpreting', in *The Mediating Person: Bridges between Cultures*, S. Bochner (ed), Cambridge: Schenkman, 181-201.

Koenen, Liesbeth and Rik Smits (1992) *Peptalk: de Engelse woordenschat vanhet Nederlands,* 2e druk, Amsterdam: Nijgh and Van Ditmar.

Kondo, Masaomi (1990) 'What Conference Interpreters Should Not Be Expected to Do', *The Interpreters' Newsletter* 3:59-65.

------ and Helen Tebble (1997) 'Intercultural Communication, Negotiation and Interpreting', in *Conference Interpreting: Current Trends in Research, Proceedings of the International Conference on Interpreting: What Do We Know and How?*, Turku, Finland, 25-27 August 1994, C. J. Taylor, Y. Gambier and D. Gile (eds), Amsterdam: John Benjamins, 149-166.

Korzybski, Albert (1958) *Science and Sanity*, 4th ed., The International Non-Aristotelian Library Publishing Company, Eaglewood (N.J.): Institute of General Semantics.

Kramsch, Claire (1993) *Context and Culture in Language Teaching*, Oxford: Oxford University Press.

Kroeber, Alfred L. and Clyde Kluckhohn (1952) *Cultures: A Critical Review of Concepts and Definitions*, Peabody Museum Papers Vol. 47, 1, Cambridge, Mass.: Harvard University.

Kuhiwczak, Piotr (1995) 'Translation as Cultural Trade', in *Sapere linguistico e sapere enciclopedico*, L. Pantaleoni and L. S. Kovarski (eds), Biblioteca della Scuola Superiore di Lingue Moderne per Interpreti e Traduttori, Forlì: CLUEB, 233-240.

Kussmaul, Paul (2000) 'Looking at Creative Mental Processes', in *Intercultural Faultlines: Research Models in Translation Studies 1. Textual and Cognitive Aspects*, M. Olohan (ed), Manchester: St. Jerome, 57-72.

Kwiewecinski, Piotr (2001) *Disturbing Strangeness*, Torun: Wydawnictwo Edytor.

Ladmiral, Jean-René (1979) *Traduire: théorèmes pour la traduction*, Paris: Payot.

Lakoff, George (1982) *Categories and Cognitive Models*, Trier: LAUT.

------ (1987) *Women, Fire and Dangerous Things: What Categories Reveal about the*

Mind, Chicago: University of Chicago Press.

------ and Mark Johnson (1980) *Metaphors We Live By*, Chicago: The University of Chicago Press.

Lalljee, Mansur (1987) 'Attribution Theory and Intercultural Communication', in *Analyzing Inter-cultural Communication*, K. Knapp, W. Enninger and A. Knapp-Potthoff (eds), Berlin: Mouton de Gruyter, 37-49.

Lanham, Richard (1983) *Literacy and the Survival of Humanism*, New Haven: Yale University Press.

Larson, Mildred (1984) *Meaning Based Translation: A Guide to Cross-Language Equivalence*, Lanham MD, University Press of America.

Leech, Geoffrey N. (1983) *Principles of Pragmatics*, London: Longman.

------ (1985) *Semantics*, Harmondsworth: Penguin.

Lefevere, André (1992) *Translation, Rewriting and the Manipulation of Literary Frame*, London: Routledge.

Lemke, Jay L. (1989) 'Semantics and Social Values', *Word* 40(1-2):37-50.

------ (1991) 'Text Structure and Semantic Choice', in *Functional and Systemic Linguistics: Approaches and Uses*, Eija Ventola (ed), New York: Mouton de Gruyter, 23-38.

Lepschy, Anna Laura and Giulio Lepschy (1988) *The Italian Language Today*, London: Routledge.

Levine, Deana R. and Mara B. Adelman (1993) *Beyond Language: Cross-Cultural Communication*, Englewood Cliffs, NJ: Prentice-Hall.

Lewis, Richard (2000) *When Cultures Collide: Managing Successfully Across Cultures*, London: Nicholas Brealey.

Lodge, David (1988) *Nice Work*, New York: Viking.

Longman (1992) *Longman Dictionary of English Language and Culture*, Harlow, Essex: Longman.

Lorenz, Konrad ([1954]1977) *Man Meets Dog*, London: Methuen.

Lull, James (1995) *Media, Communication, Culture*, Cambridge: Polity Press.

Lyons, John (1981) *Language, Meaning and Context*, London: Fontana.

MacArthur, Brian (ed) (1993) *The Penguin Book of Twentieth Century Speeches*, London: Penguin Books.

Mailhac, Jean-Pierre (1998) 'Optimising the Linguistic Transfer in the Case of Commercial Videos', in *Translating for the Media. Papers from the International Conference*: *Languages and the Media, Berlin, November 22-23, 1996*, Y. Gambier (ed), Turku: University of Turku, Centre for Translation and Interpreting, 207-224.

Malinowski, Bronislaw (1935) *Coral Gardens and Their Magic*, vol. 2, Allen and Unwin, London; reprinted 1967 as *The Language of Magic and Gardening*, Indiana University Studies in the History and Theory of Linguistics, Bloomington, Indiana: Indiana University Press.

------ ([1923] 1938) 'The Problem of Meaning in Primitive Languages', in *The Meaning of Meaning: A Study of the Influence of Language upon Thought and of the Science of Symbolism*, C. K. Ogden and I. A. Richards (eds), New York: Harcourt Brace and Co., 296-336.

Malone, Joseph L. (1988) *The Science of Linguistics in the Art of Translation. Some Tools from Linguistics for the Analysis and Practice of Translation*, Albany: State University of New York.

Maltx, Daniel N. and Ruth A. Borker (1992) 'A Cultural Perspective to Male-Female Miscommmunication', in *Her and His Speechways: Gender Perspectives in English*, G. Cortese (ed), Turin: Edizione Libreria Cortina, 171-188.

Maslowe, Abraham H. (1970) *Motivation and Personality*, 2nd ed., New York: Harper and Row.

Mason, Ian (1994) 'Discourse, Ideology and Translation', in *Language, Discourse and Translation in the West and Middle East*, R. De Beaugrande, A. Shunnaq and M. H. Heliel (eds), Amsterdam/Philadelphia: John Benjamins, 23-63.

------ (2000) 'Models and Methods in Dialogue Interpreting Research', in *Intercultural Faultlines: Research Models in Translation Studies. Textual and Cognitive Aspects*, M. Olohan (ed), Manchester: St. Jerome, 215-232.

May, Rollo (1991) *The Cry for Myth*, New York: Norton.

McLean, Alan C. (1993) *Profile UK*, London: Heinemann.

McLeod, Beverly (1981) 'The Mediating Person and Cultural Identity', in *The Mediating Person: Bridges Between Cultures*, S. Bochner (ed), Cambridge: Schenkman, 37-52.

Mead, Richard (1990) *Cross-Cultural Management Communication*, Chichester: John Wiley and Sons.

------ (1994) *International Management*, London: Blackwell.

Metzger, Melanie (1999) *Sign Language Interpreting: Deconstructing the Myth of Neutrality*, Washington DC: Gallaudet University.

Mitford, Nancy (1959) *Noblesse Oblige*, Harmondsworth, Essex: Penguin.

Mole, John (1992) *Mind Your Manners*, London: Brealey.

Montgomery, Martin (1986) *An Introduction to Language and Society*, London: Prentice Hall.

Montorfano, Emilio (1996) *Il Vero Galateo,* Torriana, FO: Orsa Maggiore.

Morley, John (1993) 'New Words for New or Destroying the Stereotypes in TV Ads', in *Shakespeare e la sua eredità*, Atti del XV Convegno dell'Assocazione Italiana di Anglistica, Parma, 22-24 Ottobre 1992, G. Caliumi (ed), Parma: Edizioni Zara, 407-418.

Mühlhäusler, Peter and Rom Harré (1990) *Pronouns and People: The Linguistic Construction of Social and Personal Identity*, Oxford: Blackwell.

Musacchio, Maria Teresa (1995) *La traduzione della lingua dell'economia dall'inglese in italiano*, Trieste: Edizioni Lint.

Myers, Greg (1994) *Words in Ads*, London: Edward Arnold.

Neubert, Albrecht and Gregory M. Shreve (1992) *Translation as Text*, Kent, Ohio: The Kent State University Press.

Newmark, Peter (1981) *Approaches to Translation*, Oxford: Pergamon Press.

------ (1988) *A Textbook of Translation*, Hemel Hempstead: Prentice Hall.

------ (1993) *Paragraphs on Translation*, Bristol: Multilingual Matters.

------ (1995) 'Translation Theory or Spoof', Lecture delivered at the SSLMIT: University of Trieste, May 1995.

Nida, Eugene A. (1964) *Towards a Science of Translating with Special Reference to Principles and Procedures Involved in Bible Translating*, Leiden: E. J. Brill.

------ (1976) 'A Framework for the Analysis and Evaluation of Theories of Translation', in *Translation: Applications and Research*, R. Brislin (ed), New York: Gardner Press, 47-92.

------ (1997) 'The Principles of Discourse Structure and Content in Relation to Translat-
    ing', in *Transferre Necesse Est: Proceedings of the 2nd International Conference on
    Current Trends in Studies of Translation and Interpreting, 5-7 September, 1996,
    Budapest, Hungary*, K. Klaudy and J. Kohn (eds), Budapest: Scholastica, 37-42.

------ and Charles R. Taber (1969) *The Theory and Practice of Translation*, Leiden: E. J.
    Brill.

Nord, Cristiana (2003) 'Function and Loyalty in Bible Translation', in *Apropos of Ide-
    ology: Translation Studies on Ideology – Ideologies in Translation Studies*, M. C.
    Pérez (ed), Manchester UK/Northampton MA: St Jerome, 89-112.

Nostrand, Howard (1989) 'Authentic Texts – Cultural Authenticity: An Editorial', *Mod-
    ern Language Journal* 73/1, 49-57.

Obler, Loraine K. and Kris Gjerlow (1999) *Language and the Brain*, Cambridge: Cam-
    bridge University Press.

O'Connor, Joseph (2001) *The NLP Workbook*, London: Thorsons.

------ and John Seymour (1993) *Introducing Neuro-Linguistic Programming*, London:
    Aquarian Press.

------ and John Seymour (1994) *Training with NLP*, Glasgow: Thorsons/HarperCollins.

O'Hagan, Minako and David Ashworth (2002) *Translation-Mediated Communication
    in a Digital World*, Clevedon: Multilingual Matters.

Ondelli, Stefano (1995) *La drammatizzazione dei titoli nei quotidiani in Italia e in Gran
    Bretagna*, Unpublished Degree Thesis , Trieste: SSLMIT, University of Trieste.

Paige, R. Michael (1993) 'On the Nature of Intercultural Experiences and Intercultural
    Education', in *Education for the Intercultural Experience*, R.M. Paige (ed), Yar-
    mouth, Maine: Intercultural Press, 1-21.

Palmer, B. J (1981) *The Concise Oxford Dictionary of Quotations*, Oxford, Oxford Uni-
    versity Press, p.135.

Palmer, Gary (1996) *Towards a Theory of Cultural Linguistics*, Austin TE: University
    of Texas Press.

Palmer, Kenneth (ed) (1982) *The Arden Shakespeare: Troilus and Cressida*, London:
    Methuen.

Parsons, Talcott (1982) 'The Pattern Variables', in *On Institutions and Social Evolu-
    tion: Selected Writings*, H. Mayhem Leon (ed), Chicago: The University of Chicago
    Press, 106-114.

Pease, Allan (1984) *Body Language: How to Read Others' Thoughts by Their Gestures*,
    London: Sheldon Press.

------ and Barbara Pease (2001) *Why Men Don't Listen and Women Can't Read Maps:
    How Are We Different And What To Do*, London: Orion Books.

Pérez, María Calzada (2003) *Apropos of Ideology: Translation Studies on Ideology –
    Ideologies in Translation Studies*, Manchester: St. Jerome.

Picchi, Fernando (2002) *Grande dizionario di inglese: inglese/italiano, italiano/inglese*,
    2nd ed., Milan: Editore Ulrico Hoepli.

Pierce, Susan (unpublished) 'American Collective Memory: How Collective, and How
    Historical?', Paper presented at *Dialogue between Cultures and Changes in Europe
    and the World*, 32nd World Sociology Congress, Trieste, 3-7 July, 1995.

Pinker, Steven (1995) *The Language Instinct*, London: Penguin.

Popovič, Anton (1970) 'The Concept "Shift of Expression" in Translation Analysis', in

The Nature of Translation, J. S. Holmes, F. de Haan and A. Popovič (eds), The Hague: Mouton, 209-2.

Pym, Anthony (2000) 'On Cooperation', in *Intercultural Faultlines: Research Models in Translation Studies I. Textual and Cognitive Aspects*, M. Olohan (ed), Manchester: St. Jerome, 181-192.

------ (2001) 'Introduction', *The Translator: The Return to Ethics* 7 (2) November, 129-139.

------ (forthcoming) 'Redefining Translation Competence in an Electronic Age'.

Quirk, Randolf and Sidney Greenbaum (1990) *A Student's Grammar of the English Language*, Harlow, Essex: Longman.

Reddick, R. J. (1992) 'English Expository Discourse', in *Language in Context: Essays for Robert E. Longacre*, Shin Ja J. Hwang and W. R. Merrifield (eds), Arlington: The Summer Institute of Linguistics and The University of Texas at Arlington, 211-223.

Reddy, Michael J. (1993) 'The Conduit Metaphor' in *Metaphor and Thought*, Andrew Ortony (ed), Cambridge: Cambridge University Press, 2nd ed., 164-201

Reiss Katherina ([1971]2000) 'Decision Making in Translation', trans. Susan Kitron, in *The Translation Studies Reader*, Laurence Venuti (ed), Manchester: St. Jerome, 160-172.

Ribiero, Branca T. (1993) 'Framing in Psychotic Discourse', in *Framing in Discourse,* D. Tannen (ed), New York: Oxford University Press, 77-113.

Riccardi, Alessandra (2002) 'Evaluation in Interpretation: Macrocriteria and Microcriteria', in *Teaching Translation and Interpreting 4*, E. Hung (ed), Amsterdam/Philadelphia: Benjamins, 115-126.

Ritchie, James E. (1981) 'Tama Tu, Tama Ora: Mediational Styles in Maori Culture', in *The Mediating Person: Bridges Between Cultures*, S. Bochner (ed), Cambridge: Schenkman, 221-245.

Ritzer, George (1993) *The McDonaldization of Society*, Thousand Oaks: Pine Forge Press.

Roberts, Roda P. (2002) 'Community Interpreting: A Profession in Search of an Identity', in *Teaching Translation and Interpreting 4*, E. Hung (ed), Amsterdam/Philadelphia: Benjamins, 157-176.

Robinson, Douglas (1997) *Becoming a Translator: An Accelerated Course*, London: Routledge.

Robinson, Gail (1988) *Crosscultural Understanding*, Hemel Hempstead, Hertfordshire: Prentice Hall International.

Rosch, Eleanor H. (1978) 'Principles of Categorization', in *Cognition and Categorization*, E. Rosch and B. Lloyd (eds), Hillsdale, NJ: Lawrence Erlbaum, 27-48.

Ross, Alan (1969) *What are U?*, London: Andre Deutsch.

Ross, Elliot D. (1988) 'Language-Related Functions of the Right Cerebral Hemisphere', in *Aphasia*, F. C. Rose, R. Whurr and M. Wyle (eds), London: Whurr, 188-212.

Ross, John R. (1970) 'On Declarative Sentences', in *Readings in English Transformational Grammar*, R. Jacobs and P. Rosembaum (eds), Waltham, Mass: Ginn/Blaisdell, 222-272.

Roy, Cynthia B. (1993) 'A Sociological Analysis of the Interpreter's Role in Simultaneous Talk', *Multilingua* 12(4): 341-363.

Russell, Bertrand (1903) 'Appendix B: The Doctrine of Types', in *Principles of*

Mathematics, Bertrand Russell (ed), Cambridge: Cambridge University Press, 523-528.

Russell, Frances and Christine Locke (1992) *English Law and Language,* London: Cassell Publishers.

Samovar, Larry A. and Richard E. Porter (1991) *Communication Between Cultures,* Belmont, California: Wadsworth Publishing Company.

Sansoni (1975) *I Dizionari Sansoni, inglese-italiano italiano-inglese,* 2 vols., Florence: Sansoni,

Sapir, Edward (1929) 'The Status of Linguistics as a Science', *Language* 5:207-214.

------ (1949) *Culture, Language and Personality,* Los Angeles: University of California Press.

------ (1994) *The Psychology of Culture: A Course of Lectures,* J. T. Irvine (ed), Berlin: Mouton de Gruyter.

Šarčević, Susan (2001) 'Preserving Multinguilism in an Enlarged European Union', *Terminologie et Traduction,* 2, 34-53.

Saville-Troike, Muriel (1986) *The Ethnography of Communication: An Introduction,* Oxford: Blackwell.

SBS (1996) *Cultural Diversity at Work. The Business Advantage* (video), Sydney, Australia: SBS.

Scarpa, Federica (1989) *La traduzione della metafora,* Rome: Bulzone.

------ (2001) *La traduzione specializzata: lingue speciali e mediazione linguistica,* Milan: Hoepli.

Schäffner, Christina (1995) 'Debate', in *Cultural Functions of Translation,* C. Schäffner and H. Kelly-Holmes (eds), Clevedon: Multilingual Matters, 32-54.

Schneider, David (1976) 'Notes towards a Theory of Culture', in *Meaning in Anthropology,* K. Basso and H. Selby (eds), Albuquerque: University of New Mexico Press, 203-206.

Scollon, Ron and Suzanne Wong Scollon (2001) *Intercultural Communication: A Discourse Approach,* 2nd ed., Oxford: Blackwell.

Searle, John R. (1969) *Speech Acts: An Essay in the Philosophy of Language,* Cambridge: Cambridge University Press.

Seeleye, H. Ned (1978) *Teaching Culture: Strategies for Foreign Language Educators,* Skokie, ILL: National Textbook Co./ACTFL.

------ and Alan Seeleye-James (1995) *Culture Clash: Managing in a Multicultural World,* Lincolnwood, Ill: NTC Business Books.

Séguinot, Candace (1995) 'Translation and Advertising: Going Global and "Debate"', in *Cultural Functions of Translation,* C. Schäffner and H. Kelly-Holmes (eds), Clevedon: Multilingual Matters, 55-86.

Selby, Henry (1975) 'Semantics and Causality in the Study of Deviance', in *Sociocultural Dimensions of Language Use,* M. Sanches and B. Blount (eds), London: Academic Press, 11-24.

Sergio Straniero, Francesco (1998) 'Notes on Cultural Mediation', *The Interpreters' Newsletter* 8: 151-68.

Severgnini, Beppe (1992) *L'inglese: lezioni semiserie,* Milan: Rizzoli.

Shin Ja, J. Hwang and William R. Merrifield (eds) (1992) *Language in Context: Essays for Robert E. Longacre,* Arlington: The Summer Institute of Linguistics and The

University of Texas at Arlington.

Sifianou, Maria (1989) 'On the Telephone Again! Differences in Telephone Behaviour: England versus Greece', *Language in Society*, 527-544.

Simons, George F., Carmen Vazques and Philip Harris (1993) *Empowering the Diverse Workforce*, Houston: Gulf Publishing.

Smith, Edward (1990) 'Categorization', in *Thinking*, D. N. Osherson and E. Smith (eds) Cambridge, Mass.: MIT, 33-54.

Snell-Hornby, Mary (1988) *Translation Studies: An Integrated Approach*, Amsterdam/ Philadelphia: John Benjamins.

------ (1992) 'The Professional Translator of Tomorrow: Language Specialist or All-Round Expert?', in *Teaching Translation and Interpreting: Training, Talent and Experience*, C. Dollerup and A. Loddegaard (eds), Amsterdam/Philadelphia: John Benjamins, 9-22.

Snelling, David (1992) *Strategies for Simultaneous Interpreters: From Romance Languages into English*, Udine: Campanotto Editore.

Sperber, Dan and Deirdre Wilson (1995) *Relevance. Communication and Cognition*, 2nd ed., Oxford: Blackwell.

Stein, John (1988) 'Physiological Differences: Left and Right', in *Aphasia*, F. C. Rose, R. Whurr and M. Wyle (eds), London: Whurr, 131-169.

Steiner, George (1975) *After Babel: Aspects of Language and Translation*, Oxford: Oxford University Press.

Sternberg, Robert J. (1984) 'Towards a Triarchic Theory of Human Intelligence', *The Behavioral and Brain Sciences* 7:269-315.

Stewart, Edward C. (1985) *American Cultural Patterns: A Cultural Perspective*, Yarmouth, Maine: Intercultural Press.

Straniero Sergio, Francesco (1998) 'Notes on Cultural Mediation', *The Interpreters' Newsletter*, 8:151-68.

Strawson, P. F. (1964) 'Intention and Convention in Speech Acts', *Philosophical Review* 73:439-460.

Stubbs, Michael (1998) 'German Loanwords and Cultural Stereotypes', *English Today*, 14 (1), 19-26.

Taft, Ronald (1981) 'The Role and Personality of the Mediator', in *The Mediating Person: Bridges Between Cultures*, S. Bochner (ed), Cambridge: Schenkman, 53-88.

Talbott, Shannon Peters (unpublished) 'Corporate Culture in the Global Marketplace: Case Study of McDonald's in Moscow', Paper presented at *Dialogue between Cultures and Changes in Europe and the World*, 32nd World Sociology Congress, Trieste, 3-7 July, 1995.

Tannen, Deborah (1985) 'Cross-cultural Communication', in *Handbook of Discourse Analysis: Vol 4: Discourse Analysis in Society*, T. Van Dijk (ed), London: Academic Press, 203-216.

------ (1992) *You Just Don't Understand: Women and Men in Conversation*, London: Virago Press.

------ (1993a) 'Introduction', in *Framing in Discourse*, D. Tannen (ed), New York: Oxford University Press, 3-13.

------ (1993b) 'What's in a Frame: Surface Evidence for Underlying Expectations', in *Framing in Discourse*, D. Tannen (ed), New York: Oxford University Press, 14-56.

------ and Cynthia Wallet (1993) 'Interactive Frames and Knowledge Schemas in Interaction: Examples from a Medical Examination/Interview', in *Framing in Discourse*,
D. Tannen (ed), New York: Oxford University Press, 57-76.

Taylor Torsello, Carol (1984) *English in Discourse: A Course for Language Specialists
I*, Padua: Cleup Editore.

------ (1987) *Shared and Unshared Information in English*, Dipartimento di Lingua e
Letterature Anglo-Germaniche, Università di Padova, Padua: Cleup Editore.

------ (1992) *English in Discourse: A Course for Language Specialists II*, Padua: Cleup
Editore.

Taylor, Christopher (1990) *Aspects of Language and Translation*: *Contrastive Approaches for Italian/English Translators*, Udine: Campanotto Editore.

------ (1998) *Language to Language: A Practical and Theoretical Guide for Italian/
English Translators*, Cambridge: Cambridge University Press.

------ (2002) 'The Subtitling of Documentary Films, in *Training the Language Services
Provider for the New Millenium*, Belinda Maia, Johann Haller, and Margherita Ulrych
(eds), Porto: Faculdade de Letras, Universidade do Porto, 153-170.

Taylor, W. L. (1953) 'Cloze Procedure: A New Task for Measuring Readability', *Journalism Quarterly* 33:42-48.

The Concise Oxford Dictionary of Quotations (1981) Oxford: Oxford University Press.

The Diagram Group (1982) *The Brain: A User's Manual*, New York: Berkeley Books.

The Open University (1993) *An Equal Opportunities Guide to Language and Image*,
Milton Keynes: The Open University.

Thompson, G. (1982) 'An Introduction to Implicature for Translators', *Notes on Translating* 1 (special edition).

Ting-Toomey, Stella (1985) 'Towards a Theory of Conflict and Culture', in *Communication, Culture and Organisational Processes*, W. B. Gudykunst, P. S. Lea and S.
Ting-Toomey (eds), Newbury Park, CA: Sage, 71-86.

Tooley, Michael (1992) *Language, Text and Context*, London: Routledge.

Tosi, Arturo (2001) *Language and Society in a Changing Italy*, Clevedon, UK:
Multilungual Matters.

Toury, Gideon (1980) *In Search of a Theory of Translation*, Tel Aviv: The Porter Institute for Poetics and Semiotics.

------ (1995) *Descriptive Translation Studies – And Beyond*, Amsterdam: Benjamins.

Townsend, Sue (1985) *The Secret Diary of Adrian Mole, Aged Thirteen and Three-
Quarters*, London: Methuen.

Trickey, David and Nigel Ewington (2003) *A World of Difference: Working Successfully Across Cultures*, London: Capita Learning and Development.

Trompenaars, Fons and Charles Hampden-Turner (1997) *Riding the Waves of Culture*,
London: Nicholas Brearley.

Tylor, Edward Barnett ([1871] 1958) *Primitive Culture*, abridged addition, New York:
Harper.

Tymoczko Maria (1998) 'Computerised Corpora and the Future of Translation Studies',
Meta, XLIII, 4, 652-659.

Ulrych, Margherita (1992) *Translating Texts from Theory to Practice*, Rapallo: Cideb
Editore.

Vaihinger, H. (1924) *The Philosophy 'As If'*, London: Routledge, Kegan and Paul.

Valdes, Joyce Merill (1986) *Culture Bound: Bridging the Cultural Gap in Language Teaching*, Cambridge: Cambridge University Press.

Van Leuven-Zwart, Kitty (1989) 'Translation and Original. Similarities and Dissimilarities', *Target* 1(2): 151-181.

------ (1990) 'Translation and Original. Similarities and Dissimilarities', *Target* 2(1): 69-95.

Vannerem, Mia and Mary Snell-Hornby (1986) 'Die Szene hinter dem Text: "scenes-and-frames semantics" in der Übersetzung', in *Überstzungswissen Schaft-eine Neuorientierung*, M. Snell-Hornby (ed), Tübingen: Francke, 184-204.

Venuti, Lawrence (1995a) *The Translator's Invisibility: A History of Translation*, Routledge: London/New York.

------ (1995b) 'Translation and the Formation of Cultural Identities and Debate', in *Cultural Functions of Translation*, C. Schäffner and H. Kelly-Holmes (eds), Clevedon: Multilingual Matters, 9-54.

------ (1998) *The Scandals of Translation*, London and New York: Routledge.

Vermeer, Hans J. (1978) 'Ein Rahem für eine Allgemeine Translationstherie', *Lebende Sprachen* 3: 99-102.

------ (2000) 'Skopos and Commission in Translational Action', in *The Translation Studies Reader*, L. Venuti (ed), London: Routledge

Victor, David A. (1992) *International Business Communication*, London: Harper Collins.

Viezzi, Maurizio (1996) *Aspetti della qualità in interpretazione,* Trieste: SSLMIT.

Vinay, Jean Paul and Jean Darbelnet ([1958]1995) *Comparative Stylistics of French and English. A Methodology for Translation*, trans. and ed J. C. Sager and M. J. Hamel, Amsterdam/Philadelphia: John Benjamins.

Vincent-Marrelli, Jocelyne (1989) 'On Cross-Purposes in Cross-Talk', in *Il muro del linguaggio: conflitto e tragedia*, Atti del X Congresso Nazionale, AIA, Sorrento, Ottobre 1987, L. Curti, L. Di Michele, T. Frank and M. Vitale (eds), Naples: Società editrice Intercontinentale Gallo, 465-90.

Waters, Malcolm (unpublished) 'McDonaldization and the Global Culture of Consumption', Paper presented at *Dialogue between Cultures and Changes in Europe and the World*, 32nd World Sociology Congress, Trieste, 3-7 July, 1995.

Watzlawick, Paul (1993) *The Language of Change*, New York: Norton.

Whitehead, Alfred N. and Bertrand Russell (1910) *Principia Mathematica*, 2nd ed., Cambridge: Cambridge University Press.

Whorf, Benjamin Lee (1956) *Language, Thought and Reality: Selected Writings of Benjamin Lee Whorf*, J. B. Carroll (ed), Cambridge, Mass: MIT.

Widdowson, Henry G. (1979) *Explorations in Applied Linguistics*, Oxford: Oxford University Press.

------ (1990) *Aspects of Language Teaching*, Oxford: Oxford University Press.

Wierzbicka, Anna (1986a) 'Does Language Reflect Culture? Evidence from Australian English', *Language in Society* 15(3):349-377.

------ (1986b) 'Italian Reduplication: Cross-Cultural Pragmatics and Illocutionary Semantics', *Linguistics* 24:287-315.

------ (1992) *Semantics, Culture, and Cognition: Universal Human Concepts in Culture-Specific Configurations*, New York: Oxford University Press.

Wilson, Diedre and Dan Sperber (1988) 'Representation and Relevance', in *Mental*

Representations: The Interface between Language and Reality, R. Kempson (ed), Cambridge: Cambridge University Press, 133-153.

Wilss, Wolfram (1989) 'Multi-Facet Concept of Translation Behavior', *Target* 1(2): 129-149.

Wittgenstein, Ludwig (1994) *The Wittgenstein Reader*, Oxford: Blackwell.

Wolf, Michaela (1997) 'Translation as a Process of Power: Aspects of Cultural Anthropology in Translation', in *Translation as Intercultural Communication*, M. Snell-Hornby, Z. Jettmarovà and K. Kaindl (eds), Amsterdam and Philadelphia: John Benjamins, 123-134.

Wolfe, Tom (1990) 'Introduction', in *The Bonfire of the Vanities*, London: Picador, vii-xxx.

------ (1990) *The Bonfire of the Vanities*, London: Picador.

Woodsworth, Judith (2002) 'Teaching Literary Translation', in *Teaching Translation and Interpreting 4*, Eva Hung (ed), Amsterdam and Philadelphia: John Benjamins, 129-138.

Zanier, Leonardo (1995) *Free ... To Have to Leave*, Istitût di culture furlane, Udine: Edizioni Biblioteca dell'Immagine.

Subject Index

Name Index